War, Strategy, and Military Effectiveness

This collection of essays represents Professor Williamson Murray's efforts to elucidate the role that history should play in thinking about the present and the future. They reflect three disparate themes in Professor Murray's work: his deep fascination with history and with those who have participated in it; his fascination with the similarities in human behavior between the past and the present; and his belief that the study of military and strategic history can be of real use to those who will confront the daunting problems of war and peace in the twenty-first century. The first group of chapters addresses the relevance of history to an understanding of the present and the possibilities of the future. The second addresses the possible direct uses of history to think through the problems involved in the creation of effective military institutions. The final group of chapters represents historical case studies that illuminate the present.

Williamson Murray is Professor Emeritus of History at The Ohio State University. Currently, he is a defense consultant and commentator on historical and military subjects in Washington, DC. He is co-editor of *The Shaping of Grand Strategy* (with Richard Hart Sinnreich and James Lacey, Cambridge, 2011), *The Making of Peace* (with James Lacey, 2009), *The Past as Prologue* (with Richard Hart Sinnreich, Cambridge, 2006), *The Dynamics of Military Revolution, 1300–2050* (with MacGregor Knox, Cambridge, 2001), *Military Innovation in the Interwar Period* (with Allan R. Millett, Cambridge, 1996), and *The Making of Strategy* (with Alvin Bernstein and MacGregor Knox, Cambridge, 1994).

War, Strategy, and Military Effectiveness

WILLIAMSON MURRAY
The Ohio State University

CAMBRIDGE
UNIVERSITY PRESS

CAMBRIDGE UNIVERSITY PRESS
Cambridge, New York, Melbourne, Madrid, Cape Town,
Singapore, São Paulo, Delhi, Mexico City

Cambridge University Press
32 Avenue of the Americas, New York NY 10013-2473, USA

Published in the United States of America by Cambridge University Press, New York

www.cambridge.org
Information on this title: www.cambridge.org/9781107614383

© Williamson Murray 2011

This publication is in copyright. Subject to statutory exception
and to the provisions of relevant collective licensing agreements,
no reproduction of any part may take place without the written
permission of Cambridge University Press.

First published 2011
Reprinted 2012
First paperback edition 2013

A catalogue record for this publication is available from the British Library

Library of Congress Cataloging in Publication Data
Murray, Williamson.
War, strategy, and military effectiveness / Williamson Murray.
p. cm.
Includes bibliographical references and index.
ISBN 978-1-107-00242-5 (hardback)
1. Military art and science – History. 2. War. 3. Strategy. 4. Military policy.
5. Military readiness. 6. International relations. I. Title.
U27.M875 2011
355.02 – dc22   2011003794

ISBN 978-1-107-00242-5 Hardback
ISBN 978-1-107-61438-3 Paperback

Cambridge University Press has no responsibility for the persistence or
accuracy of URLs for external or third-party internet websites referred to in
this publication, and does not guarantee that any content on such websites is,
or will remain, accurate or appropriate.

Dedicated to
Lesley Mary Smith
Beloved wife, valued colleague, critic extraordinaire,
and, above all, friend

Contents

	Introduction	page 1
1	History and the Future	14
2	Thucydides and Clausewitz	45
3	Clausewitz out, Computers in: Military Culture and Technological Hubris	61
4	Changing the Principles of War?	72
5	Military Culture Does Matter	83
6	History and Strategic Planning	98
7	Thoughts on Red Teaming	139
8	The Distant Framework of War	168
9	The Problem of German Military Effectiveness, 1900–1945	195
10	Reflections on the Combined Bomber Offensive	231
11	The Air War in the Gulf	265
12	Thoughts on British Intelligence in World War II and the Implications for Intelligence in the Twenty-First Century	283
13	The Meaning of World War II	311
	Index	319

Introduction

Over the past several years, I have mulled over the possibility of compiling a collection of articles I have written. These pieces have conveyed my broader sense of history to those interested in the role that historical studies might play in molding our understanding of the uses of force in the past as well as in thinking about its use in the future. I have also used such articles and essays as a means of correcting the myths and historical inconsistencies that seem to proliferate in the current policy milieu, like toadstools in a damp and corrupt climate. My editor at Cambridge, Frank Smith, expressed surprising enthusiasm for such a collection when I raised the possibility. The result was that I had to rummage over a considerable period through disparate journals and unpublished essays locked away in my files and in the various disks and thumbdrives that form the chaos that is my working environment. In the process of assembling this collection, the reviewers of the initial manuscript helped me enormously in molding the final manuscript. Their apposite comments have guided me not only in the writing of this introduction but also in the formatting and ordering of the chapters in this book.

Some of these essays reflect my recent work, and some appeared almost 20 years ago. In the case of the latter, instead of attempting to rework the footnotes, I have appended a small bibliographical paragraph of more recent books and articles that have since appeared. These short references should provide sufficient guidance for interested readers as they follow the path of historical research and arguments over the course of the intervening years.

In the end, this collection represents an overview of themes that have informed the basis of my historical work and interests since I first began my graduate studies at Yale in fall 1969. At that time, I had just completed a tour as a maintenance officer in a C-130 wing in Southeast Asia. I had three specific reasons for returning to graduate school. Two of those, I hope, are common among those engaged in the academic profession of teaching history, namely, the desire to uncover the past and convey a love of history to others. Since my earliest days in school, I have found myself fascinated by the course of human events throughout the ages – the tableau, if you will, of human beings, great and small, as they contested for power and influence. An equally important motive has been my fascination with the similarities between the past and the present in terms of human behavior despite the vast changes in culture, politics, and technology. "The more things change, the more they stay the same." Thus, it was not hard to justify to myself at the age of 28, an age when most people of my age were already firmly set in their careers, the additional five or six years in graduate school studying history.

But my third reason for returning to school was, and remains, uncommon to most in the profession of academic history. My war in Southeast Asia was an easy one. I was rarely exposed to danger. Yet, to this day I am haunted by the smell of the dead wafting through the cargo bays of the C-130s carrying body bags from the battles in I Corps for their transshipment through Saigon back to their resting places in the United States. From my first days in graduate school, I had hoped to use my study of history as a tool to help future military leaders avoid the costly, palpable mistakes that their predecessors had made in waging that dismal conflict known to Americans as the Vietnam War.[1] In the aftermath of the failures in Iraq, during what too many military and political leaders termed the post-conflict phase, I fear that much of my work has gone for naught. Yet, I have always possessed a streak of optimism to accompany my darkest thoughts. Perhaps, as the then young marine lieutenant suggested at the end of the documentary, *No End in Sight*: America can do better. It has been the avowed purpose of much of my writing to help America's military and political leaders perform more competently in the future.

In the largest sense, this collection also represents that third thread in my historical research and writings, as well as my fascination with the history of human organizations and those who lead them. These chapters

---

[1] Only in the 1990s did we learn how incompetent and dishonest America's military leaders had been in providing support to Lyndon Johnson and Robert Strange McNamara in the making of the decision to intervene in the war against the Viet Cong and North Vietnamese in South Vietnam. In this regard, see especially H.R. McMaster, *Dereliction of Duty, Lyndon Johnson, Robert Strange McNamara, the Joint Chiefs of Staff and the Lies that Led to Vietnam* (New York, 1996).

rest on the proposition that war is neither a science nor a craft, but rather an incredibly complex endeavor which challenges men and women to the core of their souls. It is, to put it bluntly, not only the most physically demanding of all the professions, but also the most demanding intellectually and morally. It is a profession whose practitioners only occasionally exercise their main task – the conduct of war, a state that they can never really replicate in peacetime. The cost of slovenly thinking at every level of war can translate into the deaths of innumerable men and women, most of whom deserve better from their leaders. It also leads invariably to the massive waste of national treasure – to which, considering the current economic situation the United States faces, Americans need to pay closer attention.

At the highest level of strategy, human conflict demands a sophisticated understanding of the international environment and the balance of power, not to mention the nature of one's opponents: their history, their culture, their religion and ideology, and their *Weltanshauuungen*. Strategy also demands a realistic evaluation of means in relation to ends. The Prussian thinker Carl von Clausewitz noted in *On War* that "no one starts a war – or rather, no one in his senses ought to do so – without being clear in his mind what he achieves by that war and how he intends to conduct it."[2] And that of course is the conundrum because the conduct of strategy throughout history suggests the opposite: states and their leaders, military as well as political, have embarked on war with only the most superficial, sloppy analysis to undergird their thinking in the rush to war.[3]

It is not surprising then that throughout my career, I have found myself profoundly influenced by Clausewitz and our increasingly sophisticated understanding of the depth and complex directions of his thought.[4] Of all the activities in which mankind engages, it is the conduct of war that envelopes it with the greatest degree of uncertainty, ambiguity, and

---

[2] Carl von Clausewitz, *On War*, trans. and ed. by Michael Howard and Peter Paret (Princeton, NJ, 1976), p. 579.
[3] See Williamson Murray, MacGregor Knox, and Alvin Bernstein, *The Making of Strategy, Rulers, States and War* (Cambridge, 1992); and the opening chapter of Williamson Murray, Richard Sinnreich, and Jim Lacey, *The Shaping of Grand Strategy: Policy, Diplomacy, and War* (Cambridge, 2011).
[4] In this regard, I have been heavily influenced by four specific works: The translation of *On War* by Michael Howard and Peter Paret that Princeton University Press published in the mid-1970s has had an enormous impact on my thinking as has Peter Paret's brilliant intellectual study of intellectual history *Clausewitz and the State* (Princeton, NJ, 1978). Two shorter works have also influenced me profoundly: Barry D. Watts, *Clausewitzian Friction and Future War* (Washington, DC, 1996) and Alan Beyerchen, "Clausewitz, Nonlinearity, and the Unpredictability of War," *International Security*, vol. 17, no. 3, Winter 1992–1993.

friction. Murphy's Law rules: "If something can go wrong, it will." The enemy's intentions and purposes will always remain an uncertain entity. As the aphorism popular among many of today's troops captures it, "the enemy always gets a vote." Unintended consequences and unforeseen second- and third-order effects bedevil the most logical and carefully thought-through approaches to war. In hard, cold fact, mankind has 5,000 years of recorded history that underlines that reality.[5]

Yet, in the 1990s, in the aftermath of the 1991 Gulf War, many in the American military, particularly the navy and air force, but even some in the army, succumbed to the belief that America's overwhelming technological superiority and the sheer crunching power of the computers possessed by the U.S. military could and would remove friction from what was termed the "battle space" – at least, for the military forces of the United States. In other words U.S. forces would be able to achieve what the Pentagon termed "battle space dominance" over America's "battlefield opponents." As Admiral Bill Owens, vice chairman of the Joint Chiefs of Staff, argued: the U.S. military would be able to see and understand everything that was happening in an area 200 miles by 200 miles and do so in real time.[6] Throughout the 1990s, analysts at think tanks wrote papers about rapid decisive operations and the new American way of war that supposedly had broken with the paradigms of the past and thus made the study of past conflicts irrelevant. In fact, information represents only disparate, chaotic fragments of reality. It is only as valuable as the ability to filter and analyze it into a relatively clear depiction of what appears to be happening.

For a few short weeks in March and April 2003 the onrush of the 3rd Infantry Division and the 1st Marine Division seemingly confirmed that vision, at least to outside observers. For those on the inside of conventional military operations during Operation Iraqi Freedom, however, matters looked considerably different. The new age of computers and rapid communications provided commanders and their staffs with a deluge of information, but little of that information was translatable into knowledge of what was actually happening in the battle space. Moreover, the frictions and misunderstandings of soldiers and marines operating under the intense pressure of combat continued to cloud the

---

[5] I am indebted to General James Mattis, a friend and critic of much of my work, for this.
[6] See William A. Owens, with Ed Offley, *Lifting the Fog of War* (New York, 2001). Such views were widespread throughout the services throughout the 1990s and informed the views of civilians like Donald Rumsfeld and Paul Wolfowitz.

picture. The chief of intelligence of the Combined Forces Land Component Command put it best in commenting to a CNN interviewer: "We're drowning in information!"

In effect, the technologies that were adopted to remove the frictions of war were creating an array of new and more complex frictions. Quite simply, information is not, and never has been, the same as knowledge. It is not surprising then that the two outstanding division commanders who led American forces into Iraq, Major General James Mattis, commander of the 1st Marine Division, and Major General Buford Blount, commander of the 3rd Infantry Division, spent most of their time with front-line units rather than back in their tactical headquarters. They did so because only at the front lines could they gain a sense of what was really happening – what the Germans term *Fingerspitzengefühl* (the feeling at the end of one's fingers). In the real world, the icons on the screens of computers can never depict reality; in effect, they represent only the pale, shimmering visage of events transpiring in a milieu of fear and uncertainty.

For the fortunes of America's post-conflict efforts, it was precisely the knowledge of the complex, fragmented nature of Iraqi culture, history, religion, and politics that was needed at the highest levels. Nevertheless, too many senior officers and civilian policy makers were sadly deficient in such understanding, as the United States stumbled into the post-conflict stage after the collapse of Saddam's evil regime. Of course, they might have read the memoirs of Lieutenant General Aylmer Haldane, who commanded the British forces that put down the rebellion of the tribes in the Mesopotamian River Valley in 1920. He noted in a comment that fit all too many generals and civilians in summer 2003, who led the effort in the first year of occupying Iraq. "I regret that on my arrival in Mesopotamia I was too much preoccupied with military matters and too little informed regarding the political problems."[7] American political and military leaders might even have studied the experiences of U.S. commanders and their forces in fighting the vicious insurgency that U.S. forces had encountered in South Vietnam in the 1960s. There is, however, little evidence that most of those responsible for addressing the growing insurgency in Iraq in 2003 and 2004 had the background to understand the events that were swirling around them in the Mesopotamian River Valley. Instead, like the Germans in the 1920s and 1930s, they had trained themselves and their subordinates to become superb tacticians – and, at the

---

[7] Lieutenant General Aylmer L. Haldane, *The Insurrection in Mesopotamia 1920* (London, 1922).

highest levels, "masters of the operational art." Thus, without reference to the historical past, they managed to repeat nearly every mistake that America's generals had made in the Vietnam War, not to mention the British difficulties in crushing the insurgency of the Arab tribes in 1920.

A number of themes in the following chapters address the issues involved in the conduct of strategy and military operations, the most important being that we *can* learn from the past. Inherent in the lessons of the past is the reality that military institutions rarely get the next war right. It is not that they focus on the last war and therefore get the next one wrong, as so many historians have suggested. Rather, it is the fact that they fail even to study the last war honestly and thoroughly. Few military institutions manage to achieve that level of competence. Instead most militaries study their profession narrowly, if at all. Then, when they face combat and the fact that war is an uncertain, high-risk endeavor, they are not prepared for reality. In peacetime, most military leaders privilege certainties and low-risk behavior, instead of preparing themselves widely and deeply by studying the history of their profession. The nature of peacetime discipline and culture more often than not results in the development of tunnel vision, usually focused on the tactical realm.

The conduct of two world wars by the German military illustrates the dangers of such a narrow focus. All too competent at the tactical and operational levels, the German military displayed an almost contemptuous disregard for the strategic issues involved in the conduct of war. As a result, during the Second World War, they managed to repeat every major strategic mistake that they had made in the Great War. The irony, given the attention that Americans showered on the German way of war in the 1980s, is the fact that it is the strategic level of war that matters most in the conduct of peace and war. If a nation's and its military's approach is largely effective in evaluating the context and realities of a potential conflict, then military organizations can adjust their tactical and operational approaches. If the strategy is fundamentally flawed, then no matter of tactical and operational virtuosity can repair the damage of strategic mistakes.

Nevertheless, if Americans have not always focused overly on tactics, they have often attempted to reduce the business of war to a search for simple, clear, engineering solutions – in other words, for "silver bullets." Their love affair with technology – and emphasis on a clear, mechanistic set of principles for the conduct of war[8] – underlines an effort to boil

---

[8] In this regard, see particularly the "Weinberger doctrine" of the 1980s.

the extraordinarily difficult down to easy-to-read briefing charts that eliminate the complex. In other words, they have too often sought to simplify and build clear but irrelevant models in the face of what will always be a nightmarish world of complexity and difficulty. In the end, military organizations tend to be unreflective and intellectually indifferent to what really matters. Their preparations for war have often turned to the simplicity of drills and training rather than to rigorous, honest study, much less than critical self-examination.

These then are the basic themes that connect the chapters in this book. The first group of chapters represents a general analysis of history and its relation to the future, accompanied by probings of historically based theory and its importance to the profession. The second examines specific historical case studies in the conduct of strategy, operations, and war.[9] The introductory chapter grapples with the largest theme in this volume: why a knowledge of, not just an acquaintance with, history represents *the* essential component in thinking about the future, even though it offers no certain path in a universe dominated by uncertainty and ambiguity. And this is because nothing else offers an understanding of the present, from which the future springs.

The following two chapters then address what might best be termed the backbone of any historical analysis of war: the fact that the great Athenian historian of the Peloponnesian War, Thucydides, and the Prussian theorist Carl von Clausewitz, the first who wrote nearly 2,500 years ago and the second nearly two centuries ago, managed to write the most serious and valuable examinations of human conflict of all the immense writings on the subject. The fact that no modern writers have managed to rise to their level of sophistication and understanding of the place of war in human affairs is indeed a sad commentary on the intellectual depth of the present age. The third chapter, written in the mid-1990s, addresses the fact that the emerging leadership of America's military appeared to be engaged in a massive effort to dismiss the past as irrelevant to understanding the future and to replace it with a technological view of the world that removed friction, ambiguity, and uncertainty from the military equation. That approach would reap bitter dividends in Afghanistan after 2001 and in Iraq after 2003.

---

[9] In 2005 Colonel Richard Hart Sinnreich, U.S. Army (ret.) and I edited a volume of essays that examined the crucial role that history should play in the education and preparation of officers throughout their careers. See Williamson Murray and Richard Hart Sinnreich, *The Past as Prologue, The Importance of History to the Military profession* (Cambridge, 2005).

That anomaly would appear to have been the result of the brilliant diplomatic and strategic maneuvering of Otto von Bismarck, the "Iron Chancellor" of Prusso-Germany. Ironically, Bismarck's methods, as well as his success, in turn may well have made a more terrible European conflict inevitable. By finessing the strategic situation in Central Europe, he prevented a great war over the unification of Germany, while waging limited wars against the Danes, the Austrians, and then the French. However, in 1875, when he threatened to launch the new German state against a France that had recovered all too quickly in his eyes from the catastrophe of the Franco-Prussian War, he confronted an enormously altered European situation from that of 1870–1871, one in which Germany confronted the possibility of waging war against a European-wide coalition of the great powers. Bismarck backed down, realizing that the possibility of a major war was something Germany *must* avoid. But his successors proved incapable of understanding his methods or the dangers that he had foreseen so clearly in the crisis of 1875. Their willful disdain for anything other than "military necessity" ensured that Bismarck's success in creating a unified German state then created the strategic disaster of the two great world wars – wars that came close to destroying Western civilization.

It was the failure of strategy that is the focus of the next chapter on German military effectiveness over most of the first half of the twentieth century. In the early 1980s, when I began emphasizing the use of history as a tool for understanding the effectiveness of military institutions, many of those engaged in similar efforts (including myself) found themselves intrigued by the German military and its performance on the battlefield.[13] It was only at the mid-point in the decade that I focused on the enormous gaps, particularly at the strategic level, but also at the operational level, in the German military performance in two world wars.[14] It was at that point that I recognized how flawed, disastrously so, was the German approach to war, an approach deeply influenced by the military culture as well as

[13] One of my earliest articles was on the coherent and effective preparation of the Wehrmacht, based on a thorough lesson-learned process that included the entire army and tied in closely with the training program, for the 1940 campaign in the west against the forces of the Western Powers: See "The German Response to Victory in Poland: A Case Study in Professionalism," *Armed Forces and Society*, Winter 1981.

[14] The gaps in strategic thinking are obvious in that the Germans managed to repeat the same strategic mistakes in the Second World War that they had made in the First World War. Given the focus of most historians on the sharp end at the operational level, the gross mistakes the Germans made in intelligence assessment and in logistics have only begun to emerge in the historical literature in the last several decades.

the extraordinary political and cultural arrogance of the military and the society at large. There are lessons in this example not only for the U.S. military but for the American people as well.

The next two chapters deal with the impact of air power in two distinct conflicts: World War II and the Gulf War of 1991. There is some irony in these essays because when I left the U.S. Air Force in 1969, I swore that I would never involve myself in the history of air power. As those who have followed my academic career know, that is not a promise I have kept. In fact, my first published book examined the factors that contributed to the *Luftwaffe*'s defeat in the Second World War.[15] In every respect, the Combined Bomber Offensive represented a bloody, ferocious campaign that wrecked Germany's cities and industrial capacity from one end of the Reich to the other. Nevertheless, beginning with John Kenneth Galbraith's thoroughly dishonest introduction to the "Strategic Bombing Survey" in the earliest days of post-war analysis, historians have argued over the precise impact that the campaign actually had on the Third Reich's war economy and the *Wehrmacht*'s ability to conduct the war against the Allies. Moreover, an increasingly strident group of historians has argued that the strategic bombing of Germany was immoral and, moreover, unnecessary because it failed to contribute significantly to the Third Reich's defeat.

The first of the two air power chapters, written in the early 1990s, addresses this question of what the Combined Bomber Offensive actually accomplished in direct, as well as indirect, terms and represents a direct rejoinder to arguments about the ineffectiveness of strategic bombing. My argument in this chapter has been considerably buttressed by the brilliant economic and historical analysis of Adam Tooze, who, by using the modern tools of economic analysis, has reached the conclusion (among others) that Bomber Command's campaign against the Ruhr in spring 1943 had a direct and major impact on Germany's ability to produce the weapons its military forces so desperately needed at the time.[16] That contribution, I would argue, makes the argument for the crucial role that the Combined Bombing Offensive played in the winning of the Second World War, even stronger. It is now clear that Bomber Command by itself in the first half of 1943 contributed in a major fashion to the

---

[15] It was first published by the Air University Press as *Strategy for Defeat, The Defeat of the Luftwaffe* (Montgomery, AL, 1983). A revised commercial edition was published by the Nautical and Aviation Press as *Luftwaffe* (Baltimore, MD, 1985).

[16] Adam Tooze, *The Wages of Destruction, The Making and Breaking of the Nazi War Economy* (London, 2006).

weakening of the Nazi war economy and Germany's ability to prosecute the war against the Reich's enemies at the war's culminating point in 1943. Thereby, it helped considerably in shortening the conflict.

The second air power chapter represents my rejoinder in the 1990s to the currents swirling around the American military that air power had managed to win the Gulf War against Saddam Hussein virtually single-handedly and that the hundred-hour ground campaign had been unnecessary. As the foundation for this piece, I used the extensive work that I had completed as the main author of the "Operations" report of *The Gulf War Air Power Survey*, the study undertaken by an independent group of scholars, at the direction of the secretary of the air force, to assess the impact of the air campaign against Iraq during the effort to defeat Iraq's armed forces and drive them from Kuwait. In fact, while the air campaign played a major role in setting the Iraqi military up for its crushing military defeat in February 1991, the ground war was absolutely necessary to underscore the complete military defeat of Saddam Hussein's forces. Without the ground campaign, there is no doubt that Saddam would have been able to claim, and would have been believed in much of the Arab world, that Iraq's military had stood (as the Germans had so willfully and falsely claimed about their army in November 1918) unbroken and undefeated in the field against the forces of the entire Western world.[17]

The penultimate chapter examines the factors that led to the success that Britain's intelligence organizations enjoyed during the Second World War. The essay was specifically written to underline the considerable differences that marked Britain's utilization of talent external to its intelligence organizations – such as mathematicians, linguists, historians, and other scholars – and America's intelligence agencies at present, which appear to be bureaucratic islands unto themselves. In the case of analysts, it is ironic to note that perhaps the most successful intelligence officer in the British effort during the Second World War was F.H. Hinsley, a Cambridge undergraduate who had not yet even earned his bachelor's degree in history when he joined Bletchley Park at the war's onset.[18] Besides his historical studies, Hinsley was also fluent in German, in fact, barely escaping being interned in Germany when he crossed the border

---

[17] For the Iraqi perspective of the war, see Kevin M. Woods, *The Mother of All Battles: Saddam Hussein's Plan for the Persian Gulf War* (Annapolis, MD, 2008).

[18] After the war Hinsley went on to become a major figure in military history and the director of the official history of British intelligence during the war: F.H. Hinsley, et al., *British Intelligence during the Second World War*, 3 vols. (Cambridge, 1984).

back into French territory on 2 September 1939, less than 24 hours before Britain declared war. And yet, today, with multi-billions of dollars being spent on America's intelligence agencies, eight years into the war on Afghanistan, America's intelligence system has yet to map the tribal and linguistic divisions of that country. Moreover, a recent study of the Central Intelligence Agency indicates that only 13 percent of the organization's personnel fluently speak or read a foreign language.

At the end of this book, I have placed a chapter that I wrote in 1994 for my friend Bob Silano, at that time the editor of *Joint Forces Quarterly*, on the fiftieth anniversary of the landings in Normandy. It summed up the deep feelings I have had when I visited the various cemeteries in Normandy, where tens of thousands of young Americans lie buried far from their homes. Those visits remind me of the grim cost involved in protecting the United States and its Allies from the evils that stalk this world. In an age of pervasive ignorance of the realities of the past and the capacity of human beings to do evil, those cold white stones are a grim reminder that only such brutal sacrifices can preserve our world from the ravages, now and in the future, unleashed by the likes of Hitler, Mussolini, Mao, and Saddam Hussein. As the Romans warned, "if you want peace, prepare for war," an adage that too many politicians, such as Neville Chamberlain in the 1930s, disregarded in their pursuit of peace at any price. Those stones at Normandy also underline the cost of a lack of military professionalism that led Omar Bradley to contemptuously dismiss what had been learned at such a cost in the Pacific theater in the amphibious landings of 1943 and 1944 – a theater, in his words, that was "just a bush league." The result was the slaughter on Omaha Beach, lying just below the cemetery. In the end, military professionalism demands the most rigorous intellectual adaptability and imagination, qualities that officers can only learn with the wholehearted commitment to the study of the history of their profession. It is with that in mind, and with considerable humility, that I offer these works to the reader.

I

History and the Future

The early Greek imagination envisaged the past and the present as in front of us – we can see them. The future invisible, is behind us.... Paradoxical as it may sound to the modern ear, this image of our journey through time may be truer to reality than the medieval and modern feeling that we face the future as we make our way forward into it.[1]

The study of history provides no clear, certain path for understanding the future. At best, its lessons are uncertain and ambiguous. No matter how sophisticated and eloquent historians may be, they can only present rough approximations of the past, much less the present or the future, both of which invariably consist of surprises as well as unanticipated changes and challenges. Yet, history, writ large, represents the best laboratory mankind possesses for understanding the future. There are, of course, other disciplines for thinking about the future, particularly when they address issues that have to do with human nature, such as anthropology, psychology, and literature.[2] But almost invariably, these disciplines

---

[1] Bernard Knox, *Backing into the Future: The Classical Tradition and Its Renewal* (New York, 1994), pp. 11–12.
[2] Leo Tolstoy's fictional descriptions of combat in the sections dealing with Austerlitz and Borodino in *War and Peace* may well represent the finest descriptions of combat ever written.

This chapter appeared in *Orbis* in Winter 2009 and is published with the permission of the Foreign Policy Research Institute. I am indebted to a number of colleagues and friends who read this work at various stages and provided insightful comments. Among those who have contributed are Karl Lowe, Colonel Jeff Lofgren, Joel Resnick, James Lacey, Lesley Smith, Rear Admiral John Richardson, and General James Mattis. The opinions expressed in this chapter, however, are entirely mine.

best address the future, when history provides a context for their use. Intelligent gaming can also approximate the future with some accuracy, such as the SIGMA games of 1965, which underlined that graduated escalation would not work against the North Vietnamese. Yet, the insights gained from those games also largely rested on the historical experiences of the French in their losing war against the Viet-Minh between 1946 and 1954.[3] This reliance on historical context in almost all predictive endeavors of utility occurs because only historically based disciplines provide the path to Sun Tsu's admonition that above all else "one must understand one's enemy," as well as oneself.[4]

Ignorance of the past, dismissal of history, or simply distortions of recent events have resulted in disastrous choices by statesmen, political leaders, and generals.[5] But that has not prevented successive generations of rulers and their political and military advisers from ignoring the lessons of history and marching down the road to disaster. And even when history makes an appearance in the decision-making processes, its users often either misunderstand or misrepresent its lessons.[6] As one of the foremost historians of Europe in the first half of the twentieth century has noted:

> The owl of history is an evening bird. The past as a whole is unknowable; only at the end of the day do some of its outlines dimly emerge. The future cannot be known at all, and the past suggests that change is often radical

---

[3] See H.R. McMaster, *Dereliction of Duty, Lyndon Johnson, Robert McNamara, the Joint Chiefs of Staff, and the Lies that Led to Vietnam* (New York, 1997), p. 90.

[4] Many of the politicians, planners, and commanders of Operation IRAQI FREEDOM would have gained considerable insight into the problems they were going to confront after conventional military operations in Iraq had they read either Lieutenant General Sir Aylmer L. Haldane, *The Insurrection in Mesopotamia* (London, 1922); or T.E. Lawrence, *Seven Pillars of Wisdom* (New York, 1991).

[5] The foremost example of such misuse and distortion of the past and its relevance for the future lay with the approach of Fascism and Marxism in their selective use of history to build ideologies that were to have extraordinarily damaging impacts on the human condition. For a specific rejection of past experience, the conduct of the Vietnam War by the U.S. military represented a rejection of the French experience in that country from 1946 through 1954 as irrelevant to the American approach. Thus, the American effort repeated nearly every mistake the French made. Beyond that dismal example lie the equally obvious ones of both Napoleon and Hitler ignoring the catastrophe of Sweden's Charles XII in Russia in the eighteenth century; the repetition by the Germans in the Second World War of every major strategic error they had made in the First World War; and failure of the French to examine the history of World War I honestly and dispassionately. The list is almost endless.

[6] In this regard, see Williamson Murray and Richard Hart Sinnreich, *The Past as Prologue, The Importance of History to the Military Profession* (Cambridge, 2006).

and unforeseeable rather than incremental and predictable. Yet, despite its many ambiguities, historical experience remains the only available guide both to the present and to the range of alternatives inherent in the future.[7]

Therein lies the crucial point, for the only way to understand the present and its potential is through a thorough study of history and the histories of allies *as well as* those of potential opponents.[8] Without that basic understanding of how the present has evolved through a perspective on the historical and cultural uniqueness of their nation's position as well as those of others, strategists have no way of understanding where they stand. If strategists do not know where they stand in the present, then any road to the future will do, as it has done in the past – all too often with disastrous consequences. A perceptive understanding of the present based on historical knowledge is the essential first step for thinking about the future.

Only history can provide the key insights into who we Americans are and how we have reached our present situation, as well as hint at the hugely differing worldviews of others.[9] Thus, history provides the crucial basis for understanding the present, in other words, the base line that any coherent and useful thinking about the future demands.[10] As one of the world's great classicists noted about Euripides, that great dramatist and analyst of human nature:

> The writer as prophet is not someone with a lucky gift of foresight but someone who foresees only because he sees, sees clearly, unmoved by prejudice, by hopes, by fears, sees to the heart of the present, the actual situation. He knows where he is. And if you know where you are, you can see where you've been and also where you are going. The poet as prophet is no vague dreamy seer but on the contrary a man of hard analytic vision who sees the here and knows truly and exactly for what it is. His face is not that of the young Shelley in the idealized portraits but the face of the prophet on the Olympia pediment, worn, sad, and loaded with the burden of terrible knowledge. The poet as prophet lives not in the past as most of us live –

---

[7] MacGregor Knox, "What History Can Tell Us about the 'New Strategic Environment,'" in Williamson Murray, ed., *Brassey's Mershon American Defense Annual, 1995–1996* (Washington, DC, 1996).

[8] I am indebted to Joel Resnick of the Joint Advanced Warfighting Division for this insight.

[9] It has been the failure to understand the other that has caused Americans – and the British as well – enormous difficulties in addressing the problems raised by emerging strategic threats. Nothing underlines this more clearly than the tragic history of the 1930s, when the democracies found it inconceivable that Hitler and the Nazis were bent on war.

[10] An historically based understanding of the present can only provide dimly lit signposts to the future, but such signposts are a considerable improvement over guesses based on idle speculation.

our attack on reality made with weapons that are already out of date – nor as others live, in dreams of the future which turn away from the world as it is, but in the present, really in the present, seeing the present.[11]

Without that historically based understanding, statesmen and military leaders "will continue, in the immortal words of Kiffin Rockwell, a pilot in the legendary World War I Lafayette Escadrille, to 'fly along, blissfully ignorant, hoping for the best.'"[12]

What then can we learn from history that is useful in understanding the future? Above all, history suggests timeless lessons about the fundamental nature of human conflict, the characteristics of human interactions, the extraordinary range of human attitudes and understandings of the world, and, perhaps most important, the larger historical, cultural, and strategic framework within which the strivings of human beings take place.[13] In physical appearance, human beings look much the same, but their cultural and historical experiences inevitably give them entirely different perspectives on the world.[14] Moreover, history underlines that human nature will remain intractable, truculent, unpredictable, and irascible; that conflict in one form or another will remain a substantial and continuous part of the human landscape; and that uncertainty, chance, and friction – the Godchildren of Carl von Clausewitz – will inevitably and often perniciously influence the course of events. And because war is always a human venture, it will remain inextricably tied to the political and historical frameworks of those states or nonstate entities that conduct it.[15]

---

[11] Knox, *Backing into the Future*, pp. 74–75.

[12] Quoted in Robert Gaskin, "The Great 1996 Non-Debate on National Security," in Williamson Murray and Allan R. Millett, eds., *Brassey's American Defense Annual, 1996–1997* (Washington, DC, 1996), p. 17.

[13] This demands the widest acquaintance with history. Thus, for those not familiar with history, its use presents an enormous challenge. For the difficulties in using history see: Williamson Murray, "Thoughts on Military History and the Profession of Arms," in Murray and Sinnreich, *The Past as Prologue*.

[14] On how differently the Chinese evaluated the Gulf War of 1991 than did Americans in the 1990s, one should consult Qiao Liang and Wang Xiangsui, *Unrestricted Warfare* (Beijing, 1999). Moreover, the level of competence among political and military leaders differs to an extraordinary extent. Sir Edward Grey, Britain's Foreign Secretary before the First World War, commented accurately on Germany's Kaiser in the following terms: "The German Emperor is ageing me; he is like a battleship with steam up and screws going, but with no rudder, and he will run into something some day and cause a catastrophe." Holger H. Herwig, *"Luxury" Fleet: The Imperial German Navy 1888–1918* (London, 1980), front piece.

[15] Clausewitz' most famous comment, often quoted, but all too often ignored, is "[w]ar is merely the continuation of policy by other means." Carl von Clausewitz, *On War*, trans.

History also underlines how ambiguous and uncertain the processes of human decision making are. In describing the outbreak of the First World War, Winston Churchill admitted that

> [o]ne rises from the study of the causes of the Great War with a prevailing sense of the defective control of individuals upon world fortunes. It has been well said, 'there is always more error than design in human affairs.' The limited minds of the ablest men, their disputed authority, the climate of opinion in which they dwell, their transient and partial contributions to the mighty problem, that problem itself so far beyond their compass, so vast in scale and detail, so changing in its aspects – all this must surely be considered... Events... got onto certain lines and no one could get them off again.[16]

This chapter aims to delineate some of the issues raised by historically based approaches to understanding the present and future and suggest the difficulties that Americans may confront in the face of inherently complex and uncertain challenges the future will inevitably throw up. It begins with a discussion of the profound impact that changes have had on the international environment and proceeds then to discussions of what history suggests about the influence of human nature on the course of future events; the future of war and its nature in the coming century; and the nature of governance and the United States; and ends with the implications of the future for the current American military. This chapter does not aim to provide answers, but rather to suggest to policy makers, strategists, and military leaders how they might better think through the complex political and cultural questions they need to be asking in the making of strategy.[17] This is the essential first step Americans need to make because if they fail to ask the right questions, then any answer will do, but all answers will prove irrelevant to the challenges the future will inevitably raise.

---

and ed. by Michael Howard and Peter Paret (Princeton, NJ, 1976), p. 87. It is worth noting that the IRA was considered a nonstate entity from 1916 to 1920 as was the Viet Minh from 1945 to 1954, but both achieved the status of states. Whatever its trappings as a fanatical religious organization, Al Qaeda has distinct political goals.

[16] Winston S. Churchill, *The World Crisis* (Toronto, 1931), p. 6.

[17] As the U.S. Naval War College's course on strategy and policy has emphasized since Admiral Stansfield Turner created it in 1972, strategy is a constantly evolving process in which states and their bureaucratic organs attempt to change and adapt to an ever changing environment. For a work deliberately focused on discussing strategy within that framework see Williamson Murray, MacGregor Knox, and Alvin Bernstein, eds., *The Making of Strategy, Rulers, States, and War* (Cambridge, 1992).

History and Discontinuities

So long as this was the general style of warfare [in the eighteenth century], with its violence limited in such strict and obvious ways, no one saw any inconsistency in it. On the contrary, it all seemed absolutely right... Suddenly [however] war again became the business of the people.... The resources and efforts now available for use surpassed all conventional limits; nothing now impeded the vigor with which war could be waged, and consequently the opponents of France faced the utmost peril.... War, untrammeled by any conventional restraints, had broken loose in all its elemental fury.[18]

In thinking about and adapting to the future, the strategist and statesman must contend with more than just human nature. Change in the modern world has almost continuously found itself driven by impersonal factors, such as technology, economic depression, natural disasters, including plagues, as well as the actions of human beings. In the 1930s, the Great Depression did as much to mold the world as did the catastrophic results of the First World War.[19] The ascent of Adolf Hitler to power in January 1933 was equally a product of that conflict – a lost war that attacked the heart of how the Germans thought of themselves – and of a Depression that threw nearly half of the German workforce onto bread lines.

Equally important in using history to think about the future must be the recognition that periods of discontinuity invariably arrive that fundamentally alter the periods of continuity to which human nature clings with such tenacity. The great problem with the discontinuities of history is that they are rarely apparent until after they have arrived. Virtually no one saw the coming of the Great Depression in 1929. Three years later, the entire world found itself mired in the worst economic slump in history. Discontinuities invariably represent periods of enormous turmoil and uncertainty and often result in great loss of human life.[20] The difficulty for strategists is that most human beings, including themselves,

---

[18] Clausewitz, *On War*, pp. 591–593.
[19] The world since 1945 has focused largely on the Second World War. Yet, in reality the First World War was more important. Admittedly it killed fewer soldiers, while its damage remained largely limited to the field of battle. Yet, it spawned the Russian Revolution and Lenin's Bolsheviks, contributed to the rise of Mussolini and Hitler, ended the great period of economic growth marking the period of globalization before August 1914, and most important ended the ingrained belief in the march of progress.
[20] It is essential to understand that discontinuities can be entirely man-made, such as the First World War or fundamental shifts in the strategic landscape, or acts of nature that fundamentally disturb the environments in which mankind lives.

invariably cling to continuities. Yet, the discontinuities invariably arrive unheralded to distort, overwhelm, and at times destroy human societies. Those that survive do so above all because of their flexibility and capacity to adapt.[21]

In the short period of thirty-one years, from 1914 to 1945, the First World War, the Depression, and the Second World War all occurred. Each by itself fundamentally changed – or warped – the course of history into new and more dangerous directions. The three together came close to destroying Western civilization as it had developed over the previous five centuries.[22] Yet the relatively long, near half-century of the Cold War and the interregnum that has followed the Soviet Union's collapse have given many in the West a sense that continuities rather than discontinuities are what the past suggests about the future. They could not be more wrong. We are sure to confront discontinuities in the future, and how well American society adapts to them will play a major role in whether it manages to preserve its values or even whether it survives.[23]

In particular, history underlines the extent of the unpredictabilities with which strategists and planners most often contend. Exacerbating the extent of the unpredictability in international relations has been the fact that mirror imaging, the failure to understand how different other nations and cultures are, has further muddied the processes of decision making. Shifts in the strategic landscape among the world powers can come with stunning suddenness. As Paul Kennedy has suggested, British military planners confronted such a shift within a period of less than five years in the 1930s:

> At the beginning of the 1930s, the Soviet Union was regarded as the greatest land enemy of the British Empire, while in naval terms the chief rivals were the United States and Japan; Italy was seen as an old friend, France was unduly assertive and difficult (but not hostile), and Germany was still prostrate. Five... years later Japan appeared as a distinct challenge to

---

[21] The Romans possessed many grand qualities both as a people and as a society, but flexibility was not one of them. And when the catastrophes of the third and fourth centuries came, the Western Empire went into a death spiral to a considerable extent caused by its failure to adapt.

[22] One should underline that those centuries, just in terms of the history of the West, consisted of enormous discontinuities, some man-made, others induced and driven by nature – the little ice age of the seventeenth century being a particularly good example of the latter.

[23] Here, survival for most Americans concerns the survival of their great political experiment and values. The discontinuity of the Soviet Union's collapse only indirectly affected those living in the United States, Western and Central Europe, and much of East Asia, and mostly in a positive sense. The opposite was the case for many in the Balkans and Caucasus.

British interests in the Far East, Germany had fallen under Nazi rule and was assessed as 'the greatest long-term danger,' and Italy had moved from friendship to enmity; whereas the United States was more unpredictable and isolationist than ever.[24]

Even the greatest of statesmen have found it difficult to foresee the outline of the future, as they struggled to make basic decisions. William Pitt, the Younger, perhaps the greatest statesman of the eighteenth century – with the possible exception of his father – announced to the House of Commons in February 1792 that "unquestionably there never was a time in the history of this country when, from the situation of Europe, we might more reasonably expect fifteen years of peace, than we may at the present moment."[25] In that same year, an unknown Corsican noble by the name of Napoleon Bonaparte was promoted to captain in a French Army, the officer corps of which was dissolving under the pressures of the French Revolution, which had already begun its dark trajectory.

Change – even drastic change – has been a theme throughout history, but the pace of major discontinuities has clearly picked up over the course of the past century and a half since the Industrial Revolution began altering the physical environment in which men live and fight.[26] There is nothing in the twenty-first century's accelerating pace of technological advances to suggest human affairs will not continue on the path of rapid and ceaseless change.[27] Yet, most individuals seek an existence in both their professional and personal lives in which change has little impact. The tension between dreams of the past's imaginary continuities and a world of ceaseless change is what provided much of the impetus for the rise of Fascism and Nazism in the 1920s and 1930s.

For those military organizations that care little about the past as it pertains to thinking about the future, institutional memories of past conflicts, i.e., experience, appear a more effective substitute. But peace time invariably washes out of all organizations the useful memories of war

[24] Paul Kennedy, "British Net Assessment and the Coming of the Second World War," in Allan R. Millett and Williamson Murray, eds., *Calculations: Net Assessment and the Coming of the Second World War* (New York, 1992).
[25] Quoted in Colin S. Gray, *Another Bloody Century, Future Warfare* (London, 2006), p. 40.
[26] For the impact of technological change on war and military organizations over the course of history, see William H. McNeil, *The Pursuit of Power, Technology, Armed Force, and Society since A.D. 1000* (Chicago, 1982).
[27] Admittedly, this was less true before the onrush of the Industrial Revolution. Peasants and unskilled laborers experienced relatively few changes in the rhythm of their subsistence-based lives, other than those caused by the changes of the seasons. Nevertheless, great changes did at times wash over their lives, particularly catastrophic events such as wars, plagues, and even climate change.

as it has always been: its horror, confusion, and innumerable frictions. Each year, the ranks of the officer corps change with a new cohort that possesses none of the experiences of those who have gone before. So experience becomes less and less of a guide to the future and more and more of an excuse for maintaining traditional ways. Moreover, experience in one conflict may have little relevance in the next, while tactical experience as a junior officer offers little knowledge or insight about the conduct of operations, much less strategy.

The larger issue for military institutions has to do with how well they innovate in peacetime and adapt in war to the actual conditions of combat. Here, there are lessons in history that suggest the paths that have led to successful military innovation in the past: a serious approach to professional military education, a willingness to study the past honestly, a culture that encourages debate within the officer corps, and a tolerance for the exceptional officer.[28] As Michael Howard has suggested, war is not only the most physically demanding of the professions, it is also the most intellectually demanding. There is a direct correlation between those military organizations that innovate intelligently in peacetime and those that adapt to the actual conditions of war effectively.[29] One might also note that institutional memory often remains flawed and warped without some larger grounding in history. After all, U.S. military forces should have discovered in Operation JUST CAUSE in December 1989 that the removal of the military, police, and government in one swift night of military operations led directly to the massive destruction of much of Panama's infrastructure, economically catastrophic looting of much of the nation's wealth, and political turmoil hard on the heals of "victory." Yet, the institutional memory of those events appears to have disappeared

---

[28] For the aspects of successful military innovation in peacetime, see among others: Thomas C. Hone, Norman Friedman, and Mark Mandeles, *American and British Carrier Development, 1919–1941* (Annapolis, MD, 1999); Harold R. Winton, *To Change an Army, General Sir John Burnett-Stuart and British Armored Doctrine, 1927–1938* (Lawrence, KS, 1988); J.P. Harris, *Men, Ideas, and Tanks, British Military Thought, and Armoured Forces, 1903–1939* (Manchester, 1995); Stephen Peter Rosen, *Winning the Next War, Innovation and the Modern Military* (Ithaca, NY, 1991); and Williamson Murray and Allan R. Millett, *Military Innovation in the Interwar Period* (Cambridge, 1996).

[29] The author is presently working on a study of adaptation in war with case studies based on combat adaptation in World War I, German tactical adaptation after Poland, adaptation in the Battle of Britain, adaptation of Bomber Command, and the Israeli Army's adaptation during the 1973 War. For further discussion of the connection between peacetime innovation and wartime adaptation, see Barry D. Watts and Williamson Murray, "Military Innovation in Peacetime," in Williamson Murray and Allan R. Millett, eds., *Military Innovation in the Interwar Period* (Cambridge, 1996), p. 414.

among the majority of military leaders and planners of Operation IRAQI FREEDOM only fourteen years later.

History, the Future, Human Nature, and the United States

Spartans, in the course of my life I have taken part in many wars, and I see among you [warriors] of the same age as I am. They and I have had experience, and so are not likely to share in what may be a general enthusiasm for war, nor to think that war is a good thing or a safe thing. And you will find, if you look carefully into the matter, that the present war which you are now discussing is not likely to be anything on a small scale... And we more than any others, can afford to take time, because we are strong.

King Archidamnus addressing the Spartan Assembly[30]

Human nature will not change. It has remained the same since the beginning of recorded history. Thucydides, that greatest of all historians,[31] noted that he had written his history of the Peloponnesian War because "[i]t will be enough for me, if these words of mine are judged useful by those who want to understand clearly the events which happened in the past and which (*human nature being what it is*) will, at some time or other and in much the same ways, be repeated in the future" (my italics).[32]

The seventeenth-century political philosopher Thomas Hobbes commented on the natural span and experience of human life that "it was nasty, brutish, and short." He was equally pessimistic about human nature itself: "[The] generall inclination of all mankind, a perpetuall and restlesse desire of Power after Power, that ceaseth only in Death."[33] Only the arrival of the Industrial Revolution, with its ability to raise the human condition above the subsistence level, created the possibility for substantial numbers of human beings, rather than a tiny minority, to live above the poverty level. The irony of that success has been a tendency of the

---

[30] His speech, given to the warrior assembly deciding whether Sparta should declare war on Athens, was a masterful exposition of the difficulties Sparta would confront in the upcoming war against the Athenians. The Spartan assembly, however, paid no attention to Archidamnus' sage advice. Thucydides, *The Peloponnesian War*, trans. by Rex Warner (London, 1954), p. 82.

[31] George C. Marshall, the great statesman and strategist, noted at Princeton in February 1947 that he doubted "whether a man can think with full wisdom and with conviction regarding certain of the basic international issues today who has not reviewed in his mind the period of the Peloponnesian War and the fall of Athens." Quoted in W. Robert Connor, *Thucydides* (Princeton, 1984), p. 3.

[32] Thucydides, *History of the Peloponnesian War*, p. 48.

[33] Quoted in Knox, "Continuity and Revolution in Strategy."

majority of those living in relative wealth to forget both the fragility of the human condition or the reality that those living in poverty might well have a lively desire to dispossess those better off of "their lives, their houses, their land, their everything."[34]

The modern world has hidden much of that reality underneath its veneer of civilization. Yet, for substantial periods of the twentieth century the conditions of brutal, ceaseless combat throughout the international environment ripped that veneer aside to reveal underneath it what the Athenians so sharply noted to their opponents on the island of Melos in the midst of the Peloponnesian War:[35]

> Our opinion of the Gods and our knowledge of men lead us to conclude that it is a general and necessary law of nature to rule whatever one can. This is not a law we made ourselves, nor were we the first to act upon it when it was made. We found it already in existence, and we shall leave it to exist for ever among those who come after us. We are merely acting in accordance with it, and we know that you or anybody else with the same power as ours would be acting in precisely the same way.[36]

Americans and their leaders may believe that they have satiated their drive for power and that the United States desires neither new territories nor dominance. Yet, simply maintaining their current position in the world will require enormous effort and a real understanding of the external world. The many beliefs that Americans hold dear challenge in fundamental ways the belief systems of much of the rest of the world, including even those of their First World allies.[37] Moreover, their existence, their wealth, and their casual ignorance of other cultures and political

---

[34] The words, used in a slightly different context by William Tecumseh Sherman, occur in a letter he wrote in spring 1864 to the mayor of a town in Alabama.

[35] For the level of savagery to which even the First World had sunk by 1945, see Max Hastings, *Armageddon: The Battle for Germany, 1944–1945* (New York, 2004); and *Retribution: The Battle for Japan, 1944–1945* (New York, 2008).

[36] Thucydides, *History of the Peloponnesian War*, pp. 404–405.

[37] One of the strengths Americans and their country have possessed over two centuries has been the ability to reinvent themselves. In many ways, they resemble the description the Corinthians gave to the Spartans about the nature of the Athenian people – a description not meant to be favorable: "An Athenian is always an innovator, quick to form a resolution and quick to carry it out.... Athenian daring will outrun its own resources, they will take risks against their better judgment, and still in the midst of danger remain confident.... [T]hey never hesitate... [T]hey are always abroad for they think that the farther they go the more they will get... Of them alone might it be said that they possess a thing almost as soon as they have begun to desire it... In a word, they are by nature incapable of either living a quiet life themselves or of allowing anyone else to do so." Most Americans would take the description as a compliment; most Europeans as an insult. Thucydides, *History of the Peloponnesian War*, p. 76.

sensibilities stir up deep antagonisms in much of the rest of the world, as well as that most basic of human feelings, *invidia*. Americans may believe that the harsh attitudes expressed by the Athenian democrats twenty-five centuries ago to the Melian oligarchs no longer reflect the realities of the world. But that is not how much of the world sees the United States or the fact that the law, which the Athenians regarded as basic to explaining the human condition, will continue to rule relations between and among states.

The great difficulty that Americans then face in the twenty-first century rests on their inability to understand the fundamental drives of those in the external world.[38] Unfortunately, the general collapse of American liberal education with its de-emphasis of the study of history and classical literature has resulted in an increasing incapacity of its political and social elites to grasp how much of the external world thinks and lives, even through the secondhand means of history and literature.[39] The skewed understanding of the nature of the world is not merely a facet that will limit considerably the ability of Americans to act realistically in a world where real and violent enemies do exist; it is perhaps an even more limiting factor in terms of how the Europeans and Japanese will act in the future. As Sun Tsu suggested more than two millennia ago, if you want to be victorious in war, then you *must* understand your enemy. And we might add that such understanding requires an understanding of his history, his culture, his strategic thinking, and his language. Only then might we gain some faint glimmerings about how he might engage us politically, strategically, operationally, and tactically. In the Vietnam War, it was precisely that failure to understand the enemy at the political and strategic levels by senior political and military leaders that led to the American defeat.[40]

---

[38] It is not that the Americans do not have the same drive; rather the peculiarities of their polity and culture, which have placed limits on how they may achieve or use power, have allowed them to channel those drives in different and more peaceful and constructive directions.

[39] The assault on the supposed classics of literature and the deconstruction of serious history has simply removed serious education in those two disciplines from the majority of our major universities and colleges. The results were brought home to this author in teaching a course at George Washington University for candidates for a master's degree, most of whom were from the most prestigious universities in the United States; of 24 students not a single one had heard of, much less read, a Greek tragedy. Robert Kaplan emphasized this point at a conference sponsored by General Anthony Zinni at Central Command in fall 1998.

[40] Here, the United States was dealing not only with Vietnamese nationalism and Communist ideology, but with a worldview that was heavily influenced by the antecedents and traditions of the French Revolution, which had a major influence on North Vietnamese

Anglo-American liberal thought of the nineteenth century has come to dominate the *Weltanschauung* (worldview) of much of the First World. That understanding of the world and history has seen peace rather than war as the basic underpinning of international relations in the world that was emerging as a result of the Industrial Revolution.[41] That view eventually mutated into a belief that peace rather than war was the natural state of mankind and that war was, for all intents and purposes, an aberration rather than an intimate, if dark, part of the human landscape.[42] Increasingly, it has become the dominant view across the First World since the start of the twentieth century.

Norman Angell's classic book, *The Great Illusion*, published only three years before the outbreak of the First World War, argued that war was an impossibility because it made no sense in either economic or political terms.[43] Angell's book enjoyed enormous popularity in the years immediately prior to the Great War – except, of course, in Germany, where the attitudes of not only the leading politicians and generals but also of the German man on the street rendered Angell's conception of the impossibility of war nonsensical.[44] In retrospect, he was right in terms of the coming war's impact on the world's first period of globalization but wrong as to human nature and its most basic drives, or for that matter how the Germans regarded war both before and after 1914.

Twenty-five years later, despite the overwhelming evidence of the dangerous course on which Nazi Germany had embarked in the 1930s, the conventional wisdom in Britain and the United States enshrined a number of dangerous illusions about the causes of World War I, its continuation, and the reaction of Europeans in general to its horrendous results.[45] On one hand, the flood of extraordinary antiwar novels, memoirs, and poetry

---

leaders, most of whom, including Ho Chi Minh and Giap, had attended French schools. There were, of course, some who saw that the United States was slowly sinking into a quagmire, as the SIGMA war games underlined.

[41] For a discussion of this intellectual and ideological process, see the seminal work by Michael Howard, *War and the Liberal Conscience* (New Brunswick, NJ, 1987).

[42] See particularly Michael Howard, *The Invention of Peace: Reflections on War and the International Order* (New Haven, CT, 2001).

[43] Norman Angell, *The Great Illusion, The Study of the Relation of Military Power in Nations* (New York, 1911), chap. 2.

[44] For German attitudes before the First World War, see MacGregor Knox, *To the Threshold of Power, 1922/33, Origins and Dynamics of the Fascist and National Socialist Dictatorships*, vol. 1 (Cambridge, 2007).

[45] In this case, the Germans waged a massive disinformation campaign to cover over or explain away the reality that they had knowingly unleashed war in July 1914. See Holger H. Herwig, "Clio Deceived, Patriotic Self-Censorship in Germany after the Great War," *International Security*, Fall 1987.

best represents the Anglo-American reaction to the war.[46] But on the German side, Ernst Jünger's ferocious works, which argued for the war as an uplifting, cleansing experience, reinforced the myths that drove so much elite and popular enthusiasm for a resumption of the struggle in Germany even before Hitler came to power.[47]

To most in Britain and the United States in the 1920s and 1930s, including political leaders, it was simply inconceivable that the Germans would again embark on another great war of world conquest. In November 1930, Adolf Hitler expressed the mood among many Germans, in a public oration, which he repeated on a number of occasions throughout the Reich: "When so many preach that we are entering the age of peace, I can only say: my dear fellows, you have badly misinterpreted the horoscope of the age, for it points not to peace, but to war as never before."[48]

Nevertheless, eight years later in the midst of a major international crisis, Nevile Henderson, British ambassador to Berlin, wrote to the Foreign Secretary, Lord Halifax, about the Runciman mission that His Majesty's government was sending to Czechoslovakia to defuse the explosive crisis that threatened war, a crisis instituted by that same Adolf Hitler, now the *Führer* of Nazi Germany: "Personally I just sit and pray for one thing, namely that Lord Runciman will live up to the role of impartial British liberal statesman. I cannot believe that he will allow himself to be influenced by ancient history or even arguments about strategic frontiers and economics in preference to high moral principles."[49] Henderson's

---

[46] Among other great works, see Fredrick Manning, *Middle Parts of Fortune* (London, 2000); Robert Graves, *Goodbye to All That: An Autobiography* (London, 1995); Guy Chapman, *A Passionate Prodigality: Fragments of Autobiography* (London, 1967); Sigfried Sassoon, *Memoirs of an Infantry Officer* (London, 1980) and *Memoirs of a Fox-Hunting Man* (London, 2006); Vera Brittain, *Testament of Youth* (London, 2006) and the poetry, of both Sassoon and Wilfred Owen. For the best collection of World War I poetry, see: John Silken, ed., *The Penguin Book of First World War Poetry* (London, 1979).

[47] Jünger not only was wounded seventeen times during the course of the war, but was awarded Germany's highest combat decoration, the coveted *pour le mérite*. See especially his brilliant *Storm of Steel* (London, 2004); and *Copse 125, A Chronicle from the Trench War of 1918* (London, 1985). Jünger's writings were typical of the German reaction to the war.

[48] Quoted in Knox, *To the Threshold of Power*, p. 361.

[49] *Documents on British Foreign Policy* (DGFP), 3rd Series, vol. 2, Doc 590, 6.8.38., letter from Sir Nevile Henderson to Lord Halifax. Along similar lines, Henderson had written Halifax in May 1938: "I... feel that however repugnant, dangerous, and troublesome the result may be..., the truest British interest is to come down on the side of the highest moral principles. And the only lasting right moral principle is self determination. The British Empire was built upon it and we cannot deny it without incalculable prejudice to something which is of infinitely greater importance to the world than apprehensions of the German menace." Public Record Office, FO 800/314, p. 49, Henderson to Halifax, 12.5.38.

missive underlines how far British thinking was removed from the realities of Europe where the Nazis were spewing out their hatred.

The lessons of the 1930s are fully relevant to those who must think about the future course of the United States in the twenty-first century. Americans, like their British predecessors in the 1930s, are predisposed to see the international environment through rose-tinted glasses. Confrontation and deterrence may well represent a leap into the darkness, but even more dangerous is the ignoring or putting off of current threats in the hope that something better will turn up. Wariness of other states as well as nonstate actors, their aims, their understanding of the world, and their potential to cause harm must form the basis of any reasonable approach to national strategy.[50]

However, given American ahistoricism, it is doubtful that many Americans understand the difficulties in "staying the course," which many political-military conflicts of the twenty-first century will require. The Roman Empire lasted as long as it did because the Romans believed in their adage: "If you want peace, prepare for war."[51] Moreover, when needed, the Romans were also willing to wield a sharp and ruthless sword. Above all, Americans should understand that the use of force is not a matter of sending signals. War is untrammeled violence and as such will inevitably bring out the worst in human nature. Again, Thucydides suggests much about the nature of war: "Then with the ordinary conventions of civilized life thrown into confusion, human nature, always ready to offend even where laws exist, showed itself proudly in its true colours, as something incapable of controlling passion, insubordinate to the idea of justice, the enemy to anything superior to itself; for, if had not been for the pernicious power of envy, men would not have exalted vengeance above innocence and profit above justice."[52]

The Future, the Nature of War, and Military Power

[A]t least one of the root sources of Clausewitzian friction lies when all is said and done, not in the weapons we wield but in ourselves. The presence of humans in the loop, with all the diverse frailties, physical and

---

[50] Few Americans within policy-making communities or in academic institutions took Al Qaeda seriously as a threat to the United States and its interests until 9/11.

[51] At least under the empire, the Romans were willing to resort to means other than war. But what made their approach work was a willingness to wage war ruthlessly to conclusion. It took the Romans a decade to settle with the Dacians, but Trajan's column in Rome underlines what the Romans meant by "settle."

[52] Thucydides, *The Peloponnesian War*, p. 245.

cognitive limits, purposes, and decisions which their presence and participation entail, alone seems sufficient to render Clausewitzian friction impossible to eliminate entirely and, in all likelihood, extraordinarily difficult to reduce greatly in any permanent sense... On this reconstruction of Clausewitz's concept, therefore, general friction arises... from fundamental aspects of the human condition and unavoidable unpredictabilities that lie at the very core of combat processes.[53]

The intervention in Iraq, as well as in Afghanistan with the support of Allied forces, has raised fundamental issues about the culture of America's military institutions, the addressing of which will be essential and difficult, particularly because they require institutional and cultural changes.[54] Exacerbating these difficulties is the fact that military institutions, at present and for the foreseeable future, confront the massive technological changes occurring at a dizzying pace throughout civil society as a whole as well as in the external world. Thus, their leaders confront the intellectual challenge of understanding and adapting not only to the cultural and historical complexities of other nations and people, but to a world more complex and interdependent with the onrush of technology.[55]

The 45-year period between 1871 and 1914 offers the only equivalent period in history, when vast technological and scientific changes resulted in enormous dislocations within the military organizations throughout the world. The extent of that technological revolution and the symbiosis between the external civilian world and that of the military go far in explaining the difficulties armies and navies faced in adapting to the challenges the First World War raised. The fact that much of scientific progress was occurring outside military institutions themselves only served to exacerbate the difficulties involved within those institutions in adapting and absorbing the social and cultural implications, not to mention the military possibilities of technological change.

---

[53] Barry D. Watts, *Clausewitzian Friction and Future War* (Washington, DC, 2004), pp. 122–123.

[54] For the essential role culture plays in military effectiveness, see Williamson Murray, "Does Military Culture Matter," *Orbis*, Winter 1999; and "Military Culture Does Matter," *Strategic Review*, Spring 1999.

[55] The issue here is not that military leaders must become practicing historians or technologists, but rather that they become familiar with those disciplines. In this regard, Air Marshal Hugh Dowding, who established Fighter Command and then fought the Battle of Britain successfully with the instrument he had created represents a standard few general or flag officers have reached. For a discussion of Dowding as military leader and innovator see Alan Beyerchen, "From Radio to Radar: Military Adaptation to Change in Germany, the United Kingdom, and the United States," in Murray and Millett, *Military Innovation in the Interwar Period*, pp. 275–287.

At present, the world has entered a period similar to that of the end of the nineteenth century – one of massive technological change and resulting social upheaval, much of it driven by the world external to the military.[56] Thus, America's military institutions confront a similar set of problems to those that emerged a century ago. Technological change is occurring in areas largely beyond their control, but with major implications for the kinds of threats the United States confronts.

The extent of those technological changes had already begun to lead the American military down dangerous paths in the last decade of the twentieth century.[57] By the mid-1990s, some senior military leaders were arguing that the technological revolution – driven by computers and communication capabilities – was creating a situation where U.S. forces not only could dominate the battle space completely, but could see and understand everything that was occurring within that space. Under the rubric of a supposed "revolution in military affairs,"[58] the line of argument went so far as to suggest that technology could remove friction and uncertainty from the battlefield – at least as far as American forces were concerned.[59] In fact, some are still describing that possibility in terms of "information dominance."[60]

American experiences in Afghanistan and Iraq have shattered many of the wilder of such claims. Nevertheless, the belief technology can overcome the uncertainties of war remains deeply embedded within the U.S. military as well as the American psyche. In the end, that may be an alluring idea, but it will inevitably lead to failure in the human arena that is war.[61] In fact, everything that modern science tells us about the

---

[56] This current state of affairs is substantially different from that of the period from 1914 through 1990, when military organizations drove technological change.

[57] See Williamson Murray, "Clausewitz Out, Computers In, Military Culture and Technological Hubris," *The National Interest*, Summer 1997; and chapter 3 this book.

[58] The concept of "revolutions in military affairs" has considerable validity in explaining the patterns of military development and innovation in the West since the Middle Ages. Unfortunately, most of the advocates of a technological revolution in military affairs simply threw out the historical precedents and embarked on an uncharted course to the future resting on untested and unprovable assumptions. For a historically based examination of what revolutions in military affairs have involved, see MacGregor Knox and Williamson Murray, eds., *The Dynamics of Military Revolution, 1300–2050* (Cambridge, 2002).

[59] For a stunning examination of the weaknesses in such an approach to future military capabilities, see Watts, *Clausewitzian Friction and Future War*.

[60] For the most extreme of these views by a senior retired officer, see: Admiral Bill Owens, vice chairman of the Joint Chiefs of Staff in the mid-1990s, with Ed Offley, *Lifting the Fog of War* (New York, 2000).

[61] For a discussion of the role of technology in future war, see Gray, *Another Bloody Century*, chap. 3.

world underlines that friction is not only an inevitable factor in war, but inherent in the nature of the universe.[62]

War will be fought in the future by human beings.[63] As in the past, it will be the human mind that will determine the outcomes of wars. Moreover, war will occur in the real world, where incalculable forces beyond the control of the participants influence the interactions between the opposing sides. In that interaction technology can only serve as a tool; knowing how to use that tool in a mechanical sense does nothing toward achieving success, unless military forces also understand the enemy, his cultural and historical framework, and *his* political goals. The opening paragraphs to the German Army's basic doctrinal manual of the 1930s best describe war's timeless environment, one that has not changed since the days of the Greek hoplite:

> War is an art, a free and creative activity founded on scientific principles. It makes the very highest demands on the human personality. The conduct of war is subject to continual development. New weapons dictate ever changing forms. Their appearance must be anticipated and their influence evaluated.... Combat situations are of unlimited variety. They change frequently and suddenly and can seldom be assessed in advance. Incalculable elements often have a decisive influence. One's own will is pitted against the independent will of the enemy. Friction and errors are daily occurrences.... War subjects the individual to the most severe tests of his spiritual and physical endurance.[64]

War is a Clausewitzian world of chance, passions, and calculation – the latter two driving not only an America involved in conflict but its opponents as well. As Alan Beyerchen has suggested about the continuing relevance of *On War*:

> Clausewitz displays an intuition concerning war that we can better comprehend with terms and concepts newly available to us: *On War* is suffused with the understanding that every war is inherently a nonlinear phenomenon, the conduct of which changes its character in ways that cannot be analytically predicted... [I]n a profoundly unconfused way [Clausewitz]

---

[62] See Watts, *Clausewitzian Friction and Future War*, pp. 79–123.

[63] Those who suggest that wars in the future will be fought entirely by machines fail to see that such scenarios suggest that when machines replace human beings, one is no longer discussing human conflict.

[64] Bruce Condell and David T. Zabecki, *On the German Art of War, Truppenführung* (Boulder, CO, 2001), p. 17. Unfortunately, the traditional as well as the current American predilection favors technology over the achievement of a Clausewitzian understanding of what history suggests about the nature of war. Concepts such as information dominance, effects-based operations, synchronization indicate a desire to return to the Napoleonic battlefield where the general in charge could see and command all.

understands that seeking exact analytic solutions does not fit the nonlinear reality of the problems posed by war, and hence that our ability to predict the course and outcome of conflict is severely limited. The correctness of Clausewitz's perception has both kept his work relevant and made it less accessible, for war's analytically unpredictable nature is extremely discomforting to those searching for a predictive theory.[65]

What is clear is that however much technology may shape and change military forces, the nature of war itself will not change.[66] Friction will continue to dominate the landscape. Individuals will continue to make mistakes, or misinterpret instructions. More information does not necessarily translate into knowledge. Instead:

> In the first place, even in an 'information-rich' environment, there is only so much that any human can absorb, digest, and act upon in a given period of time. The greater the stress, the more data will be ignored, noise mistaken for information, and information misconstrued, and the greater will be the prospects for confusion, disorientation, and surprise. Second, the spatial, and especially, temporal distribution of information relevant to decisions in war means that some key pieces will be inaccessible at any given time and place.... Third, the empirical fact of non-linear dynamics, when coupled with the unavoidable mismatches between reality and our representations of it, reveal fundamental limits to prediction, no matter how much information and processing power technological advances may one day place in human hands.[67]

Finally, those who wage war in the future will wage it for political purposes and political purposes alone.[68] History underlines that the strategic and political framework invariably determines the outcome of war. As this author and his colleague Allan Millett suggested about the importance of a coherent strategic approach to the conduct of war in summing up the military effectiveness project on the period 1914–1945:[69]

---

[65] Alan Beyerchen, "Clausewitz, Nonlinearity, and the Unpredictability of War," *International Security*, vol. 17, no. 3, Winter 1992–1993.
[66] For a clear analysis of this reality, see Gray, *Another Bloody Century*, chap. 3.
[67] Watts, *Clausewitzian Friction and Future War*, pp. 125–126.
[68] Clausewitz's statement that "war is a continuation of politics by other means" will lose none of its validity in the twenty-first century. Even so-called religious wars are ultimately with, between, and for the domination of a political entity.
[69] We also noted that "[s]trategic wisdom... is more important than tactical or operational effectiveness. The best outcome, in which prewar analysis helps to make force structures and operational concepts effective in wartime, is as rare in history as wise political leadership. Few 'got it right' in World War I, in uniform or mufti...Military success in the earliest stages of modern war does not necessarily testify to strategic judgment." Allan R. Millett and Williamson Murray, "Lessons of War," *The National Interest*, Winter 1988/1989. The military effectiveness project was funded by Andrew Marshall's Office of Net Assessment and resulted in the following publication: Allan R. Millett and

No amount of operational virtuosity... redeemed fundamental flaws in political judgment. Whether policy shaped strategy or strategic imperatives drove policy was irrelevant. Miscalculations in both led to defeat, and any combination of politico-strategic error had disastrous results, even for some nations that ended the war as members of the victorious coalition. Even the effective mobilization of national will, manpower, industrial might, national wealth, and technological know-how did not save belligerents from reaping the bitter fruit of severe mistakes [at the political and strategic levels]. This is because it is more important to make correct decisions at the political and strategic level than it is at the operational and tactical level. Mistakes in operations and tactics can be corrected, but political and strategic mistakes live forever... [70]

The difficulty in adapting flawed strategy to the realities of conflict lies in the fact that by the time statesmen realize their mistakes, it is too late to alter course because of the political consequences.[71] The history of the past century underlines that when America's leaders have made coherent and intelligent political and strategic decisions, the military forces of the United States have won victories with great long-term positive advantages to the nation. When they have not, the result has been consistent difficulties and in some cases serious consequences.[72] Given the inherent difficulties that reacting to the challenges in the international environment represents, how American leaders use or abuse history will play a crucial role in how well the nation adapts its strategy to the realities that it confronts.[73]

The Future, the United States, and the Nature of Government

Ultimately a real understanding of history means that we face nothing *new under the sun. For all the 'Fourth Generation of War' intellectuals running around today saying that the fundamental nature of war has fundamentally*

Williamson Murray, eds., *Military Effectiveness*, 3 vols., World War I, The Interwar Period, and World War II (London, 1988; Cambridge reprint 2010).

[70] Millett and Murray, "Lessons of War."
[71] Thus, Lyndon Johnson and Robert McNamara clearly recognized that they had embarked on a fundamentally flawed course by early 1967, but to have admitted so would have had political consequences for the Johnson administration. In November 1914, the chief of the German general staff, General Erich von Falkenhyn, warned the Reich's chancellor that Germany could not win the war and should make peace. The latter turned him down cold because of the war's cost thus far in the conflict.
[72] The *military* and political decision leading to large-scale involvement of U.S. forces in the ground war in South Vietnam is a case in point.
[73] Here, there is cause for worry, not only because of the ignorance Americans possess of history and other cultures, but because of the inherent resistance of the American bureaucracy to change.

> *changed, the tactics are wholly new, etc., I must respectfully say: 'Not really.' Alexander the Great would not be in the least perplexed by the enemy that we face right now in Iraq, and our leaders going into this fight do their troops a disservice by not studying (studying, vice just reading) the men who have gone before us. We have been fighting on this planet for 5,000 years and we should take advantage of their experience. 'Winging it' and filling body bags as we sort out what works reminds us of the moral dictates and the cost of competence in our profession.*[74]

In the 1990s, as globalization appeared as a major factor on the international scene, a number of political scientists and military pundits argued that the modern state would soon go the way of the dinosaurs. Their arguments could not have been more ahistorical or misleading.[75] The last great period of globalization – between 1890 and 1914[76] – had not ended with the disappearance of states but rather with a savage and ferocious war.[77] In fact, the modern state has been mutating and adapting at an ever faster rate over the past two centuries, its mutations and adaptations driven by the accelerating rate of technological, economic, and political change.

The American bureaucratic state that emerged from the Cold War was the creation of the Depression and the challenges posed by the threat of great external enemies, Nazi Germany and the Soviet Union. Both in its bureaucratic form and ability to provide substantial services to its citizens, it represented a break with the past. With the collapse of the Soviet Union, it is not surprising that many would find the American government in its current form, particularly in its defense and intelligence bureaucracies, uncapable of addressing a new and different world, in which Islamic terrorism has emerged as a potent new threat, while China appears to be a considerable uncertainty. Yet, if the bureaucratic organization of the American government has changed too slowly and inadequately to meet

---

[74] Email from General James Mattis to a professor at the National Defense University, 2003. Quoted with permission of the author.
[75] One of the more thoughtful examples of this genre of speculation by political scientists about the future is Francis Fukuyama, *The End of History and the Last Man* (New York, 2006, most recent edition).
[76] Not until the late 1990s did the percentage of international trade as a percentage of world GDP reach the same level as that reached in 1913, the last year of peace.
[77] Much like the prevailing wisdom in the 1990s, there was – at least in the Anglo-Saxon world – a literature arguing that globalization was creating a world in which war was no longer possible. The most obvious example is Norman Angell's *The Impossibility of War*. Strangely in terms of what had happened between 1914 and 1918, Angell's work was reissued in 1937 – a real case, to use Samuel Johnson's phrase about second marriages – of "the triumph of hope over experience."

that world – particularly the challenges of the external environment – it has at least begun to adapt and alter its form. Adaptation to the form and structure of government is inevitable, because governments reflect the human environment in which they exist.

Despite the accelerating rate of change over the past two centuries, the modern state has survived for a fundamental reason: human nature itself demands regulation and organization to meet the inevitable challenges of both external and internal environments. In the end, the state is the only means of providing protection and focus to large groups of human beings, as well as a certain sense of community.[78] Its most basic function is to provide security, internal as well as external, to its citizens.[79] However, in an increasingly complex and interdependent world it must also provide a buffer to the vagaries of the marketplace, while providing services beyond the mere protection to its citizens that justify its cost.

Whatever its various forms, modern states, once termed by Charles de Gaulle as those heartless, pitiless monsters, have assumed a bureaucratic form, through which they and their leaders inevitably respond to the external environment. Bureaucracies are by their nature an absolute requirement to provide the framework that creates the protection necessary to meet and thwart internal and external threats to the security of their citizens. Nevertheless, they:

> invariably define national purpose in terms of bureaucratic rather than national survival. They are happiest with established wisdom and incremental change. They cherish the myth that virtually all strategic problems are solvable in and through their own element – be it diplomacy, economic power, covert knowledge and action, ground combat, naval supremacy, or air bombardment – and that problems not soluble are not problems. When faced with the incommensurate or unquantifiable alternatives... they usually retreat to incoherent compromise... or take flight into strategy by intuition... [A]nd in the absence of driving political leadership, even structured debate may produce only paralysis.[80]

---

[78] In effect, the nation-state represents the best compromise societies have thus far devised between the economic and military inadequacies of smaller units and the socio-political stresses of larger ones.

[79] The emergence of the modern state in the seventeenth century resulted from the reintroduction of *civil* as well as military discipline to military organizations. To a considerable extent, the role of the military in the eighteenth century was as much to act as a police force for civil order as to prepare for war.

[80] MacGregor Knox, "Continuity and Revolution in Strategy," in Williamson Murray, MacGregor Knox, and Alvin Bernstein, eds., *The Making of Strategy, Rulers, States, and War* (Cambridge, 1992), pp. 615–616.

And therein lies one of the major problems that will confront policy makers in the future: the nature of bureaucratic organizations that advise and counsel them. Bureaucracies are by their nature ahistorical. To them, history exists only as a tool to justify policies and assumptions. The imaginative use of history is simply beyond their interest or focus. As the *9/11 Report* suggests, the failures that led to the catastrophic assaults on the Pentagon and the Twin Towers lay not in the availability of information that suggested such an attack might take place, given the history and culture of Al Qaeda's leadership, but in the failure of *imagination* of those charged with interpreting what that information might have indicated about the paths on which terrorists had embarked.[81] Thus, the bureaucrats in the FBI, the CIA, and the other agencies charged with protecting the United States remained focused on the interests and turf of their own bureaucratic kingdoms, rather than on the threats to America and its citizens that the information at their fingertips suggested.[82]

One can see a similar pattern in the current debate about the emerging strategic environment among the services – some arguing that China will inevitably emerge as the threat to the United States, others arguing that future threats will look much like the cocktail of local insurgencies, criminal behavior, and transnational terrorism in Afghanistan and Iraq that currently beset the United States. Unfortunately, the strategic debate is often not about the future, but rather about desires to preserve the procurement of expensive weapons systems. The real issue in the military debate should not begin with weapons systems, but rather how to create adaptable and flexible military organizations that can meet a wide range of strategic threats, especially the unexpected.

The *9/11 Report* was equally insightful in its description of bureaucratic mindsets throughout the different agencies that had grown all too comfortable in their "remembered pasts." Conformity of thought rather than imaginative thinking about the evidence was the watchword of those bureaucrats in the American government charged with thinking about the future. The issue was not only a lack of imagination but a belief that the remembered historical past of their institutions, enshrined in myth or bureaucratic practice, ensured an understanding of what the present suggested sufficient to keep positions secure. Being wrong always comes

---

[81] 9/11 Commission, *Report* (Washington, DC, 2006).
[82] Several of the agents well down on the bureaucratic food chain did recognize a substantial portion of what the raw data suggested, but their superiors had no interest in listening to them.

with risk. But being wrong in foresight sometimes is the cost of getting it right when things change.[83] However, a willingness to display both imagination and foresight within a bureaucracy often carries with it the potential for career-ending penalties, even when events prove the prophet right.

It is precisely imaginative, historically based thinking across institutional boundaries and serious thought about foreign perspectives on the United States that will require the nation to adjust to – and at times even mold – an uncertain future. Over the past 70 years, America's greatest advantage in times of crisis has been the ability of its leaders to pull into the examination of the strategic environment civilian experts who could provide serious alternatives to bureaucratic group think. Nevertheless, that ability, displayed so sharply at the beginning of both World War II and the Cold War, took place in a governmental structure that possessed a minimal bureaucratic framework compared to today's leviathan. Only the challenges raised by the Axis and Soviet Union forced Americans to expand their government massively. Thus, in the 1940s and 1950s, America's leaders – military as well as civilian – had no choice but to reach out to the worlds of business, finance, and academia for experts who possessed the imagination and knowledge to address the challenges confronting the United States.[84]

In effect, the present bureaucratic mindset represents a serious obstacle to coherent and intelligent thinking about the future. Equally deleterious has been the overregulation and legalistic perversion of the system, which has promoted a philosophy of "do nothing so that under all possible scenarios, we will do no harm." The sheer scale of regulation robs those in the bureaucracy of initiative, while those who possess initiative and drive either find themselves ground down, or leave for more imaginative environs.[85] The challenge of the future will be to adapt current prejudices and assumptions to the realities of an uncertain strategic environment. That will demand, on one hand, a willingness to reach beyond the bureaucracy, and, on the other, a ruthless willingness to prune bureaucracies of the unimaginative, the dull, and those buried in its minutia while protecting those who have still not lost imagination and hope. Here, leadership

---

[83] I am indebted to my colleague Kevin Woods for this point.
[84] It is also well to remember that U.S. military leaders, particularly George C. Marshall and Ernest King, possessed considerable ruthlessness, which allowed them to purge their services of those generals and admirals who lacked the requisite abilities to handle the global challenges confronting the United States.
[85] I am indebted to Kevin Woods for this point.

from the top must be present, because without vision and drive from senior leaders, bureaucracy will stifle the competent.[86]

Military Innovation and Adaptation and the Future

> To discover how much of our resources must be mobilized for war, we must first examine our own political aim and that of the enemy. We must gauge the strength and situation of the opposing state. We must gauge the character and ability of its government and people and do the same in regard to our own. Finally we must evaluate the political sympathies of other states and the effect that war may have on them. To assess these things in all their ramifications and diversity is plainly a colossal task.... Bonaparte was quite right when he said that Newton himself would quail before the algebraic problems it would pose.[87]

In the late 1980s a senior retired U.S. Army general, Lieutenant General John H. Cushman, commented on the effectiveness of military institutions and leaders in the first half of the twentieth century: "Thus in the spheres of operations and tactics, where military competence would seem to be a nation's rightful due, the [authors' of the various case studies] reports suggest for the most part less than general professional military competence and sometimes abysmal incompetence. One can doubt whether any other profession in these seven nations during the same periods would have received such poor ratings by similarly competent outside observers."[88]

If the record of military organizations in the first half of the twentieth century is less than impressive, one must not minimize the challenges they confronted, or the fact there were some that performed at a more consistent level than others. A historical examination of how and why past military organizations struggled in confronting past challenges suggests some important lessons for those thinking about military change in the twenty-first century. In particular, there are two areas that point to specific lessons of considerable importance: innovation in peacetime and adaptation in war.[89]

---

[86] Like the challenge that confronted General Marshall in World War II, this is ultimately a leadership, not a regulatory challenge. One cannot mandate creativity; one can only foster, promote, nurture, and ultimately recognize it.

[87] Clausewitz, *On War*, pp. 585–586.

[88] Lieutenant General John H. Cushman, U.S. Army retired, "Challenge and Response at the Operational and Tactical Levels, 1941–1945," in Millett and Murray, eds., *Military Effectiveness*, vol. 3, *The Second World War*.

[89] The recent desire to enfold military change in a single word, transformation, misses the fact that there are two different aspects to that term: innovation, which occurs in peacetime, allows military organizations the luxury of time to drive forward the processes of

The interwar period from 1919–1939 suggests that successful military innovation demands a willingness to tolerate and support those who challenge the conventional wisdom. Honest and thorough examination of recent military experience proved to be essential to effective and realistic innovation, at least at the tactical and operational levels.[90] The mantra many historians use in arguing that military institutions study the last war and that is why they do badly in the next is patently false. In fact, those few military organizations that realistically studied the combat experiences of the Great War honestly and realistically were precisely those that innovated most successfully in the tactical realm.[91] The issue is inevitably the honesty with which military institutions study not only their experiences in war, but in peacetime as well.[92]

The interwar period also indicates that professional military education played a major role in successful innovation during that period, not only in its ability to develop new and innovative concepts, but in its ability to spread those concepts throughout the officer corps where they could be evaluated.[93] It was, thus, crucial to establishing the cultural and organizational framework where innovation either succeeded or failed. Here, the U.S. military proved particularly adept in using professional military education to educate its officers for future wars as well as to test new and innovative ideas, which its graduates and faculty then carried into the

change, but often without coherent real-life experience, which war provides; adaptation, on the other hand, occurs in war and provides military organizations considerable evidence as to what works and what does not, but often without the time to consider what is relevant and what is not.

[90] The foremost example of learning through a thorough and accurate examination of what has happened on the battlefield and then folding the lessons learned into doctrine and training was the German Army in the period after the First World War. See James S. Corum, *The Roots of Blitzkrieg, Hans von Seeckt and German Military Reform* (Lawrence, KS, 1992).

[91] Here, the Germans were the major winners through their study of the 1918 battlefield. See Corum, *The Roots of Blitzkrieg*.

[92] The French during the interwar period provide an outstanding example of how not to use exercises and experiments to prepare for the next war. In almost every case, their exercises were carefully scripted, not to test doctrine and tactical concepts, but to prove them. See Eugenia C. Kiesling, *Arming against Hitler, France and the Limits of Military Planning* (Lawrence, KS, 1994).

[93] The institutions of professional military education in the United States played an essential role in the development of new concepts of operation and capabilities: the Naval War College, the operational framework for the coming war in the Pacific, as well as concepts such as carrier warfare and replenishment at sea; the Marine Corps Schools, amphibious warfare; the Air Corps Tactical School, the concepts of strategic bombing and the industrial web; and the Army's Industrial College, a coherent approach to the problems of massive mobilization.

field. The development of carrier and amphibious warfare – the former at the Naval War College and the latter at the Marine Corps Schools – is a particularly good example of the impressive influence that education can have on innovation.

However, where there was a demand for conformity of thought, there was a general inability to think through the daunting problems raised by the potential of weapons, tactics, and operations on future battlefields. Here, the French Army provides a particularly salient warning as to the damaging consequences when military leaders demand uniformity of vision.[94] On the other hand, the German Army demanded not only high standards of intellectual performance among its officers but actively encouraged debate over operational and tactical matters. The heart of the army's cultural framework for understanding war lay in the *Kriegsakademie*, with its high entrance examination and demanding curriculum, which flunked out half of the attendees for not possessing the intellectual capabilities or character to wear the crimson stripe of a general staff officer.[95]

History also suggests there is a correlation between military institutions that successfully innovate in peacetime and those that adapt to the real conditions of war.[96] Military institutions have invariably gotten the parameters of the next war wrong, largely because their conception of future war has not matched reality. In this regard, the peacetime education of officers has proven essential in providing the intellectual tools to recognize the nature of the conflict in which they are engaged. At its best, such education has not just been limited to studying the nature of war and the potential of tactical and operational innovations but to enhancing their ability to think critically. It is all too easy for even the best of military organizations to inculcate a regimented approach to problem solving when what is important to military effectiveness is disciplined, critical analysis that can see the whole as well as its contingent parts.

In particular, it is crucial that senior officers recognize the nature of their opponent and the kind of war in which they are engaged.

---

[94] Robert Doughty's study on the development of doctrine in the French Army during the interwar period is particularly insightful as to how and why the French went wrong: Robert Allan Doughty, *The Seeds of Disaster, The Development of French Army Doctrine, 1919–1939* (Hamden, CT, 1985).

[95] For the nature of the German system of professional military education see David N. Spires, *Image and Reality, The Making of the German Officer, 1921–1933* (Westport, CT, 1984).

[96] See Watts and Murray, "Military Innovation in Peacetime," p. 414.

Adaptation in war requires top-down leadership because, however, inventive individual officers may be at lower levels, without driving support from above, adaptation will occur in a higgledy piggledy fashion, while those at the sharp end will invariably fill up body bags. The British Expeditionary Force in the First World War provides a particularly good example. Field Marshal Douglas Haig and his staff took little interest in tactics; consequently, outside of technology, British adaptation fell behind that of the Germans from 1916 through the first half of 1918, a factor that added substantially to British losses on the Somme and at Passchendaele.[97] Buried in the mythology of legends about Napoleon, Haig was incapable of understanding the battlefield that he confronted, but sought great cavalry advances that had absolutely no relevance to the battlefields where his soldiers were bleeding and dying.[98]

Given the complexity of the strategic environment the United States confronts with potential threats from the emergence of peer competitors to the formless nonstate threat of Al Qaeda and the constant turmoil in the Middle East, the security of the United States demands military leaders intellectually prepared to adapt to unexpected challenges. America cannot afford to repeat the kind of ahistoricism that contributed so much to the flawed understanding of the nature of the human terrain in which U.S. forces operated after conventional operations ended in April 2003 with the collapse of Saddam's military and his regime. As a young Marine officer commented at the ending of the movie *No End in Sight*: "America can do better."

The Future: Implications for the American Military

> *Our awareness of the world and our capacity to deal intelligently with its problems are shaped not only by the history we know but by what we do not know. Ignorance, especially the ignorance of educated men, can be a more powerful force than knowledge.*[99]

It appears likely that most of the wars and military interventions involving American forces will occur – to paraphrase Neville Chamberlain – in far

---

[97] In this regard see Robin Prior and Trevor Wilson, *Passchendaele, The Untold Story* (New Haven, CT, 1996); and *The Somme* (New Haven, CT, 2005). For a brilliant evaluation of Haig and the areas where his generalship failed, see J.P. Harris, *Douglas Haig and the First World War* (Cambridge, 2008).
[98] For the intellectual failures of Haig and his generals see Tim Travers, *The Killing Ground, The British Army, the Western Front and the Emergence of Modern War, 1900–1918* (London, 1987).
[99] Michael Howard, *Lessons of History* (New Haven, CT, 1991), p. 16.

away places among people about whom we know little.[100] Chamberlain's words attempted to justify the fact that his government was about to surrender Czechoslovakia to the tender mercies of Nazi Germany. That decision turned out to be a strategic disaster for Europe and the world.[101] Similarly, the U.S. military has found itself tasked at the start of the twenty-first century to intervene with force on behalf of people about whom Americans know little.[102] And there is every prospect interventions by U.S. forces, as in Afghanistan and Iraq, will occur again in the not-too-distant future.

Because war is invariably "a continuation of politics by other means," U.S. forces will find themselves in situations were an understanding of the history, politics, and culture of the locals is not simply nice to know, but an essential ingredient of military effectiveness. If the aim of conflict is to achieve political change, then it is essential that U.S. forces also possess an understanding of the history, nature, culture, and religion of the enemy. But even if the political aim is not so broad, those forces must possess a deep understanding of the nature of their opponent. The traditional wars in which the American military found itself engaged in the last century epitomized Clausewitz's famous dictum. But that dictum is even more relevant in a world of insurgencies and nonstate actors.

Without that historical knowledge, then no matter how effective military operations may prove, those operations will more often than not address the wrong problems and the wrong political framework. In wars where the United States possesses overwhelming power *and is willing to use it*, this may not necessarily prove disastrous, but in conflicts where there are limits – either self-imposed or imposed by the international environment – on the use of force, then historically based knowledge is an absolute necessity. Blindness of the enemy's history and culture can only lead to severe difficulties, if not defeat. Admittedly, given the demand that U.S. military forces must maintain the level of combat effectiveness

---

[100] Chamberlain's words about Czechoslovakia, threatened by a massive German invasion in late September 1938, were: "How horrible, fantastic, incredible it is that we should be digging trenches and trying on gas masks here, because of a quarrel in a far away country between people of whom we know nothing." Quoted in Telford Taylor, *Munich: The Price of Peace* (New York, 1979), p. 884.

[101] For a discussion of the strategic and military aspects of Munich, see Williamson Murray, *The Change in the European Balance of Power, 1938–1939, The Path to Ruin* (Princeton, NJ, 1984), chaps. 6 and 7.

[102] Underlining the worst trends in American academic life, the American Anthropology Association has taken a position against "the weaponization of anthropology" by its members associating with the Department of Defense.

that showed clearly in the 2003 war against Iraq, the ability to develop and maintain the requisite historical and cultural knowledge represents an immense challenge.[103] But without a historical guide to the human landscape, military power is blind.

The idea of short, painless wars (at least for U.S. and Allied forces), waged by aircraft and missiles, so popular in the 1990s, will rarely, if ever, be a part of the future landscape. As the last decade has underlined, the greatest strengths of the U.S. military lie in the dimensions of the oceans and the air. There have been and there will be no real challengers in those dimensions for the foreseeable decades. But, since war is a matter of politics by other means, in the end, war will always be about the control of the ground, where history and culture dominate human society.

Consequently, military leaders must possess the historical and cultural background to offer sage political and strategic advice about the consequences involved in war.[104] Their subordinates at every level must possess a similar sensitivity not only to their own past, but to the past of those whom they will engage in the wars of the future. Admittedly, it is not possible for any single individual to absorb the histories of those whom the American military may confront in coming decades. But the familiarity with at least one other culture and its history will equip military leaders to ask the right questions about those with whom they deal.

Perhaps the most ironic statement in Clausewitz's *On War* is his comment that: "No one starts a war – or rather, no one in his senses ought to do so – without being clear in his mind what he intends to achieve by that war and how he intends to conduct it."[105] The record of humanity suggests the opposite: most political leaders, often backed by their military leaders, have started conflict with neither their aims nor the means to conduct war clear in their minds. Here, the essential prerequisite for strategic competence must lie in the ability to ask the right questions about the nature and culture of the enemy. Part of the problem lies in the inability, or unwillingness, of those who chose to use military forces to understand the nature and mind of their opponents. Without that understanding even military victory can rapidly unravel, as an uncertain and dynamic

---

[103] The Cold War presents the best indication that this can be done. Confronted with a terrible threat, the American government enlisted a number of the brightest minds in and out of government to study the Soviets both historically and currently. That effort did provide a real case of "knowing your enemy."

[104] This is not to say that it will be taken or that those senior officers who proffer it will not suffer consequences.

[105] Clausewitz, *On War*, p. 579.

political environment explodes. This is particularly true because the enemy consists of human beings who are capable of adaptation, imaginative and innovative thought, and a mindset that invariably presents surprises in how it adapts. Invariably, the enemy will exist in an entirely different cultural and historical environment.

The emerging strategic environment presents a number of diverse and formidable challenges to the American military. A globalized world depends on the American military to maintain sufficient peace, order, and stability for it to continue its expansion. Without those key elements, globalization for all intents and purposes ends. Perhaps most difficult for America's military institutions is the fact that the future strategic environment is so ambiguous and uncertain. Commitments to the protection of a globalized world will at times require the commitment of U.S. forces to missions from peacekeeping, to training indigenous forces, to combating insurgencies and terrorism, to full-scale conflicts. And those missions could take place in areas as diverse as South America, Africa, the Middle East, or the Asian-Pacific rim.

As Michael Howard has suggested, military organizations will nearly always get the next war wrong because in war, it is impossible to understand, much less predict, the context and conditions under which they will fight. The essential component in military effectiveness then is how quickly and competently a military organization can adapt to the actual conditions that it confronts. And to do that, the leaders of military forces at every level must understand the nature of the enemy they are engaging, especially his history, his politics, and his culture.

2

Thucydides and Clausewitz

We stand at the dawn of a new era in world history. The truisms and certainties of the past 60 years have disappeared in the crumbling of the Berlin Wall and collapse of the Soviet Union. How to think about the world in the new century is a crying need in a time of uncertainty, ambiguity, and flux. We can hold on to the theories and assumptions about the world, national security, and war, which have marked the efforts of those involved in political science and international relations over past decades. But such theoretical approaches have had their difficulties – not the least being that not a single one predicted even two years before it happened an event as monumental as the collapse of the Soviet Union.[1]

But to reject such theories requires that one have something to put in their place, and, here, historians have abdicated even the debate. The result has been to turn the study of current and future problems over to those who, if they do not reject history outright, are happy to rampage through the past with scant attention to its context or complexity. And in their search for absolutes and answers, they have only served to muddy the water for those who wish to gain some feel for war, power, and international relations in the coming century.

As a military and strategic historian, I have generally been suspicious of the claims of those who indulge in theoretical musings about how

---

[1] See in particular John Gaddis' challenge: "International Relations Theory and the End of the Cold War," *International Security*, Winter 1992/1993.

This chapter was presented as my inaugural lecture as a full professor at The Ohio State University in Spring 1990 and then published in the *Marine Corps Gazette* while I was the Horner Professor at the Marine Corps University.

the world works. To paraphrase Hermann Göring, when I have heard the word theory, I have reached for my gun. Nevertheless as I have aged, I have come to believe that theory, with a small t, does have its place as an organizing principle – as a means to catalog our thoughts and to extend our understanding of the complex, ambiguous, interactive phenomena that make up the real world. Particularly in the world of military institutions, theory about war (or theories about war) provides some direction for thinking about the business of "making the other poor bastard die for his country."[2]

Admittedly, theory will not win wars, nor can it ever represent a template offering the directions to strategic effectiveness, much less victory. We also must understand that it can have serious and destructive results if it seeks to reach absolute truths and certainties, particularly if it attempts to move away from that harsh auditor of human affairs: experience in the real world. Yet, the past is the only laboratory that we have, and if we are to gain some dim glimpse at the future we must have some sense of the "real" past, however contradictory that might be.

Thus, the purpose of this article is to suggest why Clausewitz, the greatest theorist of war, and Thucydides, the greatest of strategic historians, are of continuing, even vital, relevance to any understanding of the world we will enter in the next century. And so I shall examine in turn why their discussions – theoretical as well as historical – are not just "relevant," but essential as a starting point for examinations of war in the past, present, and future. Finally, I will conclude with some observations as to why most theories of war in the twentieth century have failed so dismally to capture the full range and complexity of their subject.

Clausewitz

One of the great ironies of the study of war at the sharp end is the fact that literature, rather than history, best reaches into those dark lands where men seek to kill each other. Can any history reach the power and psychological understanding that Tolstoy brings to his description of the battles of Austerlitz and Borodino? Or, for that matter, does any historical account of Gettysburg reach the psychological understanding that Michael Shaara achieved in his masterful novel *The Killer Angels*?

Yet, the literary view of war, no matter what its insights into the psychological pressures and conditions of combat, provides little in the

---

[2] Here, I am quoting that most eloquent of soldiers, George Patton.

way of an analytic framework for understanding the overarching political, strategic, and operational issues involved in conflict – those issues lying beyond the immediate concerns and impressions of the individual. In fact, literature can be downright misleading, such as when Tolstoy wanders off into näive Christianity and pacifism that marks his discussion of the causes for Napoleon's invasion of Russia in 1812: "But it happened simply because it had to happen."[3]

In order so to remedy literature's failings, we must turn to Clausewitz and Thucydides in order to place war in a large context – in its political and operational dimensions. In fact at times, particularly in the case of Thucydides, both men rise to the standards of great literature in discussing their subject. Clausewitz himself aims at no less than establishing a "general theory of war," and while Thucydides sees the world very much in historical terms, he also fits it clearly within a framework that accords closely with Clausewitz's view of a human arena dominated by ambiguity and friction. Yet, Clausewitz's general theory stands in stark contradiction to most of the philosophical and theoretical approach of the modern social sciences and their claims for what theory can or cannot do.

For Clausewitz, the purpose of theory is not to discover fundamental, unchanging truths or laws about war. Theory has the strictly utilitarian purpose of educating the mind; it cannot aim at discovering universal truths applicable to all situations, all places, all times. It forms "a guide to anyone who wants to learn about war...; it will light his way, ease his progress, train his judgment, and help him to avoid pitfalls."[4] Clausewitz continues: "[Theory] is meant to educate the mind of the future commander, or, more accurately, to guide him in his self-education, not to accompany him to the battlefield."[5] He concludes a similar argument later in *On War* with the observation that "theory is not meant to provide... positive doctrines and systems to be used as intellectual tools."[6]

The problem, as Clausewitz points out, has to do with what is knowable. "Efforts were therefore made to equip the conduct of war with principles, rules, or even systems... [B]ut people failed adequately to account of the endless complexities involved."[7] Most theories "aim at

---

[3] Leo Tolstoy, *War and Peace*, trans. by Ann Dunnigan (New York, 1968), p. 729.
[4] Carl von Clausewitz, *On War*, trans. and ed. by Michael Howard and Peter Paret (Princeton, NJ, 1976), p. 141.
[5] Ibid., p. 141.
[6] Ibid., p. 168.
[7] Ibid., p. 134.

fixed values; but in war everything is uncertain, and calculations have to be made with variable quantities."[8]

Thus, any theory that is to be of use must in the end rest on the real world, on the actual conditions of strategy, operations, tactics, and war itself. History is the only laboratory we have, and if we do not ground our theoretical examination of conflict in that reality then we are spinning webs of nonsense. As Clausewitz pointed out:

> [Theory] is an analytic investigation leading to a close acquaintance with the subject; applied to experience – in our case to military history – it leads to thorough familiarity with it. The closer it comes to that goal, the more it proceeds from the objective form of a science to the subjective form of a skill, the more effective it will prove in areas where the nature of the case admits no arbiter but talent.[9]

Any theoretical understanding of war must arise out of real acts and occurrences in human conflict; one must not impose on the world theoretical constructs or concepts arrived at independently of history and experience. Above all, Clausewitz was contemptuous of those military theoreticians in his own day who sought neat formulas to solve complex problems occasioned by war: "In short, absolute, so-called mathematical factors never find a firm basis in military calculations. From the very start there is an interplay of possibilities, probabilities, good luck and bad luck that weaves its way throughout the length and breadth of the tapestry."[10] "The jargon, technicalities, and metaphors" that passed for theory in his own time never seduced him.[11] For Clausewitz, theory could not aim at fixed values; rather "in war everything is uncertain."[12]

In the Clausewitzian universe – one which has over the past decade received considerable support from mathematical research – one looks for general knowledge instead of absolute truths. Contemporary mathematicians, and particularly researchers involved in the biological sciences, have been emphasizing more and more the importance of nonlinear mathematics to any understanding of the physical universe. In the real world, there is often a disjunction of cause and effect as a fundamental principle, that is, actions stimulate unexpected and unpredictable reactions.

The linear, Newtonian universe is disappearing under a tidal wave of fundamental rethinking about how the universe works. The implications

---

[8] Ibid., p. 136.
[9] Ibid., p. 141.
[10] Ibid., p. 86.
[11] Ibid., p. 168.
[12] Ibid., p. 136.

for the study of war and international relations are immense. Clausewitz suggests:

> The conduct of war branches out in almost all directions and has no definite limits; while any system or model, has the finite nature of a synthesis... [Most theorists] aim at fixed values, but in war everything is uncertain and calculations have to be made with variable quantities. [Most theorists] direct the inquiry exclusively toward physical quantities, whereas all military action is intertwined with psychological forces and effects. [Most theorists] consider only unilateral action, whereas war consists of a continuous interaction of opposites.[13]

Elsewhere, he indicates that "war is the realm of uncertainty; three quarters of the factors on which action in war is based are wrapped in a fog of greater or lesser uncertainty."[14] Uncertainty, chance, accident, ambiguity, and complexity all lie at the heart of Clausewitz's conception of war. At the same time, his appreciation of randomness, and his ability to recognize it, explains why so many have found his theories lacking in clarity, or utility, or even relevance. Yet, to reject Clausewitz in favor of simpler, more utilitarian theories of war, theories by and large not connected to the ambiguities of the real world, is to court disaster.

Clausewitz and Strategy

What useful lessons might we draw from Clausewitz's discussions about theory and war? First, we must understand that the Prussian has set limited goals for his study. Despite his justly famous aphorism "that war is not a mere act of policy but a true political instrument, a continuation of political activity by other means," he concentrates his analysis on the sharp, hard edge of war and leaves much of the discussion of strategy and policy and issues of morality to others.[15]

Despite the fact that he spends relatively little time in examining the strategic-political level of war, Clausewitz recognizes the crucial relationships between politics and war:

> War is no pastime; it is no mere joy in daring and winning, no place for irresponsible enthusiasts. It is a serious means to a serious end... When whole communities go to war whole peoples, and especially civilized

---

[13] Ibid., pp. 134, 136.
[14] Ibid., p. 101.
[15] Ibid., p. 87.

peoples – the reason always lies in some political situation, and the occasion is always due to some political object. War therefore is an act of policy.[16]

If we are to gain an understanding of war, Clausewitz argues, we cannot divorce it from its societal and political context – a basic theoretical insight that informs all of his discussions about the interface among politics, strategy, and military operations. His contribution to our theoretical understanding of conflict at the strategic and political levels is best embodied in his depiction of war "as a remarkable trinity – composed [first] of primordial violence, hatred and enmity ... [second] of the interplay of chance and probability within which the creative spirit is free to roam; and [third] of its element of subordination, as an instrument of policy that makes it subject to reason alone."[17] The actual conduct of war finds itself suspended between these three great influences and, torn between external pressures and influences, war follows its unpredictable and nonlinear course.[18]

Clausewitz and Friction

This last point brings us to Clausewitz's greatest contribution to our understanding of war – namely his concept of friction. Commentators on Clausewitz have tended to focus on friction as one of a number of factors described in Book I that impede the general flow and conduct of military operations. In fact, as Barry Watts has persuasively argued, Clausewitz uses *Friktion* as an overarching concept that encompasses the enormous difficulties that confront nations, political leaders, commanders, military organizations, and soldiers in the field in their conduct of war.[19] It is in its conceptualization of friction that *On War* achieves its greatest analytic triumph.

Clausewitz argues that friction, both of the natural variety and of simple human nature, pervades all elements of war and life, although it has its most obvious impact in war. Bad intelligence, incompetence, misunderstandings, personal likes and dislikes, contempt for the enemy, carelessness, stupidity – all the factors that contribute to making any human endeavor involving more than one person difficult – place enormous

[16] Ibid., p. 86–87.
[17] Ibid., p. 89.
[18] In this regard, see particularly Alan Beyerchen, "Clausewitz, Nonlinearity, and the Unpredictability of War," *International Security*, Winter 1992/1993, pp. 69–70.
[19] See Barry Watts, *Clausewitzian Friction and Future War* (Washington, DC, 1996).

impediments to the conduct of war at every level. "Everything in war," he writes, "is very simple, but the simplest thing is difficult. The difficulties accumulate and end by producing a kind of friction that is inconceivable unless one has experienced war."[20] Clausewitz aptly describes the effort involved in waging war as comparable to the attempt to run through water.[21] "Countless minor incidents – the kind you can never foresee – combine to lower the general level of performance, so that one always falls short of the intended goal."[22]

As Winston Churchill described the Gallipoli catastrophe, "the terrible ifs accumulate." An obscure Turkish Colonel, Mustafa Kemal, happens to pass the Anzac landings; the Australians take their time in scaling the cliffs overlooking the landing site; the British colonels at Y Beach have no instructions and, consequently, do nothing despite the gunfire indicating the slaughter of their comrades on the beaches at the tip of the peninsula; the minesweepers are manned by British fishermen who are willing to risk their lives to remove mines but who refuse to expose themselves as targets for Turkish artillery and machine guns; British forces land at Sulva Bay and for three days do nothing despite the fact that there are no Turks in front of them. The list of *ifs* is almost endless, but there they are, the frictions of Gallipoli that ruined the only strategic possibility for avoiding the slaughter of the Western Front – a slaughter that would last another three years. If we wish to understand war even in a theoretical sense, the fundamental Clausewitzian reality is that war "is the realm of chance. No other human activity gives it greater scope."[23] Thus, the terrible *ifs* accumulate.

Clausewitz makes clear that an understanding of friction is fundamental to any understanding of war because friction pervades any conflict from beginning to end and at every level. To add to the environmental frictions – weather, confusion, bad communications, incompetence, truculence, and irascibility, among a host of others and all of which beset military organizations even in the best of times – is the fact that war presents us with living, breathing opponents who are attempting to do no less than kill us and our comrades. That simple thought is enough to turn some soldiers' blood to ice. "In war, the will is directed at an animate object that reacts."[24] Above all commanders and leaders lack knowledge

---

[20] Clausewitz, *On War*, p. 119.
[21] Ibid., p. 120.
[22] Ibid., p. 119.
[23] Ibid., p. 101.
[24] Ibid., p. 149.

of how the enemy will react; what they must know is that his every action will be calculated to undo everything they are trying to do. "War is thus an act to compel our enemy to do our will."[25] But the enemy has exactly the same intention as far as we are concerned; and he will be willing to go to any length to achieve that objective, including killing us.

What one needs in order to master the innumerable frictions that hinder and hamper every action in war "is a sense of unity and a power of judgment raised to a marvelous pitch of vision, which easily grasps and dismisses a thousand remote possibilities which an ordinary mind would labor to identify and wear itself out in so doing."[26] Indeed, only the extraordinary intellect still functions "in the dreadful presence of suffering and danger ... in this psychological fog [where] it is so hard to form clear and complete insights."[27] But in war this kind of presence is all too rare, and military organizations are left to muddle through with all that muddling through entails in terms of long, endless rows of tombstones.

Thucydides: The Clausewitzian Historian

Indeed, it is anachronistic to call Thucydides, the fifth-century B.C. Greek historian, a Clausewitzian historian. Yet, in every respect his analysis of war, strategy, power, and international relations prefigures the theoretical framework that Clausewitz established in the early nineteenth century. Nowhere, of course, does Thucydides lay down a specific theory or theories of war. He does make an extraordinary claim: "It will be enough for me, however, if these words of mine are judged useful by those who understand clearly the events which happened in the past and which (human nature being what it is) will, at some time or other and in much the same ways, be repeated in the future. My work is not a piece of writing designed to meet the taste of the immediate public, but it was done to last forever."[28] Let me suggest that most of us who today study strategic and military history would fully agree with that claim.[29]

What makes *The History of the Peloponnesian War* the greatest book ever written about war is its range. Unlike Clausewitz, Thucydides is

---

[25] Ibid., p. 75.
[26] Ibid., p. 112.
[27] Ibid., p. 108.
[28] Thucydides, *The History of the Peloponnesian War*, trans. by Rex Warner (London, 1954), p. 48.
[29] For the relevance of Thucydides to the modern strategic world, see in particular Bernard Knox, "Thucydides and the Peloponnesian War: Politics and Power," *The Naval War College Review*, Winter 1973.

willing to examine the full range of war's complexities from the highest levels of policy making and strategy to the psychological collapse of soldiers and armies on the battlefield. And again, unlike Clausewitz, he is willing to confront the moral parameters within which human societies interact in time of war.

Nevertheless, as John Keegan has pointed out in *Face of Battle*, Thucydides is one of the few historians who manages to bring to his account a real sense of the psychological and physical terror and confusion of the battlefield. In Thucydides' account chance, ambiguity, fog, all the frictions that Clausewitz lays out and more, dominate the landscape of the great contest between Athens and Sparta for hegemony of Greece. It is in his depiction of the Peloponnesian War as a contest of independent human wills that Thucydides also lays out the fundamental nature of war. And that contest as he makes clear again and again – often distorted in translation – is one where chance [*tyche*] dominates.[30]

Nothing makes his Clausewitzian universe clearer than a short examination of his description of the attempted *coup de main* by the Thebans against the town of Platea at the beginning of the war. At first, everything works flawlessly. A small Theban attack party crosses Platean territory unseen and arrives at the gates of Platea at first darkness. Conspirators within the city have overpowered the guards and unlocked the gates. Platean resistance collapses before it can begin. The major force of Thebans to solidify the hold on the city is already on the march from their city over a distance that measures only eight miles as the crow flies. Platea appears firmly in the hands of the Thebans and the Platean traitors.

But is it? A heavy rain begins. The Asopus overflows its banks. The torches of the relieving force sputter and go out. The relieving Thebans get lost on the mountain track. Meanwhile in the beleaguered, confused city, the Plateans realize how few enemies are within their walls. In the darkness and confusion of a strange city, Theban cohesion and confidence collapses. Isolated attacks from the rooftops further the confusion. In the strange alleyways and streets, Platean hoplites strike at the invaders. The Thebans collapse and those who are not immediately butchered fall into Platean hands as hostages. The relieving force arrives to find its comrades in enemy hands and the gates barred. "The terrible ifs accumulate."

Since the late nineteenth century, the Anglo-American intellectual consensus has increasingly tended to regard war as an anomaly, as an event

---

[30] And according to my good friend Don Kagan, *tyche* is not always translated by the translators of the Peloponnesian War because of its prevalence throughout the text.

or occurrence entirely foreign and unnatural in human affairs. Despite a slight increase in the interest in military and strategic history in the United States, it is well to remember that most American colleges and universities still have no courses that deal with military history – in effect no examination of the impact of war on society. Only a country whose intellectual elites are entirely removed from reality could write history as if wars had never occurred. In that sense, both Thucydides and Clausewitz are out of step with current American views and understandings of the world.

The larger intellectual framework within which Thucydides casts his history represents a recognition that the coin of international exchange is power: economic power, financial power, and, above all, military power. Nations and states may, or may not, express this last aspect of power; but power, whenever and however expressed, is the basic determinant of human affairs. Thucydides believes that power has no moral attributes; it is amoral in character, but always present in the exchanges and dealings of nations and human beings. Thus, he tells us that the great cause of the Peloponnesian War lay in "the growth of Athenian power and the fear this caused in Sparta."[31] Later in the war, the Athenian negotiators are equally explicit in their dialogue with the Melian oligarchs:

> Our opinion of the Gods and our knowledge of men lead us to conclude that it is a general and necessary law of nature to rule wherever one can. This is not a law we made ourselves, nor are we the first to act upon it when made. We found it already in existence and we shall leave it to exist forever among those who come after us. We are merely acting in accordance with it, and we know that you or anyone else with the same power as ours would be acting in precisely the same way.[32]

Yet, Thucydides does have the Athenians say to the Spartans that those who are especially deserving of praise are those who display a regard for justice beyond what was called for in the situation.

If Thucydides considered the Athenian-Spartan clash as inevitable, the policy errors and idiosyncratic decisions of statesmen, the element of chance, the faulty assumptions of the opposing sides, and the pressures of public anger determined the actual course of events that led directly to the war that broke out in 431 B.C. The precipitating events came far from the epicenter of the Spartan-Athenian clash. On the western coast of Greece a quarrel between Corinth and Corcyra over their colony, Epidamnus, drew in the great powers. The crucial factor was Corcyra's navy and location,

---

[31] Thucydides, *The History of the Peloponnesian War*, p. 49.
[32] Ibid., pp. 404–405.

both of which pushed the Athenians to intervene. The Corinthians, in turn furious at Athens for its interference in what they regarded as their own matters, turned to Sparta, and events moved inexorably toward war.

But even as the Greek city states tumbled over the edge, there were those who tried to hold back the rush to war. Archidamus, one of the Spartan kings, a man with long experience at war, warned the Spartan assembly: "Spartans, in the course of my life I have taken part in many wars, and I see among you many people of the same age as I am. They and I have had experience and so are not likely to share in what may be a general enthusiasm for war nor to think that war is a good or safe thing."[33]

Archidamus continued on to warn his listeners about the economic and military strengths the Athenians possessed – a situation that would allow the Athenians to fight a war entirely foreign to Spartan experience. Looking at the wreckage of the Peloponnesian War 30 years later, it is hard to see how he could have been more prescient. Yet, he might as well have been speaking on the moon. The Spartans voted for war with great enthusiasm. It was the miscalculations of Spartan statesmen and military leaders who created the plausible scenarios and simple, easy, operational and tactical answers to intractable strategic and political problems.

Those Spartan leaders who urged war undoubtedly believed the mere appearance of their phalanx before the walls of Athens would force the Athenians to come out and fight – a prospect that none of them could conceive of resulting in anything other than victory. The enemy, of course, would come out and do what was expected of him. But the Athenians did not come out and fight; instead, they remained impregnable behind their walls for the next 30 years. On the other hand, the Athenian leader, Pericles, calculated that by relying on its economic and maritime power, by refusing to meet Sparta on land, and by waging a war of "exhaustion," Athens would eventually force Sparta to recognize the Athenian state as the other "superpower" of Greece. Ironically, Athens achieved much of this in the Peace of Nicias.

But Pericles was dead when the contestants agreed to that peace. New and aggressive leaders came forward with grander designs; and the cost of "victory" so embittered and infuriated the Athenians that the Peace of Nicias collapsed shortly after agreement. Dissatisfied with the fruits of victory, the Athenians pursued total victory over Sparta by supporting their traditional enemy Argos, by destroying the city of Melos, and eventually by launching the great expedition to Sicily that ended in catastrophe.

[33] Ibid., p. 82.

War had clearly slipped out of the hands of those who sought to control it; the cool, rational strategies with which the contestants had begun the war had foundered; and the conflict had degenerated into an eye-gouging fight to the finish. War is uncontrollable because it is so inextricably linked to the human emotions. Here, Thucydides was in complete agreement with what Clausewitz was to write twenty-two hundred years later.

Most perceptively, Thucydides underlines that war carries with it the moral degradation and collapse of civilized values within the societies that wage it. It inevitably results in the general loss of humanity as the opposing sides become accustomed to slaughter. "[W]ar is a stern teacher; in depriving [men] of the power of easily satisfying their daily wants, it brings most people's minds down to the level of their actual circumstances."[34] He then adds: "[W]ith the ordinary conventions of civilized life thrown into confusion, human nature, always ready to offend even where laws exist, showed itself proudly in its true colors, as something incapable of controlling passion, insubordinate to the idea of justice, the enemy to anything superior to itself; for if it had not been for the pernicious power of envy, men would not have so exalted vengeance above innocence and profit above justice."[35]

And so the history of the Peloponnesian War represents a descent into hell. What would have been unthinkable at the war's beginning becomes normal practice as it continues. At the start of the conflict, the Athenian position in the Aegean is threatened by a revolt by their ally, Mytilene. After considerable debate, the Athenians eventually decided to spare the innocent and kill only those active in the revolt. Twelve years later at Melos, under similar circumstances, they did not even bother to debate the question but instead slaughtered the men and sold the women and children into slavery – an incident that Euripides' great, dark play, *The Trojan Women*, celebrates.

One of the most bizarre spectacles of our century has been the predilection for comfortable, middle-class intellectuals to believe that revolution is a "good" thing. Since 1789, they have enshrined revolution in the temple of virtue. Today with the wreckage of 70 years of the Soviet Union exposed to the light of day, Thucydides' dark wisdom stands as a sad reminder of how little mankind has learned from the past. Foreshadowing Orwell, Thucydides noted about the civil war in Corcyra (modern-day Corfu): "Words too had to change their meaning. What used to be

---

[34] Thucydides, *The History of the Peloponnesian War*, p. 242.
[35] Ibid., p. 245.

described as a thoughtless word of aggression was now regarded as the courage one would expect to find in a party member; to think of the future and wait was merely another way of saying one was a coward; any idea of moderation was just an attempt to disguise one's manly character; ability to understand a question from all sides meant that one was actually unfitted for action."[36]

In a chilling parallel to the contest between Stalin and Trotsky, Thucydides notes the following about the contest for power during the civil war on Corcyra:

> As a rule those who were least remarkable for intelligence showed the greatest power of survival. Such people recognized their own deficiencies and the superior intelligence of their opponents; fearing that they might lose a debate or find themselves out-maneuvered in intrigue by their quick-witted enemies, they boldly launched straight into action; while their opponents, overconfident in the belief that they would see what was happening in advance, and not thinking it necessary to seize by force what they could secure by policy, were the more easily destroyed because they were off their guard.[37]

Like Clausewitz, Thucydides lays out no template for the future. He only provides a deep and thorough analysis of how men acted in his time. Yet, that singular claim, quoted at the beginning of this section – that his account would analyze "events which happened in the past and which (human nature being what it is) will, at some time or other and in much the same way, be repeated in the future" – stands as a tribute to a history that allows us to understand our own times and motivations in a clearer, less ambiguous light. If we truly seek to understand international relations, strategy, and war in real terms, then we must come to grips with the intricately constructed account that Thucydides has left us.

Theory and the Twenty-First Century

What to make of the claims of modern theories to our understanding of war and military institutions over the past century? Here, the record is hardly an impressive one. The great theorists from Mahan to Douhet to Liddell Hart and Fuller to the theories of nuclear deterrence have thrown minimal light on the dark paths stretching before them. They have sought answers and certainties where there are none; they have

[36] Ibid., p. 244.
[37] Ibid., p. 244.

consistently sought to make facts fit theory; and in their simplifications, they have pushed aside the real world of difficulties. As Wolfe said before Quebec, "War is an option of difficulties." And more often than not within a short time of their writing, such theories have seen the real world rise up to underline their flawed assumptions and conclusions.

Mahan's greatest contribution may have been to mislead the German Navy in its preparations for two world wars into believing that submarine warfare did not represent a viable option for the Reich's naval strategy, but such a "triumph" is hardly one for theory. In the air power arena, the theories of Douhet, Trenchard, and the Air Corps Tactical School may have justified the creation of air forces. But they also provided a theory of strategic bombing that was close to ideology in its rigidity. Moreover, when the new conflict came, such theories littered Central Europe with the wreckage of aircraft and aircrew, largely because commanders, indoctrinated by theory, ignored the evidence that unescorted bomber formations could not survive without long-range escorts. With the success of air power in the Gulf War, we have seen claims that air power has at last realized the dreams of its early prophets. *The Gulf War Air Power Survey*, however, suggests that the air campaign in that war with its frictions and ambiguities underlines the continuing relevance of Clausewitz more than the triumph of early air power theories.

The fundamental problem with most theories of war in our century has been the fact that theorists have sought simple, comfortable answers to the intractable and insoluble problems raised by war. In fact, theories that provide answers and solutions have invariably led to dead ends. At its best, theory, as Clausewitz suggests and Thucydides implies, can only indicate the most important kinds of questions we might ask. There are no templates.

The German success in armored warfare in the first years of World War II is instructive about how theory can contribute to impressive military capabilities. The Germans learned little directly from theorists; rather in Clausewitzian terms they focused their efforts in the interwar period on a close examination of what history suggested about the tactical lessons of the last war.[38] Then, through careful study of exercises and combat experience they honed their combat capabilities in a fashion that thoroughly intertwined experience (both historical and current) and theory. Their philosophy of war was infused with a Clausewitzian sense of the ambiguities of war.

---

[38] See Williamson Murray, "Armored Warfare," in *Innovation in the Interwar Period*, ed. by Williamson Murray and Allan R. Millett (Cambridge, 1996), pp. 6–49.

Yet, there is a warning in the German performance in the interwar year. Because, while the Germans studied the tactical lessons of the last war with great care, they paid almost no attention to the strategic lessons of the last conflict; and they and their nation would pay a terrible price for that blindness.

It is essential that Americans not believe they possess such enormous wisdom that they can dismiss the past. Throughout America's short span of existence as an independent nation, Americans have had a tendency to dismiss history. As Henry Ford so eloquently stated: "History is bunk." At times, they have paid a price for that contempt, but, for the most part, they have escaped because of the distance of the United States from other powers and its great economic power. However, we now live in a world where the distances have shrunk and where the lethality of weapons has vastly increased. Whether Americans like it or not, they live in a world still governed by the same rules, the same general patterns that existed in Thucydides' time. Above all war has not changed its fundamental nature of ambiguity, uncertainty, and friction.

The great advantage of Clausewitz and Thucydides is the fact that their theories of power and war remain consistently tied to the real world of human experience. Their world, whether it be in its theoretical construct or its historical understanding, remains one in which ambiguities, contradictions, chance, uncertainty, and discontinuities are the basic building blocks.

What this author finds particularly worrying in current discussions within the U.S. military about "military technical revolutions," or the "coming information war" are the underlying assumptions that the advances that have occurred over the past decade and that may continue into the future will allow us to comprehend the complexities of war in a fashion that has never been the case in the past. What Clausewitz and Thucydides suggest, however, is that such assumptions – so driven and influenced by an increasingly narrowly focused American *Weltanschauung* – remain as flawed and idiosyncratic as similar theories did in the early 1960s when a poor, technologically inferior opponent refused to play by the rules and theories established by America's brilliant military and civilian technocrats. And we lost. We should not forget that defeat.

Additional Reading

Over the past two decades since this work was first presented at Ohio State and published five years later, a number of important works have appeared on Thucydides, the Peloponnesian War, and Clausewitz. For

Thucydides, Professor Donald Kagan, a man who kept me in this profession by his enthusiasm, wisdom, and encouragement, has continued his masterful examination of what has been his life's work: Thucydides and the Peloponnesian War. Thus, I would urge the reader to begin any additional exploration of the subject of Thucydides with Professor Kagan's abridgement of his masterful four-volume study of the Peloponnesian War (*The Peloponnesian War* [New York, 2003]), which he has followed up with a commentary on that greatest of all historians (*Thucydides, The Reinvention of History* [New York, 2009]). Equally important is Victor Davis Hanson's *A War Like No Other, How the Athenians and Spartans Fought the Peloponnesian War* (New York, 2005).

For Clausewitz, there are several short commentaries on that greatest of all theorists on war that provide wonderful introductions to that difficult and complex, as well as enlightening work. Hew Strachan's *Clausewitz's On War* (New York, 2007) provides an insightful, concise, and sharp examination of the evolution of the Prussian theorist's thinking. The collection of essays that he edited with Andreas Herberg-Rothe is also well worth consulting: *Clausewitz in the Twenty-First Century* (Oxford, 2007). Peter Paret's *The Cognitive Challenge of War, Prussia 1806* (Princeton, NJ, 2009) places Clausewitz's thinking solidly within the intellectual milieu of his own time. Both works, however, suffer from ignoring the impact of the beginnings of the scientific revolution at the time Clausewitz was writing. Here, the reader should consult the brilliant article by my former colleague at Ohio State, Alan Beyerchen, "Clausewitz, Nonlinearity, and the Unpredictability of War," *International Security*, Winter 1992/93. It appeared two years after I gave this lecture. Finally, a must read is the late Michael I. Handel's *Masters of War: Classical Strategic Thought* (London, 2000).

3

Clausewitz out, Computers in: Military Culture and Technological Hubris

One of the greatest understudied aspects of military history concerns the institutional cultures through which officer corps come to grips with the dynamic and ambiguous problems of war and peace. That institutional culture shapes the understanding of the strategic, operational, and tactical choices before the professional soldier, and it also implants broader assumptions concerning the historical framework in which those choices find their meaning. It is a process that proceeds by means of formal education, informal acculturation, and practical experience. Actual events on the battlefield have traditionally exercised the principal reality check on the understandings and assumptions of institutional military culture, this despite ample evidence that military institutions sometimes prove astonishingly resistant to learning from their experiences.[1] And as difficult as they are to learn in combat, how much harder must it be to learn the lessons of war in peace, absent the harsh, unpredictable, and unforgiving world of death and destruction. Consequently, it is doubly important that in peacetime military professionals work to frame the right kind of questions and generate realistic assumptions.

For the most part, however, the historical record suggests peacetime military institutions postulate answers rather than questions, and adopt assumptions that speak more to their own intellectual comfort zones than to reality. American military culture has generated exceptions to

---

[1] See in particular Andrew Krepinevich, *The Array in Vietnam* (Baltimore, 1986); and Timothy Travers, *The Killing Ground, The British Army, the Western Front, and the Emergence of Modern War, 1900–1918* (London, 1987).

This chapter was presented as a lecture at the Army War College in 1995 and then published in the *National Interest* in 1996.

this rule during the past century, in some cases dramatically so. But a major cultural shift now appears to be underway that does not bode well for the future, one that is liable to return us to a part of our past experience that is better discarded.

At the turn of the twentieth century, the American military reflected the peculiar insularities of the great republic it served. The nation had fought two great wars to that point in its history; the first, the Revolutionary War, hardly represented a standard of military professionalism, and the second, the Civil War, involved considerable tensions between the nascent professional services and the novel demands of massive mobilizations of citizen soldiers and economic power. Otherwise, the American military had for the most part chased Indians and sailed on lonely stations as an annex to the Royal Navy.

But following the Philippines War, the American military entered a period of resolute professionalization. Senior military leaders and far-sighted civilians founded serious academic institutions, such as the staff college at Fort Leavenworth and the Army and Navy War Colleges to educate as opposed to train officers. How those institutions functioned in peacetime explains a great deal about the successful adaptation of the American military to the challenges of the First World War. West Point and Annapolis, meanwhile, were *not* institutions of professional military education in the nineteenth century – and many would argue they still are not. They were engineering and training schools to turn young men into officers. Giving virtually no attention to military history, the conduct of operations, or strategy, they were in the business of turning out lieutenants.

By the 1920s the American military services were firmly established with cultures that identified their officers as professionals, possessing a body of significant knowledge they could only gain through systematic training, experience, and education. In that period the services received minimal funding from their civilian masters – to the extent that when war broke out in Europe in 1939, the army of the United States ranked in capabilities with the South American republics rather than with its future opponents and allies. And yet, in less than three years, the U.S. Navy's carrier aviation had destroyed much of the Japanese Navy's carrier force. U.S. Marines had executed an amphibious landing on Guadalcanal, and the Army was preparing for landings in North America. Within another two years, American military might would bestride the world from the ravaged cities of Germany to the battlefields of Normandy and the Pacific.

How to explain this extraordinary transformation? Undoubtedly, the massive arsenal of American industry was a factor. But of great importance was also the cultural and intellectual verve of the U.S. officer corps that the war colleges and staff colleges had nurtured during the interwar period. The institutional ethos established there not only insisted that it was important for officers to go to school, but that many of them should serve on the faculties of those institutions as well. The future Admiral Raymond Spruance attended the Naval War College as a student and then went on to serve two separate tours on the faculty. Ernest King was promoted to rear admiral while at the war college. A substantial number of their air leaders in the Second World War not only attended the Air Corps Tactical School at Maxwell but served on that school's faculty; the Army's colleges and schools developed a generation of sophisticated leaders for the future. Across the services, too, a broader cultural framework of serious professional reading and thinking encouraged the careers of the best officers. When General of the Armies George Marshall commented in a lecture at Princeton after World War II that one could not understand strategy unless one had read Thucydides, he reflected the educational ethos of an entire generation of American military professionals.

These educational institutions were not just repositories for book learning. The Naval War College played a crucial role in the development of carrier aviation. The Infantry School at Fort Benning, under Marshall's leadership, identified many of the best in the Army and attracted them to its faculty. The Marine schools at Quantico helped to develop the amphibious concepts and doctrine without which the Pacific campaigns would have been impossible.

When the Second World War was over, this educated military elite returned home filled with praise for the part that their education had played in preparing them for the trials of war. Admiral Chester William Nimitz wrote, "I credit the Naval War College for such success [as] I achieved in strategy and tactics during the war."[2] For his last assignment before retirement, Spruance returned by choice to become president of the Naval War College, while Dwight D. Eisenhower founded the National War College, which began its life with luminaries like George Kennan on its faculty and brigadier generals among its student body. By the early 1960s, however, that cultural framework had dramatically changed. The faculties of the war and staff colleges had become repositories for officers whose careers were over. It was now the kiss of death for an officer to receive an assignment to teach on the faculty of any school. In the U.S. Navy, it had become fashionable for officers to be selected for senior

---

[2] E.B. Porter, *Nimitz* (Annapolis, MD, 1976), p. 136.

service school but not to attend. In fact, the service cultures have retained a solid belief through to the present day that assignment to teach in any senior school is anything but career enhancing.

It was not just in their attitude toward professional military education that service cultures changed so radically in the early part of the Cold War. There was also a decline of intellectual seriousness. General William Westmoreland's memoirs reflect well this latter shift:

> Beside my bed I kept... several books; a bible; a French Grammar; Mao Tse-tung's little red book on guerrilla warfare, *The Centurions*, a novel about the French fight with the Vietminh; and several works by Dr. Bernard Fall, who wrote authoritatively on the French experience in Indochina... I was usually too tired in late evening to give the books more than occasional attention.[3]

The general was, of course, a man of his word: *The Centurions* is after its first chapters about the war in Algeria.

How had this change come about? Largely, it was the result of the emerging leadership in the 1950s and early 1960s having gone to war in 1941 as first lieutenants and junior captains with no exposure to professional military education. By 1945 these officers were colonels (or navy captains) and in some cases brigadier generals (or rear admirals). Their attitude seems to have been that since they had not needed professional military education to be successful both on the battlefield and in their careers, education could not be all that important. The results of this cultural change show clearly in a comparison of the 1954 and 1965 decisions concerning whether to intervene in Indochina. In the earlier case, the thoughtful warnings of Generals Matthew Ridgway and James Gavin – that the political and strategic gains of intervention, as well as the uncertainties of the situation, were not worth the costs that the United States would incur – persuaded President Eisenhower not to take the dangerous path of supporting the French as they went down to defeat at Dien Bien Phu. And, of course, Eisenhower himself was a well-educated military professional who knew how to listen to Ridgway and Gavin. Barely a decade later, however, the leadership of the American military – now a different generation – discussed the question of intervention in Southeast Asia exclusively in operational and tactical terms. The larger political and strategic framework, which a real education would have supplied, had simply disappeared from sight.

---

[3] William Westmoreland, *A Soldier Reports* (New York, 1989), p. 364.

Moreover, by the mid-1960s, the American military culture had been fundamentally corrupted by the dominating personality of Robert Strange McNamara and his approach to national security policy as Secretary of Defense. McNamara's expertise as a number cruncher had pushed him to the presidency of Ford Motor Company, and he brought the current methods of American business, a cost accounting mentality and a rigid engineering view of the world, to the business of managing the Defense Department. In his astonishing memoirs – astonishing in that they display virtually no understanding of what their author had done to the American military in the 1960s – McNamara claims that "the military tried to gauge its progress [in Vietnam] with quantitative measurements such as enemy casualties (which became infamous as body counts), weapons seized, prisoners taken, sorties flown, and so on."[4] But, of course, it was precisely such statistical, quantitative measures of efficiency that McNamara himself had *demanded* the military use to judge every situation from weapons procurement to the face of battle. And without an educational and cultural compass to guide its responses, the professional American military cloned itself on the Secretary of Defense. By the mid-1960s, on the cusp of the Vietnam intervention, it was out-McNamaring McNamara.

The U.S. military thus addressed the strategic and operational questions raised by Vietnam in terms of quantitative and technological measures: how many weapons captured, how many villages pacified, how many enemies killed, how many ton miles of cargo flown, how many bombs dropped. Little else mattered. History on the one side and the uncertainties and ambiguities of the battlefield on the other disappeared into a set of technological and game-theoretical assumptions. Thus, the United States marched into the Vietnam War with what was, in retrospect, an incredible ignorance. Americans had scant knowledge of the language, culture, traditions, and history of the people on whose behalf the United States was intervening, and, what was worse, neither the civilian leadership at the Pentagon nor the professional military even *desired* such knowledge. Clearly, a cloud of mechanistic hubris had essentially trumped the key purposes and functions of professional military education.

Underlying this hubris was the general cultural enthusiasm for "modern technology" that characterized the period and that was assumed to be the source of an unprecedented U.S. economic superiority. It followed that technological sophistication spelled superiority in the military sphere

---

[4] Robert S. McNamara, *In Retrospect: The Tragedy and Lessons of Vietnam* (New York, 1995), p. 48.

as well.[5] And there the American academic community played a role in making the mess in Vietnam. Academic spinning of game and deterrence theories proliferated like mutant Ebola viruses as prominent professors flocked to Washington in the early 1960s to remake not only American society but its foreign policy as well. The "decisive" technology was the computer, the application of which in the social sciences only reinforced the predilection among academics to believe they were on the trail of quantitatively guaranteed predictive capabilities with respect to human affairs. Between the secretary of defense, his whiz kids, and the supportive academic environment around them, a common theme developed in American defense policy making that saw American technology and the coming of the computer age as rendering factors such as history, culture, and the traditional understanding of war irrelevant.

The American military came back deeply scarred from Vietnam. Army and marine officers who had survived two or three tours in Southeast Asia returned deeply suspicious of the predictive universe that Robert McNamara and their senior officers had imposed on the war's conduct. Drugs, indiscipline, and bad morale all exacerbated the feeling of malaise that drove a reexamination of the military's culture and values among mid-level and junior officers. From that effort, the American military managed to overcome the collapse that followed the war. The intellectual ferment that marked the post-Vietnam War period represented a substantial departure from the attitudes characterizing much of the 1960s. There was an instinctive revulsion against quantitative measurements of efficiency – exchange ratios, body counts, the mechanistic tabulation of data for its own sake. But there was more than that, too.

The changes in America's military culture after Vietnam took time to develop. The army's first cut in 1976 at a new edition of its basic operations manual, FM 100–5, was a regurgitation of the mechanistic, firepower-intensive approach that had dominated the army in Vietnam. But while senior leaders stuck with the old, the culture of the emerging leaders was embracing a new edition of Clausewitz's *On War*, edited by Michael Howard and Peter Paret in 1975. That translation made Clausewitz accessible to the generation of officers returning from the wreckage of Vietnam, and they found in his writings an intellectual statement for their deepest belief that war was inherently unpredictable, uncertain, and ambiguous at every level. Indeed, as Alan Beyerchen has emphasized, Clausewitz's continuing relevance is largely due to the fact that he is

---

[5] For a particularly vivid example, see "South Vietnam," *Time*, October 22, 1965.

a profoundly nonlinear thinker in a world that is widely, but wrongly, thought to be linear.[6]

It was the Clausewitzian understanding of friction, uncertainty, and chance – gained at such cost in Vietnam – that dominated American military thought in the last decade and a half of the Cold War. American grand strategy sought to turn the competition with the Soviets onto grounds that represented *our* strengths, not those of our opponents. The "competitive strategies" approach of the Pentagon's Office of Net Assessment found an audience among the services. And in choosing whether to use military force – that most crucial of political decisions – the Weinberger and Powell doctrines appeared. Many have argued that those doctrines were so restrictive that the United States would not have fought the Revolutionary War, or even the Second World War. Yet, whatever their problems, they reflected a Clausewitzian belief in the primacy of politics in the fighting of war.

It was not that the emerging leadership rejected technology, computers, or science. Rather, it subordinated those factors to an appreciation of the centrality of the human factor in war. The most impressive monuments to this Clausewitzian project were the basic doctrinal manuals that came out of the army and marine corps in the 1980s. The army's 100-5 operational doctrinal manual of 1986 represented a fundamental revolt against the mechanistic, predictive, and top-down approach of the 1970s iteration. As the manual warns its readers: "Friction, the accumulation of chance errors, unexpected difficulties, and the confusion of battle – will impede *both* sides. To overcome it, leaders... must be prepared to risk commitment without complete information, recognizing that waiting for such information will invariably forfeit the opportunity to act [emphasis added]."[7]

General Al Gray, commandant of the marine corps, then drew heavily from the army's approach in casting a new basic doctrinal statement, FM-1, for the marines. In a similar vein the various training centers led by the army's National Training Center, but also including the marines' Twenty-Nine Palms, the air force's Red Flag, and the navy's Top Gun programs, represented a substantial and successful effort to grapple with a world in which friction, fog, and chance are dominant factors. The Gulf War of 1991 represented the culmination of the Clausewitzian era.

---

[6] Alan Beyerchen, "Clausewitz, Non-linearity, and the Unpredictability of War," *International Security*, Winter 1992/1993.
[7] Field Manual 100-5, "U.S. Army Blueprint for Air/Land Battle," 1986, p. 16.

In every respect, American forces had trained and prepared themselves over the previous decade and a half within a Clausewitzian approach; the army's second-year course at Leavenworth, the School of Advanced Military Science (SAMS), created in 1983 with the enthusiastic support of the army leadership, rested entirely on a Clausewitzian conception of the study of war. The success in the Gulf represented the fundamental payoff for an officer corps that had learned at great cost that the world offers little of the predictive, mechanistic philosophy that so enamored their superiors, political and military, in Vietnam.

In the aftermath of the American success in the Gulf in 1991, one heard many echoes of President George Bush's famous comment that: "The specter of Vietnam has been buried forever in the desert sands of the Arabian peninsula." Certainly, in terms of time, Americans are indeed putting Vietnam behind them. They are now 32 years [written in 1997] past the escalation of 1965; those standing at the outset of the Second World War were only 25 years away from the beginning of the Great War, while the U.S. Marines coming ashore at Danang in 1965 were only 20 years distant from the end of the Second World War. By the turn of the century, time will have washed virtually all of the Vietnam experience out of the officer corps of the various services, only very senior generals will have had that experience.

With the passing of the Vietnam War generation, another major shift in the cultural and intellectual framework of the American military appears to be occurring. The Clausewitzian universe is under attack by a new generation with no experience in Vietnam. A leader in this attack has been Admiral William Owens, recently the vice chairman of the Joint Chiefs of Staff. Owens has made extraordinary claims:

> Technology could enable U.S. military forces in the future to lift the 'fog of war'... Battlefield dominant awareness – the ability to see and understand everything on the battlefield – might be possible.
>
> When you look at areas such as information warfare, intelligence, surveillance, reconnaissance and command and control, you see a system of systems coming together that will allow us to dominate battlefield awareness for years to come... And while some people say there will always be a 'fog of war,' I know quite a lot about these programs.
>
> The emerging system of systems promises the capacity to use military force without the same risks as before – it suggests we will dissipate the 'fog of war.'[8]

---

[8] William Owens quoted in, respectively, Thomas Duffy, "Breakthrough Could Give Forces Total Command of Future Battlefield," *Inside the Navy*, January 23, 1995; Peter Grier, "Preparing for 21st-Century Information War," *Government Executive* (August 1995); and his own "System of Systems," *Armed Forces Journal* (January 1996).

Owens is not alone; his views represent a major trend in the culture of the American military. This new *Weltanschauung* represents in essence a return to the McNamara paradigm, a belief that American technological superiority will allow U.S. forces to achieve quick, easy victories over their opponents with relatively few casualties. The air force is leading the charge toward the technological utopia "battlespace dominance." Its *New World Vistas* suggests: "The power of the new information systems will lie in their ability to correlate data automatically and rapidly from many sources to form a complete picture of the operational area, whether it will be a battlefield or the site of a mobility operation."[9] In 1995 a senior army general announced to a group of marine officers that "the digitization of the battlefield means the end of Clausewitz." And just recently the army's chief of staff has commented that if the U.S. Army had possessed the information technologies available today, the United States might well have prevailed in Vietnam.[10]

These trends have again found a receptive echo in the academic world, not surprisingly among political scientists. In March 1996 the recently retired Admiral Owens collaborated with the current dean of the Kennedy School of Government at Harvard, Joseph S. Nye, Jr., on an article that transferred Owens' arguments about battlespace dominance to the world of international affairs and international relations:

> This information advantage can help deter or defeat traditional military threats at relatively low cost... [It] can strengthen the intellectual link between U.S. foreign policy and military power and offer new ways of maintaining leadership in alliances and ad hoc coalitions... America's emerging military capabilities... offer, for example, far greater pre-crisis transparency. If the United States is willing to share this transparency, it will be better able to build opposing coalitions before aggression has occurred. But the effect may be more general, for all nations now operate in an ambiguous world, a context that is not entirely benign or soothing.[11]

The danger in the belief that technology will offer the U.S. military total battlespace and foreign policy dominance in the next century does not lie in the technology itself. Technology indeed offers substantial leverage against future opponents. What is dangerous about the new technocratic view is the same thing that was dangerous about the older version: it

---

[9] *New World Vistas: Air and Space Power of the 21st Century* (Washington, DC, 1995). The thinking in this report is so linear that the mathematical theory to describe combat devised by F.W. Lanchester to describe attrition in war is cited as having "survived remarkably well." It has not.

[10] Quoted in *Inside the Pentagon*, October 17, 1996, p. 11.

[11] Joseph S. Nye Jr. and William A. Owens, "America's Information Edge," *Foreign Affairs*, March/April 1996, pp. 20–36.

is wholly disconnected from what others think, want, and can do. Precisely because Americans have a long track record of overestimating their technological superiority as well as their understanding of the ability of their opponents to short-circuit U.S. advantages, this represents a form of hubris in which the nation cannot afford to indulge again. This is also why many of the overtones one hears today about the coming "revolution in military affairs" are so disheartening.

Much of the literature on the "system of systems" as a revolutionary military event emphasizes the removal of friction and ambiguity from the battlespace. At its heart is the presumption that the future revolution in military affairs will be largely technological. History suggests, however, a different perspective. The three most important elements in all past revolutions in military affairs were not technological in nature, but rather conceptual, doctrinal, and intellectual.[12] Those military institutions in the 1920s and 1930s (the RAF, the U.S. Army Air Corps, and the innovators of the British army), which attempted to leap into the future without reference to the past, ended up making mistakes that killed thousands of young men. The succession of new gadgets notwithstanding, successful innovation in the past only worked when it rested on a realistic appreciation of what was *humanly* possible.

Inherent, too, in the anti-Clausewitzian approach is the belief that what military organizations need is more quantifiable data, more "information." A vast array of sensors and computers all tied together will supposedly reduce friction from the military equation to manageable and controllable levels. But the processing of ever more information may easily clog up military organizations with a flood of indigestible data. Worse, current claims about information dominance miss the essential difference between information and knowledge. America's leaders did not need more information at Pearl Harbor, and it is doubtful that future leaders will need more information in the future. What they will need in the next century is a deeper understanding of the political context of war and the historical and cultural attributes of their opponents as well as the very different set of assumptions their opponents will possess. They will require knowledge of foreign languages, cultures, religious beliefs, and above all history, precisely what technocrats ignore because such knowledge cannot be quantified or measured. What matters most in war is what is the mind of one's adversary, from command post to battlefield point-of-contact. This is a truth well illustrated by a scene from the Gulf

---

[12] See A. J. Bacevich, "Morality and High Technology," *The National Interest* (Fall 1996).

War. As two marine generals stood over a relatively undamaged and well-stocked Iraqi bunker complex the coalition forces had captured with minimum casualties and a large haul of prisoners, one quietly commented: "Thank God the North Vietnamese weren't here."[13]

How can it be that the emerging American military culture is throwing history and all its associated intangibles overboard not 30 years after the United States paid such a high price in Vietnam for ignoring them? The tragedy of the post-Vietnam War experience of the American military is that its deeper understanding of war was never institutionalized within its educational system. Despite the instinctive attractions of the Clausewitzian approach for American officers in the post-Vietnam period, there has been no abiding change in the military's cultural attitudes toward education. Teaching duty on the faculties of professional military schools is still not "career enhancing"; the navy still refuses to send a substantial number of its best officers to any school of professional military education; the Army War College, despite an impressive faculty, is an institution where war rarely appears in the curriculum; the army has turned one of its few truly innovative educational experiments of the 1980s, SAMS, into a humdrum planning exercise; the Air War College, after a short period of professional military education, has returned to the golf course; and finally, the National War College remains buried within the army's budget, where it simply fails to get the support it needs.[14] Thus, it is not surprising that we are seeing a significant change in the military culture away from the Clausewitzian form of the past two decades. What Americans should have learned the hard way in Vietnam is being thrown away, with barely a thought for the consequences. Current trends suggest that the new military culture is already preparing our officer corps to repeat the Vietnam War, except that this time, at some point in the twenty-first century, the United States may lose even more disastrously.

---

[13] I am indebted to Lieutenant General Paul Van Riper, USMC ret., for this story.
[14] For one measure of the change over the last decade, see my "Grading the War Colleges," *The National Interest* (Winter 1986/87).

4

Changing the Principles of War?

The mere fact that the Office of Force Transformation in the Department of Defense would have funded a contest as well as several conferences about whether the principles of war have changed now that the world has entered the twenty-first century says much about the "American way of war" – and not necessarily in a positive vein. It is not that I am against the idea of conferences or intellectual argument. Indeed, I am delighted to praise the office for its effort to spark intellectual debate in a town (Washington) of contentless briefs and irrelevant joint concepts.

Let me begin with the question as to whether there is any validity to the remake or even to the concept of what has traditionally been termed the "principles of war." The "principles" have been around as a plaything for military academics and theorists for at least two hundred years. They have littered the landscape of supposed intellectual discourse about the employment of military forces for that entire time. Every military organization has possessed its own slightly different set of principles. Not surprisingly, generals have added their two cents to the discussion. Even that severe critic of military orthodoxy and iconoclast, the British general and pundit in the period between World War I and World War II, J.F.C.

This chapter was presented at a conference sponsored by the Office of Force Transformation at the Johns Hopkins Applied Physics Laboratory on whether technological changes over the past two decades demanded fundamental changes in the principles of war. This work argued that the principles of war are in fact a useless and misleading attempt by the lazy to characterize in formulae what is an inherently chaotic and uncertain human activity.

Fuller, could not resist the opportunity to come up with his own set of principles.[1]

Napoleon Bonaparte, that great misleader of military thought, commented from exile at St. Helena that: "War should be made methodically, for it should have a definite object; and it should be conducted according to the principles and rules of the art."[2] Yet, in looking at Napoleon's spectacular career, one is hard put to see where he ever waged war methodically or followed any set of principles except the one principle Nathan Bedford Forest enunciated – to get there "furstest with the mostest."[3] In fact, Napoleonic war at its best displayed a stunning contempt for rules and a willingness to fly in the face of conventional wisdom. That reality, among many others, was a major factor in the emperor's brilliant victories.[4]

The first years of the American Civil War saw the military forces of the Union stumble as too many senior officers attempted to connect the principles of the French theorist, the Baron de Jomini, to the complex problems of the war that they were now confronting. In 1848, Henry Halleck, that pedant turned soldier, who was to play such a negative role in U.S. Grant's career and almost lose the war for the North, commented in his treatise on war, itself largely a regurgitation, if not outright plagiarism of Jomini, that: "War is not, as some seem to suppose, a mere game of chance. Its principles constitute one of the most intricate of modern sciences; and the general who understands the art of rightly applying its rules, and possesses the means of carrying out its precepts, may be morally certain of success."[5] There is, of course, no evidence that Halleck divined such rules, even if they existed, given his abysmal performance as a field commander in the west in the first half of 1862. About the best one can say about his generalship is that having insured himself

---

[1] How idiosyncratic Fuller was is suggested by the book he published immediately after his retirement, the title of which was: *Generalship: Its Diseases and Their Cure: A Study of the Personal Factor in Command* (London, 1936).

[2] Quoted in Robert Debs Heinl, Jr., *Dictionary of Military and Naval Quotations* (Annapolis, MD, 1966), p. 249.

[3] For Napoleon's career see particularly David Chandler's monumental work *The Campaigns of Napoleon* (London, 1966). For the Forrest quotation see Heinl, *Dictionary of Military and Naval Quotations*, p. 63.

[4] However, he would have done far better had he recognized Clausewitz's yet unwritten dictum that war is a continuation of politics by other means. "We see, therefore, that war is not merely an act of policy but a true political instrument, a continuation of political intercourse, carried on with other means." Carl von Clausewitz, *On War*, trans. and ed. by Michael Howard and Peter Paret (Princeton, NJ, 1976), p. 87.

[5] Quoted in Heinl, *Dictionary of Military and Naval Quotations*, p. 249

against every possibility, he never achieved anything, except to prevent others from launching operations that might have hurt the Confederacy and its military forces.

Other commentators on human conflict have had less truck with the idea that there is any such thing as the "principles of war." Not surprisingly, Grant himself – the author of one of the great works of American literature and one of the few honest memoirs by a general – a supreme realist on the subject of the conduct of war – noted negatively on the influence of such theoretical constructs on the conduct of Union generals in the Civil War's early years: "If men make war in slavish obedience to the rules of war, they will fail."[6]

Carl von Clausewitz, the Prussian combat veteran and theorist of war, was even more caustic about those attempting to boil the nature of war into neat aphorisms and theories. In describing what passed for theory and principles in his own day, he commented:

> Efforts were therefore made to equip the conduct of war with principles, rules, or even systems.... It is only analytically that these attempts at theory [and principles] can be called advances in the realm of truth; synthetically in the rules and regulations they offer, they are absolutely useless. They aim at fixed values, but in war everything is uncertain, and calculations have to be made with variable quantities. They direct the inquiry exclusively toward physical quantities, whereas all military action is intertwined with psychological forces and effects.[7]

As with most bad intellectual things in this world, the concept of the principles of war largely derive from French military traditions – a derivative of the efforts by Jomini to simplify the complex and nightmarish processes involved in war and combat. Jomini himself argued: "There exist a small number of fundamental principles of war, which may not be deviated from without danger, and the application of which, on the contrary, has been in all times crowned with glory."[8] Jomini derived his principles by analysis of Napoleonic warfare, which he had observed firsthand. But he entirely misunderstood the substance of the emperor's approach to war and substituted geometric and geographic nostrums that he believed would inevitably lead to success. In short, the principles of war to Jomini represented an effort to simplify for the soldier (or sailor, or marine, or airman) what is inherently the complex and opaque lessons of past conflicts.

---

[6] U.S. Grant, *The Memoirs of U.S. Grant* (New York, 1885).
[7] Clausewitz, *On War*, p. 136.
[8] Heinl, *Dictionary of Military and Naval Quotations*, p. 249.

Changing the Principles of War?

The Israeli historian of military thought Azar Gat has commented on Jomini in the following terms:

> Jomini claimed that all military history from 'Scipio and Caesar to Napoleon' had been guided by the principles he had extracted from Napoleonic warfare, and referred to all periods of history that clearly contradicted this claim as undeveloped or degenerate... rather than understanding Frederick [the Great's] strategy against the background of the political and military conditions of the time, Jomini maintained that Frederick had not been operating according to Napoleonic principles because military thought had not yet developed enough to recognize these principles.[9]

It was an extraordinary claim, and almost immediately in the American Civil War reality disproved his theories.

Since Jomini first popularized the idea of principles, they have been popular among all too many in the military profession because they represent a simple guide – taught from the earliest days of an officer's career in ROTC and service academy classrooms – that obviates the difficult task of *studying* and *understanding* one's profession in the midst of the demanding day-to-day challenges of the military profession. How satisfactory they are for really being able to understand the dynamics of politics, operational concerns, or the integration of technologies into tactical concepts, and the all-pervasive nature of war – its ambiguities, uncertainties, and its psychological pressures at every level – is another question. The British general Archibald Wavell, who commanded British forces in the western deserts of North Africa in 1940 and 1941, commented in a lecture in 1930: "I would give you a warning on the so-called principles of war, as laid down in the *Field Service Regulations*. For heaven's sake, don't treat those as holy writ, like the Ten Commandments, to be learned by heart, and as having by their repetition some magic, like the incantations of savage priests. They are merely a set of common-sense maxims, like 'cut your coat according to your cloth,' 'honesty is the best policy,' and so forth."[10]

Britain's prime minister and leader in the last two years of the First World War, David Lloyd George, best summed up the kind of officer to whom the principles of war appeal in an entry in the index of his memoirs titled: "military mind."

> **Military mind**, narrowness of, 3051; stubborness of, not peculiar to America, 3055; does not seem to understand arithmetic, 3077; its attitude in July

---

[9] Azar Gat, *A History of Military Thought, from the Enlightenment to the Cold War* (Oxford, 2001), p. 124.
[10] Heinl, *Dictionary of Military and Naval Quotations*, p. 249.

1918, represented by Sir Henry Wilson's fantastic memorandum of 25/7/18, 3109; obsessed with North-West Frontier of India, 3119; impossibility of trusting, 3124; regards thinking as a form of mutiny, 3422.[11]

Bernard Brodie, the great American strategic analyst during much of the Cold War, was almost as cynical about the utility of the principles to the intellectual preparation of the military mind. A student of Clausewitz, he found himself in full agreement with the Prussian thinker's distrust of theories that attempt to organize war into neat categories:

> It may be that the consideration of a catalogue of numbered principles (usually fewer than a dozen) with the barest definition of each may be necessary to communicate to second-order minds... some conception of what the business is all about...
>
> In short, the catalogue of principles must be recognized for what it is, which is a device intended to circumvent the need for months and years of study of and rumination on a very difficult subject, presented mostly in the form of military and political history and the 'lessons' that may be justly derived therefrom.[12]

In fact, the greatest generals have forgotten the principles of war well before they command a company, while the worst never learned them to begin with.

What makes the principles of war relevant to a discussion of the "American way of war" – and here I am sure that Russell Weigley would be in complete agreement were he alive – is the fact they fit so well within the American tradition of approaching war as an engineering problem. That belief has been particularly congenial to Americans because it suggests that one can break conflict down into its constituent parts, which then can be examined and then solved.

Recent events over the past three years in Iraq have underlined this in spades. We have seen the American military divide the Iraq War nice and neatly into distinct phases. Thus, with a clear separation between Phase 3 and Phase 4, planners and operators could first solve the operational, campaign portion of defeating the Iraqi Army and removing Saddam from power, before turning to the "post-conflict" situation. With that clear break in place the American military turned the Coalition Force Land Component Commander (CFLCC) into Combined Joint Task Force-7

---

[11] David Lloyd George, *War Memoirs of David Lloyd George*, vol. 6 (London, 1936), p. 3497.

[12] Bernard Brodie, *War and Politics* (New York, 1973).

(CJTF-7), which became V Corps' responsibility instead of Third Army's, while at the same time replacing the V Corps commander with a general who had no experience at that level of command and allowing General Tommy Franks to head off into the sunset of retirement.

Were the American military Clausewitzian in its culture, there would have been no separation in thinking and planning between Phases 3 and 4 because commanders and planners alike would have recognized that the goal – a democratic, or at least less murderous Iraq – demanded a coherent focus from the onset of operations on achieving the *political* goals for which the United States and its leaders decided to fight the war. Naturally, the pure military problem of defeating the Iraqi military would then have formed only a portion of the far larger political problem.

But then the American military, with a few exceptions, has never been Clausewitzian in outlook. Rather by education and culture, its officers have been students of the Baron de Jomini since the earliest days. West Point was founded as an engineering school as well as a military academy to provide the United States not only with soldiers but also with the engineers it needed to provide technical help in taming a continent. Not surprisingly, an engineering mentality has dominated the curriculum at the United States Military Academy through to the present day. Significantly, until the 1960s, even military history remained the preserve of the topography department, and a real history department was not established at West Point until the late 1960s. Moreover, right through to the present, the Naval Academy has remained the preserve of engineers. But in fairness to the academies, American culture has had an even greater role in molding the American military to the point where the services could regard the "principles of war" as something significant.

Ironically, the U.S. military at present finds itself confronting a world in which by its extraordinary virtuosity – and the extraordinary stupidity of most of its opponents – it has eliminated virtually all of the conventional threats on land, at sea, and in the air.[13] Many would suggest that, in effect, the success of America's military over the course of the twentieth century has made the study of conventional military history an arcane art – especially since the appearance of a peer competitor is simply not in the cards, unless American policy makers make monumental

---

[13] For the less than impressive strategic approach of the Axis Powers during the Second World War that maximized the potential of their opponents see Williamson Murray and Allan R. Millett, *A War to Be Won, Fighting the Second World War* (Cambridge, MA, 2000); and Gerhard L. Weinberg, *A World at Arms, A Global History of World War II* (Cambridge, 1994).

strategic mistakes over the coming decades. Unfortunately, the last decade has underlined that history is not dead, but rather it has made the study of campaigns, such as the guerrilla warfare in Spain against Napoleon's forces, of direct relevance to the battle against the insurgency in Iraq.[14]

The real problem is that the search for a new set of principles to address the vast technological changes yesterday, today, and tomorrow taking place in the world reflects a military culture at odds with everything that history has suggested about the nature of war. And military cultures are extraordinarily difficult to change. Usually only war itself brings reality to those military cultures that have failed to study the past.

The confusion and uncertainty marking much of the 1990s reflected a recognition on the part of the American military that no one remained on the playing fields of war, at least in terms of conventional war.[15] That same situation obtains today. The real strategic issue that confronts the United States at present is the problem of how to hold together what some call globalization, what others call the "American Empire," and others – the First World.[16] The fact that China and India are rapidly joining the older industrialized world suggests opportunities for a more peaceful world than was the case with the twentieth century.

The great danger to the First World – a world that the United States has played *the* key role in constructing since 1945 – lies in the gap between the cultures of its various diverse parts and the cultures and values of the rest of the world, most particularly that of the Islamic world. History has condemned the Islamic world to adapting to a world that it has taken the West 600 years and innumerable world wars to create.[17] Thus, in innumerable ways the United States will find itself the spectator of and

---

[14] For a stunning example of the value of history to understanding what is currently occurring in Iraq, the reader is urged to consult John Lawrence Tone, *The Fatal Knot, The Guerrilla War in Navarre and the Defeat of Napoleon in Spain* (Chapel Hill, 1995).

[15] Of course, time has almost entirely washed out the experiences of the Vietnam War except for a few senior officers, while the study of the war's lessons did not occur, nor were those lessons inculcated into the system of professional military education. Instead the services focused on deterring the Soviets from using their immense conventional strength on the plains of Europe.

[16] For a superficial examination of the current strategic environment see Thomas Barnett. Unfortunately, Barnett is almost entirely ignorant of history and foreign cultures. Thus, his arguments entirely miss the depth of rejection of Western values throughout the Islamic world, particularly in the Middle East.

[17] In addition to World War I and World War II, the historian must add The War of Spanish Succession, The War of Austrian Succession, The Seven Years' War, the Wars of the French Revolution, and the Napoleonic Wars to his or her list of world wars.

participant in the troubles that will accompany the Islamic world in its adjustment to a world of globalization that challenges so many of its cultural norms. Consequently, more often than not the military forces of the United States will find themselves pulled into the messy business of nation building and stability operations that have involved them over the past two years in Iraq [written in 2005]. How well they do in such environments will play a major role in the stability of the region and the world. And where exactly the principles of war will fit into this confusing world of intermittent guerrilla war, terrorism, peacekeeping, and peace enforcement is difficult to say.

Thus, in answering what kind of military forces the United States will need for much of the twenty-first century, one might begin by suggesting that not only air and sea control, but logistical capabilities will be the *sine qua non* for projecting much of America's military power from North America to the trouble spots of the world. The logistical capabilities will be crucial because America's military forces have increasingly been coming home from the foreign deployments that marked the Cold War. In thinking about air and sea control, it is doubtful that future opponents of the United States will dare to challenge America directly, given the kinds of capabilities that America already enjoys. Instead, if challenged at all in those environments, it will be by opponents who will attempt to deny the use of those capabilities common to forces deploying from the United States.

In the end, as has been the case throughout history, what will matter are the boots that the United States is able to put on the ground. The bloodless wars by long distance air power and technology that so many defense experts in Washington predicted during the Clinton administration will rarely, if ever, happen. What will matter will be the ability of the United States to execute its political and strategic designs and aims within and among cultures and historical frameworks that are by and large foreign to the education and thinking of Americans and their representatives in uniform. This is a Clausewitzian universe, most definitely not one where the principles of war make the slightest difference, especially against uncertain and ambiguous enemies who play by their own rules. As Retired Major General Robert H. Scales has suggested, the wars the United States will fight in the twenty-first century will be wars where an understanding of the cultural environment will form the essential basis to achieving political success.

Americans have fought such wars in the past. In some, such as in the Philippine insurrection in the early twentieth century, U.S. military forces have done very well.[18] But the Vietnam War was a disaster, largely because of an almost willing ignorance of the local culture and political conditions that senior American military leaders displayed from 1965 through 1968.[19] The current troubles in Iraq suggest many of the same difficulties that beset U.S. forces in Vietnam. Almost from the moment of the toppling of Saddam's statues in Baghdad, Coalition forces have had to play catch up in a political and cultural world of which few at any rank had any deep understanding.[20]

The issue then is how to prevent the repetition of such mistakes in the future. Here technology provides few answers. Technological capabilities have played an important, but not decisive role in the wars of the past century. Those capabilities have certainly not changed the fundamental nature of war. Admittedly, no one in the last century armed with stone-age weapons has managed to win against technologically sophisticated opponents. But technological superiority by itself has never guaranteed success. The Germans had technologically inferior tanks and artillery in 1940; nevertheless, they won one of the greatest operational victories in the history of the twentieth century.[21] In the 1944–1945 campaigns, the Germans possessed by far and away the most sophisticated fighter aircraft, the most sophisticated heavy tank, the most sophisticated medium tank, the most sophisticated submarine, and the best machine gun. *And they went down to catastrophic defeat.*[22]

[18] In a conversation with this author in late March 2005, Colonel Greg Fontenot, U.S. Army retired), suggested that American success in the Philippines resulted from two factors: the soldiers, mostly farm boys from a nation that was still largely agricultural in its makeup, could understand and communicate relatively easily with the locals. Second, the officer corps had been involved in stability operation on the Western frontier and hence, supported by the progressive ethos of the time, were far better able to deal with the problems that confronted them during the course of the insurgency.

[19] Perhaps the most obvious was the inability to grasp the truly revolutionary symbiosis between French and Vietnamese cultures and radical nationalism. To this day, Giap prefers to speak French when he discusses political matters.

[20] There were ironically first-rate books about the nature of Saddam's tyranny that certainly would have suggested the difficulties that were going to occur in the postconflict phase once Saddam's tyranny and disfunctional regime was overthrown. Unfortunately, there is not much evidence that they exercised much influence over thinking in the U.S. government. The best of these was the 1989 book by Kayan Makiya published at the time under a pseudonym. See Samir al-Khalil, *The Republic of Fear, The Politics of Modern Iraq* (Berkeley, 1989).

[21] The best recent examination of the campaign is Karl-Heinz Frieser, *Blitzkrieglegende, Der Westfeldzug, 1940* (Munich, 1995). In English the best overview of the campaign remains Telford Taylor, *The March of Conquest, The German Victories in Western Europe, 1940* (New York, 1958).

[22] For the catastrophic nature of that defeat see Max Hastings, *Armageddon, The Battle for Germany, 1944–1945* (New York, 2004).

What will matter to the military forces of the United States in the twenty-first century is how well American military leaders at all levels *understand* their opponents: their history, their culture, their political framework, their religion, and even their languages. Thus, to an extent that has never been true in the past, the American military is going to have to place education at the center of how it prepares its officers to confront the uncertain and ambiguous world of the twenty-first century. History is crucial to the intellectual preparation of officers because immersion in its lessons is the only way not only to build an understanding of the larger issues involved in conflict, but because it represents the only way to understand foreign cultures without living in them. Similarly the study of language provides a crucial path to understanding how different and complex the thinking framework of other nations is – at least from the vantage point of Americans. Learning "principles of war" is the last thing that they need.

Yet, the study of military history, or history in general, has only been the preserve of a few exceptional officers in the American military. Unfortunately, the general ahistoricism of American culture is deeply imbedded within the services, with the possible exception of the marine corps. But there is a larger problem here because pervasive ahistoricism is only a symptom of a contempt for serious professional military education that marks the services and the joint world – a contempt reinforced by the current civilian leadership in the Department of Defense. If, as a number of prestigious government panels have suggested, America needs more flexible and intellectually adaptable officers in its military services, then someone at the senior level is going to have to address the personnel systems that play such a crucial role in careers. The reality is that one can only create intellectually adaptable officers through serious education.

Providing officers a rest in their busy careers, providing them a single hour to mull over Clausewitz at the war college, and asking them to read materials chosen at the lowest common denominator will not provide any significant cultural change. Nor will it prepare them to deal with the challenges of the twenty-first century. The current approach to professional military education – with few exceptions – is not serious education at all.

Already, the myth makers are at work in blaming the troubles over the past two years on the Pentagon's senior civilian leadership. In reality, the senior military leadership deserves a substantial share of the blame. Too many officers at senior levels in 2002 and 2003 lacked the educational background to challenge the facile assumptions that issued from the Pentagon's E ring. And given the similar experiences in stability operations of U.S. military operations in Vietnam, Panama, Haiti,

Bosnia, the United States deserved better advice from its senior military leaders.

Conclusion

I am afraid that the contest to come up with a new set of the principles of war sets all too comfortably in the current intellectual milieu of service cultures as well as that of the emerging joint culture. At the highest levels, profoundly ahistorical concepts and doctrine march in mad array across a barren landscape – developed by officers and contractors supposedly versed in the nature of war. The words Clausewitz used to describe the theories and doctrines of his own time are equally applicable to current efforts to define war into nice, neat categories that have little to do with the ugly street brawl that recently took place in Fallujah [written in 2005]:

> A... serious menace is the retinue of *jargon, technicalities, and metaphors* that attends these systems. They swarm everywhere – a lawless rabble of camp followers. Any critic who has not seen fit to adopt a system – either because he has not found one that he likes or because he has not yet got that far – will still apply a scrap of one as if it were a ruler....[23]

[23] Clausewitz, *On War*, pp. 168–169.

5

Military Culture Does Matter

Professional military cultures differ greatly from service to service and from nation to nation. Yet, they represent an essential component of military effectiveness. How armies, air forces, marine corps, and navies think about war guides their peacetime innovations and determines the patterns of successful or unsuccessful adaptation of war.[1] The military profession is not only the most demanding physically of the professions, it is also the most demanding mentally.[2] But there is another side that military historians and pundits often exclude from their examinations of military culture. That is the portion of the landscape that deals with the physical, physiological, and psychological preparation of military organizations for *war*. As the Prussian military theorist, Carl von Clausewitz, suggests: "The end for which a soldier is recruited, clothed, armed, and trained, the whole object of his sleeping, eating, drinking, and marching *is simply that he should fight at the right place and the right time.*"[3]

War places extraordinary demands on the individual. In effect, military organizations require the soldier to remain on the battlefield in an arena of danger where *his enemy aims to kill him*. They demand that he maintain

---

[1] I have examined some of the attributes of professional military culture in "Does Military Culture Matter?" *Orbis*, Winter 1999. One of the major lacunae in the works of military historians has been the subject of military culture. Brian Bond's *British Military Policy between the Two World Wars* (Oxford, 1980) remains one of the main exceptions. The reader should note that this essay appeared in *Strategic Review* in Spring 1999.

[2] There have been those who argue that there is no such thing as a military ethic or ethos. As philosophers, they have not had to produce any evidence. But all the evidence of the history of the past four hundred years suggests otherwise.

[3] Carl von Clausewitz, *On War*, trans. and ed. by Michael Howard and Peter Paret (Princeton, NJ, 1975), p. 95.

himself in an environment in which every human instinct suggests that he should leave immediately. Clausewitz brilliantly depicted that terrifying challenge in *On War*:

> As we approach, the rumble of guns grow louder and alternates with the whir of cannonballs... shots begin to strike close around us. We hurry up the slope.... Here the cannonballs and bursting shells are frequent.... Suddenly someone you know is wounded; then a shell falls among the staff. You notice that some of the officers act a little oddly.... Now we enter the battle raging before us, still more like a spectacle, and join the nearest division commander. Shot is falling like hail, and the thunder of our own guns adds to the din. A noise is heard that is a certain indication of increasing danger – the rattling of grapeshot on roofs and on the ground. Cannonballs tear past, whizzing in all directions, and musketballs begin to whistle around us. A little further we reach the firing line, where the infantry endures the hammering for hours.... The air is filled with hissing bullets that sound like a sharp crack if they pass close to one's head. For a final shock, the sight of men being killed and mutilated moves our pounding hearts to awe and pity.[4]

Across the ages war has represented the darkest and most terrifying of human experiences.[5] What was true for the Greeks in the fifth century BC was true for the Romans in the second century BC, was true for the Prussians of Clausewitz's time, and will be true for soldiers and marines in the next century.

The Historical Parameters of Military Culture

History suggests a great deal about the kinds of cultures military organizations in the Western World have developed over the past 400 years to keep the soldier on the battlefield. It is military culture, rather than technology, that explains the extraordinary record that Western military institutions have achieved over this period. In fact, the "rise of the West" was almost entirely due to the culture of discipline that European armies developed in the first half of the seventeenth century.[6] Unfortunately, in

---

[4] Ibid., p. 113.
[5] Beginning with John Keegan's *Face of Battle* (New York, 1975), military historians have paid greater attention to the psychological dimensions of war. In this regard, see also Victor David Hanson, *The Western Way of War, Infantry Battle in Ancient Greece* (Berkeley, CA, 1989). Hanson's book is about the culture of military organizations in the largest sense.
[6] The term "the rise of the West" largely derives from William McNeil's brilliant cross-cultural comparison: *The Rise of the West, A History of the Human Community* (Chicago, 1964). McNeil then moved on to fill in the military dimension of that problem: *The Pursuit of Power, Technology, Armed Force, and Society since AD 1000* (Chicago, 1984).

their contempt for history, Americans are on the brink of losing their understanding of how and particularly *how and why* Western military institutions developed disciplined cultures that were so different from what had been the general pattern throughout history, and on which the cultures of military organizations in the Western model have rested for the past four centuries.[7]

The "Western Way of War" reaches back to the Greeks and Romans.[8] The former developed the first true army as opposed to armed mobs. The Greek hoplite formations represented the *social* discipline of the *polis* and, to a great extent (Sparta, possibly the one exception), it was social cohesion that kept the Greek citizen soldier on the battlefield.[9] However, the phalanx represented a system that was culturally dependent, one that could not be transferred to other cultures. In the fourth century, BC the *polis* lost its social and political cohesion and hence its ability to call upon its citizens for the defense of the city; thus, it came to depend on mercenaries who possessed neither the loyalty nor commitment to defend the city.

The Romans began their rise to domination of the Mediterranean world with a system that closely resembled that of the Greek city states. But somewhere at the beginning of the wars with Carthage, they developed a military culture in which the Roman military organization rather than societal pressures imposed discipline on the legions. By the end of the second century BC, the Romans possessed a ruthlessly disciplined force that year in and year out replicated itself, that placed disciplined and articulated military forces on the battlefield, and that demanded that the Republic's legionaries remain completely obedient to the orders of their officers, the centurions. The ancient battlefield was as terrifying as the modern battlefield. And the Romans mastered human fear by a regime of discipline captured best by the historian of the Roman-Jewish War, Flavius Josephus: "The Romans are sure of victory... for their exercises are battles without bloodshed, and their battles bloody exercises."[10]

---

[7] This is, of course, because the Western model has been copied with great success by the Japanese, the Israelis, and the Indians among others.

[8] For the best book on the nature of Greek warfare in the classical age, see Hanson, *The Western Way of War*.

[9] This was less true of the Spartan hoplite, who spent virtually his entire life training and preparing for war – a major factor in Sparta's centuries-long domination of the battlefields in the Peloponnesus.

[10] Robert Debs Heinl, Jr., ed., *Dictionary of Military Quotations* (Annapolis, MD, 1966) p. 328. Another more literal translation puts Josephus' arguments in the following form: "their military exercises by no means fall short of the tension of real warfare, but every soldier is every day exercised, and that with real diligence, as if it were in time

In fact, the badge of rank for the centurions, beside their wounds, was a club, with which they beat their men. The Roman system carried over into the empire and for nearly a quarter of a millennium, with the exception of two short periods of civil war, the legions guaranteed the internal as well as external peace of the Mediterranean world.[11] Somehow in the catastrophe of the third and fourth centuries AD, that system collapsed. A military commentator on that collapse might well have written:

> The loss of discipline became most pronounced under the Emperor Constantine who felt that he could defend the empire most successfully by relying on German cavalry and mercenaries instead of the legions. Thus, the honoraria [bonuses] the legionaries and centurions received disappeared. Centurions no longer received the respect that their rank had once entailed; many left for service in other branches of the Imperial domain, while those that remained no longer could discipline the soldiers. The legions themselves were broken up because they were politically unreliable, while discipline and good military order were no longer the mark of what were still called legions, but were in effect nothing more than armed mobs increasingly incapable of fighting the barbarians or of maintaining civil discipline.[12]

Over the next 13 centuries, the survivors of the collapse of the Roman Empire exhibited great interest in the empire, whose roads and monuments underlined how far the current crop of Europeans had regressed from the technological and military accomplishments of their predecessors.[13] But every attempt at recreating the Roman way of war foundered on the inability of European armies to reintroduce discipline into their organizations. At times, the social cohesion of peculiar subgroups within Europe – most notably the Welsh and Yorkshire archers of England and the Swiss pikemen – could bring some societal discipline to the battlefield. But neither the Swiss nor English armies possessed any greater civil discipline than their opponents. Thus, the English armies of the Hundred Years' War burned and raped their way across the French

---

of war, which is the reason they bear the fatigue of battle so easily... nor would he be mistaken [who] would call those their exercises unbloody battles, and their battles bloody exercises." Flavius Josephus, *The Great Roman-Jewish War*, trans. by William Whiston (New York, 1960), p. 121.

[11] For the Roman Army in the first two centuries of the empire, see Graham Webster, *The Roman Imperial Army of the First and Second Centuries A.D.* (New York, 1979).

[12] Our sources on particularly the third century, but also the fourth, are so sparse and unclear that the historian can only surmise what happened.

[13] For the deep interest in Roman military practices in Shakespeare's time, see *Henry V*, act 3, scene 2.

countryside, thereby ensuring that their armies had no chance of winning the conflict.

That was the great problem not only of war but of European states until the early seventeenth century: military organizations were so ill-disciplined that they were hardly effective instruments of military *and political* power, and they were capable of the most frightful acts of indiscipline, such as the mutiny at Antwerp of the Spanish Army in 1574, an act that undermined entirely the Spanish government's political policies in the Low Countries.[14] One of the first acts of early modern governments, after they had decided to embark on war and recruited military forces, was to ensure that their armies immediately moved onto someone else's territory. There were, of course, no permanent standing armies, because governments lacked the means to pay military forces. Machiavelli put his finger at the heart of the problem. "Good laws are necessary for good arms; and good arms are necessary for good laws." In other words, there must be, according to Machiavelli, a symbiotic relationship between the ability of the state to enforce its laws and the quality of its military institutions and between its military institutions and the framework of law and discipline that govern armed forces.

That was the conundrum that European military institutions were in when Maurice of Orange and Gustavus Adolphus began the process of recreating the Roman model in the early seventeenth century – in other words, of creating an army rather than an armed mob.[15] The tactical formation of choice at the time was *tercio;* it depended on the cohesion of a large ill-disciplined group on the battlefield. The lack of discipline in a civil sense resulted in political catastrophes, such as Antwerp, as well as military ineffectiveness. Militarily the *tercios* minimized the potential of firepower weapons. The only way military reformers could utilize the potential of gunpowder weapons was to spread out formations, but in so doing those formations immediately lost the group cohesion on which they depended.

Hence, the difficulty that military reformers confronted: how to introduce external discipline – discipline imposed from above on "soldiers," who possessed little sense of discipline or obedience. One of the key statements in Gustavus' *Articles of War* was the statement that soldiers must dig when they were told to dig – obviously something that had not

---

[14] Geoffrey Parker, *The Dutch Revolt* (Ithaca, NY, 1977), p. 164.
[15] See in particular Hans Delbrück, *The History of the Art of War*, vol. 4, *The Dawn of Modern Warfare*, trans. by Walter J. Renfroe, Jr. (Lincoln, NB, 1985), pp. 155–159.

happened in 1,300 years.[16] Beginning with Maurice of Orange and Gustavus Adolphus, the Europeans managed the difficult process of reinventing the Roman legion in modern guise – not only with the march commands of the legion, but the ruthless, ferocious discipline that had characterized those legions. The French General Jean Martinet, who played a major role in the transition process, gave his name to an attitude and approach to military organization that has not entirely disappeared in the late twentieth century.[17] Indeed, the centurions of the first century AD would have felt quite comfortable in the company of Frederick the Great's NCOs who used their swords against those who wavered in their position in the formation.

Moreover, as William McNeill has persuasively argued, the process of inculcating discipline by what the British accurately term "square bashing" addressed fundamental psychological needs of men in groups.[18] Ironically, Liddell Hart, who was a great military pundit, but not a first-rate military historian, argued that "square bashing" was antiquated and irrelevant to the process of creating "modern" soldiers. Of course, his favorite army of the twentieth century, the *Wehrmacht*, suggested that there was a clear connection between the discipline of the parade ground and that of the battlefield.

There were two crucial elements to the creation of armies in the seventeenth century. In the largest sense, they provided the kick start, which contributed in a significant fashion to the creation of the modern Western state. Virtually everything in that process was military dependent. The civil discipline of military organizations allowed state authorities to create increasingly effective governmental bureaucracies. Those state bureaucracies, backed up by disciplined military forces, allowed for the more efficient collection of taxes, which in turn supported the increased professionalization of armies and navies. Behind the increasing power of the state lay the power of its military institutions to impose

---

[16] On Gustavus Adolphus' contribution to the creation of modern military organization, see Michael Roberts, "The Military Revolution, 1560–1660," in *Essays in Swedish History* (London: 1960).

[17] Martinet was much more important than merely a drill master. As Louis XIV's first inspector general of infantry, he was instructed by the War Minister: "You ought to make all the officers that command units understand that the intention is that they reestablish obedience without reply in regard to officers who are their subalterns...." John A. Lynn, *Giants of the Grand Siècle, The French Army, 1610–1715* (Cambridge, 1997), p. 281.

[18] McNeill, *The Pursuit of Power*, p. 131. See also William H. McNeill, *Keeping Time Together, Dance and Drill in Human History* (Cambridge, MA, 1998), chap. 5.

the laws of the state. And, whether Americans like it or not, the power and success of the modern state depends on its ability to compel its young men (and perhaps in the future, its young women) to serve in military organizations and perhaps give up their lives in defense of the nation.

But equally important was the fact that beginning with Gustavus Adolphus, the new model, disciplined European armies were able to thin out the line of battle in order to bring increasing amounts of firepower to bear on their opponents – as their opponents were able to do to them.[19] This process, which was extraordinarily painful even in military terms, involved the imposition of absolute obedience to superior officers, the harsh discipline of the barracks square, and even the clothing of soldiers in the same pattern of uniform – something that had not happened since the Romans. Thus began the tactical evolution that has continued to the present day – the thinning out of the battle line. The success of that process depended absolutely on the ability of armies to maintain discipline in the ranks – to keep the soldier in line, even if it were to be a single firing line. Thus, discipline was the glue that made the individuals composing an army stay on the field of battle, no matter how terrible the conditions of fear, death, and mutilation might be. Without that discipline, armies were not armies, but armed mobs, incapable of maintaining cohesion, tactical formations, or obedience. The victory of the West over what Paul Kennedy has called the "rest" resulted from the organizational cultures of Western armies and navies as much as from superior Western technology.

In the early twentieth century, the inventiveness of Western science and technology changed the battlefield beyond all recognition. In the First World War, the battle line entirely disappeared in the catastrophic battles from Tannenburg on. But the imperatives on which Western military organizations had built their success remained. In fact, in some ways those imperatives became even more important. What had to replace the massed assaults typified by the first day on the Somme were smaller and smaller unit attacks that depended on fire and maneuver to succeed on a battlefield. By 1917, in the German system of defense in depth the front was no longer a line of trenches, but rather sprinkled with a thin covering of machine gunners. The battlefield had become a lonely place indeed. The glue that now had to keep the soldiers on the front was a disciplined culture of military obedience and obligation.

---

[19] See in particular Michael Roberts, "The Military Revolution, 1560–1660."

German *Auftragstaktik* (mission-oriented orders), which developed out of the changes on the First World War battlefields, depended on the discipline of storm troopers to remain steadfast in the terrifying conditions that combat in the modern world inevitably creates.[20] During World War II, there was a direct connection between the *Wehrmacht's* battlefield performance and its discipline, which historians have now discovered to have been a ruthless combination of ideological and military discipline.[21] One of the brightest German general staff officers of the period, General Erich Marcks, eventually chief planner for Barbarossa, suggested in his diary immediately after victory over the French in 1940 that the *Wehrmacht's* success had largely resulted from the ideological motivation and discipline of the attacking troops – not from the result of the sophisticated application of new armored tactics or operational concepts. "The change in men weighs more heavily than in technology. The French we met in battle were no longer those of 14–18. The relationship was like that between the revolutionary armies of 1796 and those of the [first] coalition – only this time we were the revolutionaries and Sans-Culottes."[22]

Military Culture in the Next Century

What do such historical ruminations have to do with thinking about military culture and the performance of the American military in the twenty-first century? A great deal. Let us first examine the potential pressures of combat that U.S. military organizations will confront in the next century and then turn to various processes occurring in civil-military relations – processes that are quite worrying in their potential impact on the creation of U.S. military culture in the next century. The operative word is war. There is a crucial debate occurring at present within the American military over the nature of war in the next century. Ironically this debate, which is fundamental to understanding the requirements of American military culture, is occurring on the fringes of what passes for

---

[20] For the development of German tactics, see: Bruce I. Gudmundsson, *Stormtroop Tactics, Innovation in the German Army, 1914–1918* (New York, 1989).

[21] During the Second World War the Wehrmacht executed somewhere between 13,000 and 15,000 soldiers as a result of regular court martials for breaches of discipline (this total does not include those who died as a result of assignment by court martials to disciplinary battalions). See Omar Bartov, *Hitler's Army, Soldiers, Nazis, and War in the Third Reich* (Oxford, 1991), p. 96.

[22] Quoted in MacGregor Knox, *Common Destiny: Dictatorship, Foreign Policy, and War in Fascist Italy and Nazi Germany* (Cambridge, 2000), p. 186.

intelligent discourse in Washington.[23] Yet, this debate lies at the heart of the professional and cultural ethos of the American military, and the results of the debate will exercise considerable influence over the performance and effectiveness of American military forces. The outcome of the debate will also exercise considerable influence over the culture of discipline and military ethos of those who will have to fight.

On one side, the cultures of the United States Air Force and the United States Navy as well as a number of prominent military leaders have entirely resurrected Robert McNamara's technological, mechanistic vision of war.[24] Their argument, simply put, is that history is irrelevant; that the technologies of the next century will allow us to see and *understand* everything in whatever battle space U.S. forces fight; and that the U.S. military will have near perfect knowledge and comprehension in the wars the United States will fight. As a senior Army general told the Marine Corps War College in 1996, "the digitization of the army represents the end of Clausewitz."

This view of war argues that the American military will stand off and, by using precision strike coupled with instantaneous satellite pictures, destroy the enemy almost as if one were playing a video game. This vision also sees small numbers of ground forces able to operate against and defeat numerically superior enemies by the successful use of technology – particularly air support.[25] And, of course, the enemy will have no chance to adapt or counteract American moves. In such a world, the disciplined responsiveness of individuals is less of a problem because they will rarely have to confront the factors that have so bedeviled military organizations in the past, above all fear and uncertainty. In Cold War terms, one might characterize the new military theories as "zap a commie for mommy." If one accepts this view, as much of the air force and navy already do, then the rest of this discussion is irrelevant.

On the other hand, there are others, including this author, who argue that whatever technological changes occur in the next century, the fundamental nature of war will not alter. As Clausewitz suggested about

---

[23] This essay was written in the late 1990s. However, there is nothing in Donald Rumsfeld's Department of Defense, especially on the civilian side, that suggests that this comment needed to be changed.

[24] See Williamson Murray, "Clausewitz Out, Computer In," *The National Interest*, Summer 1997, pp. 57–64; chapter 3 this collection.

[25] This was Donald Rumsfeld's vision for the Iraq War in 2003. Left out of his equation was the necessity of military operations to influence the political context within which the post-conflict phase would take place.

military theorists in Book I of *On War:* "Kind-hearted people might of course think there was some ingenious way to disarm or defeat an enemy without too much bloodshed, and might imagine this is the true goal of the art of war. Pleasant as it sounds, it is a fallacy."[26] In the future, the United States will confront adaptive enemies who have thought long and hard about American weaknesses.[27] Above all, human strengths and weakness will still dominate the conduct and outcomes of war. Future battlefields will remain places of fear, ambiguity, uncertainty – in other words, places where the courage and discipline of individual soldiers, marines, airmen, or sailors will be essential not only to survival but to combat effectiveness.[28]

In the twenty-first century a number of trends in the "Western Way of War" will continue. Units will spread over greater and greater distances. The "thin red line" will become even thinner. Any opponent who is a real threat to American interests will possess precision weapons, perhaps even precision stealth cruise missiles. Consequently, major air bases and ports will come under attack from the onset of hostilities. There will be no clear delineation of front and rear. Of course, this latter aspect of war should not represent a new concept even to air force officers who served in South Vietnam between 1965 and 1972. Unfortunately, that is part of the current cultural problem with the services – time has almost completely washed the experiences of the Vietnam War out of the officer corps.[29] Units will have to operate in small, highly maneuverable packages, both to call in fires and to maximize the psychological pressure on the enemy. Such units will have to fight with great distances between themselves and other friendly units, whether they are in cities or deserts.

Thus, the heart of the cultural framework within which the American military must work will be one that demands steadfast, cohesive organizational discipline. Does it mean that the American military has to reinvent the *Wehrmacht's* unrelenting vision of discipline? Of course not! But it does demand that the services pay attention to factors that will influence their cultures in the coming century. These include a recognition that

---

[26] Clausewitz, *On War*, p. 75.
[27] See in particular Major General Robert Scales, U.S. Army, "Adaptive Enemies," *Strategic Review*, Spring 1999. And that is precisely what has happened in Iraq.
[28] Lt. Gen. Paul Van Riper and Maj. Gen. Robert Scales, "Preparing for War in the 21st Century," *Strategic Review*, Summer 1997.
[29] What is clearly going to mitigate this comment is the fact that the experience of fighting the insurgencies in Iraq and Afghanistan is going to educate a whole new generation of officers, particularly in the army and the marine corps, as to the realities of combat.

war will place extraordinary demands on the psychological and physical stability of combatants.

If America's opponents do everything in their power to strike the U.S. base structures in and out of theater, how will the noncombat elements of the American military do if they come under sustained attack? Military history suggests that catastrophic defeats usually begin in the rear. That is why the Greeks put a substantial portion of their best hoplites in the rear ranks. In May 1940 military collapse began in the French rear areas.[30] Military success for American forces in the Battle of the Bulge in December in the same area resulted to a great extent from the sustained resistance that a number of rear area formations put up.[31]

Here, there are worries, given current service approaches to acculturating incoming recruits. At present, only the marine corps puts all incoming recruits through the harsh, unremitting pressures that have characterized effective boot camps throughout history. The combat side of the army equation is clearly similar to that of the marines. But the recruits on the army's support side receive an attenuated and mild basic training.[32] It is unlikely that such training will produce support soldiers who can stand up to the pressures of sustained and terrifying attacks on rear areas. The navy has fallen from what was in the nineteenth century a harsh, unremitting discipline, best characterized by Winston Churchill, as "rum, sodomy, and the lash" to time-out cards for stressed out recruits.[33] Throughout its short history the air force has never viewed basic training as anything other than a socialization process, rather that an acculturation process aimed at inducing rigorous discipline. If the precision strike, battle space dominance crowd is right, such approaches to basic training will have little effect. However, if the distant punishment theorists are wrong, then such attenuated training will have a catastrophic impact, especially if U.S. opponents strike U.S. rear areas.

There is an additional problem with U.S. military culture, and that has to do with the external and internal pressures increasingly at work on the American military. There are major demographic changes occurring in the

---

[30] For the best account of the French collapse in 1940, see Alistar Horne, *To Lose a Battle, France, 1940* (Boston, 1969).

[31] See in particular, Charles B. MacDonald, *The Battle of the Bulge* (London, 1984).

[32] In this regard, see Thomas E. Ricks, *Making the Corps* (New York, 1997), pp. 171–174. The disaster that happened to the 507th Maintenance Company in An Nasariyah in the early days of the Iraq War has led the army to reinstitute serious combat training for all those passing through basic training, whatever their specialty.

[33] The navy has abandoned time-out cards in its basic training program, but the philosophy that made such an approach possible remains alive and well.

external society as well as those that have occurred recently within U.S. military organizations. These changes will exercise considerable, if unpredictable, effects. The first has to do with the disappearance of the World War II generation, which is dying off at the rate of 1,000 veterans per day. Over the past 50 years, that generation has exercised an important influence over the American body politic. Most importantly it has understood the importance of military organizations in the defense of the United States and its interests. The World War II generation also possessed a basic understanding of the importance of military culture and institutions. In the largest sense, that understanding has translated into a realism within the larger body politic about the use of military force and nature of military institutions. That generational common sense may well disappear with the World War II generation.

The second societal change has been the increasing remove of the American elites from the services that protect them. There are two great dangers in this. The most obvious has been the willingness of political leaders to use military institutions in a haphazard and careless fashion, as a general reflection of the inability of those who cast U.S. foreign policy to understand how the world works.[34] A number of commentators have stressed this possibility. And the arguments of "military experts" about the potential of technology to remove the pain from war with total battle space knowledge and network-centric war has already found an eager and enthusiastic audience among civilians within Washington's Beltway.

On the other hand, an uninformed and ignorant civilian leadership is capable of doing enormous harm to American military culture in time of extended peace. The remarks of Undersecretary of the Army Sarah Lister about the marine corps' troglodytic maintenance of its culture suggests the kinds of dangers that lie ahead for those islands of military culture that remain devoted to preparing the U.S. armed forces for *war*. In this regard, the collapse of serious historical studies from America's leading universities and colleges in favor of deconstruction and gender studies is of considerable worry. There remain a few outposts where serious military history remains in the curriculum – Ohio State, the University of North Carolina, Kansas State, and Yale still retain major graduate programs in military history, but that is it.[35] And it will get worse. The

---

[34] The performance of the Clinton and the two Bush administrations over their time in office certainly justifies this comment.
[35] Of the service academies, only West Point forces all of its students to take a two-semester course in military history and offers a substantial number of upper division courses in war and strategy.

result is going to be a political and intellectual elite in the United States that is not only removed from the American military by a lack of service, but an elite that is fundamentally ignorant of military and strategic issues that a broad education might provide.[36]

There is a larger point here. As Robert Kaplan suggested in a conference at Tampa Bay in April 1998, the destruction of the serious study of literature and history in our schools, colleges, and universities is producing a generation of Americans incapable of understanding the tragic, even through the medium of books.[37] This new generation will find it all too easy to attack military cultures that lie beyond their intellectual comprehension. And the military, or those inclined to join its ranks, will vote with their feet. We have already seen a shift in the services of choice among Hispanics from the army to the marine corps as a result of their belief that army culture is not sufficiently *machismo*. The next step could be that substantial portions of the society that have traditionally provided the backbone of the services, namely Hispanics, Blacks, and White southerners, will no longer join unless they are out of work. And the military, if it is to succeed on the battlefields of the next century, must be something more than just a job.

Finally, there are significant changes within the military culture itself because of a generational shift in the experiences of the officer corps – whose services have provided little understanding of their profession. Officers with experience in Vietnam are rapidly disappearing from the services; only a few at the highest level remain, and they will soon be gone. Moreover, it is now eight years since the Gulf War and ten years since the end of the Cold War [written in 1999]. That means that over half of the officers currently on active duty have had their impressions of the profession of arms formed in historical cultures, largely removed from the kinds of threats that formed previous generations of American officers, reaching back to World War II. Only the marine corps, with its astonishing interest in military history – astonishing in comparison to the

---

[36] Along with these lines, see the devastating critique by Charles Krauthammer, "A World Imagined, The Flawed Premises of Liberal Foreign Policy," *The New Republic*, March 15, 1999, pp. 22–25. See also Williamson Murray, "The Emerging Strategic Environment. An Historian's View," *Strategic Review*, Spring 1999.

[37] Along these lines, in informal polls taken of the approximately 65 students that I have taught at George Washington University over the past three semesters at the graduate level (drawn from among the most prestigious colleges and universities in the United States), only five indicated that they were exposed at university or high school to a single Greek tragedy. Only one had read *War and Peace*.

other services – seems willing to provide a historical compass to its officer corps.

The emerging military culture may have a number of dangerous attributes, particularly if the American military confronts a sustained period of peace. After all, not all interwar periods last twenty years, like the gap between 1919 and 1939; instead, the United States may confront a period of fifty or sixty years, such as that after the Congress of Vienna in 1815. In that case, the capacity of military leaders, uninformed as their professional cultures have made them about the historical parameters of war, may simply surrender to ill-thought-out demands by civilians to bring the military into line with what civilian leaders regard as the politically correct pattern of civil society.

Conclusion

Military culture has played a crucial role in the effectiveness of military institutions throughout history. In fact, it was a determining factor in the rise of the West. Considering what the past suggests, there is no reason to expect that the fundamental nature of war will change in the next century.[38] The culture of discipline has characterized the "Western Way of War" for the past four centuries; it has provided the glue that has kept armies on the battlefield under the most terrifying of circumstances.

Unfortunately, the trashing of the Kassebaum Report, which provided trenchant criticism of gender integrated basic training by the army, air force, and navy underlines the distinct possibility that military leaders will surrender on crucial cultural issues without even a whimper.[39] And it is interesting to note that the Kassebaum Report covered far more than just the issue of gender-integrated training, but addressed crucial issues such as the level of discipline the services must inculcate into the new recruits. On the most specious basis, those who make up the world of

---

[38] For the fundamental nature of war in the last decade of the twentieth century, see Mark Bowden, *Black Hawk Down, A Story of Modern War* (New York, 1999).

[39] "Report of the Federal Advisory Committee on Gender-Integrated Training and Related Issues to the Secretary of Defense," December 16, 1997 (Washington, DC, 1997). What is particularly sad about the fate of the Kassebaum Report is the fact that not only did it examine gender-integrated training, but it made a number of serious recommendations on recruiting and basic training in general. Yet, from its publication date the report ran into a massive disinformation campaign that suggested its members had done no research (not true) and that the report was ideologically motivated (again untrue). What is truly astonishing is that this disinformation campaign resulted in the air force, army, and navy rejecting the report out of hand without even examining whether they had a problem.

journalism in the United States viciously attacked the report. That, of course, was to be expected. But the army, navy, and air force dismissed the findings out of hand, even when there was no pressure from their civilian masters to reject its findings. In fact, they refused even to examine its findings or recommendations. That simple fact should warn us of the shoals ahead. There are already too many U.S. service leaders who will willingly dispense with what is militarily, correct in favor of what is politically correct. That does not bode well for the American military in the next century.

Additional Works Not Cited

Since this essay appeared a decade ago, there has been one major addition to the few works dealing with military culture: Isabel V. Hull's outstanding *Absolute Destruction: Military Culture and the Practice of War in Imperial Germany* (Ithaca, NY, 2005).

6

History and Strategic Planning

From Rome to 1945

This chapter aims to examine the development of strategic planning from its origins in the eighteenth century through the Second War. It will not examine how different organizations accomplished the task, but rather the demands that strategy invariably has raised for strategic planners as well as the underlying reasons that have made strategic planning succeed or fail. In the end, competence in strategy and policy is the most important component in the success or failure in the conduct of war over the past 400 years. As the author and his colleague, Allan Millett, have noted about the first half of the twentieth century, "it is more important to make correct decisions at the political and strategic level than it is at the operational and tactical level. Mistakes in operations and tactics can be corrected, but political and strategic mistakes live for ever."[1]

Yet, what is meant by strategy? This essay at least will define strategy in Clausewitzian terms: the use of military means to achieve political goals. Inherent in such a definition is the belief that intelligent strategy demands a careful weighing of the means available and the extent of the goals to be achieved to ensure that there is a coherent connection between goals sought and means available. But it is to the political end that

---

[1] Allan R. Millett and Williamson Murray, "Lessons of War," *The National Interest*, Winter 1988.

This chapter is largely drawn from my experiences in teaching the "Strategy and Policy" course at the Naval War College in Newport over the academic years 1985–1986 and 1991–1992 and in leading the "Making of Strategy" project that resulted in the book *The Making of Strategy, Rulers, States, and War*, edited by Williamson Murray, MacGregor Knox, and Alvin Bernstein (Cambridge, 1992). It has never before been published.

planners must pay particular attention. Above all, strategy and its planning involve complex processes through which statesmen, military leaders, and their planners adapt to the actual conditions, in both peace and war, that they confront.[2] It is invariably a messy business for those engaged in its formulation. Strategists and strategic planners must inevitably grapple with the accumulated baggage of their national history and culture as well as the complex problems raised by logistics and operations, few of which offer simple or easy solutions. Moreover, statesmen, soldiers, and planners must make and articulate strategy in an extraordinary, fluid environment. The Cold War was an anomalous period in history precisely because so little change in the nature of the threat occurred.

The business of strategic planning must begin with the provision of an intelligent framework through which statesmen and military leaders can understand the world and through which adaptation to real challenges and threats can take place. In thinking through the problems posed by strategy, consistency is the hobgoblin of small minds. At the same time, strategic planners must bring coherence to the strategic problems they confront in order to provide some clarity to the ambiguous and uncertain challenges they confront. To exacerbate their difficulties, the enemy will inevitably make his own strategic and operational plans, which rarely accord with what planners expect. The great Moltke is reputed to have said that no military plan outlasts first contact with the enemy. What he probably meant to suggest is that all plans inevitably confront the unexpected. Even more than operational planners, strategic planners must form plans that are flexible enough, in both the short- and long-term, to flow with the ambiguities and uncertainties that events will invariably throw up.

Strategic planners confront the difficulty of translating strategy into coherent plans that allow for the effective mobilization of a nation's economic and military power into the directed projection of military power. To paraphrase Clausewitz, strategy is a relatively simple matter, but in war the coherent and effective articulation of strategy is an extraordinarily complex and difficult matter. Partially, this is the result of the fact that the enemy is an independent factor; partially it results from the fact

---

[2] For a discussion of the nature of the strategic process and the considerable number of components that one must consider in understanding why those processes differ so greatly from nation to nation and time period to time period, see particularly Williamson Murray and Mark Grimsley, "Introduction: On Strategy," in *The Making of Strategy, Rulers, States, and War*, chap. 1.

that war, more than any other human endeavor, is governed by chance; and, partially, because friction, uncertainty, and ambiguity will always confront the strategic planner in an incalculable fashion.[3]

Moreover, the great difficulty for the strategic planner is that war by its nature is suffused with political factors and influence. And as in the operational environment, those factors and influences are inevitably subject to ebb and flow. Thus, the planner stands in the quicksands not only of operational chance and change but of political and strategic changes as well. In commenting on a military exercise that posited an Austrian operational threat to Prussia without presenting any political context, Clausewitz noted:

> War is not an independent phenomena, but the continuation of politics by other means. Consequently the main lines of every strategic plan are *largely political in nature*, and their political character increases the more the plan applies to the entire campaign and to the entire state. A war plan results directly from the political conditions of the two warring states, as well as their relations to third powers. A plan of campaign results from the war plan, and frequently – if there is only one theater of operations – may be identical to it. But the political elements even enters the separate components of a campaign; rarely will it be without influence on such major episodes of warfare as battle, etc. According to this point of view, there can be no question of a *purely military* evaluation of a great strategic issue, or of a purely military scheme to solve it.[4]

Yet, the historian must confront the fact that much of the planning and formulation of strategy will remain opaque and unrecoverable, even in the present day. Much of what transpires between individuals in the day-to-day business of strategic planning simply disappears from the record. As one of the foremost historians of Britain's emergence as a great power has noted about the making of strategy in eighteenth century Britain:

> Parliamentary debates and gossip remain, but thousands of other informal discussions in salons, taverns, dinner parties, balls, and random encounters are lost. Unofficial correspondence exists only where key figures retreated to their country estates or were otherwise absent, and official documents tend to reflect decisions rather than the processes that created them. The compromises, trade-offs, and private deals characteristic of advanced systems of clientage are often lost to recorded memory. Decisions were usually compromises, and those who dissented could only grumble and criticize until

---

[3] For why Clausewitz is correct in his argument that war more than any other activity is governed by chance, see Alan Beyerchen, "Clausewitz, Nonlinearity, and the Unpredictability of War, *International Security*, vol. 17, no. 3, Winter 1992/1993.

[4] Peter Paret, *Clausewitz and the State* (Oxford, 1976), pp. 379–380.

victory dismissed their complaints or misfortune made them next year's policy.[5]

Strategic Planning: Its Origins

Strategy has been a facet of the "Western way of war" since at least the Middle Ages. Thus, one might suppose that strategic planning has been an integral part of the wars that Western states have waged against each other as well as against outsiders.[6] Surprisingly, it has not.[7] Admittedly, at times ad hoc approaches to strategic planning have appeared, usually driven by the increasing complex strategic problems that Western states and their military organizations have confronted. But it has taken centuries rather than decades for an understanding of the art of strategic planning to emerge as the basis for the projection of military forces across continental distances.

That is not to say that strategic conceptions have not driven Western warfare from the beginning of the West's rise to global supremacy. There is no doubt that the Romans, particularly during the period of the Empire, possessed effective strategic planning processes to control the vast expanses of territory that ranged from Britain and the North Sea to Syria and the Euphrates.[8] During the period between 30 BC and 235 AD the Romans held their frontiers with no more that 150,000 legionaries in approximately 30 legions, supported by 150,000 auxiliaries.[9] The projection of those forces as well as the sustainment of the world's first

---

[5] William S. Maltby, "The Origins of a Global Strategy from 1559 to 1713," in Murray, Knox, and Bernstein, eds., *The Making of Strategy, Rulers, States and War*, p. 165.

[6] For an outstanding examination of one of the earliest uses of strategy to achieve political goals in Western history, see Clifford J. Rogers, *War Cruel and Sharp, English Strategy under Edward III, 1327–1360* (Woodbridge, Suffolk, 2000).

[7] This is surprisingly so because of the fact that wars in the West have been directly linked to the achievement of political objectives, as Clausewitz so aptly noted in *On War*. Yet, strategic planning has largely been an attribute of the British and American approach to war.

[8] For an interesting examination of the developments in Roman strategy over the early centuries of the empire, see Edward Luttwak, *The Grand Strategy of the Roman Empire, From the First Century A.D. to the Third* (Baltimore, MD, 1976).

[9] Gibbon's comment about this period was that "In the second century of the Christian era, the empire of Rome comprehended the fairest part of the earth, and the most civilized portion of mankind. The frontiers of that extensive monarchy were guarded by ancient renown and disciplined valour. The gentle, but powerful, influence of laws and manners had gradually cemented the union of the provinces. Their peaceful inhabitants enjoyed and abused the advantages of wealth and luxury." Edward Gibbon, *The Rise and Fall of the Roman Empire* (New York, 1946), pp. 1, 61.

truly professional army required complex planning processes not only in the innumerable military campaigns the Romans waged, but in times of peace as well.

For most of the period after Julius Caesar's conquest of Gaul, the Romans were content to "manage" the frontier districts that bordered the empire. Such management involved the bribery of tribal chieftains, manipulation of inter- and intra-tribal conflicts among the barbarians, support for puppet kingdoms, and, at times, ferocious military campaigns and punitive expeditions, when the natives threatened real trouble that could extend to the left bank of the Rhine. Only in four cases after the destruction of three Roman legions by the Germans in the Teutoburgerwald did the Romans actively seek to expand the Empire's borders: the conquest of Britain at mid-point of the first century AD, the conquest of Dacia – modern day Romania – late in the first and early second centuries, the conquest of Persia shortly thereafter, and a series of smaller wars that sought to expand the frontier confronting the German tribes during the first and second centuries to include most of Bavaria and Austria.[10] The first two efforts involved complex strategic planning that brought together legions and auxiliaries from across the Empire, the creation of a vast logistic base, and, if necessary, the creation of fleets, roads, and other infrastructure to support the operational effort that focused Roman power on the empire's enemies. All of this undoubtedly took careful, detailed, and sophisticated planning throughout the imperial bureaucracy, of which virtually none has survived.[11]

With their military superiority, enabled by the discipline and training of the legions, the Romans won all of these campaigns. But they only fell back on military conquest as a last resort. Then as now, military operations were immensely expensive, and the Empire, which rested to a considerable extent on a subsistence economy, could only afford war when there was no other choice.[12] Conquests like Germany simply could

---

[10] The last of these involved a gradual encroachment and incorporation of territory to improve the empire's strategic frontier by connecting the Rhine defenses with those of the Danube.

[11] In this regard the loss of Trajan's memoirs recounting his conquest of Dacia must be regarded as a serious loss, for they would certainly have provided a glimpse of how strategic planning proceeded during the high empire.

[12] One authority suggests that the annual tax base of the empire was approximately 3.5 percent, which was minuscule compared to what modern states rely on to finance their expenditures. Yet, that percentage was the maximum taxation the empire could support. When the threat significantly increased in the late second century and the base appeared to have shrunk as a result of plagues, the Roman Empire entered an economic decline from which it never recovered. See Chester G. Starr, *The Roman Empire, 27 B.C.– A.D. 476, A Study in Survival* (Oxford, 1982).

not pay for themselves, and the Romans were content to use other means to protect their territories. This must have required sophisticated planning and calculations on the right balance between military force, diplomacy, and special operations to encourage the locals to do the Romans' job for them.

The Romans most probably made complex calculations in their decision not to conquer northern Scotland but rather to defend Britain at the natural frontiers between Britain and Scotland, to create the means for great engineering projects such as Hadrian's Wall, and then to maintain that fortified defense for offensive as well as defensive purposes.[13] Similarly, after Trajan's conquest of Parthia, the emperor Hadrian and his advisers calculated that holding the Mesopotamian Valley was beyond the Empire's resources – that it would cost less and take less effort to defend on the Syrian frontier.[14] The problem for the historian is that none of the documents has survived, and thus any understanding of how the Romans planned at the strategic level can only exist in conjectures. The reality is that for nearly three centuries the Romans projected effective military forces by land and sea as well as diplomatic initiatives over the empire's distances and enforced the *pax Romana* across the Empire's frontiers until the mid-third century.[15]

There were others in the centuries that followed the Romans through the eighteenth century who appear to have had a sense of strategy and strategic vision, as well as some willingness to plan strategically. But they were very much the exception. In the mid-fourteenth century, Edward III

---

[13] Hadrian's Wall and the slightly later Antonine Wall are the ultimate example of the careful strategic planning that allowed the Romans to defend the empire with a true economy of force.

[14] A modern historian, quoting an ancient source, notes the following on the grand strategy of the Empire and the prudence that guided strategic policy planning: "As Appian put it in the preface to his *Roman History*, 'possessing the best part of the earth and the sea the emperors wish rather to preserve their Empire by the exercise of prudence' and reject rule over 'poverty-stricken and profitless tribes of barbarians... They surround the Empire with great armies and they garrison the whole stretch of the land and the sea like a single stronghold.'" Starr, *The Roman Empire*, p. 123.

[15] Such planning included the careful construction of a vast road system that ran the length and breadth of the empire to facilitate movement of legions and auxiliaries as well as communications among the empire's far-flung military forces, so that they could concentrate with great rapidity. Europe would not see the construction of a similar system until the nineteenth century with the creation of the interconnected railroad lines, many constructed for strategic purposes. The conquest of Britain resulted in the creation of a road system for military and strategic purposes that "for the first time knit together the various habitable belts in one unified transportation network, which for the most part radiated from London [already Britain's greatest port]." S.S. Frere, *Britannia* (London, 1978), p. 16.

of England developed a complex strategy of destructive raiding, which combined with the tactical superiority of his armies to devastate Valois France. The strategic approach forced the French to fight battles they could not win. The English king came close to destroying the French monarchy. In the late 1340s, he executed his strategy by planning military operations that brought together the archers and men-at-arms in England. Supported by coordinated reinforcements from his Continental allies, he deployed those forces by amphibious operations to the Continent and then conducted complex campaigns supported by pre-planned logistics.[16] But Edward III was clearly a military genius, capable of planning and achieving results far in advance of his time. He would have few equals in strategic planning until the early eighteenth century.[17]

Another figure of note in the early seventeenth century, Cardinal Richelieu, set France's strategic policy for the next 200 years. His policies aimed at ensuring that no single power would dominate the area known at the time as the Germanies.[18] Thus, despite the fact that he was a great prince of the Church, Richelieu provided the financial and strategic support that made it possible for Sweden, a Protestant power, to intervene in the Thirty Years War. The victories of Gustavus Adolphus, the Swedish king and military genius, prevented the Catholic Hapsburgs from dominating the German lands across the Rhine and creating a coherent German state. Over the next two centuries, Richelieu's concept was eminently successful in guiding France's strategic policy of keeping Germany divided – at least until Bismarck's wars of unification in the nineteenth century. But

---

[16] See particularly Clifford Rogers' discussion of the Crecy–Calais campaign of 1346 and Poitiers campaign of 1356 – the latter saw three separate but coordinate efforts that came close to destroying the French monarchy. At times, the planning failed to achieve the larger conception, but then Edward and his planners were operating under conditions of fog, friction, and ambiguity that have governed war throughout history. Clifford J. Rogers, *War Cruel and Sharp, English Strategy under Edward III, 1327–1360* (Woodbridge, UK, 2000), pp. 217–272, and 325–384.

[17] Two possible acolytes would clearly be Henry V, whose assault on the French monarchy in the early fifteenth century nearly placed an English king on the French throne, and Gustavus Adolphus who nearly destroyed the power of Habsburg Austria in his campaigns in the 1630s. But both warrior kings, who possessed considerable planning abilities at the strategic level, proved exceptions in their times, while their deaths ended their strategic designs.

[18] One might point to Elizabeth's intervention in the Dutch Revolt against Spain in the sixteenth century as an equally successful strategic concept – one that has guided English and British statesmen in interventions on the Continent to prevent the Spanish (during Elizabeth's reign), the French (in the War of Spanish Succession and the Revolutionary and Napoleonic Wars), and then the Germans (World War I and World War II) from dominating the Low Countries.

in all of this, there was little of what today would be regarded as strategic planning as a coherent process of weighing and assessing the risks and opportunities that military operations might involve.

Strategic Planning: The Early Phases, 1700–1815

The Wars for Empire

Strategic planning appears for the first time in a coherent, bureaucratic sense in the eighteenth century.[19] In the War of Spanish Succession, the British government, under the leadership of the Duke of Marlborough, confronted both the old and new.[20] On one hand, in order to fight the greatest power on the European Continent, France, the British had to conduct the conflict with the support of Continental allies. On the other hand, this war represented something new in history, a global war for empire. For the first time, the effectiveness of naval power allowed the British to fight a war of global proportions. Both forms of war required substantial planning to undergird the projection of British military power onto the continent and across great oceans to North America, the Carribean, and India, as well as into the Mediterranean.

In the case of war's traditional form – war on the Continent – neither the genius of the Duke of Marlborough nor the size of the British Army were sufficient to achieve significant results against Louis XIV's massive resources without substantial help from allies – logistically as well as militarily. Two significant allies provided the wherewithal to augment British military power on the continent: the Dutch Republic and the Hapsburg Empire. Marlborough was indeed one of the great captains of military history. He may not have been as skillful on the battlefield as Napoleon, but, unlike Napoleon, Marlborough was a great strategist.[21] His handling

---

[19] It may well have occurred in the highest levels of the Roman Empire in the first and second centuries AD, as we suggested in the introduction. However, our sources remain too sparse to provide any clear guidance on this subject except that the extent of the empire and the coherence and effectiveness of several of its most impressive campaigns – against Britain in the mid-first century and against Dacia (modern-day Rumania) in the early second century – suggest that something akin to strategic planning existed. For an imaginative but in the end, speculative examination of this issue, see Luttwak, *The Grand Strategy of the Roman Empire*.

[20] The most impressive account of the British side of the War of Spanish Succession remains Winston S. Churchill's magisterial *Marlborough, His Life and Times*, 4 vols. (London, 1933–1938). See also David Chandler, *Marlborough as Military Commander* (London, 1973).

[21] For Napoleon's masterful grasp of operational art and battlefield command see David Chandler, *The Campaigns of Napoleon* (New York, 1966).

of Britain's allies, in particular the Protestant Dutch and the Catholic Austrians, as well as his sophisticated understanding of sea power, allowed the coalition to come close to breaking the power of France.

The campaign of 1704 underlines the extent of allied strategic planning. In the opening years of the war, the Dutch had been unwilling to support Marlborough's desire to fight a major battle against the French. Over the winter of 1703–1704, the Duke determined to unite his British army – then located in Holland – with the Austrians under Prince Eugene in southern Germany. To accomplish this goal, Marlborough and the Austrians negotiated with the minor German states and then established a series of supply dumps along the Rhine and at other locations so that the English Army could march south as fast as possible without having to forage. The campaign proceeded almost like clockwork; the allied armies united in Bavaria and at Blenheim administered to the French one of the most decisive defeats in history.[22]

At the same time, the British were mounting major maritime expeditions, some successful, some not. These efforts required massive preparations and planning to bring together the ground and naval forces (in some cases combined as well as joint) for what would today be termed expeditionary warfare. In 1704 the Royal Navy, supported by ground forces, including a regiment of foot from Hanover, seized Gibraltar to provide access to the Mediterranean.[23] Other expeditionary forces sailed from the British Isles to attack the French in North America, India, and Spain. These efforts were not as successful as the campaigns later in the century, but they underline a capacity to move from conception, to preparation, to execution in expeditionary war – planning capabilities that provided the British with considerable advantages over the French for the remainder of the century.

---

[22] The Battle of Blenheim was decisive not just in terms of its immediate operational effect – it gave the Allies the initiative for the rest of the war – but because it undermined the claims of Louis XIV's theorists that the divine right of kings represented the natural order of things. To them, absolute monarchy also provided the most effective and efficient forms of government. However, it was hard to make such arguments after the devastating defeats of Blenheim, Ramillies, and Oudenarde. Thus, those French military defeats created an intellectual atmosphere of disillusionment within France. The result of that disillusionment was the movement known today as the "enlightenment." Its suspicion of tyranny and ancient government was eventually to be a contributing factor to the French Revolution and the overthrow of the French monarchy at the end of the eighteenth century. I am indebted to Professor Paul Rahe of the University of Tulsa for this point.

[23] The great German novelist and war hero Ernst Jünger fought during the First World War in a Hanoverian regiment that had served in the capture of Gibraltar and that in 1915 still had the Rock of Gibraltar as its cap badge.

What suggests how far Marlborough had moved beyond his European allies are two of his later campaigns. In 1707 he pushed Eugene and the Austrians to launch an attack from Italy over the Alps against the French naval base at Toulon, the basis of Louis XIV's power in the Mediterranean. Marlborough promised the Royal Navy's support to provide the necessary supplies for the advance so that the Austrians could strike swiftly before the French were ready. However, mistrustful of naval support, Eugene and his Austrians, burdened by heavy, land-based logistics, moved far too slowly, and the French successfully defended Toulon. The following year Eugene moved north and joined Marlborough and the Dutch for a campaign in the Low Countries. Again the campaign could not have taken place without extensive planning and logistical preparations. At Oudenarde, the allies won their third great victory over the French in six years. Louis XIV's France appeared on the brink of collapse. Marlborough then proposed allied armies move through the last line of French defensive fortresses and switch their logistics to the English Channel. He had already prepared the admiralty to support such a move. His allies demurred. They simply were unwilling to have their forces depend on seaborne sustenance. Marlborough, despite his prestige, bowed. Thus, was lost the last chance to defeat France in the War of Spanish Succession and thereby break the power of the French monarchy.[24]

In the end, the allies imposed a severe peace on Louis XIV's exhausted kingdom and brought an end to French hopes of creating a European hegemony – at least until the end of the century. But the allies had pursued too many projects – the Austrians in Italy, the British and Austrians in Spain, the Dutch, the British, and the Austrians in the Low Countries, and the British on the world's oceans in pursuit of France's colonies – to achieve decisive strategic results. But those in charge of Britain's efforts had learned valuable lessons that affected how Britain waged the great conflicts of the mid-eighteenth century.

The Seven Years' War, 1756–1763

In 1756 the Seven Years' War broke out – a conflict that determined much of the world's political course over the next two hundred years.[25]

---

[24] For a discussion of these issues, see Churchill, *Marlborough, His Life and Times*, pp. 625–632.

[25] This may appear to be an extreme statement, but the collapse of French political power in North America and India had the result that English was to become the dominant language on the world stage.

In this conflict the British fought a very different war from that of the War of Spanish Succession. They committed a bare minimum of military force to the Continent. Britain's strategic policy rested on the assumption that Frederick the Great's military genius could hold off the combined power of Russia, Austria, and France, while British forces attacked France's colonies and strategic possessions around the globe.[26] Only a small British land force contributed to the defense of the Germanies, while major financial subsidies from Britain sufficed to keep Frederick and his Prussians in the war. While Frederick was fending off his enemies on the Continent, the British concentrated on destroying France's worldwide empire. There were three arenas where the British and French contested for global hegemony: North America, the sugar islands of the Caribbean, and India. Such a war required the massing of forces, the planning of great expeditions, and the coordination of strategy among various theaters of operation. During the first years of the war, the British had a rocky start, particularly in North America, where General Braddock's expedition against the French in the Ohio Valley met a disastrous defeat on the banks of the Monongahela.[27]

But in William Pitt, Britain possessed one of the great strategists and war leaders in history. Moreover, its leaders had by this time refined the processes of translating a strategy of expeditionary warfare and the military means required to realize that vision into coherent and effective plans for action. The experiences of the War of Spanish Succession and the War of Austrian Succession (1746–1749) had honed the British ability to plan in strategic terms. Thus, they were able to plan, coordinate, and execute strategic expeditions in a fashion the French failed to match. In addition, they focused their energy and resources almost entirely on the maritime war for empire, while the French concentrated much of their military power and national resources on the war against Prussia – a war they were fighting in part because of insults that Frederick had tossed at Madame Pompadour, Louis XV's mistress.

---

[26] In the end, they were right, but barely. By the last year of the war, Frederick's position was so desperate he contemplated suicide. Only the death of the Czarina, Frederick's mortal enemy, saved Prussia by bringing her son, an enthusiastic admirer of Frederick, to the Russian throne and ending the coalition of Russia, Austria, and France.

[27] This discussion of the war for North America – a part of the global war known as The Seven Years' War to Europeans and The French and Indian War to Americans – draws much from Fred Anderson's brilliant study: *Crucible of War, The Seven Years' War and the Fate of Empire in British North America, 1754–1766* (New York, 2000).

Unlike other British statesmen, Pitt understood how to motivate the American colonials to participate in a grand design of eliminating French power from Canada: a combination of financial inducements appealing to their sense of greed and the granting of military commissions that recognized their ambitions. Three years into the war the British were prepared for the difficulties involved in executing their plans and strategies. In 1759, Major General James Wolfe destroyed a French army on the Plains of Abraham near Quebec City, a victory that set the stage for the final destruction of the French position in North America the following year.

In spring 1760 almost exactly on time to catch the breakup of the ice in the St. Lawrence River, a British fleet arrived with reinforcements and supplies, just six days before the French and in time to thwart French preparations to assault British forces holding Quebec. Their arrival was most fortuitous because the victors of 1759 were in desperate straits from the Canadian winter. That summer, British commanders led a three-pronged advance against the French: the first, up the St. Lawrence from Quebec City; the second, north from Albany and Lake Champlain; and the third, down the St. Lawrence by British and Colonial forces which had swung west along the Mohawk River toward Oswego and then advanced on Montreal from the southwest. The designer of the plan, General Jeffrey Amherst, aptly commented: "I believe that never three Armys [sic] setting out from different & very different Parts from each other, Joyned in the Centre, as was intended, better than we did, and it could not fail of having the effect of which [we] have just now seen the consequence."[28] Equally decisive events were occurring on the other side of the globe. Here, British resources, military support, and the military genius of Robert Clive combined to eliminate the French position in India. The Indian subcontinent now formed the jewel of the British Empire.

Yet, there were limits to what British strategic planning could achieve when their strategic appreciations went askew. Pitt certainly understood and respected the American colonists. But those who came after consistently underestimated American will, truculence, and nascent strengths. Political arrogance led to a failure of strategic conception and an absence of strategic planning. As the confrontation with the colonies reached the exploding point in the 1770s, the British government was dismembering Britain's military power in the name of economy at the same time it deliberately courted a political and military confrontation in North America.

[28] Ibid., p. 409.

When war exploded, the British were so short of troops they had to hire German mercenaries.[29]

Since basic political and strategic assumptions were flawed, strategic planning for a campaign on the other side of the Atlantic proved incapable of bridging the gap. The American colonists put up a far more sophisticated defense than had been the case with the French in Canada. Moreover, throughout the Seven Years' War, the British possessed secure bases – the colonies – from which they could coordinate and conduct their strategic plans. In the War of American Independence, the British planned their strategy in London and executed it in North America. Of Lord Germaine's approximately sixty-three letters of instruction to Sir Henry Clinton from 1778 to 1781, six took less than two months to arrive in the colonies, twelve took approximately two months, twenty-eight took two to three months, eleven took three to four months, four took four to five months, and two took five to seven months.[30]

Is it any surprise then that the Saratoga campaign ended in disaster when strategic planning in London had so little relevance to what was occurring in the colonies? Nevertheless, one should not forget that beginning in 1778 the British again confronted a global war when both France and Spain declared war against them. They made the sensible decision to write off the colonies and defend the rest of their empire against the French and the Spanish. In that longer conflict, their ability to tailor resources, planning, and capabilities to the needs of the moment allowed them to hold onto the rest of the empire – a victory of sorts.

The French Revolutionary and Napoleonic Wars

As previously suggested, strategic planning for Napoleon occurred almost entirely within one of the great minds of human history. For the British, however, the problem in these wars was the fact that the French were no longer targetable for their foreign possessions. Moreover, France and its new army had entirely overturned the framework of European war with the massive mobilization of the French people and its resources.[31]

---

[29] In a gesture of contempt for his former allies, Frederick the Great made the German princes, who hired out troops to the British, pay a cattle tax on their soldiers who crossed his territory.

[30] Piers Mackesy, *The War for America, 1775–1783* (London, 1975), p. 73.

[31] In effect, the French were creating the second great military revolution in Western History. For the significance of that revolution, see MacGregor Knox, "Mass Politics as Military Revolution: The French Revolution and After," in MacGregor Knox and Williamson

For the British the problem was twofold: strategic planning that addressed global issues was not necessarily capable of addressing a purely Continental opponent. In addition, Britain's allies on the Continent proved incapable of standing up in the field against the fury of French arms and military effectiveness even before Napoleon arrived on the scene. British subsidies and strategic planning that included a massive blockade of the European Continent could not counterbalance the Grand Army's military superiority. Coalition after coalition collapsed, while Britain found it impossible to maintain substantial forces on the Continent. "Not until [European] statesmen had at last perceived the nature of the forces that had emerged in France, and had grasped that new political conditions now obtained in Europe, could they foresee the broad effect all this would have on war; and only in that way could they appreciate the scale of the means that would have to be employed, and how best to employ them."[32]

In 1808 the tide turned with Napoleon's disastrous intervention in Spain. That action allowed the British to deploy a substantial, well-led military force to the Iberian Peninsula.[33] Throughout these great wars, one simply cannot speak of strategic planning by the French. Napoleon's marshals and ministers were there simply to execute what the great man ordered, while the emperor consistently confused strategy with decisive victory on the battlefield. Eventually, such an approach foundered on the inability of one man to plan and organize everything – especially when his nation was taking on the rest of Europe. Napoleon's invasion of Russia in 1812 opened the door for a successful and united counterattack by his opponents.

In the 1813 campaign British financial and economic resources allowed the other major powers to keep sufficient forces in the field to overwhelm, if not directly defeat, the emperor.[34] Here, alliance strategic planning at last established a framework within which the allies could pursue a

---

Murray, eds., *The Dynamics of Military Revolution, 1300–2050* (Cambridge, 2002). See also the introductory essay to that volume – "Thinking about Revolutions in Warfare" – which discusses the difference between military revolutions and revolutions in military affairs.

[32] Carl von Clausewitz, *On War*, trans. and ed. by Michael Howard and Peter Paret (Princeton, 1976), p. 609.

[33] The best work on the campaigns of Napoleon remains Chandler's *The Campaigns of Napoleon*.

[34] Napoleon won virtually all the major battles in the 1813 campaign (Bautzen, Lützen, Dresden), but lost the campaign because his enemies kept coming at him regardless of their losses until they finally overwhelmed his forces at the Battle of Leipzig.

multi-faceted campaign. They were able to concentrate their superior resources in manpower to defeat Napoleon's marshals while holding the emperor at bay. At the same time the Royal Navy's blockade continued its strangling of the French economy, while the Duke of Wellington broke the back of French military power in Spain and crossed the Pyrenees into southern France. The allied cause was particularly helped by the fact that the Prussians had created the first educated and trained group of staff officers: the Prussian general staff. But strategic planning still remained an idiosyncratic feature of the overall European military landscape, an important facet of how the British waged war, but only of casual interest to most on the Continent. The Europeans, including the French, simply did not possess the intellectual framework to undertake serious strategic planning that balanced economic resources, risk, political objectives, and military forces.

The Industrial Revolution

The Crimea

In the late eighteenth century, a new factor – perhaps the most momentous in history – began to impinge on the conduct of war: the Industrial Revolution.[35] It had no direct impact on tactics or the conduct of battles up to 1815, but it provided Britain with the financial basis on which its statesmen – and strategic planners – could support the vast fleets that the Royal Navy put to sea to enforce the blockade, an increasingly strong army in Spain under Wellington, and the subsidies that allowed Britain's Continental allies to place ever larger armies in the field for longer periods of time in the last years of the war against Napoleon.

By mid-point in the century, the Industrial Revolution was having a direct impact not only on the mobilization of military forces, but also on their tactical and operational capabilities. The railroad, the telegraph, and rifles exercised a direct and important influence over the conduct of military operations. In the Crimean War (1854–1856), the British and French fought the Russians for reasons that were obscure even to the participants. While considerable planning went into the projection of the Anglo-French expeditionary force that eventually carried the war to the siege of Sebastopol, the disasters suffered by both sides over the

[35] For a discussion of the impact of the Industrial Revolution on military affairs in the nineteenth century, see Murray and Knox, "Thinking About Military Revolutions," in Knox and Murray, eds., *The Dynamics of Military Revolution*, chap. 1.

winter do not suggest sophisticated planning. Thus, one can hardly talk of strategic conceptions or of strategic planning driving the conduct of military operations.[36]

Nevertheless, the Industrial Revolution, both in terms of communications and transportation, had a number of crucial effects on the conduct and planning of strategy. It allowed statesmen and military organizations to undertake more coherent and effective planning for the projection of military power. Above all, it allowed strategic planners to make corrections to military strategy, while statesmen were in a position, if they wished, to adapt their strategic conceptions to the reality of the conflict they actually confronted. And finally, it allowed the projection of military power on a more coherent and timely basis.

The American Civil War
The situation at the start of the American Civil War hardly suggested strategic planning at its beginning – at least in terms of a strategy for attacking the Confederacy at its heart. Almost immediately, the U.S. Navy developed a strategy with support from the army for seizing bases around the South's periphery to enforce a blockade.[37] But there was no real strategic planning for dealing with the Confederacy on land at the beginning of the war. In the east Union armies wandered toward Richmond in the hope that the defeat of Lee's army and the capture of Richmond would end the war. At least in the West, Union commanders understood that opening up the Mississippi River could contribute to the overall strategic picture.

Only a few generals possessed a glimmer of a strategic conception. General Winfield Scott, the decrepit commander of the Union Army at the start, argued for something he called "the Anaconda" strategy, whereby the Union would strangle the Confederacy to death. In early 1862 President Abraham Lincoln articulated the concept of projecting Union forces from different theaters at the same time to break the cordon defense the Confederates had established. But the leading Union general, George McClellan, dismissed Lincoln's thoughts as the musing of a baboon. In 1863, the Union launched three great offensives, Major General Joseph Hooker against Richmond, Major General Ulysses S. Grant against Vicksburg, and Major General William Rosecrans against

---

[36] For the Crimean War, see: Cecil Woodham-Smith, *The Reason Why* (New York, 1960); Christopher Hibbert, *The Destruction of Lord Raglan, A Tragedy of the Crimean War* (London, 1961); and particularly Andrew D. Lambert, *The Crimean War, British Grand Strategy Against Russia, 1853–1856* (Manchester, UK, 1990).

[37] I am indebted to Colonel Kevin Weddle, Professor, U.S. Army War College, for this point.

southeastern Tennessee. Significantly, there was no overall strategic direction behind these three drives: the Mississippi and Virginia offensives began in late April and early May; that in Tennessee in late June. Because of a lack of coordination, only Grant's succeeded, but General Henry Halleck immediately squandered the strategic advantages of seizing Vicksburg. Halleck possessed no strategic conception for winning the war. Thus, instead of concentrating on what was strategically and operationally useful – Grant had suggested a move on Mobile – Halleck dissipated Grant's forces to pursue tactical objectives.

It was not until Grant took over as commander of the Union Army in early 1864 that one can talk of a strategic conception behind the overall operation of Union forces and the planning to translate that conception into reality. Grant, in one of the clearest strategic orders ever issued to subordinate commanders, laid out the strategic framework for the 1864 campaign. It was to launch the Union armies at the same time in concentric attacks to destroy the South's economic and political heart. Grant's orders to Sherman, commander of Union forces in Tennessee, made explicit the overall strategy for the coming campaign:

> It is my design, if the enemy keep quiet and allow me to take the initiative in the spring campaign, to work all parts of the army together, and somewhat toward a common centre [sic]. For your information, I now write you my programme, as at presently determined upon.... I will stay with the Army of the Potomac, increased by Burnside's corps of not less than twenty-five thousand men, and operate directly against Lee's army, wherever it may be found.... You I propose to move against Johnston's army, to break it up and to get into the interior of the enemy's country as far as you can, inflicting all the damage you can against their war resources. I do not propose to lay down for you a plan of campaign, but simply lay down the work it is desirable to have done and leave you free to execute it in your own way. Submit to me, however, as early as you can, your plan of operations.[38]

Unfortunately, for the prospects of a Union victory in 1864, only Sherman and Meade possessed the operational competence to live up to Grant's strategic concept.[39] Nevertheless, Grant's framework bore fruit in spring 1865. The Union produced the means; its military commanders,

---

[38] Ulysses S. Grant, *Personal Memoirs of U.S. Grant*, vol. 2 (New York, 1886), pp. 130–131.

[39] Nevertheless, Grant never complained in his memoirs about the failure of his other army commanders to live up to his expectations. They were political generals and Grant understood their participation in the campaign had been crucial to Lincoln's victory in the presidential elections of fall 1864.

particularly Major Generals William T. Sherman and George Thomas, produced the victories; Union logisticians provided the supplies over continental distances; and Lincoln provided the political glue that held everything together despite the gloomy days of summer 1864. Undergirding all was sophisticated planning and adaptation that allowed the Union to move forces over enormous distances by railroads and steamships to meet changing strategic situations.[40] Yet, one should not forget the cost of creating these strategic capabilities from nothing. The cost of developing strategic wisdom, vision, and planning was the aimless slaughter of the war's first two-and-a-half years.

The German Wars of Unification

At the start, the German Wars of Unification (1866 and 1870–1871) showed a higher degree of operational planning than was the case with the American Civil War.[41] This was, of course, a reflection of the Prussian General Staff's interest in and understanding of the importance of railroads to mobilizing and then deploying forces into the various theaters of operations – an interest that Prussia's geographic vulnerabilities reinforced.[42] The result was that in both the Seven Weeks' War and the Franco–Prussian War, the Prussians gained significant operational advantages over their opponents – advantages they were then able to translate into some of the most decisive victories – operationally as well as strategically – in Western military history. But there is no evidence that the general staff and its head, Field Marshal Count Helmut von Moltke, ever considered the strategic ramifications of what they were doing. Thus, the importance of strategic planning, at least in the terms Clausewitz had laid out forty years earlier, never appeared in their deliberations.

Luckily for the Prussian generals, there was someone above them who was in charge of strategic thinking and execution: Prince Otto von Bismarck. The "Iron Chancellor" may well have been the greatest strategist of all time, but it is hard to find direct evidence of strategic planning

---

[40] The foremost example of this was the movement of General Schofield's corps from central Tennessee to and then across the Ohio River and then by railroad to the east coast, where it then embarked on steamers to move to North Carolina to reinforce Sherman's forces, which were driving north from Georgia and South Carolina.

[41] For an examination of these wars, see Dennis Showalter, *The Wars of German Unification* (London, 2004).

[42] For a discussion of the impact of railroads on Prussian strategic thinking and preparations for war see, Dennis Showalter, *Railroads and Rifles, Soldiers, Technology, and the Unification of Germany* (Hamden, CT, 1975). See also Showalter's "The Prusso-German RMA, 1840–1871," in *the Dynamics of Military Revolution, 1300–2050*, chap. 6.

beyond what went on in the great man's head. Like Napoleon's instinctive understanding of operational art, Bismarck's grasp of strategy was that of a genius: intuitive, decisive, and in almost all cases effective. In 1866, he immediately stepped in after the victory at Königrätz and ordered a halt to the Prussian columns closing in on Vienna.[43] To their annoyance, the Prussian generals would get no victory parade in Vienna.[44] Bismarck offered the Austrians, who were looking directly in the face of political as well as military collapse, a peace in which they would suffer no territorial losses – the territorial concessions would all come at the hands of their allies, the other German states.

In the Franco–Prussian War of 1870–1871 Bismarck again manipulated the strategic framework so that Moltke and his generals would only have to fight an isolated France.[45] As the war continued, the chancellor placed onerous – at least from the point of view of the generals – restrictions on the movements of Prusso–German military forces. He refused to allow them to move west or northwest of Paris. He aimed to ensure that German forces would not approach Belgium or the English Channel, since a move toward either would alarm British sensibilities about the area immediately adjacent to their shores. Similarly, Bismarck pushed Moltke to start military operations against Paris before his generals were ready because of fears that other powers might intervene in the conflict if it were not to end quickly.

The larger effect of Bismarck's genius was to create an operational framework within which Prussia's military forces could destroy the inferior military forces brought to the fight by their opponent. But there was no planning process at the strategic level, except for what occurred in Bismarck's mind, and the great man rarely, if ever, bothered to inform his subordinates of his strategic conceptions. The result would have a significant and disastrous impact on the next generation of Germany's political and military leaders, who, as the Franco–Prussian War receded into the past, increasingly came to disregard the contribution that Bismarck's strategy had made to the unification of Germany.

---

[43] For the most recent examination of the Seven Weeks' War, see Geoffrey Warrow, *The Austro-Prussian War, Austria's War with Prussia and Italy in 1866* (Cambridge, 1998).

[44] For Bismarck's conflicts with the Prussian generals and Moltke in particular, see Gerhard Ritter, *The Sword and the Scepter, The Problem of Militarism in Germany*, vol. 1, *The Prussian Tradition, 1740–1890*, trans. by Heinz Norden (Coral Gables, FL, 1969), chap. 8.

[45] For the Franco-Prussian War see Michael Howard's masterful treatment: *The Franco-Prussian War, The German Invasion of France, 1870–1871* (New York, 1969). For a more recent history, see Geoffrey Wawro, *The Franco-Prussian War, The German Conquest of France in 1870–1871* (Cambridge, 2003).

As a result, they came to believe that Prussia's great victories in 1866 and 1870 had resulted almost entirely from the military genius of Moltke and the operational and tactical superiority of Prussia's military forces.[46] Thus, strategy, including serious strategic planning, disappeared from the German lexicon until 1945, when Bismarck's creation disappeared.[47]

Strategic Planning and World War I

One of the major factors contributing to the tragedy of World War I, the most disastrous war in human history, had to do with the tragic lack of effective strategic planning before, during, and after the conflict on all the contending sides.[48] That is not to say that innumerable plans did not exist throughout the general staffs and war ministries of Europe in 1914. Nevertheless, virtually all of these plans had to do with operational matters, designs that aimed to achieve decisive victory over their opponents. When those plans failed, the result was not to rethink the strategic and political assumptions, nearly all faulty, that underlay those plans, but rather to double the bet.[49] The hope was that strategic success would eventually result from a Napoleonic decisive victory, so heavily emphasized in the staff colleges before the war.[50] For the most part, the politicians were satisfied to watch the generals butcher a generation of European youth.

[46] For a discussion of the increasing confusion in Germany in the period between 1890 and 1914 of operational necessity with strategy, see Holger Herwig, "Strategic Uncertainties of a Nation-State: Prussia-Germany, 1871–1918," in *The Making of Strategy*, chap. 9. For a discussion of these issues within the context of German military innovations during this period, see Eric Dorn Brose, *The Kaiser's Army, The Politics of Military Technology in Germany during the Machine Age, 1870–1918* (Oxford, 2001).

[47] For the weaknesses in German strategic planning and strategic conceptions, see Williamson Murray, *German Military Effectiveness* (Baltimore, MD, 1992), chap. 1.

[48] As for the statement that World War I was the most disastrous war in human history, one might note that how it was conducted and ended made a second great world war inevitable. In terms of its political impact, it ended only in 1989 with the fall of the Berlin Wall and reunification of a Europe sundered by the military events of the period between 1914 and 1919.

[49] The one moment of strategic insight that occurred in Germany during the war came in November 1914, when the new chief of the general staff, General Erich von Falkenhayn, suggested to the Chancellor, Theobald von Bethmann Hollweg, that Germany could not win the war and, therefore, should seek peace. Bethmann Hollweg turned Falkenhayn down cold. Holger Herwig, *The First World War, Germany and Austria-Hungary, 1914–1918* (New York, 1997).

[50] The irony is that there were no decisive victories after Napoleon's defeat of the Prussians at Jena-Auerstadt. Yet, as late as the Passchendaele Offensive in 1917, Field Marshal Douglas Haig was still aiming at achieving a decisive Napoleonic victory over the Germans. See Robin Prior and Trevor Wilson, *Passchendaele, The Untold Story* (New Haven, 1996), and Leon Wolff, *In Flanders Fields, The 1917 Campaign* (New York, 1958). Far and away the best biography of Haig is H.P. Harris, *Douglas Haig and the First World War* (Cambridge, 2008).

The Germans epitomized the inability to think in strategic terms. Confronted with the possibility of a two-front war, they gambled all on a massive invasion of France through Belgium and Luxembourg.[51] Thus, they initiated a two-front war by invading France through the Low Countries over an obscure quarrel in the Balkans. The failure to achieve victory over the French in early September 1914 confronted the Germans with a blockade that had an increasingly severe effect on their economy as each year of the war passed. So badly prepared for a blockade were they in terms of strategic planning that they possessed only minimum stocks of nitrates, crucial to the making of explosives. Only the desperate efforts of the German Jewish scientist Fritz Haber created the ability to synthesize nitrates from the atmosphere. Nevertheless, the economic difficulties of the war's first months were insufficient to prevent the Germans from introducing gas war in spring 1915, which in turn allowed the British to tighten the blockade to include most foodstuffs. There was no consideration by German military leaders of the political and strategic backlash that might occur from resorting to chemical warfare, which the Hague conventions had explicitly forbidden.[52]

The continued triumph of military and operational necessity over strategic planning led the Germans to introduce unrestricted submarine warfare in January 1917, which in short order brought the United States into the war and sealed Germany's fate. In effect, the Germans fought the war as a series of eight six-month campaigns with no overall strategic concept, much less strategic planning, to guide their conduct of military operations.[53] A recent work on the culture of the German military before and during the First World War has the following to say about the lack of any kind of strategic appreciation in the Kaiser's Reich:

> The structural and institutional barriers to strategic planning meant that military viewpoints were not coordinated with or subordinated to political-economic-legal calculations but were free to develop according to their own unexamined internal logic. The new challenges posed by the war... meant that no expert in any field had an obvious policy remedy. In wartime

---

[51] The traditional picture given by historians of the nature of German military planning and the Schlieffen Plan in the period before the First World War has been challenged by Terence Zuber, "The Schlieffen Plan Reconsidered," *War in History*, 1999, 6 (3). His work is not convincing.

[52] Nor did the Germans consider the tactical implications of using gas, since the winds in France blow from west to east most of the time (toward German lines). For the advantage that the Allies gained, see particularly Albert Palazzo, *Seeking Victory on the Western Front: The British Army and Chemical Warfare in World War I* (London, 2002).

[53] I am indebted to Dr. Bradley Meyer of the USMC's School of Advanced Warfighting at Quantico for this point.

military expertise seemed most apposite. But no degree of military expertise could have overcome Germany's strategic deficits.... The longer the war continued the more the power discrepancy tipped to Germany's disadvantage. Genuine strategic planning would have been forced to acknowledge that Germany was too small to become a world power, or to win a world war. For those who wanted to avoid this conclusion, purely military thinking was attractive. For the German military had developed its culture on the very premise of over achievement, of using quality, daring, and tactical proficiency to overcome strategic disadvantage. By acquiescing to German military culture, civilians could conveniently deny the discouraging truth of Germany's situation.[54]

At least the British did think in terms of a blockade of the Reich, but that was as much guided by the fact that at the onset of hostilities, the British Army lacked the means to win a major battle, as by any significant strategic planning. The Royal Navy's abominable staff work only resulted in the formulation of the concept of a distant blockade in the last years before the war.[55] That change resulted from the amateurish briefing that the navy gave to the cabinet in 1911 on its recommended approach to a war with Germany, which finally forced it to establish a staff college and alter its strategy. The cabinet was so appalled that it fired the First Lord of the Admiralty and sent Winston Churchill to fix the problem. Up to that point, the British had thought in terms of a close blockade with their battle fleet, which would have had disastrous consequences given the new technologies of mines and submarines. In late 1914 Winston Churchill came up with the one strategic alternative to the Western Front with his proposal for an attack on the Dardanelles.[56] But bad strategic and operational planning and cooperation resulted in

---

[54] Isabelle V. Hull, *Absolute Destruction, Military Culture and the Practices of War in Imperial Germany* (Ithaca, NY, 2005), p. 206.

[55] Many of the Royal Navy's senior officers preferred a close blockade, which with the danger of submarines and mines might well have resulted in a disastrous British defeat. For the strategic and operational arguments within the Royal Navy, see Nicholas A. Lambert, *Sir John Fisher's Naval Revolution* (Columbia, SC, 1999).

[56] In his note to the prime minister, Churchill warned there was no solution to the stalemate on the Western Front except for the continued slaughter of hundreds of thousands. The debate over Churchill's Dardanelles strategy has raged ever since. What is significant from our point of view is that Churchill proposed this approach precisely because he recognized that the only direct solution to the stalemate on the Western Front would be the slaughter of vast numbers of soldiers. The advantage of success at the Dardanelles would not have lain in the ability to ship arms to the Russians (the Western Allies had few surplus arms); rather, it would have lain in the pressure that success would have had on Austria in the Balkans, and that pressure in turn might have forced the Germans to postpone their great summer offensive in the east and devote those forces to rectifying a deteriorating situation in the Balkans.

the failure of the Royal Navy to open up the Straits without the help of ground forces. When those forces became available, flawed operational and tactical execution resulted in a series of missed opportunities. British and Dominion troops withdrew from Gallipoli in November–December 1915, the great amphibious effort to open the Straits a shambles. Well might Churchill write in his account of the First World War: "The terrible ifs accumulate."

The war then turned into a long, drawn out struggle of attrition. Here, British and French strategic and economic planning far surpassed that of the Germans. The control of the world's oceans, unchallenged throughout the war – allowed the Western Allies to draw from the great world economy, including much of the world's agricultural production, while Germany's economic situation grew increasingly grave.[57] Only once, at the end of May 1916, did the High Sea Fleet challenge the Royal Navy's control of the North Sea. It was able to claim a tactical victory, but British naval superiority remained intact, and the High Sea Fleet never again reached deep into the North Sea.[58] Meanwhile, in 1916, the *Materialschlacht* (battle of materiel) on the Somme underlined for the Germans how far behind they had fallen.

The so-called Hindenburg Plan, with the impossible demands for weapons and ammunition production that it put on the German economy, ended up breaking morale at home, with no chance of matching the swelling Allied economic superiority – a superiority that America's entrance into the war as a result of German miscalculations only served to increase. The revolutionary improvements the German Army was able to make in combined arms tactics in 1917 and 1918 could not make up for a complete absence of strategy and strategic planning in the conceptions of the Ludendorff-Hindenburg team.[59] In the end, German tactical developments only served to prolong the war and make the peace that much harder.[60]

---

[57] In this regard, see Avner Offer, *The First World War: An Agrarian Interpretation* (Oxford, 1989).

[58] Many historians do not even regard Jutland as a tactical victory: two German battle cruisers returned to harbor with their decks awash. For a discussion of how and why the British failed to achieve a greater success at Jutland, see Andrew Gordon, *The Rules of the Game, Jutland and British Naval Command* (London, 1996).

[59] David T. Zabecki, "Operational Art and the German 1918 Offensives," Ph.D. thesis, Cranfield University, 2004.

[60] For the improvements the Germans made to combined-arms tactics, see Timothy Lupfer, *The Dynamics of Doctrine: The Changes in German Tactical Doctrine During the First World War* (Leavenworth, 1981).

Strategic Planning: The Interwar Years and World War II

The Axis

Interestingly, while the military institutions of the various powers made extraordinary efforts to grapple with the lessons of World War I, the lessons about the crucial importance of strategic planning – not to mention strategy – largely seem to have gone by the boards.[61] Military institutions studied lessons from the last war in areas in which they had done well and ignored what suggested less than impressive military competence.[62] Not surprisingly, the Germans concentrated on improving the effectiveness of combined-arms tactics and marrying that improvement to the tank. But nowhere does the German military appear to have examined the strategic lessons of its defeat. In fact, almost to a man, they accepted the massive disinformation campaign waged by their government that Germany had not caused the war and that the collapse of 1918 had resulted from the fact that the Jews and communists had stabbed an undefeated Imperial Army in the back.[63]

There was one brief moment in the late 1920s and early 1930s when some coherent strategic planning took place. The minister of defense, retired General Wilhelm Groener, one of the most competent general staff officers during World War I, demanded that German exercises play not only the operational and tactical aspects of future war realistically but the harsh strategic fact that Germany in 1930 simply did not possess the means to defend itself.[64] Groener drew the conclusion that the Republic must accordingly cast its strategic and political plans in accordance with that reality. But that short window of realistic assessment – one that drew scant approval from most of Germany's military leaders – lasted only until 1931 when Groener lost his job in a coup engineered by senior generals, who wanted the officer corps to play an active role politically. It did, and the result was Adolf Hitler.

---

[61] For the effectiveness of military institutions in the interwar period, see Allan R. Millett and Williamson Murray, eds., *Military Effectiveness*, vol. 2, *The Interwar Period* (London, 1988).

[62] For a discussion of military innovation and military institutions during this period, see Williamson Murray and Allan R. Millett, eds., *Military Innovation in the Interwar Period* (Cambridge, 1996).

[63] See Holger H. Herwig, "Clio Deceived, Patriotic Self-Censorship in Germany after the Great War," *International Security*, Fall 1987.

[64] For a discussion of this, see Williamson Murray, "German Net Assessment in the Interwar Period," in *Calculations, Net Assessment and the Coming of the Second World War*, ed. by Williamson Murray and Allan R. Millett, eds. (New York, 1992).

Hitler's arrival in power started with a massive rearmament program that was far beyond Germany's economic means. The Führer's demands for massive rearmament clearly pointed toward another great European war. The generals were delighted with a blank check for rearmament, and few questioned the underlying assumptions of Nazi plans.[65] Only in 1938 did a senior military leader challenge Hitler's drive to war with military forces still largely unprepared. The then chief of the general staff, Ludwig Beck, raised serious strategic objections to the Führer's policies, but the pusillanimous surrender of Britain and France at Munich in September of that year ended whatever qualms might have existed among the other generals. Thereafter, they were content to follow in Hitler's wake – their extraordinary tactical and operational talents winning a number of devastating operational victories without solving the Third Reich's strategic quandary of a strategy that consistently refused to address the question of insufficient means. As Manstein suggested in a letter to Beck in August 1938, Hitler had been right so far in his political and strategic calculations. Thus, according to the man who supposedly possessed the brightest strategic mind among the German generals, there was no reason not to continue doubling the bet.[66]

In invading the Soviet Union, Hitler, with the full concurrence of his generals, made one of the most disastrous mistakes of the war. Strategic planning for the war against the Soviets rested on a series of superficial and unrealistic assumptions: 1) the invasion would catch and destroy the bulk of the Red Army in the frontier districts; 2) the Soviets possessed no substantial reserves; 3) the *Wehrmacht* would overcome the logistical problems posed by Russia's distances by will and expedients; 4) the weather would pose no significant difficulties; and 5) most disastrously of all, Stalin's tyranny would collapse in a matter of weeks because of its subhuman, Jewish nature.[67] One must emphasize that such assumptions were those of military planners and most of the leading generals as well as Hitler.[68]

---

[65] For a discussion of Germany's strategic position in the 1930s, see Williamson Murray, *The Change in the European Balance of Power, 1938–1939, The Path to Ruin* (Princeton, NJ, 1984), chap. 1.

[66] "Hitler has so far always estimated the political situation correctly." Telford Taylor, *Munich* (Garden City, NY, 1979), p. 695.

[67] For a fuller discussion of the nature of German strategic planning for Barbarossa, see Williamson Murray and Allan R. Millett, *A War To Be Won, Fighting the Second World War* (Cambridge, 2000), pp. 110–120.

[68] For these issues, see Horst Boog, Jürgen Förster, Joachim Hoffmann, Ernst Klink, Rolf-Dieter Müller, and Gerd R. Ueberschär, *Das Deutsche Reich und der Zweite Weltkrieg*, vol. 4, *Der Angriff auf die Sowjetunion* (Stuttgart, 1983).

Thus, there were no contingency plans should the invasion run into difficulties, nor did the Germans examine the economic consequences of the invasion.[69] Hitler provided the strategic rationale for Barbarossa early in the planning processes in July 1940. In a conversation with the commander-in-chief of the army, Field Marshal Walther von Brauchitsch, and the chief of the general staff, General Franz Halder, he suggested that the only factor keeping the British in the war was the hope that the Soviet Union and the United States would intervene. They in turn were delighted with Hitler's strategy of invading the Soviet Union, since it would keep the focus of German armament policy and war-making on the army.[70] Therefore, the obvious solution to British intransigence was to invade the Soviet Union!

The greatest strategic mistake of the war followed on the heels of the invasion of the Soviet Union. On 11 December 1941, Hitler declared war on the United States in response to the Japanese attack on Pearl Harbor. Again, the Führer had the full support of his generals and admirals.[71] In fact, the *Kriegsmarine* had argued in favor of such a decision throughout summer 1941. No discussions took place in the German high command, while Hitler announced his decision to thunderous applause in the Reichstag. He immediately authorized the *Kriegsmarine* to begin the unrestricted submarine warfare it had been so enthusiastically advocating off the American coast, but so ill-prepared was Admiral Karl Dönitz that he found it hard to place half a dozen boats off North America at the end of December 1941.[72] Most astonishingly, virtually no one in the senior levels of the Reich paid the slightest heed to America's economic strength – at least until 1943, and by then it was too late.

One can speak of strategic planning to an even lesser degree with respect to Germany's allies. Planning never seems to have existed in Mussolini's bizarre state.[73] Almost immediately upon the German

---

[69] The fact that the Germans were drawing nearly 20 percent of their raw materials from the Soviet Union might have given planners pause. It did not.

[70] Franz Halder, *The Halder War Diary, 1939–1942*, ed. by Charles Burdick and Hans-Adolf Jacobsen (Novato, CA, 1988), p. 242.

[71] For a discussion of the issues revolving around Hitler's decision to declare war on the United States, see Murray and Millett, *A War To Be Won*, pp. 135–136.

[72] For a discussion of the German Navy's strategic planning regarding the United States, see Holger Herwig, *The Politics of Frustration: The United States in German Naval Planning, 1889–1941* (Boston, 1976).

[73] For an examination of the systemic factors contributing to the military incompetencies of Mussolini's Fascist state, see MacGregor Knox's *Mussolini Unleashed, Fascist Italy's Last War* (Cambridge, 1984).

invasion of France and the Low Countries in May 1940, the Italians began preparing to declare war. Such efforts, however, did not include preparations to attack Malta, or to recall the Italian merchant marine (half of which was outside the Mediterranean). In effect, there was no serious analysis of Italy's ability to conduct a war beyond the defeat of France and especially of Italy's ability to sustain a serious war against Britain in the Mediterranean. Within a week of demobilizing the army's reserve divisions in October 1940, the Duce and his generals began planning for an invasion of Greece. Their plans took into account neither the coming winter nor the inability of Albania's logistical infrastructure to support additional Italian forces. Those forces in Albania were already outnumbered by the Greeks on the other side of the frontier. In effect, the Italians undertook the invasion of Greece to pay back Hitler and the Germans for their unilateral occupation of the Rumanian oil fields in August 1940.

The Japanese certainly possessed impressive military capabilities, but the deep rivalries between the army and the navy prevented even the semblance of coordinated, joint planning in operational matters. As for strategy, just like the Nazis, the Japanese embarked on war with the United States without the slightest willingness to grapple with the implication of America's enormous industrial capacity.[74] In fact, in order to persuade the army to support the navy in its desire for war in summer 1941, the navy staff agreed to reallocate 100,000 tons of its steel to the army. Such was the level of analysis that took place in Japan.[75] The absence of strategic planning led the Japanese Army to continue to emphasize the war in China to the exclusion of the battles in the Solomons through 1943.[76] Even in 1944, the bulk of the army remained in China, where it fought a fruitless campaign to subjugate the Chinese and bring them within Japan's "Co-Prosperity Sphere." In both Guadalcanal and New Guinea, the Americans and the Australians held despite the fact they were fighting both campaigns on a shoestring. When the Japanese woke up in 1943, the Americans had won naval and air superiority in the central and southern Pacific, and it was too late to move sufficient ground forces out

---

[74] The commander of the Japanese fleet, Admiral Yamamoto, did recognize America's industrial potential and argued against war. But his decision to attack Pearl Harbor ensured the United States would enter the war united in its desire to destroy the Japanese Empire.

[75] I am indebted to members of the military history department at Japan's National Institute for Defense Studies for this gem.

[76] For the battles in the Solomons around Guadalcanal, see Richard Frank, *Guadalcanal, The Definitive Account of the Landmark Battle* (New York, 1990).

to the Solomons. It was even too late to prepare adequate defenses for the Marshalls and the Marianas.

The lack of strategic planning showed particularly with regard to Japanese preparations to protect their merchant fleet, upon which their military outposts throughout the South Pacific and their whole economy depended. The Japanese made *no* preparations to defend that merchant shipping, and only faulty American torpedoes and weak skippers prevented a disaster in 1942.[77] But the disaster, though postponed, came in 1943. By 1944 the Japanese economy was in collapse, with the nation on the brink of starvation, most of its merchant fleet at the bottom of the sea, and the great American amphibious drives slicing toward the Marianas and Philippines.

Strategic Planning: The Allies

The British

British and American military institutions were unprepared for the conflict that broke on their nations – in Britain's case in September 1939 and America's case in December 1941. The British disasters in the early years of the war had little to do with a lack of strategic planning. In the 1920s and 1930s, under one of the more sophisticated administrative bureaucrats in history, Sir Maurice Hankey, the British created the first truly modern system for strategic planning.[78] Beginning with the chiefs of staff committee and several military subcommittees, which included intelligence and planners, the British funneled coherent military advice to the Committee of Imperial Defence – which included not only military members but also leading civilian administrators and ministers – and then to the Cabinet. This provided the means for the British to examine complex strategic questions in a coherent, systematic fashion.[79]

The problem in the mid-to-late 1930s was the fact that the Chamberlain government refused to provide a reasonable level of resources to its military organizations – especially considering the nature of the threats. Moreover, there was a tendency in the British bureaucracy, military as

---

[77] For the Japanese military's attitude toward protecting the nation's sea lines of communication, see Mark Parillo, *The Japanese Merchant Marine in World War II* (Annapolis, MD, 1993).

[78] Stephen Roskill, *Hankey, Man of Secrets*, vol. 2, 1919–1931, and vol. 3, 1931–1963 (Annapolis, MD, 1972, 1974).

[79] For a discussion of how the system worked, see Murray, *The Change in the European Balance of Power*, chap. 2.

well as civilian, to manipulate assessments to prevent coherent responses to the Nazi and Fascist threats and thus keep expenditures on rearmament to a minimum.[80] All that changed when Winston Churchill became prime minister on 10 May 1940.[81] From that point on, Churchill provided the drive that made Britain's system of strategic planning function. His government was willing to make hard strategic choices in the face of the overwhelming military and economic power the Third Reich presented in summer 1940.[82] For over a year the British stood alone with only aid from the United States to keep them in the fight. Britain confronted a number of terrifying challenges throughout that period. To begin with, there was the *Luftwaffe* and its day and night offensive against the British Isles.[83] Second, the Royal Navy had taken terrible losses in destroyers as a result of the Norwegian and Dunkirk operations. In virtually every theater, the British military started from scratch and on a weak economic base to boot. Both from historic experience and from the lesson of fighting the Germans on the continent, British planners chose the Mediterranean as the line of least resistance upon which to attack the Axis. In addition, Churchill supported a massive bombing offensive against German cities, although his expectations were less than those of the Royal Air Force (RAF).

The German invasion of the Soviet Union helped the British psychologically. They were no longer alone in the war. But the desperate straits in which the Soviets soon found themselves forced the British to send extensive military aid that their own forces desperately needed. The diversion of aircraft to the Soviets in late summer contributed to the disaster in Malaya. In the long run the entrance of the United States into the conflict represented a Godsend. But in the short run it also contributed to the pressure on Britain. The flow of Lend–Lease slowed, as U.S. forces, desperately mobilizing, absorbed much of America's production. Moreover, the U.S.

---

[80] For the extent of these problems, see ibid., chap. 2.

[81] As one of his military assistants characterized the change: "The days of mere 'coordination' were out for good and all.... we were now going to get direction, leadership, action with a snap to it." General Sir Leslie Hollis, *One Marine's Tale* (London, 1956), p. 66.

[82] The myth has it that Churchill bullied his generals and admirals into making decisions with which they disagreed. In fact, Churchill never overruled his commanders. For the relationship between Churchill and his military, see Eliot Cohen, *Supreme Command, Soldiers, Statesmen, and Leadership in Wartime* (New York, 2002).

[83] In fact, the German night bomber offensive might have posed the most serious threat had not a young British scientist, R.V. Jones, stumbled on the fact that the Germans possessed blind-bombing capabilities. See R.V. Jones, *The Wizard War, British Scientific Intelligence, 1939–1945* (New York, 1978), pp. 92–103, 127–145.

Navy was unprepared to defend the convoys plying the east coast of the United States, while its commanders proved unwilling to learn from the British. The heavy losses that ensued added to the burden British planners confronted in addressing the strategic problems raised by a global conflict.

In summer 1942 the Anglo–American Allies took the crucial decision to land in North Africa, a decision that reflected British arguments about the centrality of the Mediterranean war. To the British the weaknesses of the Italians as well as their own weaknesses on the ground in comparison to the Germans made the Mediterranean a natural choice. Moreover, British planners viewed opening the Mediterranean to Allied convoys as essential to easing the burden on global shipping commitments. In retrospect, the British were correct. In view of their military and economic weaknesses, they could not gamble on fighting the Germans on the Continent until there was virtually no chance of failure.[84] By forcing Allied strategic planning to address the Mediterranean first, the British achieved a number of advantages. It allowed the Anglo–American powers to fight the Germans in North Africa, where the Axis logistical system was incapable of fighting a sustained battle. It provided time to win the Battle of the Atlantic. Of crucial importance, it also provided a raw and untried American military another year to learn the business of war against first-class opponents. With the conquest of Sicily, the Allies saved somewhere between six and eight million tons of shipping, which was of immense importance to powers whose military forces were fighting across the globe.

Nevertheless, the war in the Mediterranean represented only a small portion of British commitments and the necessity for strategic planning. Throughout 1942 and 1943, the Royal Navy carried the bulk of defending Atlantic convoys against German U-boats. At the same time, the Special Operations Executive engaged in a massive intelligence operation and in sabotage campaigns to support resistance movements throughout Western Europe. Through late 1943, the RAF's Bomber Command carried the bulk of the air campaign, which finally brought the war home to the Germans. All of these diverse efforts required exquisite strategic planning that coordinated and allocated resources among these and many other diverse endeavors.

If the British won the first arguments over Allied strategy, the Americans were fast learners. Strategic planning for the alliance had, by late

---

[84] To a considerable extent, this explains Montgomery's caution in his use of the British Army in 1944 and 1945.

1943, become increasingly influenced by American strategic aims and desires. That fact reflected two factors: first, as American power grew, British power and influence declined. And, second, the Americans were fast becoming adept at strategic planning for both the Pacific and the European wars. Thus, it is not surprising that their vision would increasingly come to dominate inter-Allied discussions.

The Americans

The American military began strategic planning as a serious exercise in the 1920s. There was some cooperation between the services in terms of bureaucratic niceties, but they looked in different directions and came up with differing conceptions.[85] The navy and marine corps looked to the Pacific; the army either looked toward Europe or simply focused on the defense of North America. There was a joint board where the navy and army met to talk about planning for a number of scenarios, which were color-coded depending on the potential opponent. Perhaps because it was so badly funded and a potential European enemy seemed so unrealistic – at least until the late 1930s, army strategic planning remained to a considerable extent unfocused and unrealistic.[86] The navy's situation was somewhat better. Not only was it better funded throughout the interwar period, but its rearmament programs began in 1938 two years before those of the army. Moreover, whatever the attitudes of civilians in charge of the American government, there was a real and palpable Japanese threat in the Pacific throughout the 1920s and early 1930s. The Imperial Japanese Navy represented a first-class force, while America's colonial possessions – particularly the Philippines – were vulnerable to a Japanese thrust.[87]

Not surprisingly, from the early 1920s on, the navy focused its war games, exercises, and strategic planning on dealing with that threat. By the mid-1920s, naval planners at Newport had gained significant insights into the potential for carrier operations but had also recognized there was

---

[85] For a clear discussion of American military planning before the Second World War – army as well as navy – see Mark A. Stoler, *Allies and Adversaries, The Joint Chiefs of Staff, the Grand Alliance, and U.S. Strategy in World War II* (Chapel Hill, NC, 2000), chap. 1.

[86] To a considerable extent this reflected the split among the combat branches in the army. The army air corps focused on strategic bombing, the coastal artillery on coastal defense; and the infantry and cavalry on a repetition of the war in Europe they had fought in 1917–1918.

[87] This vulnerability did lead some within the army to suggest that the United States should give up the Philippines.

not going to be a great Mahanian battle in the seas off Japan.[88] Instead, in a war with the Japanese, the Americans were going to have to seize bases from which to project naval power farther across the Pacific. Consequently, logistics would represent a key component in any American strategy. The consequences of such thinking were immense: the emphasis on carrier war, amphibious operations, and eventually underway replenishment would lead to the development of revolutionary capabilities by the end of the interwar period.

Nevertheless, the war that came surprised planners in both navy and army. The collapse of France in spring 1940 undermined a number of assumptions American planners held: There would be no base on the continent from which to fight the Germans; the *Wehrmacht* clearly represented a greater threat than its predecessor, the Imperial German Army; and America now confronted the possibility of a two-front war against two different kinds of opponents – the Germans, a continental power, and the Japanese, a maritime power. As a worsening international situation broke on American planners, they had to make significant changes in how they thought about a future war. In November 1940 the chief of naval operations, Admiral Harold Stark, set out in clear fashion the strategic framework within which the United States would fight the coming war.

Stark's "Plan Dog" memorandum – described by Louis Morton, one of the leading American historians of the war, as "perhaps the most important single document in the development of World War II strategy" – focused on the defeat of Germany as the essential target for American strategy. In the largest sense Stark recognized that the issue was not just that Germany represented the greatest threat, but that the restoration of a balance of power in Europe was essential to America's long-term strategic interests.[89] Nevertheless, throughout summer 1940, Roosevelt confronted serious opposition from his military advisers and planners to providing American materiel to the hard-pressed British. In 1941 they were no happier to see the president push for major aid to the Soviet Union after the beginning of Barbarossa.

Stark's view certainly became the heart of the army's position in December 1941. Nevertheless, as army planners attempted to pursue a Germany-first strategy, they discovered that the American public, furious

---

[88] For the development of carrier warfare and the influence of the war games at the Naval War College at Newport, see particularly Thomas C. Hone, Norman Friedman, and Mark D. Mandeles, *American and British Aircraft Development, 1919–1941* (Annapolis, MD, 1999).
[89] Stoler, *Allies and Adversaries*, pp. 29–37.

over Pearl Harbor, was demanding that the U.S. military wreak vengeance on the Japanese. Moreover, the new chief of naval operations, Admiral Ernest J. King, was taking a stand directly in contradiction to that taken by Stark. The Pacific was the only theater that mattered to King. As Dwight Eisenhower, at the time Marshall's chief planner, noted despairingly in his diary: "We've got to go to Europe and fight, and we've got to stop wasting resources around the world – and still worse – wasting time."[90] For Marshall and Eisenhower, the obvious strategic direction would be a landing on the European Continent as soon as possible with a strategic defensive in the Pacific. But in the world of political reality, such an approach was not in the cards. The draw to the Pacific appeared almost irresistible. Midway in 1942 at least halted Japanese momentum, but the threat posed by Japanese possession of Guadalcanal and its new air base aimed at dominating the Solomons forced King to commit the 1st Marine Division to seize and then defend that island. Meanwhile, Douglas MacArthur's scratch force of army units and Australians battled the Japanese over the Owen Stanley range of mountains to the north of Port Moresby in New Guinea.

Marshall and his army planners seemed caught between the demands of the Pacific and the British, whose intransigence blocked the concept of a landing on the coast of northwest Europe in 1942. They appeared no more enthusiastic about such an endeavor in 1943. For a brief moment Marshall considered moving the American emphasis to the Pacific. However, in summer 1942 President Franklin Roosevelt stepped in: there *would be* American operations in Europe, but that effort would be a combined effort with the British to seize French North Africa and attack Rommel from the west. In overruling his military advisers, Roosevelt made one of the most important decisions of the Second World War. In retrospect, it was the correct one: it committed American forces to a theater where the Germans were at a severe disadvantage geographically and logistically. The clearing of the Mediterranean in 1943 would provide the Anglo–American powers with considerable relief in terms of pressures on their shipping. Moreover, the additional year would provide the U.S. Army with additional time to train, and allow the U.S. Army Air Forces time to defeat the *Luftwaffe* in the skies over Europe.[91]

In retrospect, American strategy could not have worked out better. It resulted in a balance between the theaters, so that the war in the

---

[90] Ibid., p. 71.
[91] For a discussion of how the Allies won air superiority in 1943 and 1944, see Williamson Murray, *Luftwaffe* (Baltimore, MD, 1985).

Pacific ended almost concurrently with the war in the European Theater of Operations. The challenges to strategic planning, however, almost defy imagination. American planners had to deal with the tugs of three different theaters – the Pacific, the Mediterranean, and the European; they confronted a great naval and amphibious war in the former; in the latter they confronted the ferocious skills of the *Wehrmacht*; they had to win the Battle of the Atlantic in order to deploy American forces to Europe; they had to plan for, and wage, a great strategic bombing offensive against both Germany and Japan; and while American industry produced prodigious amounts of war materiel, much of its weapons production went to supporting America's allies, Britain and the Soviet Union. In coordinating this massive effort, what is surprising is how few mistakes were made. Undoubtedly, the decision for an 89 division army was a mistake – a decision that placed great pressure on the divisions engaged in constant combat in Europe, from their landing on the Continent to the end of hostilities. However, outside of that decision, which reflected the huge pressures on American resources, there were no other major errors.

While the American planning effort drew extensively from prewar efforts and thinking in the services – the creation of what is today the Industrial College of the Armed Forces is a particularly good example – what made it so exceptional was the willingness of the American military to draw on civilian expertise.[92] Thus, major business figures found themselves suddenly brigadier or even major generals in charge of complex supply, training, or mobilization commands. Moreover, the two years of relative peacetime mobilization between September 1939 and December 1941 allowed senior military leaders to gain a sense of the multiple tasks and conflicting and competing priorities they would confront with hostilities.

The extent of the challenges that the American services confronted in strategic planning is suggested not by only the variety of demanding campaigns they had to fight, but the fact that most of these theater-level campaigns involved decision making at the operational level – which had not been done by American officers since the Civil War. In retrospect, the Americans proved to be fast learners, particularly in the Pacific, where the distances and the nature of amphibious and maritime operations demanded interservice cooperation. Many of these campaigns also

---

[92] Roosevelt himself led the push to emphasize America's enormous productive strengths in the conduct of the war. As early as 1938 at the height of the Munich crisis, he pushed for major increases in aircraft production, although not fully understanding the support structure needed in bases, training, and maintenance.

represented joint and combined efforts, which depended on the integration of service efforts as well as close cooperation with allies, again a facet of warfare with which the American military had had little experience.[93] But those tasks Dwight Eisenhower was to master in the European Theater of Operations.

Conclusion

In looking at history, it is astonishing to see how little a role serious strategic planning has played in great wars, which all too often have been the mark of Western civilization. In fact, it would appear that for at least three centuries, strategic planning was the unique preserve of the maritime powers, first Britain and then the United States. The question then arises as to why this should be. The connection between maritime power and strategic planning would seem to go back to Thucydides' account of the Peloponnesian War. In contrasting speeches, the great historian has the Spartan ephor Sthenelaidas declaring for war simply on the basis of Spartan military superiority and Athenian bad behavior. "And let no one try to tell us that when we are being attacked, we should sit down and discuss matters."[94] Sthenelaidas' approach sums up the level of strategic planning that most nations and their military organizations have taken throughout history.

On the other hand, Pericles, the Athenian politician and general, laid out a detailed strategic argument of why Athens should risk war against the Peloponnesians, as well as the sort of war that would best address the quandary that confronts a sea power in fighting a land power. "In a single battle the Peloponnesians and their allies could stand up to all the rest of Hellas, but they cannot fight a war against a power unlike themselves, so long as they have no central deliberative authority..."[95] The difference between the sense of strategic ambiguity and complexity in Pericles' speech and Sthenelaidas' simple-minded belief that all the

---

[93] In World War I, the United States had been an associated rather than an Allied power, while only in fall 1918 were there sufficient American troops to play a major role in the Allied offensives that defeated the Germans.

[94] Admittedly, the Spartan king does give a clear-headed strategic analysis of why Sparta should put off a war until the Peloponnesians possessed the resources in ships and money to fight the Athenians at sea. The Spartan assembly rejected his advice. For the speeches before the Spartan assembly, see Thucydides, *The Peloponnesian War*, trans. by Rex Warner (New York, 1954), p. 86.

[95] Thucydides, *The Peloponnesian War*, p. 120.

Spartans had to do was to show up and that the ensuing and inevitable battle would end the war immediately underlines the fundamental issue that land powers are where the wars are, while maritime powers have to get to the war – a task that invariably requires long-term planning.

In the largest sense, maritime powers cannot think in terms of decisive maritime battles, because victory at sea at best translates into control of the sea, which may not even prove permanent. Victories at sea can provide navies with the ability to project military power onto shore or the ability to deny economic sustenance to Continental powers. Thus, maritime powers have had to think about war in a sustained, long-term framework, because naval battles, whether at the start of a war or at some other time, serve only to open up possibilities for further lines of advance. They cannot pursue war with the aim of fighting a short, decisive battle, in which defeat in battle would lead to the enemy's collapse. Napoleon's devastating victory at Austerlitz in December 1805 led the Austrians to sue for an armistice in a matter of days; his victory at Jena-Auerstädt in September the following year led to the collapse of the Prussian state in a matter of weeks. But no matter how decisive Nelson's victory in 1805 at the Battle of Trafalgar might have been in maritime terms, the French fought on for another ten years.

The fact that maritime battles have been thought of in terms of future operations on land has resulted in a very different mindset from that of the statesmen and generals of Continental powers. War from the British point of view had to involve sustained military action at sea and on land. And that in turn, demanded long-term planning, the division and allocation of resources among competing conceptions and lines of approach, the search for and utilization of allies and their military power, and the mobilization of Britain's financial and economic resources.[96]

From the early eighteenth century, the British confronted and, for the most part, solved difficult choices regarding the allocation of military and economic resources. They could not entirely abandon war on the Continent; one of the key components of their strategic approach was that no single European power should be allowed to dominate the Continent. Thus, they confronted the question of how much was enough to keep their allies in the war not only in terms of financial resources, but also in

---

[96] A major British advantage was that they had developed the first truly modern system of borrowing on the national wealth. See John Brewer, *The Sinews of Power, War, Money, and the English State, 1688–1788* (New York, 1989), and D. W. Jones, *War and Economy in the Age of William III and Marlborough* (Oxford, 1988).

terms of commitment of ground forces from the United Kingdom. They also confronted the possibility that the French might actually launch an invasion of the British Isles, a threat usually more pointed directly at Ireland than at England or Scotland.[97] Thus, the British had to deal with both these strategic commitments as well as the problems involved in projecting their military power to places as far away as India. All of this took sophisticated planning and conceptualization because it involved both land and naval power.

Nevertheless, at least in three of the great wars of the eighteenth century – the War of Austrian Succession, The Seven Years' War, and the War of American Independence – the British were able to get away with war on the cheap, at least as far as Continental commitments were concerned. Luckily for British strategic planners for most of the eighteenth century, Britain did not confront a formidable opponent on the Continent, with the exception of the War of Spanish Succession. But beginning in 1792, that strategic approach broke down. The French Revolutionaries were able to put sufficiently effective forces into the field to overwhelm the great coalitions that British financial support and diplomacy stitched together, while there were no longer French colonies worth conquering. Britain then confronted the necessity of putting major ground forces on the Continent – an operational commitment its statesmen and army were not able to master for more than a decade, until the Duke of Wellington seized on the advantages of Portugal and far western Spain to confront the French.

The strategic situation darkened when Napoleon took over the French government because there was now a military genius, perhaps the greatest in history, in control of a revolutionary France fully able to mobilize its economic and popular resources. The emperor's victories between 1805 and 1807 created a situation where no amount of manipulation or control of the global oceans could directly address the Continental threat. Only a change in how the other European powers addressed the threat beginning in 1809 opened up the Continent to British strategic planning. As Clausewitz suggests, "[n]ot until [European] statesmen had at least perceived the nature of the forces that had emerged in France, and had grasped that new political conditions now obtained in France, could they foresee the broad effect all this would have on war..."[98]

---

[97] William III, the Dutch Stadtholder, in 1688 invaded England with the support of the Dutch fleet and army in November and replaced the Catholic James II on the British throne. Since he enjoyed widespread support among the Protestants, the great majority in Scotland and England, he was welcomed with open arms.
[98] Clausewitz, *On War*, p. 609.

The British were to find themselves in a similar situation in the twentieth century in both world wars against the Germans. In the first they were able to devote considerable resources to attacking Germany's colonies around the world and then drive the Turks out of the Middle East; but that was not enough because there remained the problem of handling German military and economic power. As Michael Howard has suggested about the nature of the German problem for British strategists, "[i]t was... precisely the failure of German power to find an outlet and its consequent concentration in Europe, its lack of any significant possessions overseas, that made it so particularly menacing to the sprawling British Empire and which make so misleading all arguments about 'traditional' British strategy drawn from earlier conflicts against the Spanish and French Empires, with all the colonial hostages they had to offer fortune and the Royal Navy."[99]

As a result, the British had to commit major ground forces to the Continent to address the problems involved in defeating the Imperial German Army in the field. And given the weaknesses of their own forces, it would take four long years and involve the terrible killing battles of the Somme, Passchendaele, and the 1918 offensives. In the Second World War, the British again confronted the fact that the strategic problem raised by Germany could only be addressed by ground war on the Continent. To a certain extent, the catastrophe of 1940 allowed them to follow a more traditional strategy of attacking on the perimeter, at least until Overlord in June 1944. But as suggested earlier, the war in the Pacific and British commitments to the Mediterranean and to the strategic bombing of Germany placed an almost intolerable burden on the British economy and people. They mastered these commitments, but only by the most careful strategic planning, which in the early war years mitigated and addressed the problems raised by their military weaknesses. In the latter portions of the war, strategic planning – and balancing – allowed Britain to box "well above its weight class."[100]

In many ways, America's strategic position has resembled that of Britain. However, for the early part of its history the removal of the United States from the rest of the world by two great oceans allowed it to remain aloof from the wars and conflicts that beset Europe and Asia. The American Civil War was the great exception. The extent of the South's commitment to its dream of a great slave-holding, independent Confederate States of America forced the Union to develop not only a maritime but

---

[99] Michael Howard, *The Continental Commitment* (London, 1972), p. 32.
[100] A phrase still in use among British politicians and defense correspondents.

also a continental strategy in pursuit of total victory. The Union won because it was able to put into action complex operational movements, supported by economic and political mobilization back home.

What is truly astonishing is that with almost no apparent effort in the Second World War, the Americans were able to replicate British strategic planning on a far larger scale than the British had ever managed. In effect, the United States fought and won a two-front war over global distances, while supporting its allies with massive economic aid, an effort that also required a massive logistical effort. There were, of course, mistaken assumptions in American planning, but perhaps even more so than operational planning, strategic planning requires the ability and the willingness to adapt to the actual conditions a nation confronts. Admittedly, the Americans ran some extraordinary risks, particularly in the Pacific. The Guadalcanal operation that began in August 1942 ran on a shoestring, one that the catastrophic defeat at Savo Island made even tighter. But the Japanese, instead of striking hard, which would have overwhelmed the American defenders, launched incremental attacks, each of which failed by a narrow margin. The Pacific theater undoubtedly received more attention than the strategic planners might have wished in 1942 and 1943, but they bowed to the political necessity of popular opinion in the United States. Similarly, they had to bow to Roosevelt's insistence that American troops be committed to the fight in Europe in 1942, even if it meant a Mediterranean operation. To paraphrase one commentator: the making of strategy is like making sausage – inevitably messy. But in the end the American strategic approach, tempered early in the war by British wisdom, achieved the extraordinary success of bringing about the defeat of the Third Reich and Imperial Japan within three months of each other.

There are a number of generalizations that one might make about strategic planning from the earlier discussions. The most obvious is that strategic planners must have a clear idea from their masters of why the war is being fought. To repeat Clausewitz: "No one starts a war – or rather, no one in his senses ought to do so – without first being clear in his mind what he intends to achieve by that war and how he intends to conduct it."[101] The conduct of the war and the ends sought demand a realistic appraisal of means at hand and the difficulty of the task. In particular, this aspect of strategic planning demands that planners be willing to challenge the basic operational as well as strategic assumptions

[101] Clausewitz, *On War*, p. 579.

underlying the rationale for war. The record in this regard is dismal; in fact, the historical landscape of the twentieth century is littered with the faulty assumption that undergirded decisions to go to war in 1914, 1939, not to mention Indo-China in 1947, Vietnam 1964–1965, and the Middle East in 1967.

The challenging of assumptions is only a starting point for strategic planners. Obviously, they must expend considerable effort in balancing the means–ends equation. But equally, they must involve themselves in prioritizing and focusing the emphasis in strategic and operational choices on what really matters. Here again, to paraphrase Clausewitz: there is a subtle, but crucial warning that while strategy is a relatively simple matter, in war the simplest thing is difficult. As Allan Millett has suggested about America's Pacific strategy, a child could have outlined the two most effective routes to reach the Japanese Home Islands.[102] But as with operational planning, the difficulties in strategic planning lie in the details. The translation of military forces and resources into what became a two-pronged drive toward Japan represented strategic planning at its best. That there were two drives, when one would have done the job as well without the attendant risks of splitting U.S. forces, underlines the fact that politics, interpersonal relations, and interservice rivalries will inevitably intrude into the world of the strategic planner.

Strategic planners, even more so than operational planners, must also consider the enemy as he is rather than as they would like him to be. This is particularly difficult to do because inevitably human prejudices and stereotypes influence even the best informed. Yet, the enemy, his culture, his history, the nature of his government, his putative war aims, are essential elements in strategic planning. Without some coherent ability to understand the opponent the "other," strategic planning becomes a futile exercise that can have disastrous consequences. The whole strategic planning that framed German operational moves in 1941 resulted in national catastrophe and the destruction of the Third Reich. Similarly, the faulty assumptions of American strategic planners at the highest levels about the nature of their North Vietnamese opponent made U.S. defeat in the Vietnam War inevitable.

There is one more crucial element in the world of the strategic planner. Even more so than the operational planner, he or she must live in the future. The great Allied victories of 1944 in Europe and the Pacific were the result of the thoughtful calculations of strategic planners who in 1942

[102] Conversation with Allan Millett, Columbus, Ohio, April 2004.

made decisions based on how they thought military operations and the strategic situation would evolve over the coming years. Those calculations and decisions reflected estimates that had to be flexible enough to take into account major shifts in requirements they could not foresee. Only so could the great landing craft shortages of late 1943 and early 1944 be overcome. The Germans in two world wars proved incapable of thinking in terms of the future; hence, their decisions consistently focused on the short term and the immediate operational advantage. On the strategic level, thinking in future time is to a considerable extent a matter of intuition; one can only speak of what the Germans called *Fingerspitzengefühl* – the intuition that comes from a knowledge of history, culture, and languages. For senior commanders and their staffs, confronting strategic planning is a matter of how well they have educated themselves over the course of their careers – not a matter of how well they have been trained. In the final analysis, strategic planning is an art, not a science.

Additional Readings

Since I completed this chapter, a number of important works have appeared. In particular, on the planning for World War I, see Holger H. Herwig, *The Marne, The Opening of World War I and the Battle that Changed the World* (New York, 2009). For the most recent examination of British strategy, see H.P. Harris, *Douglas Haig and the First World War* (Cambridge, 2008). On the German 1918 offensive, David T. Zabecki's outstanding dissertation has been published and is now available in paperback: *The German 1918 Offensive: A Case Study in the Operational Level of War* (London, 2009). For British strategy between 1937 and 1945, see Williamson Murray, "British Grand Strategy, 1931–1942," in Williamson Murray, Richard Hart Sinnreich, and Jim Lacey, eds., *The Shaping of Grand Strategy: Policy, Diplomacy, and War* (Cambridge, 2010).

7

Thoughts on Red Teaming

In the twenty-first century, the United States and its allies will confront a number of disparate challenges. Enemies will prove adaptive and effective in preparing their military forces to attack, disturb, disorient, and prevent the projection of U.S. military power onto their territory and to deny the United States political and strategic victory. Moreover, they will undoubtedly fight within diverse strategic, operational, and tactical frameworks – frameworks largely determined by their societal, religious, and political cultures, all differing from those of the United States and its allies.[1] America's potential opponents are already preparing to fight the U.S. military and, over the past decade, they have had two spectacular demonstrations of what its forces can do. The great difficulty for the armed forces of the United States lies in the fact that at present – and for the foreseeable future – they confront enormous ambiguity and uncertainty about their potential enemies; the conditions under which war will occur; as well as the staying power, military capabilities, and operational courses potential opponents might employ.

The question, then, that confronts the U.S. military is how to prepare forces to fight against opponents, the nature and aims of which are at

---

[1] The Vietnam War should be a constant reminder to U.S. military planners in the twenty-first century that military superiority at the tactical level does not necessarily translate into political and strategic victory.

This chapter was written for Dr. James Miller, when he was with Hicks and Associates and was Deputy Undersecretary of Defense for Advanced Systems and Concepts, to examine how the Pentagon might better incorporate red teaming into its examination of present and future capabilities.

present unclear.[2] However much one might be tempted to prepare those forces on the basis of capabilities, such an approach will inevitably lead to mirror imaging. Thus, it would seem that red teaming U.S. forces and concepts from the highest to lowest levels represents the best alternative to learning on the battlefield, where military organizations learn by killing their own. This paper will use the term red teaming to mean the willingness to establish independent teams or other means to challenge the assumptions and preconceptions that military organizations often make.[3] Such teams demand independent, perceptive officers and players unhindered by the strictures and mindsets of service cultures and bureaucratic restraints. War games, exercises, and maneuvers that prepare military forces for the future must involve red forces and red teams that can utilize asymmetric approaches, operational concepts, and tactics to challenge the plans and concepts of America's military. If they do not, they simply become one more method of validating the status quo, and historically the price paid for such an approach has been in blood and national treasure.

What might history suggest about red teaming? In the broadest sense, the past suggests that red teaming has been a major factor in the preparation of effective military forces for war. Where there has been a willingness and ability to imbue red teams with honest, realistic abilities to challenge the capabilities and assumptions of national military power in exercises and experiments, national military forces have invariably been better prepared to handle the terrible challenges of combat. Where red teaming either did not exist or was carefully managed to ensure that it did not challenge the status quo, the results were almost uniformly dismal. Moreover, red teaming, where used honestly, has invariably been a means to improve the processes of transformation and change.

A close look at the history of military institutions and their performance at the tactical, operational, and strategic levels suggests that red teaming has been a crucial component in, and a barometer of, military

---

[2] For the nature of that strategic environment see Williamson Murray: "The Emerging Strategic Environment: An Historian's Thoughts," *Strategic Review*, Winter 1999. See also MacGregor Knox, "What History Can Tell Us About the 'New Strategic Environment,'" in Williamson Murray, ed., *The Mershon American Defense Annual, 1995–1996* (Washington, DC, 1996).

[3] One of the dangers for the creation of effective military forces in a time of prolonged peace (e.g., the periods 1815–1854 and 1874–1914 for Europe's continental armies) is the ease with which military institutions can slide into comfortable assumptions about the harsh, unforgiving realities of combat. For the sad results of the prolonged period of maritime peace between 1815–1914 on the Royal Navy and its culture, see Andrew Gordon, *The Rules of the Game: Jutland and British Naval Command* (London, 1996).

effectiveness. Through service in a number of different roles, red teaming has extended and improved the concepts, doctrinal framework, and understanding of the military organizations, where it has been in use. Therein lies the rub because, for the most part, military institutions have disregarded red teaming in their preparation for war. As a result, military institutions that have fought modern wars have, for the most part, gone into combat unprepared and incapable of adapting to the harsh realities of the battlefield.[4] Only after terrible losses have most finally recognized that their vision of future war was fundamentally flawed.[5]

The purpose of this chapter is not to present a history of red teaming, but rather to examine the issues and areas of red teaming which have made contributions to military effectiveness.[6] One might divide these areas into six parts: 1) the instruction and evaluation of officers; 2) the examination of war plans; 3) the testing of doctrinal and combat conceptions through experiments and exercises; 4) the development of an understanding of the enemy as he is, rather than as we would like him to be; 5) red teaming's contribution to the training of troops; and, finally, 6) its potential role in examining the assumptions of policy makers and strategy.[7]

Across the areas in which red teaming has been employed, there are several prerequisites for it to be effective. The first is an absolute requirement

---

[4] One senior retired U.S. Army general commented on a study of the effectiveness of military institutions in the following terms: "Thus, in the spheres of operations and tactics, where military competence would seem to be a nation's rightful due, the twenty-one [reports by authors in this study of military effectiveness] suggest for the most part less than general military competence and sometimes abysmal general incompetence. One can doubt whether any other profession during the same periods would have received such poor ratings by similarly competent outside observers.... [I]t is clear that operational and tactical performance is a virtue to be sought by those who are responsible for military forces. Yet from these auditors' reports, most national forces failed to achieve a high performance in either category." Lieutenant General John A. Cushman, U.S. Army retired, "Challenge and Response at the Operational and Tactical Levels, 1914–1945," in Allan R. Millett and Williamson Murray, eds., *Military Effectiveness*, vol. 3, *The Second World War* (London, 1988), p. 322.

[5] As Michael Howard has suggested on a number of occasions, the basic issue for military institutions is not to get the next war absolutely right, but rather to get it less wrong than their opponents, and thereafter to adapt more quickly to the actual conditions they encounter.

[6] For an examination of the history of red teaming, see Williamson Murray, "Red Teaming: Its Contribution to Past Military Effectiveness," DART Working Paper #02-2, Hicks and Associates, Inc., September 2002.

[7] One of the surprising aspects of military history over the past half century is the absence of serious studies, to include articles, on the impact, or lack thereof, that serious red teaming has had on military effectiveness.

for free play and honest, vibrant interaction. Red teams must have the opportunity to utilize their capabilities to maximum effect. The corollary is the need for intellectual honesty in evaluations of the interactions between red and blue in exercises and experiments and the examination of plans. The second facet of successful red teaming is the requirement that red teams consist of competent, imaginative officers and other participants, capable of thinking outside the box. Members of red teams must also understand the culture not only of the enemy's military, but also of his society. Without an intellectual basis that understands the possibility that the enemy will think and act differently than one's own side, red teaming is likely to fail. The third prerequisite is perhaps the most obvious, but it has not always been met: those who evaluate and receive reports of war games, exercises, and other forums where red teaming plays a significant role must actually pay attention to the results.[8] Finally, red teaming must extend beyond the tactical and operational levels to the strategic level to help leaders avoid winning battles and losing wars.

In the largest sense, history suggests that the commitment to serious red teaming is a general indication of the health of military organizations. Where red teaming exists in active and vigorous forms, military organizations have almost invariably outperformed their opponents. Moreover, the red teaming of concepts and doctrine in peacetime – in other words, the willingness to challenge assumptions – has invariably better prepared military organizations to adapt to the actual conditions of war. Red teaming has allowed them to alter their perceptions of what future war will look like to match reality – instead of attempting to make the realities of the battlefield fit preconceived notions.[9] It is the latter approach, for example, that resulted in Field Marshal Sir Douglas Haig's ill-thought out and disastrously costly offensive in Flanders in 1917.[10]

---

[8] This is particularly difficult to do when policy makers and military leaders believe their assumptions are correct and when such individuals do not possess the intellectual integrity to allow those assumptions to be challenged.

[9] Along these lines, there are two works that underline the cost to military institutions and their nations that have followed the latter path. See Timothy Travers, *The Killing Ground, The British Army, the Western Front, and the Emergence of Modern War, 1900–1918* (London, 1987); and Andrew Krepenevich, *The Army in Vietnam* (Baltimore, MD, 1986).

[10] For the resulting battle, see particularly Robin Prior and Trevor Wilson, *Passchendaele, The Untold Story* (New Haven, CT, 1996). See also Leon Wolff, *In Flanders, The 1917 Campaign* (New York, 1958) and Peter H. Liddle, ed., *Passchendaele in Perspective, The Third Battle of Ypres* (London, 1997).

Above all, red teaming must not involve an attempt to "validate" existing doctrine or weapons systems. Throughout the period 1920–1939, the French validated their weapons systems and doctrine – encompassed in the slogan "the methodical battle" – in innumerable exercises and experiments. They found nothing wrong with either.[11] But as the premier historian of the French Army has pointed out: "[t]he methodical battle was appropriate only if the enemy fought in a similar fashion, but the concept [of Blitzkrieg) was as different from the methodical battle as an envelopment is from a frontal assault."[12] The result was that, even though on the banks of the Meuse on 13 May 1940, the French got the infantry-artillery battle, for which they had prepared, and the Germans had to conduct one of the most difficult of all military operations – an opposed river crossing – the French defenders were incapable of matching the speed and ruthlessness with which German infantry moved. Validation instead of serious red teaming by the French military throughout the interwar period had laid the seeds for disaster.[13]

Red Teaming in the Instruction and Evaluation of Officers

Red teaming originated in the early decades of the nineteenth century. It was the child of the Prussian general staff's educational and organizational system. Prussia's military reformers created the system in response to the catastrophe of the double battle of Jena/Auerstadt, in which Napoleon's Grand Army crushed the Prussian Army in a single day in October 1806. The Prussians created the general staff to institutionalize military effectiveness by developing an educated and competent staff. To do so, they founded the *Kriegsakademie*, which was the single means through which officers could enter the general staff and the prestige

---

[11] In fairness to the French, there was nothing wrong with their military equipment. Their armor, for example, was superior to that possessed by the Wehrmacht. The problem lay in how the French incorporated that armor into their concepts and doctrine. The best work on French doctrine in the interwar period remains Robert Doughty, *The Seeds of Disaster, The Development of French Army Doctrine, 1919–1939* (Hamden, CT, 1985).
[12] Ibid., p. 179.
[13] The French failure to red team was confirmed in a conversation with Colonel Robert Doughty, U.S. Army. Doughty emphasized not only was there no red teaming in the French Army in the interwar period, but at times during exercises umpires would change the results or even projected capabilities if they suggested possibilities beyond what current doctrine stated. Phone conversation with Colonel Robert Doughty, 22 March 2002.

that accompanied the wearing of its crimson stripe. Only a select few Prussian officers gained entrance to this first school of professional military education, and then a substantial number failed and were dropped from the two-year course.

Concurrently, with the rise of the general staff and *Kriegsakademie* to a position of influence within the Prussian system came the development of the first war game, the *Kriegspiel*, which was initially a derivative of chess. By the early 1820s, one of the derivatives had become a sophisticated board game that allowed simulation not only of terrain but of the movements of cavalry, artillery, and infantry, as well as the results of combat engagements. When the chief of the general staff, General Phillip Baron von Muffling, had the game demonstrated to him in the early 1820s he exclaimed: "It is not a game at all! It's training for war! It is of value to the whole army."[14]

In effect, the Prussians had stumbled onto a powerful tool for testing and expanding the potential of their forces. *Kriegspiel* demanded the use of red teams in one form or another to challenge the operational and tactical thinking of the next generation of leaders. By mid-century, red teaming was playing an important role in military planning. But its first use by the Prussians was as an educational tool. It became a standby in the Prussian military's educational system not only at the *Kriegsakademie*, but in the education of officers at every level and stage of their careers. Out of the *Kriegspiele* developed sand table exercises, map exercises, general staff rides (many led by the chief of the general staff himself), and exercises, including the great fall maneuvers each year.

In a pedagogical sense, the *Kriegspiel* was a means to judge the competence and ability of officers to make decisions under pressure. Under the watchful eyes of senior officers, junior officers conducted *Kriegspiele*. These games were not merely an educational tool; they were an evaluative tool aimed at determining which officers had the mental ability and imagination to serve at higher levels. One historian has noted: "[The *Kriegspiel*] was a testing vehicle for personnel. Officers were pitted against each other under the watchful eyes of their superiors. Careers were made, put on hold and accelerated at war games."[15]

By the mid-point of the nineteenth century, the Prussians had embedded the *Kriegspiel* deeply within their military culture. As a result, their

---

[14] Quoted in Colonel Trevor N. Dupuy, U.S. Army (retired), *A Genius for War, The German Army and the General Staff 1807–1945* (Englewood Cliffs, NJ, 1977), p. 51.
[15] Arden Bucholz, *Moltke and the German Wars, 1864–1871* (New York, 2001), p. 19.

army, with its system of professional military education, became the first military organization to place a high value on how officers performed in what were largely mental exercises. This was, of course, not the only method of evaluation the Prussians used. As with all military organizations, other factors played in the calculus of promotion to higher ranks, and it would not be until Hans von Seeckt's reforms in the early 1920s that the general staff's culture came to dominate that of the army as a whole.[16] Nevertheless, this ability to use war games and their inherent red teaming as an educational and evaluative tool created a culture of honest criticism between the different levels of the officer corps. The nature of the *Kriegspiel*, with general staff officers making up the red teams, resulted in a deeper understanding of the possibilities open to the enemy.[17]

In 1866, in the Seven Weeks' War against the Austrians, and then in 1870–1871 in the Franco–Prussian War against Louis Napoleon's empire, the Prussians gained two of the most decisive victories in European military history.[18] European armies as well as the U.S. Army and Navy rushed to follow the Prussian example.[19] However, in nearly every case they confused style with substance; virtually none of them imported the German military culture of rigorous red teaming as a tool to evaluate officer suitability for the higher levels of command and staff. That situation has continued to the present. There are some exceptions; not surprisingly, the German educational system remains largely intact. On the other side of the North Sea, the British have instituted a course called the Higher Command and Staff Course for 0–6 promotables and newly promoted 0–7s. The performance of officers on that course and its final war game seems

---

[16] For the reforms that Seeckt carried out in the downsizing of the German Army's officer corps and in making the General Staff's culture dominate that of the Reichsheer, see James Corum, *The Roots of Blitzkrieg, Hans von Seeckt and German Military Reform* (Lawrence, KS, 1992).

[17] For a variety of reasons the Germans did not carry over this tradition of honest red teaming from the tactical and operational levels to the strategic and political levels, not to mention logistics. The end result of this minimization of strategy and politics was to lead to catastrophe in two world wars. See among others, Williamson Murray, *German Military Effectiveness* (Baltimore, MD, 1992), chap. 1.

[18] For the most thorough studies of those campaigns, see Geoffrey Waro, *The Austro-Prussian War, Austria's War with Prussia and Italy in 1866* (Cambridge, 1966); and Michael Howard, *The Franco-Prussian War, The German Invasion of France, 1870–1871* (London, 1961).

[19] In the European case only the armies immediately set about creating schools of professional military education. The Royal Navy, for example, did not set up a staff college until immediately before World War I. The U.S. Navy, however, established the Naval War College in the 1880s.

to play a role in the selection of officers for joint commands at the highest levels. But the general practice has been that professional military education and performance in free play war games has rarely been used as a tool to evaluate the suitability of officers for promotion and assignment.[20]

Red Teaming and War Planning

Here, the Germans provide an instructive lesson in both what one can gain through effective red teaming and the weaknesses that result from too narrow a perspective. The development of the *Kriegspiel* provided the Prussians and eventually the Germans with a substantial advantage over their opponents at the tactical and operational levels. It was not that the skills of effective campaign planning could not be learned in combat. At the beginning of the American Civil War, substantive operational planning – or any other planning for that matter – simply did not exist. But by fall 1863, the Union's high command was able to take a whole corps of 25,000 men, their horses, guns, and logistical support, and ship the whole lot over 1,200 miles from Maryland to Tennessee in ten days. But that planning ability had only been learned at a huge cost over two-and-a-half years of war. What enabled the Prussians to gain such an advantage over their opponents was that through red teaming they had developed a thorough system of planning great troop movements in peacetime.

Thus, the Prussians reached an impressive state of military competency in their planning before the wars of unification broke out. Part of this had to do with the geographical reality that Prussia was surrounded by three of the great powers of Europe. She simply had to get her armies into play before potential enemies moved onto her territory, as was the case not only in 1806 but also during the course of the Seven Years' War in the eighteenth century.[21] The war games of the mid-nineteenth century

---

[20] Why this should be so remains an interesting question. Perhaps it is a reflection of the larger dynamic of careerism in military cultures that in nearly all cases are also deeply anti-intellectual, partially as a result of what they are called upon on to do. For anti-intellectualism in the military, see Col. Lloyd J. Matthews, U.S. Army retired, "The Uniformed Intellectual and His Place in American Arms: Parts I and II," *Army Magazine*, July, August 2002.

[21] For the influence of geography on strategy and military culture, see Williamson Murray and Mark Grimsley, "Introduction: On Strategy," in Williamson Murray, MacGregor Knox, and Alvin Bernstein, eds., *The Making of Strategy, Rulers, States, and War* (Cambridge, 1992), pp. 1–23. See also Williamson Murray, "Some Thoughts on War and Geography," in Colin S. Gray and Geoffrey Sloan, eds., *Geopolitics, Geography and Strategy* (London, 1999), pp. 201–217.

underlined the importance of deployment games to an even greater extent. By utilizing Prussia's modern railroad system, Prussian forces were able to deploy into the field before their opponents. The chief of the general staff after 1857, Helmut von Moltke, played a major role in channeling Prussia's construction of new railroads into meeting the army's deployment needs.[22]

In the Seven Weeks' War against the Austrians in 1866, prewar planning for deployment allowed the Prussians not only to deploy three armies concentrically around Bavaria but to march those armies into Bohemia and unite them on the battlefield of Königgrätz. There they won one of the most decisive victories in military history. Moltke had understood that by red teaming the deployment possibilities, the Prussian Army would gain an inestimable advantage in the conduct of operations. Moreover, by war gaming the possibilities open to the Prussian and Austria armies in a campaign centering on Bohemia, the Prussians gained an understanding of the importance of time and the concomitant difficulties involved in getting logistical support forward to support the armies. That allowed the full initialization of railroads and prewar planning to ensure the required logistical system would be in place if war occurred. In the end, the advantages the Prussians gained by deploying before their opponents gave them the initiative they never lost.

Moltke is often reputed to have said operational plans never survive first contact with the enemy. Yet, to a considerable extent that is a misrepresentation of how the Germans war gamed the possibilities of a campaign. The aim of such games was to gain insights into the possibilities open to the enemy. It was not that one could predict his actions, but rather that one could better understand how he might react. One historian has noted: "[War gaming] was a means of testing and evaluating plans in a simulated situation, of trying out, of competitively testing many possibilities."[23] War gaming and red teaming did not predict the actual course of the wars of unification. Nor could it prevent surprises from occurring. The Prussians were after all fighting against complex adaptive

---

[22] As one of his biographers noted: "Hardly a single important railroad line was built... in Prussia or for that matter in Germany, without Moltke submitting an opinion on the most favorable routing, or the construction of bridges, tunnels, etc... Moreover, he endeavored to make clear the general viewpoints influencing his thinking in memoranda to the responsible authorities in order to create understanding for the interests of the military and give them emphasis." Dennis E. Schowalter, *Railroads and Rifles, Soldiers, Technology, and the Unification of Germany* (Hamden, CT, 1975) p. 39.

[23] Bucholz, *Moltke and the German Wars, 1864–1871*, p. 19.

opponents. Ironically, the Austrians and the French probably performed more incompetently during the course of those campaigns than did the red forces in the gaming before the conflicts. But war gaming prepared Prussian commanders to react to the unexpected and to take advantage of their enemies' mistakes.

In the period before the First World War, the Germans failed to replicate the level of success they enjoyed in the 1860s and 1870s. War gaming and red teaming performed an extraordinary job in setting up the deployment of German forces to launch the so called Schlieffen plan, which was the opening move in the fighting on the Western Front. German troop trains crossed the Rhine River bridges with only a 30-second gap between each train – a monumental triumph of technical and logistical planning, which was one of the reasons the French were to be so surprised by the size and extent of the German move on the far side of the Meuse, a move that allowed the Germans to avoid the great French defenses along the Franco–German frontier.[24]

However, once German forces got beyond the Liege gap, the execution of the invasion of France by the drive through Belgium suggests that German red teaming of the coming campaign could only have taken place at the most superficial level. Underestimating the adaptiveness of their adversary, the Germans were caught by surprise at the tenacity and effectiveness of the Belgian defense of Liege; by the speed with which two Russian armies invaded East Prussia; by the withdrawal of the Belgian Army to Antwerp, from which it threatened German lines of communication (and forced the Germans to deploy two corps off their advance southward); by the appearance of the British Expeditionary Force, covering the left flank of the French deployment; by the fact that the French were able to transfer troops from their right wing to their left wing swiftly; and by the fact that the French launched a significant counterattack from the fortress city of Paris. There were simply too many surprises in the execution of the invasion of Belgium and France for any other explanation other than that the general staff had not red teamed its operational concept with rigor.

Things did not significantly improve with the conduct of World War I by the Germans. Red teaming played no role in examining the

[24] The French were also surprised because they refused to believe that their opponents might act differently than they did – in this case by the willingness of the Germans to employ reserves as front-line troops, something the French high command was unwilling to consider.

fundamental assumptions of the plan for the Verdun offensive, drawn up by the chief of the general staff, Erich von Falkenhyn.[25] In 1918 a red-on-blue war game conducted by Army Group Prince Rupprecht, responsible for the upcoming spring offensive, indicated that there was only the slightest chance of success.[26] When Rupprecht reported the results to General Erich Ludendorff and asked the overall commander of the German army what the operational goal of the upcoming offensive was, the latter replied: "We will punch a hole into [their line]. For the rest we shall see."[27]

In the period after the First World War, the Germans displayed considerable skill in refocusing the army on the culture Moltke had emphasized.[28] Red teaming became an even more important tool in the education and evaluation of officers. The 1940 offensive against France and the Low Countries was carefully gamed. In fact, much of the plan's final form took shape only through the war games that took place during February and March 1940. Again, as in Moltke's day, the aim was to prepare officers to address the unexpected, both favorable and unfavorable, that might arise in the course of the coming campaign.[29]

The war games did not aim to plan every detail of the coming move through the Ardennes. And it was that sense of the possibilities open to the French – developed by red play in those games – that created the tension between the German high command and the generals at crucial moments of the breakthrough. It was Guderian who sensed that the French had no effective response to the growing breakthrough on 14 and 15 May. But no serious war gaming could possibly have suggested the extraordinary incompetence of the French high command, and General Maurice

---

[25] Thus, Falkenhyn's strategic memorandum justifying the Verdun offensive suggested on one hand that Britain was Germany's greatest opponent and that the Allies would win a war of attrition, and then on the other that the solution should be to wage a massive battle of attrition against the French Army at Verdun. The disconnects are so startling that they underline the complete absence of red teaming. The best history of the Battle of Verdun remains Alistair Horne, *The Price of Glory, Verdun, 1916* (New York, 1962).

[26] General der Infanterie a.D. Rudolf Hoffman, "War Games," Manuscript # P-094, U.S. Army Historical Division, p. xi.

[27] Crown Prince Rupprecht, *Mein Kriegstagebuch*, vol. 2 (Munich, 1920), p. 179.

[28] For the influence of military culture on the development of German mechanized, combined arms tactics during the interwar period, see particularly Williamson Murray, "Armored Warfare," in Williamson Murray and Allan R. Millett, eds., *Military Innovation in the Interwar Period* (Cambridge, 1996).

[29] For a new look at the 1940 campaign, see Williamson Murray, "May 1940: Contingency and Fragility of the German RMA," in MacGregor Knox and Williamson Murray, eds., *The Dynamics of Military Revolution, 1300–2050* (Cambridge, 2001).

Gamelin in particular, which had moved the entire French operational reserve, the Seventh Army, from Rheims to the far left of the Allied line. Thus, the senior leadership had real reason to fear Guderian's drive to the west that increasingly exposed the German flank to a possible French counterattack.

The weakness in the German red teaming in the Second World War was not apparent in the early campaigns of the Second World War, but it would play a crucial role in the disastrous strategic mistakes of 1941. In neither the strategic nor the logistical side of war did the German military exhibit the slightest interest in red teaming or its results. In October 1940, a logistical war game carried out under the direction of the *OKH (Oberkommando des Heeres*, the German Army's high command) indicated that the supply system could only function relatively effectively up to Smolensk, two-thirds of the way to Leningrad and just beyond Kiev. Yet, these sobering results had no effect on the operational planning for Operation Barbarossa. The infamous August pause was in fact the result of the near collapse of the Wehrmacht's logistical system – in this case a complete failure to pay attention to what war gaming had suggested.

Equally disastrous was the fact that the German military had not considered the strategic and operational, much less the productive implications of an American entrance into the war. In fact, the *Seekriegsleitung* (the navy's high command) spent much of summer and fall 1941 trying to persuade Hitler to declare war on the United States, while neither the *Luftwaffe* nor the army had any interest in examining the implications of such a war. The result was that on 11 December 1941 Hitler declared war on America and failed to get anything in return from his Japanese allies.[30] Admittedly, by this point in the war, the Führer had no interest in any system that presented a challenge to his "unalterable" decisions. But the German military was no more willing or able to game the long-term implications of such a decision than was its beloved Führer.[31]

Red teaming at the operational level would seem to be a *sine qua non* for the effective outcome of military planning. As disastrous as not red

---

[30] For a discussion of Hitler's decision to declare war on the United States, see Williamson Murray and Allan R. Millett, *A War To Be Won, Fighting the Second World War* (Cambridge, MA, 2000), pp. 135–136.

[31] For a discussion of the German military's unwillingness and inability to judge the strategic level of war, see Williamson Murray, "Net Assessment and Nazi Germany in the 1930s," in Williamson Murray and Allan R. Millett, eds., *Calculations: Net Assessment and the Coming of World War II* (New York, 1992).

teaming the possibilities open to an opponent have been the ignoring of the operational and strategic implications of red teaming. The most egregious example may be the fact that one of the French war games in 1938 indicated that the Germans could transit the Ardennes in 60 hours (it actually took them 58 hours). That warning was entirely ignored by the French high command. With his main reserves now out on the far left of the Allied line, Gamelin was left in the position that, when queried by Churchill in the midst of the catastrophic German breakthrough along the Meuse, as to where the operational reserve was, he could only laconically reply: "Aucune (none)."[32] Given the large numbers of steps French troops might have taken to delay the German advance in the Ardennes – such as demolitions, delaying actions, blocking actions – the fact that the French had taken none of these actions as well as having left themselves with no operational reserve is an extraordinary indictment of their military competence. It is also a clear indication of a failure to utilize red teaming to challenge planning assumptions. The result of their ignoring the clear warnings that red teaming had suggested – that the Germans might move rapidly through the Ardennes – was catastrophic military defeat.

Testing Doctrine and Developing Operational Concepts: The Processes of Experimentation

With the onrush of technological change in the twentieth century, the development of new operational concepts and doctrine has come to play an increasingly important role. Here, red teaming has been a major player in identifying and examining the possibilities. The development of new concepts of operation, experimentation, and the influence of both on doctrine, written and unwritten, was to be a major factor in successes on the battlefields of World War II. Red teaming was crucial in exercises and experiments for providing a realistic forum for innovators and military bureaucrats alike. Where it did not exist, doctrine and concept development either stagnated or moved into the world of faulty assumptions.

The U.S. Navy

Of all the world's military organizations, the U.S. Navy had the most outstanding record in the interwar period. It all began at the Naval War College in the early 1920s with a heavy emphasis on war gaming under

---

[32] Winston S. Churchill, *The Second World War*, vol. 2, *Their Finest Hour* (Boston, 1949), p. 46.

the guidance of Admiral William Sims.[33] These games aimed to achieve two distinct purposes: the first was to educate the officer students. The second was to examine the possibilities that modern technology, including aircraft carriers, might offer the fleet beyond simply providing more of the same. These games provided a number of crucial insights. One commentator on the development of war games has noted that the games "contributed substantially to the development of ideas about how to employ aircraft."[34]

The most important insight was that the dynamics of offensive carrier operations differed fundamentally from battleship engagements. When battleships engaged, as at Jutland, the fires from the two sides concentrated more or less in steady streams, with each side redirecting its stream of fire onto the enemy's surviving ships as the engagement progressed. However, the war games in the early 1920s indicated that carrier strikes should come in pulses of combat power rather than in continuous streams.[35] The red-on-blue fleet games underlined that the first strike and its power would be the crucial factor in the air war at sea. Hence, the fundamental measure of effectiveness for carrier aviation was a function of not only the number of aircraft that carriers could carry but the number of aircraft they could launch at one time.

What is indeed astonishing is the fact that this crucial insight was gained before the navy possessed a single operational aircraft carrier. When the first carrier, the *USS Langley*, finally became available, Joseph M. Reeves, a future admiral and one of the veterans of the Newport games, became its captain and immediately set about experimenting with the ship and its aircraft.[36] Within a year Reeves had shortened take off

---

[33] The emphasis on professional military education by the navy's leading admiral in Europe during World War I, Admiral Sims, and by one of its leading admirals in World War II, Raymond Spruance, both of whom returned from their operational command assignments to become presidents of the Naval War College, stands in marked contrast to today's navy, which is more often than not ambivalent toward its war college. The great irony of that attitude lies in the fact that the Naval War College remains the only world-class academic institution in the American system of professional military education for the study of strategy.

[34] Peter P. Perla, *The Art of Wargaming: A Guide for Professionals and Hobbyists* (Annapolis, MD, 1990), p. 71.

[35] Norman Friedman, Thomas C. Hone, and Mark D. Mandeles, *American and British Aircraft Carrier Development, 1919–1941* (Annapolis, MD, 1999), p. 34.

[36] Reeves had attended the senior officers course at Newport in 1923 and after graduation had become the head of the tactics department, where he had supervised the 1924–1925 games. Stephen Peter Rosen, *Winning the Next War, Innovation and the Modern Military* (Ithaca, NY, 1991), pp. 40–43.

and landing times for larger numbers of aircraft, created crash barriers and deck parks and a system of marshalling large of numbers of aircraft in the air. The result was that the *Langley* was able to operate 48 aircraft off its deck, instead of the 14 with which it had initially gone to sea.

The example of the war gaming at Newport in the early 1920s carried over into annual fleet exercises. In these red-on-blue exercises, Newport provided the initial planning based on the experiences of war gaming at the college. The college also provided its instructors as umpires for the exercises. Those instructors then fed the results back into the war gaming that took place at the college during the winter. That interaction was important in defining the potential of carrier aviation, as well as pushing the navy to develop aircraft capabilities that would revolutionize naval warfare and eventually play a major part in the success U.S. aviation was to enjoy in World War II.[37] The use of war college instructors as umpires represented a recognition that independent adjudication is essential to the intellectual rigor of such exercises.

It is also worth noting that the war gaming at Newport, with the U.S. fleet opposing a surrogate Japanese fleet, suggested many of the larger parameters of the coming Pacific War in the early 1920s. In 1923 the future commander of the Central Pacific drive, Chester Nimitz, noted the following about the operational and strategic framework of a possible war against Imperial Japan in his student thesis:

> [T]he operations imposed [in a future Pacific war] on Blue will require the Blue Fleet to advance westward with an enormous train, in order to be able to seize and establish bases on route. The possession by Orange [the Japanese] of numerous bases in the western Pacific will give her fleet a maximum of mobility while the lack of such bases imposes on Blue the necessity of refueling at sea en route or of seizing a base from Orange for this purpose, in order to maintain a limited degree of mobility.[38]

From such thinking, based on solid red teaming, the U.S. Navy developed a grasp of what it would need at the strategic and operational levels in the

---

[37] Here, the Navy's choice of the radial engine, which was much easier to maintain than in-line engines on the pitching decks of carriers, eventually led to the development of radial engines that were nearly the equal of in-line engines – a technology which engineers had not thought possible. Thus, when World War II came, all of the U.S. Navy's aircraft and many of the army Air Forces' aircraft would use radial instead of in-line engines. In Europe, only the German Folke-Wolf 190A, of all the Luftwaffe and RAF front-line aircraft, used a radial engine.

[38] Chester W. Nimitz, "1923 Naval War College Thesis," *Naval War College Review*, Nov–Dec 1983, pp. 12–13.

coming Pacific War, as well as an understanding of the logistical support that such a campaign would require.[39] Out of these war gaming and fleet exercises came the push to develop aircraft capabilities, amphibious war, the logistical fleet train that supported the fleet underway at sea, and the conception of island hopping. Moreover, the habits of mind created at Newport carried on into the conduct of the Pacific war. From the Marianas on, Nimitz spent several days war gaming and red teaming the possibilities open to upcoming operations with his staff and principal commanders.[40]

The German Army

On the other side of the world, the Germans also gained considerable insights in their creation of mechanized, combined-arms tactics through the use of red teaming in *Kriegspiele* and on maneuvers.[41] As suggested earlier, that effort emphasized the tactical application of combined-arms units on the battlefield but failed to red team either a strategic or wider operational framework effectively. Still, the creation of *Blitzkrieg* capabilities was one of the most impressive innovations in military history, as one of the few instances in modern warfare where tactical virtuosity came close to overturning strategic incompetence.[42]

The German success in developing combined-arms warfare grew out of their success at the end of World War I with the development of decentralized infiltration tactics that contained a strong element of combined-arms war.[43] But the problem the Germans confronted in 1918 was that while

---

[39] The red teaming at the tactical level in the interwar years did not have as impressive an outcome for the navy. The navy's performance in the early days of the Pacific War – not just at Pearl Harbor, but at Savo Island and the following night battles in the Solomon – represents a depressing catalogue of tactical and command ineptitude. See Williamson Murray and Allan R. Millett, *A War To Be Won, Fighting the Second World War* (Cambridge, MA, 2000), pp. 210–217.

[40] Unpublished paper, Barry D. Watts, "Diagnostic Observations on Theater Level War Gaming," presented at National Defense University's "Thinking Red in War Gaming" Conference, 23–25, April 1985, p. 7.

[41] The term blitzkrieg tactics is still in favor among even historians who should know better. In fact, what the Germans were developing can best be characterized as mechanized, combined-arms warfare. For that effort, see Murray, "Armored Warfare," in *Military Innovation in the Interwar Period*.

[42] For the difficulties the Germans confronted, see Williamson Murray, *The Change in The European Balance of Power, 1938–1939, The Path To Ruin* (Princeton, NJ, 1984); and for the ambiguities, see Murray, "May 1940: Contingency and Fragility in the German RMA," in *The Dynamics of Military Revolution*.

[43] For the development of that capability, see particularly Timothy T. Lupfer, *The Dynamics of Doctrine: The Changes in German Tactical Doctrine During the First World War*

their tactical system was able to create a rupture of the enemy's front line, their forces did not possess the maneuverability to exploit that success to achieve operational objectives. In 1920 Hans von Seeckt took over the German Army and confronted the demands of the victorious powers for a radical downsizing of the officer corps in the aftermath of World War I. In meeting those demands, Seeckt ensured the general staff and its culture would dominate the culture of a reborn German Army.[44] The first task of that new officer corps was to learn the lessons of the last war.[45] The second task was through experiments and exercises to probe the potential of emerging technologies. After the army's first experiment with motorization in the Harz Mountains, Seeckt commented on the cover sheet of the lessons-learned report that he had circulated through the army:

> I fully approve of the Harz exercises's conception and leadership, but there is still much that is still not clear about the specific tactical use of motor vehicles. I therefore order that the following report be made available by all staffs and independent commands as a topic for lectures and study. Troop commanders must see to it that experience in this area is widened by practical exercises.[46]

Red teaming and rigorous testing of assumptions, just as in Moltke's day, lay at the heart of Seeckt's legacy to the interwar German army. As he suggested in a memorandum in 1924: "It is of fundamental importance that our subordinate leaders be trained to think and act independently."[47] Thus, the Germans emphasized red teaming and free play in their exercises

---

(Leavenworth, KS, 1981); see also Bruce I. Gudmundsson, *Stormtroop Tactics, Innovation in the German Army, 1914–1918* (Westport, CT, 1989).

[44] For Seeckt's contribution, see Corum, *The Roots of Blitzkrieg*. For the influence of that culture on German officers who were not members of the general staff, but rather "muddy boots" soldiers, see Sir David Fraser, *Knight's Cross, A Life of Field Marshal Erwin Rommel* (London, 1993).

[45] Historians consistently argue that military organizations study the last war and that is why they perform badly in the next conflict. Nothing could be farther from the truth. Only the German Army made a careful, thorough, and honest study of what had been happening on the battlefields of 1918 and then made a major effort to inculcate those lessons into its doctrine and preparations for the next war throughout the interwar period. That is why it performed so well in the first battles of World War II. Seeckt ordered that the 57 different committees, which he established to learn the lessons of the Great War, produce "short concise studies on the newly gained experiences of the war..." Quoted in Corum, *The Roots of Blitzkrieg*, p. 37. For the German evolution of combined-arms, mechanized warfare, see particularly Murray, "Armored Warfare."

[46] Reichswehr Ministerium, Chef der Heeresleitung, Betr: "Harzülbung, 8.1.22," National Archive and Record Service, Captured German Records, T-79/65/000622.

[47] David N. Spires, *Image and Reality, The Making of the German Officer, 1921–1933* (Westport, CT, 1984), p. 105.

in a fashion that was far in advance of the practices in other European armies. By 1933 a rigorous culture of testing and examining assumptions at the tactical level was already in place.[48] In the ensuing period of massive rearmament, the army's leaders ensured that this culture of demanding examination and evaluation extended to the extensive experimentation that took place throughout the period.[49] Initially, with neither motorized nor mechanized units available, the army established a number of independent tank battalions with armored fighting vehicles that were already bordering on obsolescence – but they were the only vehicles that German industry was capable of producing at the time.[50]

So rapid were the processes of testing and red teaming that the army's commander-in-chief decided to establish three test panzer divisions at the conclusion of the fall maneuvers in 1935. Nevertheless, the army's senior leaders were not about to put all their eggs in a single basket. At the same time, they established motorized infantry divisions, so-called light divisions, which were a combination of cavalry and motorized infantry with a few tanks thrown in, and independent tank regiments to support the infantry. Not until late 1938 did the army leadership decide to establish another three panzer divisions and disestablish the independent tank battalions, a direct result of extensive red teaming and experimentation in the intervening period. And not until the following year after the conclusion of the Polish campaign did the army decide to transform the light divisions into full-fledged armored divisions – in this case, as the result of the lessons of the battlefield. The simplistic accounts of *Blitzkrieg* developed after World War II have severely distorted the actual processes of experimentation and red teaming that allowed the Germans to evaluate

---

[48] However, this was not the case with the Germans in their examination of strategic problems. In 1928, for example, the future field marshal, Werner von Blomberg, almost ended his career because of the completely bizarre strategic framework that he designed for the study tour that year. See Wilhelm Deist, *The Wehrmacht and German Rearmament* (London, 1981), p. 16.

[49] It is worth noting that, when the German Army began rearmament at Hitler's direction in February 1933, it did not possess a single tank. Yet, the new doctrinal manual that had just been finished in 1932 by the army's future commander-in-chief, Werner von Fritsch, and the future chief of the general staff, Ludwig Beck, had extensive discussions of how tanks might be used to further the possibilities of exploitation at the operational level. The Wehrmacht would fight World War II with that doctrinal manual as the basis of its warfighting doctrine – a doctrine that emphasized decentralized leadership, ruthless exploitation, and effective combined-arms tactics. See Chef der Heeresleitung, *Truppenfuhrung* (Berlin, 1933).

[50] Not until late 1938 with the first production of the Mark III and Mark IV tanks were the Germans finally able to field modern tanks.

and evolve the possibilities of armored mechanized warfare more clearly than their opponents in the opening campaigns of World War II.[51]

The British Army

One of the great ironies of World War II, especially considering the British Army's performance in that conflict, is the fact that its leaders in the late 1920s and early 1930s ran an extraordinarily imaginative and innovative set of experiments with mechanized forces.[52] Before World War I the British had had a lackadaisical attitude toward red teaming in exercises. In the 1911 exercises on the Salisbury plain, the commander of one of the maneuver forces could not even be bothered to come down from London for the day.[53] Nevertheless, the British did a better job of running imaginative and challenging experiments on the Salisbury plains in the period between 1925 and 1934.

The success of these experiments rested on the fact that they posited two independent forces (of approximately division size) fighting against each other. In the 1927 exercise, the army established an experimental armored unit to test out the possibilities a mechanized force might realize.[54] During that exercise, the experimental unit achieved a number of notable successes. One portion of the force, commanded by future general Frederick Pile, advanced nearly 40 miles to avoid the opposing side's patrols and seized key bridges in the maneuver area.[55] It then caught

---

[51] For those campaigns, see Murray and Millett, *A War To Be Won*, chapters 3–4.
[52] For the British Army in the interwar period, see Brian Bond, *British Military Policy Between the Wars* (Oxford, 1980). See also Brian Bond and Williamson Murray, "British Military Effectiveness in the Interwar Period," in Allan R. Millett and Williamson Murray, eds., *Military Effectiveness*, vol. 2, *The Interwar Period* (London, 1988).
[53] Travers, *The Killing Ground*, p. 27.
[54] Astonishingly, the military reformer, J.F.C. Fuller, then a lieutenant colonel, was offered command of the experimental unit by the chief of the imperial general staff and by the general commanding the exercise. However, in a fit of pique Fuller made a set of impossible demands and then, when all of his demands were not met, proceeded to turn down the command in what one of his biographers quite correctly termed as "probably the worst decision of his life." Anthony John Tryhall, *"Boney" Fuller: The Intellectual General, 1878–1966* (London, 1977), p. 136. See also the splendid study on the British Army and the tank: J. P. Harris, *Men, Ideas, and Tanks: British Military Thought and Tanks, 1903–1939* (Manchester, 1996), p. 216.
[55] Pile was one of the more effective officers in the British Army when the Second World War broke out. For most of the war, he commanded Britain's anti-aircraft defenses despite the fact that he had had extensive experience in mechanized experiments during the interwar period. The problem seems to have been that the chief of the imperial general staff, Field Marshal Alan Brooke, had taken a dislike to Pile sometime during their army careers and ensured that Pile would never receive an operational command.

one of its opponent's columns in the open, where it was destroyed by aircraft. The exercise's overall commander, General Sir John Burnett-Stuart, commented in the hot wash:

> I know that a lot of you will not like the tactics which you saw employed by the light [mechanized] group in these maneuvers. You will think them risky. But I assure you that in armored war these things will be tried, they will probably come off, there will always be people who will chance their arm in this way, and you have got to be prepared to meet them when they do.[56]

In the following years, the British used their experimental armored force, usually established each year, to examine the possibilities of mechanized warfare further. Since free play between the opposing sides occurred frequently, the British gained a number of critical insights on the future of armored warfare. Among them was the fact that efforts to incorporate infantry units that possessed no organic transport would hinder the tanks' mobility. The obvious lesson was that only with mechanization could infantry and artillery units participate in mobile warfare. Moreover, wide-ranging, rapid operations underlined that radio communications were going to be an absolute necessity in coordinating the movements of mechanized forces. Finally, the experiments indicated that close air support might be an important enabler of mobile operations.[57] Ironically, the Germans would learn the most from these experiments, a fact that the German tank pioneer Oswald Lutz made clear to the British general, Sir John Dill, in 1935.[58]

But the British failed to incorporate the lessons of these experiments into the army's preparation for war. There were a number of reasons for this failure. First, the national strategy minimized the commitment of British troops to the Continent until February 1939, when the government finally relented and recognized the German danger. Second, and more important, the army possessed no coherent, combined-arms doctrine into

---

[56] Quoted in Harold R. Winton, *To Change an Army, General Sir John Burnett-Stuart and British Armored Doctrine, 1927–1938* (Lawrence, KS, 1988) pp. 80–81.

[57] Unfortunately, the Germans watched what was happening on the Salisbury plain all too closely. They, rather than the British, picked up most of the important lessons and incorporated those lessons into their forces as they began the processes of developing their own capabilities in mechanized war. For the German analysis of the British experiments, see particularly: Reichswehrministerium, Berlin, 10.11.26, "Darstellung neuzeitlicher Kampfwagen," National Archives and Records Service, Microfilm T-79/62/000789; Reichswehrministerium, Berlin 1929, "England: Die Manover mit motorisierten Truppen, September 1929," National Archives and Records Service, Microfilm, T -79/30/000983.

[58] Murray, *The Change in the European Balance of Power*, p. 35.

which the experiences of mechanized experiments could be incorporated. Third, and perhaps most important, the army's culture remained hostile to change and new ideas if they involved the serious study of the military profession.[59] As Michael Howard has suggested: "The evidence is strong that the army was still as firmly geared to the pace and perspective of regimental soldiering as it had been before 1914; that too many of its members looked on soldiering as an agreeable and honorable occupation rather than as a serious profession demanding no less intellectual dedication than that of the doctor, the lawyer, or the engineer."[60]

Understanding the Enemy
One of the spin-offs from successful red teaming, when done correctly, is the development among those who play on red teams of a deeper understanding of potential opponents and how they might think about waging conflict. These insights can then be passed along to the larger body of the officer corps both through interaction in war games and by members of the team themselves. Unfortunately, as with so much of the history of red teaming, this has been a rare occurrence. The penalty for not developing such understanding, on the other hand, has been high. While there are a number of sources for developing an understanding of the enemy, red teaming offers one of the better methods for connecting intelligence with an actual understanding of how the enemy might utilize his capabilities.

Not surprisingly, at least in the 1930s, the Germans made a consistent effort to include the enemy's military system in their war games. While the Germans never established permanent red teams to portray the enemy, they paid close attention to how their enemy would fight, as well as the emerging technological possibilities that might be available to future red forces. In the case of the former, one historian has noted the following: "Foreign operational doctrine was translated [by the Germans] and studied so that officers playing the roles of that nation's force commanders in war games and maneuvers could act realistically and not simply 'mirror image' German doctrine. Realistic problems were posed in major maneuvers – for example, a war with Poland or France. Modern forms of ground and air organization were first tried out in these games."[61]

---

[59] In this regard, see particularly Bond, *British Military Policy Between the Wars*.
[60] Michael Howard, "The Liddell Hart Memoirs," *Journal of the Royal United Services Institute* (February, 1966), p. 61.
[61] James S. Corum, "A Comprehensive Approach to Change, Reform in the German Army in the Interwar Period," in Harold Winton and David R. Mets, eds., *The Challenge of Change, Military Institutions and New Realities, 1918–1941* (Lincoln, NE, 2000), p. 48.

But as with all things concerning the German military in the first half of the twentieth century, there were limits to the willingness and ability of the *Wehrmacht* to use red teaming to gain insights into the nature of their opponents. Operation Barbarossa, the invasion of the Soviet Union, is a particularly good example of the inability of the Germans to challenge their assumptions beyond those concerning the tactical.[62] German operational planning, despite its extensive red teaming, never examined the larger political and organizational possibilities open to the Soviets. *Wehrmacht* military leaders accepted the ideological preconceptions of the political leadership that the Jewish–Bolshevik state (the Soviet Union) would be incapable of organizing or sustaining prolonged resistance once German forces had crushed the Red Army in the border areas.[63]

Instead, the Germans confronted a state capable of mobilizing its massive manpower resources and industrial potential for a prolonged struggle. As early as August 1941, within less than two months of the start of the invasion, the chief of the general staff, *Generaloberst* Franz Halder, was bemoaning that:

> The whole situation [in the war in Russia] shows more and more clearly that we have underestimated the colossus of Russia.... This conclusion is shown both in the organizational as well as the economic levels in the transportation, and above all in the infantry divisions. We have already identified 360. [The Germans had expected to meet 150.] The divisions are admittedly not armed and equipped in our sense, and tactically they are badly led. But there they are, and when we destroy a dozen, the Russians simply establish another dozen.[64]

But matters were no better on the other side of the hill. Not surprisingly, real red teaming, the challenging of basic assumptions, never entered into the picture in Stalin's Soviet Union. In late December 1940 and early January 1941, the Soviets ran a series of war games on a potentia Nazi–Soviet conflict. Unfortunately, the preconceptions on both the

---

[62] The German conception of operations largely excluded logistics and intelligence from serious consideration – a defect that reflected Germany's position at the heart of Europe.

[63] For the nature of those ideological assumptions and the ready acceptance of them by German military leaders see Horst Boog, Jürgen Forster, Joachim Hoffman, Ernst Klink, Rolf-Dieter Müller, Gerd R. Ueberschär, *Das Deutsche Reich und der Zweite Weltkrieg*, vol. 4, *Der Angriff auf die Sowjetunion* (Stuttgart, 1983). It is worth underlining that the Wehrmacht continued to underestimate substantially the operational sophistication of its Soviet opponents throughout the entire Second World War – a factor that contributed significantly to the success that Soviet maskirovka (deception) enjoyed in disguising the location of every single major Soviet offensive from 1943 to the end of the war.

[64] Franz Halder, *The Halder War Diaries, 1939–1942*, edited by Charles Burdick and Hans-Adolf Jacobsen (Novato, CA, 1988), p. 506.

political and operational levels made it impossible for the Soviet high command to gauge the extent of the danger.[65] As the military historian John Erickson has noted:

> Here were two grave mistakes in assessing [German] intentions. The first was Stalin himself [and his ideological assumptions]... The second derived from the failure of the professional military to draw accurate conclusions about German war doctrine in its broadest sense. The latter was compounded in the spring of 1941, when the 'new methods' demonstrated by the German Army [in the French campaign] went largely ignored.... *The failure to comprehend the essentials of German military doctrine in a tactical, operational sense and German 'war doctrine' in its widest context was the prime cause of the disaster; the effects of this was and had to be devastating, for such a failure impeded and inhibited effective operational planning.* [italics in the original][66]

But it is not only tyrannies based on ideology that failed to use red teaming to understand their opponents. Whatever the successes of their free play experiments with mechanized forces, the British failed to place their red teams within a framework that resembled what the Germans were doing on the Continent.[67] The result of this failure to portray and understand their potential opponents led to a general failure to understand the nature of German tactical and operational doctrine throughout the entire course of World War II. That failure had its roots in a failure to develop red teaming that represented and portrayed a realistic picture of German doctrine and how the Germans would fight. Thus, in 1935 Sir John Dill, eventually to become the chief of the imperial general staff early in World War II, wondered during a visit to German maneuvers at Tannenburg in 1935 "how the Germans had achieved such success despite the notorious disobedience of their junior officers."[68] As late as the Normandy battles, British infantry marveled at what seemed to be the pattern of reverse slope positions used by the Germans, "something

---

[65] On the political level the Soviet leaders, influenced by their Marxist ideology, posited that Nazism, representing the last stages of capitalism, would be fully satisfied by the capture of Western European markets and that Hitler's obsession with conquering the territories of European Russia for Lebensraum was simply a propaganda device.

[66] John Erickson, "The Soviet Union, 1930–1941," in *Knowing One's Enemies, Intelligence Assessment Before the Two World Wars*, ed. by Ernest R. May (Princeton, NJ, 1984), pp. 418–419.

[67] One might suggest that the complete failure of the French to use red teaming at any level was the major factor in the catastrophe of 1940.

[68] Quoted in David French, *Raising Churchill's Army, The British Army and the War Against Germany, 1919–1945* (Oxford, 2000). Of course, what Dill had been seeing was the conduct of decentralized, mission-oriented tactics being exercised by German infantry units.

that we had never envisaged," despite the fact that such an approach had been a basic principle of German doctrine since 1917.[69]

The record of red teaming's use to understand the enemy is thus rather dismal. Intelligence organizations rarely possess a clear idea of the tactical framework within which their own forces fight; thus, for the most part they are incapable of understanding what aspects of the enemy's approach to war their own forces need to know. In fact, we are dealing with more than an intelligence problem, but rather, a cultural problem – one that generally results in systemic failure to understand the enemy. Intelligent red teaming that actually presents how the enemy may fight is one of the best methods of challenging the tactical assumptions and preconceptions that are generally so costly in the first clash of arms. Moreover, red teaming offers insights into understanding how one's opponents might adapt and change on the battlefield.

Red Teaming and Training

Red teaming has had less of a role in the training of military forces than one might expect, even in the twentieth century. Yet, the absence of red teaming, as represented by realistic opposition forces (OPFOR), has consistently resulted in stylized, unimaginative training regimes that have produced military organizations incapable of adapting on the battlefield. The general unwillingness of the French to use serious, independent OPFORs in their training maneuvers, even in force-on-force exercises, contributed to an atmosphere in which no one at any level challenged the preconceptions and assumptions of the high command.[70] The implications for French maneuvers were dismal. Exercises and maneuvers were entirely scripted for both sides, while no free play was allowed to occur in any phase.[71]

---

[69] Quoted in Max Hastings, *Overlord, D-Day and the Battle for Normandy 1944* (London, 1984), p. 141.

[70] In 1935 Gamelin, shortly after taking over command of the French Army, established the high command as the sole arbiter for doctrine. From that point on, all articles, lectures, and books by serving officers had to receive approval by the high command before publication. As the future general André Beaufre noted in his memoirs: "Everyone got the message, and a profound silence reigned until the awakening of 1940." André Beaufre, *1940, The Fall of France* (New York, 1968), p. 43.

[71] Conversation with Colonel Robert Doughty, U.S. Army, the leading expert on the French Army in the English speaking world. Colonel Doughty indicated that sometimes during exercises, umpires would change the projected capabilities of weapons systems if there were a suggestion that possibilities other than those prescribed by French doctrine might exist. Phone conversation with Colonel Robert Doughty, 22 March 2002.

Thoughts on Red Teaming

There were two driving forces behind the tight control the French high command exercised over its training. The first was the "looking-good" syndrome – a desire to ensure that none of the participants in or observers of maneuvers came away with the slightest hint that the army's leadership was not in complete control. The second driving force was the desire to "validate" the army's doctrine of the "methodical" battle.[72] The impact on training was catastrophic. Even Gamelin was embarrassed by the results of a training exercise in 1931. One historian of the army during this period has noted:

> Attending [the 1931] maneuvers as inspector general, Gamelin was chagrined at the 'sporadic and feeble' actions and embarrassed to hear that a German attaché had wondered whether [the] 'infantry did not know how to attack.' Gamelin [himself] dismissed the operation as 'not an attack but a funeral procession... [T]he infantry following the tanks like hearses.[73]

Things failed to improve in the late 1930s. The French continued to view maneuvers as "impressive demonstrations of [the] approved method of fighting." Thus, French training, with its absence of red teaming, could only replicate a doctrine that removed all initiative from its officer corps and left nothing to chance. Thus, on the banks of the Meuse, even though the French got the battle for which they had trained, their troops could not even apply the army's doctrine with speed and dispatch.

There have, of course, been significant success stories in the influence of red teaming on tactical training. Here, the American military shone in the period after Vietnam. The less than impressive air-to-air record of U.S. fighter aircraft in aerial combat over North Vietnam during Rolling Thunder (1965–1968) led the navy to establish Top Gun in the late 1960s, in which red teaming aggressor pilots, flying aggressor aircraft, challenged navy fighter pilots. Electronic ranges ensured pilots could no longer claim imaginary successes, but rather had to address their real weaknesses. The startling improvement of navy fighter pilots during the Linebacker air campaigns of 1972 then forced the air force to establish Red Flag and put its fighter pilots into a realistic training environment, in which they had

---

[72] For the development of the French Army's doctrinal framework during the interwar years, see Robert Doughty's brilliant study, *The Seeds of Disaster*.

[73] Quoted in Eugenia C. Kiesling, *Arming Against Hitler, France and the Limits of Military Planning* (Lawrence, KS, 1995), p. 139.

to contend not only with aggressor red teams flying dissimilar aircraft, but also ground systems that replicated those of the Warsaw Pact.[74]

Similarly, the army and marine corps established complex ranges for ground combat in the deserts of Southern California. With extensive electronic monitors and computers, those exercise areas trained a new generation of officers by confronting them with an active, effective red force that, in retrospect, was probably superior to anything the Soviets and their allies were capable of putting in the field. The larger point is that the establishment of serious tactical red teaming played a key role in significantly improving the capabilities of U.S. military forces in the last decade of the Cold War. That competitive edge would show with startling clarity in the devastating air and ground victories that the United States military achieved in Desert Storm.

Red Teaming and Strategic Assumptions

It is at the strategic level that red teaming is most useful in challenging dangerous assumptions.[75] Yet, it is at this level where red teaming has been the least used; and even when used, its results have, more often than not, been rejected or disregarded. In the run up to World War I, none of the powers appeared to have used red teaming to examine the possible results of either strategic or operational moves on potential opponents. Before 1914, the German general staff appears to have passed along a precis of its plan to invade the Low Countries to its Foreign Office and political leaders, who in turn abdicated their responsibilities to examine the ramifications through some form of red teaming. The German military historian, Gerhard Ritter, has pointed out:

> However admirable Schlieffen's great operational plan of 1905 may have been as a technical military achievement, the fact remains that its basic approach was accepted by the top political leadership in Germany without any real discussion of the grave countervailing political arguments... this [was] one of the most incomprehensible acts of omission of the Wilhelmian

---

[74] For the aerial combat over North Vietnam, see Marshall L. Michell, III, Clashes, *Air Combat Over North Vietnam, 1965–1972* (Annapolis, MD, 1997).

[75] It is *not* a matter of having politicians simply call in military leaders for their "military" advice. As Clausewitz suggests: "We can now see that the assertion that a major military development, or the plan for one, should be a matter for *purely military* opinion is unacceptable... Nor indeed is it sensible to summon soldiers, as many governments do when they are planning a war, and ask them for purely *military advice*." Carl von Clausewitz, *On War*, trans. and ed. by Michael Howard and Peter Paret (Princeton, NJ, 1975), p. 607.

Reich – or perhaps it would be more accurate to say that it can be understood only in the light of the deficiencies within the German governmental and army system...[76]

This state of affairs continued throughout World War I. The fateful decision to resume unrestricted submarine warfare in 1917, which would bring the United States into the war and seal Germany's fate, occurred entirely on the basis of the German Navy's "pure military advice," without the slightest effort to red team the strategic and economic consequences of launching unrestricted submarine warfare.[77]

Perhaps even more distressing than the general unwillingness or inability to red team the enemy at the strategic level are those few cases where red teaming did in fact suggest the paths open to the enemy, but where policy makers and military leaders either disregarded or dismissed the results. In the 1950s and early 1960s, the military and academic worlds in the United States developed sophisticated strategic games to examine the possibilities that might lead to nuclear war. In 1964 two pol-mil (political-military) games, SIGMA I-64 and SIGMA II-64, were run to examine the strategic and political framework that an American intervention in South Vietnam might face. Both had a Cassandra-like quality with respect to the eventual outcome of that intervention:

> In response to U.S. military action, North Vietnam and the Vietcong raised the tempo of attacks in the South and conducted terrorist attacks on U.S. installations and personnel. The game's final report concluded that 'a small expenditure of iron bombs' led the United States to commit sizeable forces and funds to defeat the North, while the war in the South continued with less attention and fewer resources. The paper warned that the U.S. public and Congress would not support a strategy based on graduated pressure. In fact, the officers who played the North Vietnamese leaders in the game exposed fundamental flaws in the assumptions that underlay graduated pressure. First, it showed that North Vietnam was capable of responding to U.S. escalation by intensifying the war on the ground. Second, it suggested that the United States was underestimating Hanoi's resolve.[78]

---

[76] Gerhard Ritter, *The Sword and the Scepter, The Problem of Militarism in Germany*, vol. 2, *The European Powers and the Wilhelminian Empire, 1890–1914*, trans. by Heinz Norden (Coral Gables, FL, 1970), p. 205.

[77] For the discussions and processes by which the Germans resumed unrestricted submarine warfare in 1917 see Holger H. Herwig, *The First World War, Germany and Austria-Hungry, 1914–1918* (London, 1997). Matters were no better before World War II. See Murray, "Net Assessment and Nazi Germany in the 1930s."

[78] H.R. McMaster, *Dereliction of Duty, Lyndon Johnson, Robert McNamara, The Joint Chiefs of Staff, and the Lies that Led to Vietnam* (New York, 1997), p. 90.

The results of SIGMA II were no more encouraging.[79] Yet, policy makers and military leaders in Washington largely dismissed the implications of the games. Not surprisingly, given the actual course of events, the games played no role in the decision to commit massive military forces to a conflict that was not in the best interests of the United States.

It appears that red teaming the highest level strategic decisions of the U.S. government may represent the most significant contribution that red teaming might make. Unfortunately, it is probably the most unlikely because, if done well, such an approach will inevitably challenge not only the military assumptions of generals and admirals, but even more dangerously the assumptions of politicians and senior bureaucrats. Only great statesmen such as Winston Churchill have had the moral courage to withstand challenges to their assumptions and preconceptions without executing the messenger. Integrity at the highest levels demands a willingness to grapple with the idiosyncratic and difficult questions that red teaming might present. It is the only method that can assure assumptions and preconceived notions receive the test they deserve and that America's young men and women are not placed in harm's way on the basis of feckless hopes.

Conclusion

What then might the experience of red teaming in the past suggest? Clearly, effective military organizations – ones that have realistically innovated in times of peace and that have adapted to the real conditions of war – have developed organizational cultures in which the challenging of assumptions has formed an intimate part of their world view. Red teaming has been one of the more effective ways in which the members of a military organization could challenge its assumptions. It would seem that effective red teaming can only be reflective of a larger culture that prizes serious intellectual assessments. It must also reflect the willingness of military organizations to tolerate honesty among the different levels of command, a culture in which subordinates can suggest other paths and alternatives other than those proposed by their superiors, without detriment to their careers. Equally important to military effectiveness is a culture that takes the intellectual preparation for war as seriously as the physical preparation. By itself, red teaming cannot create such a culture.

[79] Ibid., p. 157.

Red teaming can inform; it can educate; it can challenge assumptions; but, it cannot by itself change a culture that is unregenerate.

Simply grafting red teams onto organizations that possess few of the traits suggested previously will not produce an effective military organization. Human beings will instinctively understand and follow the cultural norms that really matter. If organizational leaders are disingenuous, if they display little interest in the "inky-fingered" side of preparing for war, and if they execute the bearers of bad news, all the red teaming in the world will make not the slightest bit of difference.[80] Unfortunately, it is the latter culture that has dominated military organizations in the twentieth century and earlier. "Muddy boots" soldiering, no matter how intense, can only go so far in preparing military organizations for war.

Red teaming will not prevent surprises. Surprise is inherent in a world dominated by chance, ambiguity, and uncertainty. But red teaming can prepare military organizations to deal with surprise. In particular, it can create a mental framework prepared for the unexpected, and it is the skillful, intelligent adaptation to the actual conditions of war that best leads to victory. The real issue that lies behind the facade of red teaming is the kind of military and political culture that can best protect the national interests. The business of war is the most complex and difficult that human beings undertake. The use of red teaming to challenge the assumptions and preconceptions of military planners as well as political leaders, to prepare and train forces for the challenges they will confront, and to educate and evaluate the intellectual acuity of officers could significantly improve the combat capabilities of U.S. military forces, but only if red teaming exists in a wider culture of honesty, rigor, and intellectual professionalism. Above all, red teaming could allow American policy makers and military leaders to gain insight into the nature of our opponents as they really are, as opposed to how policy makers would like to picture them.

---

[80] The phrase "inky fingered" was used by British officers to disparage those officers who actually read books. I am indebted to Major General Jonathan Bailey, Director General of Doctrine in the British Army, for this phrase.

8

The Distant Framework of War

In August 1914, a catastrophic war exploded on a European Continent, a continent that at the time seemed far removed from the travails of war, slaughter, and rapine that had marked earlier centuries. The ensuing conflict represented a watershed in European history, largely determining the erratic and murderous course of the twentieth century. While there had been a number of conflicts on the Continent in the 99 years between 1815 and 1914, none had come close to the violence, length, and destruction that the Revolutionary and Napoleonic Wars had caused. Nor had any of those wars approached the violence and ferocity of what was to come in the Great War.

Yet, the First World War did not represent a new phenomena in European history. In his classic *On War*, Carl von Clausewitz had accurately described the French Revolution's impact on Europe in the following terms:

> [B]ut in 1793 a force appeared and beggared all imagination. Suddenly war again became the business of the people – a people of thirty millions, all of whom considered themselves to be citizens.... The people became a participant in war; instead of governments and armies as heretofore, the full weight of the nation was thrown into the balance. The resources and efforts now available for use surpassed all conventional limits; nothing now impeded the vigor with which war could be waged, and consequently the opponents of France faced the utmost peril.
>
> War, untrammeled by any conventional restraints, had broken loose in all its elemental fury. This was due to the peoples' new share in the great affairs

This chapter was given at a conference at the Mershon Center dealing with the origins of the First World War. It has never been published before.

of state; and their participation in turn, resulted partly from the impact that the revolution had on the internal conditions of every state and partly from the danger that France posed to everyone.[1]

Clausewitz then posed to his nineteenth-century readers the fateful question for the coming 100 years of European history: "Will this always be the case in the future? From now on will every war in Europe be waged with the full resources of the state, and therefore be fought only over major issues that affect the people?"[2]

The near century of peace that followed Napoleon's defeat at Waterloo seemed to suggest that Clausewitz's question could be answered in the negative: the European powers had, for the most part, learned to work through their differences. Instead of disastrous conflicts involving all the powers, only smaller conflicts between two or at most three powers had broken Europe's tranquility in the aftermath of the Napoleonic Wars. The most violent, the Franco–Prussian War of 1870–1871, hardly lasted a year. While that war occasioned a number of fierce engagements – St. Privat and Gravelotte spring to mind – the casualty bill nowhere approached those of Napoleonic battles, such as Eylau, Leipzig, or Dresden. Moreover, the lower casualty rate occurred at a time when weapons of increasing technological sophistication and lethality were in the hands of the opposing armies. Thus, the sustained period of peace in the nineteenth century has led historians into the mistaken belief that World War I represented a new phenomenon – in effect leading them to miss the continuities in European history that had been operative since the beginning of the eighteenth century.

There had, of course, been the American Civil War. Nevertheless, despite the fact that the contestants were mostly of European extraction, few in Europe took much notice of its length or ferocity. That conflict had seen not only a war of the people, but the impact of the Industrial Revolution, which like the French Revolution had exploded at the end of the eighteenth century. For European military experts, that conflict had been one between ill-trained and ill-disciplined militias, as Graf von Moltke, the Prussian chief of the general staff is reputed to have pointed out. And certainly, the images of even the premier spit-and-polish troops of the Civil War, the Army of the Potomac, underlined a certain lack of regard for the military standards of appearance that ranks with the

---

[1] Clausewitz, *On War*, pp. 591–593.
[2] Ibid., p. 593.

disregard for the sartorial niceties of the military profession that the Israeli Defense Forces have displayed in the last half of the twentieth century. Moreover, given the distances to North America, it is not surprising the Europeans would either disregard events far from their shores or, as in the case of a generation of British military historians, distort the Civil War into a depiction of Southern knighthood fighting and losing only because of the hopeless odds confronting them on the battlefields of Virginia – a picture that the comfortable upper-class Victorians and Edwardians of the British Army found particularly congenial.[3]

However, by 1919, it was apparent that the American Civil War, with its deadly combination of the Industrial and French Revolutions, had been the harbinger of the next great European war.[4] By that point, it was too late. The horror of World War I – its length, its casualties which had swallowed up an entire generation of European youth, and its economic costs which had destroyed Europe as the engine of world prosperity, and even destroyed its belief in progress – all resulted in social and political revolutions that dwarfed the wreckage of what the French Revolution had brought in its train. In addition, World War I gave birth to monstrous experiments in social engineering: in Russia, with the Bolshevik Revolution and in Germany, with Hitler's National Socialists. In fact, one can argue that the social and political divisions that World War I caused did not end until 1989, when the Berlin Wall finally came down and the Bolshevik Revolution, born in 1917, collapsed.

Winston Churchill best caught the extent of the storm that swept over his Edwardian world in the opening paragraphs of *The World Crisis*:

> It was the custom in the palmy days of Queen Victoria for statesmen to expiate upon the glories of the British Empire, and to rejoice in that protecting Providence which had preserved us through so many dangers and brought us at length into a secure and prosperous age.
>
> Children were taught of the great war against Napoleon as the culminating effort in the history of the British people, and they looked on Waterloo and Trafalgar as the supreme achievements of British arms by land and sea. These prodigious victories, eclipsing all that had gone before, seemed the

---

[3] In this regard, see Jay Luvaas, *The Education of an Army: British Military Thought, 1815–1940* (London, 1965).

[4] For a discussion of the connection between the French and Industrial Revolutions in the American Civil War and then in the First World War, see Williamson Murray and MacGregor Knox, "Thinking about Revolutions in Warfare," in *The Dynamics of Military Revolution, 1300–2050*, ed. by MacGregor Knox and Williamson Murray (Cambridge, 2002).

fit and predestined ending to the long drama of our island race.... Three separate times in three different centuries had the British people rescued Europe from military domination. Thrice had the Low Countries been assailed. Thrice had British war and policy, often maintained single-handed, overthrown the aggressor. Always at the outset the strength of the enemy had seemed overwhelming, always the struggle had been prolonged through many years and across awful hazards, always the victory had at last been won.

Surely that was the end of the tale as it was so often the end of the book. History showed the rise, culmination, splendour, transition and decline of States and Empires. It seemed inconceivable that the same series of tremendous events through which since the days of Queen Elizabeth we had three times made our way successfully, should be repeated a fourth time and on an immeasurably larger scale. Yet that is what happened, and what we have lived to see.[5]

Perhaps it is not surprising then that World War I has become a picture in our historical consciousness of a dark and astonishing explosion that broke 99 years of almost unbroken peace in Europe. Moreover, one can only explain the Second World War in terms of the revolutionary movements that the Great War had spawned. Neither the Bolshevik seizure of power in 1917 nor that of the Nazis in 1933 is explicable without reference to the collapse of the Russian and German Empires at the end of World War I. Yet, even after the passage of nearly a century [this work was written in 2002], the origins of World War I have remained opaque and uncertain enough to support innumerable historians and academic careers.[6]

In the largest sense, the puzzlement among historians over the war's eruption has resulted from two factors: the conflict's seemingly interminable length and cost – in both economic and human terms – and the distortion over the course of the nineteenth century of historical patterns that had begun in the late seventeenth century. In fact, the First World War was not the *first* world war, but it was the first world war in over a century. Therein lay much of the problem for those who conducted the war both on the battlefield and in the political and strategic arenas. This chapter attempts to place the Great War within two

---

[5] Winston S. Churchill, *The World Crisis* (Toronto, 1931), p. 3. The three wars, to which Churchill refers where Britain had saved European civilization, were the wars of Philip II of Spain, of Louis XIV of France, and of the French Revolution and Napoleon.

[6] Of all the works that explain the origins of the First World War, the greatest and most thorough still remains Luigi Albertini's masterpiece: *The Origins of the War of 1914*, 3 vols. (New York, 1952–1957).

contexts: the first, the strategic patterns of European wars beginning in the eighteenth century and continuing into the nineteenth century; and second, the difficulties that military institutions confronted in adapting to the major technological changes that had occurred over the previous four decades before 1914, a crucial factor in the prolongation and cost of the conflict.

The Patterns of War

In the late seventeenth century, Louis XIV appeared close to achieving a hegemony over Europe that would have allowed France and its military power to dominate the central and western portions of the Continent in a fashion not seen since the collapse of the Roman Empire. By 1700, the French Army had the reputation of being the most advanced and technologically proficient in Europe.[7] The French fleet was among the most powerful among the maritime powers. In every respect, France was at the point of dominating the European Continent.

In terms of Louis XIV's enemies, Habsburg power in Austria and Germany was under assault from both the west (France) and southeast (the Ottoman Empire). As recently as 1688, the Turks had besieged Vienna, and while it is clear today that their power was on the wane, that reality was not apparent to the statesmen of the time. To the west, Spain had entered a period of decay, its power and influence rapidly disintegrating. As a military power, England, at least on its record in the seventeenth century, hardly mattered, whatever the discipline and tactical proficiency Oliver Cromwell had provided to his 'New Model Army.' Only the Dutch, with their obstinacy and tenacity, had managed to hold the French at bay over the course of the Nine Years' War at the end of the century. Exhausted from that conflict, the combatants cobbled together a peace they hoped would last. But tensions among the European powers now existed not only on the Continent but in the territories and colonies they had seized around the world over the previous two centuries.

Thus, the peace did not last. In 1699 the king of Spain died with no direct heir. In his last will and testament, he turned the Spanish Empire over to Louis XIV's grandson, in effect combining the power of France and Spain in Europe, as well as throughout the world. This represented a state of affairs the other powers refused to accept, and the War of Spanish Succession (1701–1714) broke out, a war that was to be the *first* world

---

[7] For the French Army in this period, see particularly John Lynn, *Giant of the Grand Siècle, The French Army, 1610–1715* (Cambridge, 1997).

war. For a variety of reasons, historians, including Winston Churchill, have focused on the Duke of Marlborough's brilliant campaigns in the Low Countries and southern Germany.[8] In those two theaters, with the cooperation of the great Habsburg general, Prince Eugene, the allies came close to breaking the power of the French monarchy.

In 1704 Marlborough and Eugene united their armies in southern Germany and annihilated a French and Bavarian army at Blenheim. At one stroke their victory destroyed Louis XIV's strategic position. So devastating was the impact of their victory on French military power that France would remain on the defensive for the remainder of the war. Two years later a combined Anglo–Dutch force under Marlborough wrecked another French army at Ramilles, and in 1708 the allies won their third signal victory at Oudenarde. France appeared to be on the brink of collapse. Only the battle at Malplaquet the next year, where the allies barely drove the French off the field, restored some luster to French arms and undermined Marlborough's prestige sufficiently for his enemies in London to drive his supporters from power.

Nevertheless, while the attention of Europe's leaders centered on these momentous campaigns along the frontiers between France on one side and the Low Countries and Belgium on the other, the opposing sides were contending across the world in a series of campaigns that projected military power at distances never before occurring in history. In effect, the War of Spanish Succession was also a world war. In 1704, British and Hanoverian regiments, including one in which the German novelist Ernst Jünger would later serve during the First World War, seized Gibraltar.[9] By 1707 British control of the Mediterranean was sufficient to support Prince Eugene's attempt to capture Toulon. Elsewhere, British and French forces were contending for control of the Caribbean's lucrative sugar, while in India the duel for the Indian subcontinent was already underway. Even in North America British and French forces were feeling each other out in what the colonists in America called Queen Anne's War. In fact, these initial battles in North America and India represented the opening round between the British and the French for control of world empire.

---

[8] Not surprisingly, given the fact that he was a direct descendant of the Duke of Marlborough, Churchill was to write a biography of his ancestor, perhaps his greatest historical study and one of the great works of English literature, as well as historical analysis, in the twentieth century. See Winston S. Churchill, *Marlborough, His Life and Times*, 4 vols. (London, 1933–1938). For a more modern look at Marlborough see David Chandler, *Marlborough as Military Commander* (London, 1973).

[9] Jünger proudly noted in his memoirs, *Storm of Steel*, the cap badge of his Hanoverian regiment still displayed Gibraltar during its battles in the First World War.

The worldwide nature of the conflict reflected the drastic social, political, and military changes that had occurred during the seventeenth century with the creation of the modern state and its bureaucratization of military forces.[10] That process rested on the creation of responsive and obedient military organizations – military organizations that possessed both internal discipline, so the state could maintain order within its frontiers, and external discipline, so that it could project its power beyond its borders in coherent and well-supplied campaigns. The creation of admiralties and war offices ensured disciplined and well-trained military forces. The state now provided the resources and financial support to provide soldiers and sailors not only military equipment and supplies required for long campaigns but regular pay, sustenance, and barracks in peacetime as well as in war.

The world had not seen such effective political and military institutions since the time of the Roman Empire, when 30-odd legions (roughly 150,000 legionaries) and an equivalent number of auxiliaries had guaranteed the security of the entire Mediterranean world for nearly 250 years.[11] The crucial point is that the creation of the modern state with its trained and organized military forces allowed the contestants to conduct coherent and effective military operations over long periods of time not only in Europe but across the broad expanses of the world's oceans out onto which the Europeans had first ventured two centuries earlier.

The War of Spanish Succession settled little in terms of the worldwide contest between Britain and France. The struggle between the British and French for control of North America, India, and the Caribbean remained open for dispute and resolution at a later date. Nevertheless, the heavy casualties accompanying Marlborough's efforts to support the Habsburgs and the Dutch on the Continent led to a furious debate in Britain about the wisdom of a Continental or oceanic strategy against France. Jonathan

---

[10] For discussions of the nature of military revolutions during the course of the seventeenth century, see among others: Clifford J. Rogers, *The Military Revolution Debate, Readings on the Military Transformation in Early Modern Europe* (Boulder, CO, 1995); William H. McNeill, *The Pursuit of Power* (Chicago, 1982); Gunther Rothenberg, "Maurice of Nassau, Gustavus Adolphus, Raimondo Montecuccoli and the 'Military Revolution' of the Seventeenth Century," in Peter Paret, Gordon A. Craig, and Felix Gilbert, eds., *Makers of Modern Strategy* (Oxford, 1986); Geoffrey Parker, *The Military Revolution: Military Innovation and the Rise of the West, 1500–1800* (Cambridge, 1988); and Williamson Murray and MacGregor Knox, "Thinking about Revolutions in Warfare," in Knox and Murray, eds., *The Dynamics of Military Revolution* chap. 1.

[11] On the Roman Army, see Graham Webster, *The Roman Imperial Army of the First and Second Centuries A.D.* (London, 1969); and Adrian Keith Goldsworthy, *The Roman Army at War, 100 BC – AD 200* (Oxford, 1995).

Swift's biting satire, *On the Conduct of the Allies*, represented as furious an assault on the idea that Britain had anything to gain in supporting Continental allies as anything written by antiwar authors in the late 1920s and 1930s disparaging the active participation of Britain's army on the Continent in the First World War.[12] But whatever the failures involved in the conduct of worldwide operations during the War of Spanish Succession, the breadth and extent of those campaigns over oceanic distances as well as the capacity of European states to sustain military forces at war for considerable periods of time represented a revolutionary departure in the conduct of war in terms of historical precedents.

If the results of this *first* world war were anything but clear, the results of the *second* and *third* world wars were decisive for the course of world history over the next two centuries.[13] The second world war actually involved two conflicts, the war of Austrian Succession (1740–1748) and the Seven Years' War (1756–1763).[14] The short interval of peace between the two conflicts saw a major realignment of European alliances, but the essential point was that Britain and France remained on opposite sides of the struggle. The conflict in Europe revolved around the seizure of provinces and territories, with the War of Austrian Succession beginning with the utterly unprincipled seizure of the province of Silesia by Prussia's Frederick the Great.[15] For the most part, European conflicts in the eighteenth century remained limited in goals and the unwillingness of the participants to inflict damage on enemy territory.[16] As Clausewitz

---

[12] In this regard, the military pundit B.H. Liddell Hart coined the term "the British way in war" in the 1930s to describe a British strategic approach that utilized Continental allies, while the Royal Navy with support from the army picked off vulnerable colonial possessions of the nation's enemies. What Liddell Hart ignored was the fact that in nearly every case in these wars Britain also had to make substantial efforts, financial as well as military, on the Continent to support those allies. Moreover, the Germans in the world wars of the twentieth century had few colonial possessions that were vulnerable to British attack.

[13] MacGregor Knox, in his section of *The Mainstream of Civilization*, fifth edition (New York, 1989), p. 89, refers to these wars quite correctly as the first world wars.

[14] Julian S. Corbett's *England in the Seven Years' War*, 2 vols. (London, 1907) still remains a classic on the conduct of that war by the Royal Navy. Fred Anderson's *Crucible of War, The War for Empire in North America, 1756–1765* (New York, 2003) is a brilliant piece of writing and historical analysis. His *The French and Indian Wars* (New York, 2005) is also worth consulting.

[15] Frederick announced that he was putting the province of Silesia under Prussian "protection" to aid the new Empress of Austria, Maria Teresa, as she assumed power in the Habsburg lands.

[16] There is a particularly sharp discussion of limited war in the eighteenth century in MacGregor Knox, "Mass Politics and Nationalism as Military Revolution: The French Revolution and After," in Knox and Murray, eds., *The Dynamics of Military Revolution*.

suggested eighty years later, "Not only in its means, therefore, but also in its aims, war increasingly became limited to the fighting force itself. Armies with their fortresses and prepared positions, came to form a state within a state in which violence gradually faded away."[17]

But the war for empire was on a wholly different plain.[18] The British aimed at eliminating their French rivals from the colonial competition for territories that both nations coveted. The struggle for world empire ranged from India to the Caribbean to the primeval forests of North America. In 1745 in the middle of the war of Austrian Succession, a combined British and American colonial force seized the great French fortress of Louisbourg on Cape Breton Island; two years later the Royal Navy annihilated two French fleets escorting convoys from the West Indies. In the end, because the French had captured Madras in India, both sides agreed on a peace treaty at Aix-la-Chapelle that largely represented the *status quo ante bellum*.

Thus, the War of Austrian Succession settled little. Particularly the French and the British felt that there were strategic issues that only war could decide. The struggle broke out again in Europe in 1756, the official start of the Seven Years' War, one of the most decisive contests in human history. But the fighting had already begun two years earlier in North America when a young and incompetent George Washington led a Virginia expedition deep into the forest gloom of western Pennsylvania against a French and Indian fort on the site of modern-day Pittsburgh.[19] General George Braddock's disastrous expedition, which the French and Indians soundly crushed, soon followed Washington's defeat. But initial French victories in North America and India proved ephemeral. An incompetent French monarch, Louis XV, embroiled his nation in both oceanic and Continental wars, the latter partially because Frederick the Great had insulted his mistress. As a result, the French fought neither war well and bankrupted the state to boot.[20] Frederick the Great's Prussians

---

[17] Clausewitz, *On War*, p. 591.
[18] During the Seven Years' War, Admiral John Byng failed to accomplish his mission to land troops on Minorca and allowed a French fleet to escape with minimum damage. He was tried by court martial and then executed by firing squad. On the other hand, Lord Sackville, commander of allied cavalry at the Battle of Minden, refused three times to obey the order to charge the disorganized French. He was not executed for dereliction of duty. The message was clear: Britain would hold the Royal Navy to a higher standard than it would hold the British Army. Twelve years later as Lord Germain, Sackville would direct the war against the American colonists and play a major role in the loss of the North American colonies.
[19] Anderson's *Crucible of Empire* is outstanding on this.
[20] The financial difficulties occasioned by the Seven Years' War would only be exacerbated by the French participation in the American War of independence and contribute directly

soon humiliated the French at Rossbach, while even greater disasters occurred in the war for empire. In 1757 near Calcutta, Robert Clive led British forces to victory at Plessy and largely destroyed France's position on the Indian subcontinent.

In 1759, a year the British termed the "year of miracles (*annus mirablis*)," a British army under Major General James Wolfe destroyed the French Army defending Quebec on the Plains of Abraham. British amphibious forces captured the main sugar islands in the Carribean. And the Royal Navy pursued and destroyed a French fleet under a full gale over the unchartered reefs of Quiberon Bay. When the smoke cleared, the Royal Navy had gained Britain domination over the world's oceans. A great new world empire stretched from North America to India. The French, on the other hand, had suffered not only catastrophic defeats on the world stage, with results that would make English the *lingua franca* of world business and diplomacy into the twenty-first century, but their army had suffered complete humiliation at the hands of Frederick the Great's armies. Moreover, the monarchy accumulated a mountain of debts that would lead to the revolution. Slightly more than a decade later, a major revolution would break out in Britain's North American colonies, the course of which would bring the French in to challenge Britain's position.[21] But with the exception of the American colonies – a fractious and disobedient lot, Britain remained in control of its world empire, while France had nothing to show for its efforts other than American gratitude. And events would soon show that there was precious little of that.

Revolutionary War

The wars at the end of the eighteenth and beginning of the nineteenth centuries, however, dwarfed every war that had occurred before in history. Their protracted course reflected the fact that two great social and economic revolutions in human affairs now fueled the engine of war: the French Revolution and the Industrial Revolution. Begun in 1792, the Wars of the French Revolution led directly to the Napoleonic Wars. For nearly a quarter century between 1792 and the Battle of Waterloo in

---

to the outbreak of the French Revolution and the destruction of the monarchy. For a clear examination of Byng's execution and how it pushed the Royal Navy in the right direction, see Arthur Herman, *To Rule the Waves, How the British Navy Shaped the Modern World* (New York, 2004).

[21] And the only reason lying behind the French decision to intervene in the American Revolution seems to have been a desire to avenge France's defeat in the Seven Years' War.

1815, Europe was at war. The political, social, and ideological consequences of the French Revolution and the equally widespread effects and consequences of the first stages of the Industrial Revolution in Britain changed the face of European and world history.

Yet, one of the more remarkable facets of this period of constant warfare was that to a great extent these two revolutions remained separate and distinct phenomena. The revolutionary enthusiasm allowed the French to mobilize their population and resources to an extent never before seen in history. As the republic decreed in its *Levée en Masse*:

> From this moment, until our enemies have been driven from the territory of the Republic, the entire French nation is permanently called to the colors. The young men will go into battle; married men will forge weapons and transport supplies; women will make tents and uniforms and serve in the hospital; children will make old cloth into bandages; old men will have themselves carried into public squares to rouse the courage of the warriors and preach hatred of kings, and the unity of the Republic.[22]

Thus, it was not revolutionary new technologies or tactical systems that led to the ensuing French successes. In fact, until Napoleon's eruption into Italy in 1796, the French consistently lost more battles than they won.[23] But losses did not matter to the new revolutionary armies, supported as they were by the almost inexhaustible resources of manpower the *levée en masse* was able to supply. The republic's masters were willing to shovel reinforcements and new battalions into the struggle until they overwhelmed France's opponents. A French nation that supported its military establishment with unlimited numbers of volunteers and conscripts could afford terrible casualties, while the *ancien régimes* opposed it with armies made up of long-service, highly trained professional soldiers who took several years and considerable expense to train to the standards of their armies. As Clausewitz suggested:

> Suddenly war again became the business of the people – a people of thirty millions, all of whom considered themselves to be citizens.... The people became a participant in war; instead of governments and armies as heretofore, the full weight of the nation was thrown into the balance. The resources and efforts now available for use surpassed all conventional limits; nothing now impeded the vigor with which war could be waged and consequently the opponents of France faced the utmost peril.... War

---

[22] *Archives parlementaires de 1789 á 1860, première série* (Paris, 1907), vol. 72, p. 674, translation by MacGregor Knox.
[23] The most thorough discussion of Napoleonic warfare remains David Chandler's brilliant *The Campaigns of Napoleon* (New York, 1966).

untrammeled by any conventional restraints, had broken lose in all its elemental fury.[24]

Thus, France's opponents could not sustain the terrible casualties that war now entailed until nearly two decades later when they adapted systems of conscription that were similar to those of the French. The difficulties they confronted were only exacerbated when Napoleon seized control of the Revolution's military system and applied it with even greater effectiveness due to his brilliance as an operational commander.

In the end the French were brought down by two factors. First, the other European powers finally drew on the nationalism of their own populations. In a desperate attempt to reform the Prussian monarchy after the catastrophic defeat of Jena-Auerstedt in 1806, Baron von Hardenberg, one of the leading Prussian military and civil reformers, warned his monarch in 1807 that "the illusion that we could withhold the revolution most effectively by holding fast to the old has itself resulted in the promotion and ever greater extension of the revolution. The power of its principles is so great, they are so generally recognized and widely spread, that the state that fails to take them up voluntarily will either suffer destruction or be compelled from outside to accept them."[25]

The extent of the Prussian humiliation in 1806, in which the proud military and state of Frederick the Great had collapsed in less than a month, provided Prussia's reformers with a handle to force a conservative and unwilling monarch to execute a series of major civil and military reforms. In the long run the liberal civil reforms failed to stick, but in the short run they allowed Prussia to harness the national outrage throughout the Germanies at the French occupation to drive and support the mobilization of Prussia's military forces for the battles of 1813, 1814, and 1815. Unfortunately for the eventual course of European history, the military reforms stuck: the efforts to create an educated, professional officer corps, embodied in the great general staff, set the Prusso–German Army on the road to its invention of modern war in the period from 1916 through 1918.[26]

---

[24] Clausewitz, *On War*, pp. 592–593.
[25] Georg Winter, ed., *Die Reorganisation des Preussischen Staates unter Stein und Hardenberg* (Leipzig, 1931), vol. 1, pp. 305–306. Translation by MacGregor Knox.
[26] See among others MacGregor Knox, *Common Destiny: Dictatorship, Foreign Policy, and War in Fascist Italy and Nazi Germany* (Cambridge, 2000), chap 5; and Martin Samuels, *Command or Control? Command, Training and Tactics in the British and German Armies, 1888–1918* (London, 1995).

In Spain, nationalism, led by the church and peasants, resulted in a ferocious guerrilla war.[27] By 1810 the British were providing substantial help to the rebels, while the Duke of Wellington's forces, based in Portugal, provided a growing threat to the French position throughout the Iberian Peninsula. Likewise in Russia, the monarchy mobilized both the church and the peasants to the cause of nationalism against the foreign invader. The combination of guerrilla war, Russia's distances, the harshness of winter conditions, and the fierceness of Russian resistance at Borodino combined to destroy the Grand Army in the 1812 campaign. In the end, only nationalism, in its many different forms, could defeat the French.

But there was also an equally important factor that contributed to the defeat of the French: the Industrial Revolution.[28] The impact of that revolution on the course of the wars between 1792 and 1815 was less direct than that of revolutionary nationalism; it was certainly less obvious to the participants.[29] Yet, behind the "storm-beaten ships" of the Royal Navy that protected Britain from the French armies, the British had been undergoing a great shift in the means of production.[30] Napoleon is reputed to have described the British as "a nation of shopkeepers." He could not have been more incorrect. It was the French who were, and remained for much of the nineteenth century, "a nation of shopkeepers."

The British, on the other hand, were developing in the late eighteenth century the first sustainable basis for industrial production.[31] As the partner of James Watt, the inventor of the steam engine, commented: "I sell,

---

[27] For the factors lying behind the revolutionary situation in northern Spain, see John Lawrence Tone, *The Fatal Knot, The Guerrilla War in Navarre and the Defeat of Napoleon in Spain* (Chapel Hill, 1994).

[28] For the relationship of these two great revolutions, see Murray and Knox, "Thinking about Revolutions in Warfare."

[29] See McNeill, *The Pursuit of Power*, chap. 6.

[30] "They were dull, weary, eventless months, those months of watching and waiting of the big ships before the French arsenals. Purposeless they surely seemed to many, but they saved England. The world has never seen a more impressive demonstration of the influence of sea power on history. Those distant, storm-beaten ships, upon which the Grand Army never looked, stood between it and the dominion of the world." Alfred Thayer Mahan, *The Influence of Sea Power upon the French Revolution and Empire, 1793–1812* (Boston, 1894), p. 118.

[31] One can, of course, quibble that the sustained period of industrial development in England, which began in the 1770s and lasted for decades thereafter, was not a revolution because of its length. Certainly the processes of change were evolutionary, but the results were revolutionary in their impact on first British and then human society and the economic framework within which much of the world would work in the future. For the first time muscle of either man or animals had been replaced to a great extent.

Sir, what the world desires to have – power."[32] Nevertheless, the technologies of the time were not yet ready to impact the actual battlefield. The armies of the French Revolutionary and the Napoleonic periods fought with weapons that replicated in almost every respect the weapons in use during the War of Spanish Succession 100 years earlier. The French had only altered the social, tactical, and operational framework of war, not the technological framework within which the armies of the late eighteenth and early nineteenth centuries operated.

But the productive base created by the Industrial Revolution provided the British with the financial resources to maintain complete dominance over the world's oceans, support a major army on the Iberian Peninsula, *and* provide the money that helped to keep the armies of the great coalitions that eventually defeated Napoleon in the field. France herself had been wealthy enough to support the mobilization of its population to an unheard of degree, but none of the empires of Central or Eastern Europe (Prussia, Austria, or Russia) possessed sufficient financial strength to mobilize their population to a similar extent. But Britain, with the swelling profits of the Industrial Revolution as well as those of her great worldwide empire, was able to make up the deficit.

The Continental powers were not the only ones to gain from Napoleon's defeat. In the largest sense, Allied victory, confirmed at the Congress of Vienna, solidified Britain's hold over a world empire which stretched from Canada to India and which further pushed the pace of technological change – first, in Britain, eventually in the rest of Europe, and then in the world. Peace came in 1815 and, with the Corsican ogre safely packed away to St. Helena, the European powers could safely turn from the pursuit of war to rebuilding a ravaged Continent.[33]

A Century of Peace?

Nearly 25 years of constant war, accompanied by the slaughter of millions of soldiers and the wastage of vast resources, resulted in the peace of the exhausted in 1815. Historians have often seen the ninety-nine years of peace following Waterloo as a single continuum that reflected a

---

[32] Stanley Chadorow, MacGregor Knox, Conrad Schirokauer, *The Mainstream of Civilization*, 5th edition (New York, 1989), p. 685.
[33] The exception was Britain, which like the United States in 1945 emerged from the wars with its territory untouched and its economy swelling from the profits of war. On visiting London shortly after the Battle of Waterloo, Field Marshal Blücher is reputed to have exclaimed: "Lord what a city to loot."

coherent balance of power and agreement among the great powers – one that began to break down only in the early years of the twentieth century. The story is, however, more complex. In the immediate aftermath of the French–Revolutionary–Napoleonic Wars, the major Continental powers established a commonality of aims, embodied in the League of the Three Emperors. However, the British soon fell away from Continental entanglements to focus on their empire. In particular, they were less than enthralled with the reactionary nature of the goals propagated by the Austrian statesman Clemens von Metternich. Metternich himself was attempting to put the genie of nationalism back in the bottle – admittedly an impossible task, but one that would have spared Europe the catastrophe of the first half of the twentieth century.

Metternich's world unraveled with the revolutions of 1848. In the succeeding 25 years a number of wars occurred among the European powers. For the most part, these wars remained conflicts of single powers against other single powers, while the span of conflict in terms of geography and time remained limited. Thus, the fighting rarely approached the intensity and violence of the wars of the French Revolution or Napoleon. How and why this was so played a role in creating the conditions that made possible the catastrophic surprise of 1914. While technological change was of increasing importance in all of these conflicts, the fusion of the Industrial Revolution with the French Revolution's mobilization of the nation, which was the great mark of the First World War, only occurred in the American Civil War; however, there were some elements of such a fusion in the Franco–Prussian War of 1870–1871.[34] The long-term result was that, for the most part, the Europeans failed to grasp the grim lessons of what modern war would entail, which would have been the case had a conflict similar to the American Civil War occurred.

After 1848 Europe remained in flux, with neither a dominant hegemon nor a stable balance of power. In the 1860s, however, the Prussians under Otto von Bismarck's leadership overturned the centuries-old framework of European power by uniting the center, an area that had derisively been termed for centuries as "the Germanies."[35] Guided by Bismarck's statesmanship, the Prussians fought three major wars. The result of their victories was the creation of a united German state that dominated Europe

---

[34] McNeill, *The Pursuit of Power*, pp. 250–254.
[35] The basis of Cardinal Richelieu's policy, exemplified by his support for the Protestant Swedes in the late 1620s, was to keep the Germanies divided and to prevent any single power, in this case the Catholic Hapsburgs, from dominating the region.

diplomatically and strategically for the next 75 years.³⁶ To all intents and purposes, the new Prusso–German state had gained a position of semi-hegemony in Europe after 1871. But there were limits. In 1875, worried by France's quick recovery, Bismarck threatened renewed war against the French. The other major powers, led by the British, however, made it clear that they would not stand apart from a second Franco–Prussian War. Thus, Bismarck had to be content with a strategic situation that placed Berlin at the center of an increasingly complex diplomatic web that he manipulated until he was finally removed from office. Nevertheless, the other European powers maintained considerable latitude in the conduct of their international policies.

With Bismarck's dismissal in 1888, the Reich lost its rudder. Those who followed thought they understood Europe and Germany's future place in it better than Bismarck. But they understood nothing. They busily engaged in disconnected and aggressive policies that led much of the rest of Europe to perceive Germany as a threat, drove Republican France and Tsarist Russia into an alliance that eventually attracted the British, and tied the German state to the irresponsible and decaying Austro–Hungarian Empire. In effect, while Germany was steadily becoming more powerful in its economic and military strength, its flawed strategic policies were creating an anti-German alliance system of even greater strength.³⁷ Thus, the Reich created the very encirclement that its leaders denounced. In the end, Germany's leaders attempted to break the alliance system that surrounded them by embarking on a catastrophic war that came close to destroying European civilization.

The Wars of Mid-Century

The first major conflict to erupt after the revolutionary tide of 1848 had run its course was the Crimean War (1854–1856).³⁸ That conflict

---

[36] Tragically for European history, most Germans attributed Prussia's enormous strategic successes to the military rather than to Bismarck's statesmanship, which had created the possibilities that the Prussian military were able to take advantage of.

[37] The historical profession continues its implicit and explicit examination of German strategic and military policies that contributed to the outbreak of the First World War. Among others, see Isabel V. Hull, *Absolute Destruction, Military Culture and the Practices of War in Imperial Germany* (Ithaca, NY, 2005); Holger Herwig, *The First World War, Germany and Austria, 1914–1918* (London, 1997); and Roger Chickering, *Imperial Germany and the Great War, 1914–1918* (Cambridge, 1918).

[38] Among others on the Crimean War, see Andrew D. Lambert, *The Crimean War, British Grand Strategy against Russia, 1853–1856* (Manchester, 1990); and Christopher Hibbert, *The Destruction of Lord Ragland* (London, 1963).

pitted Britain and France as allies against Tsarist Russia in defense of the moribund Turkish Empire. The major cause of the war had to do with British and French fears that the Russians were about to topple the Ottoman Empire, correctly described as Europe's sick man, and penetrate into the Mediterranean. Whatever the politics of the situation, the war involved opponents at the far ends of Europe, with no common frontier across which to wage war. Thus, despite the excitement of British and French public opinion, there was no chance for either side to wage a war that aimed at overthrowing the other. The allies eventually cobbled together expeditionary forces and, supported by their combined navies, projected those forces into the Black Sea and eventually onto the Crimea.

That deployment represented the first direct impact that the technologies of the Industrial Revolution were to have on the conduct of war between the major powers. The steam ship allowed the allies to deploy forces far more quickly and support them more reliably than had ever been the case before.[39] The Russians, however, who had invested less in railroads than the rest of Europe, found it more difficult to deploy and sustain substantial military forces in the Crimea far from their center, even though it was their own territory. The technologies of the Industrial Revolution also provided allied armies with another major advantage. Armed with the *minié* bullet, which allowed rifled muskets to reach out and kill at greater ranges than smooth-bore muskets, British soldiers at the Battle of Alma devastated the great columns of attacking Russian infantry, equipped with the latter. Thus was born the legend of the "thin red line."

Moreover, the telegraph not only allowed Whitehall and Paris to keep in touch with their military forces almost immediately, but enabled journalists to send reports to their newspapers on battlefield results as well as the sorry state of allied supply, particularly that of the British forces. However, while technology altered the battlefield in major ways, the Crimean War remained a cabinet war – closer to the wars of the eighteenth century in Central Europe than to the wars of the twentieth century. The results of the war were hardly impressive. In the end, the Russians agreed only to the demilitarization of the Black Sea and to the maintenance of the decrepit Ottoman Empire.

Before the decade was out, Napoleon III, Emperor of France and nephew of the great Napoleon, had embarked on another major war – this

---

[39] The travails of the British expeditionary force over the winter in spite of modern technological support suggest a great deal about how matters had gone in earlier times.

time in Italy. The emperor was a strong supporter of nationalism and encouraged the Piedmontese to embark on a struggle of national liberation to drive the Austrians out of northern Italy and unite the peninsula under their suzerainty. However, the horrors of the Battles of Magenta and Solferino between the Franco–Piedmontese armies and the Austrians were sufficient to persuade the emperor, who possessed little of his uncle's ruthlessness, to end the war. The Piedmontese gained Lombardy as their reward, while a revolutionary tide of nationalism which the war had unleashed soon added Sicily and Naples to the new Italian state. The Austrians retained Venetia, but they soon lost it as well. Nevertheless, Europe escaped the possibility of a major conflict that would have resulted, had the other major powers intervened.

The Prussian Wars and the Remaking of Europe

The 1860s and 1870s brought a greater number of conflicts, all of which underlined the growing importance of technology as well as the increasing pace of technological change. In the last of these conflicts, the Franco–Prussian War, the contestants came close to unleashing a war that combined the Industrial and French Revolutions. But the major strategic anomaly of these wars, which overthrew the European order established by the great French statesman, Cardinal Richelieu, in the seventeenth century, lay in the fact that despite the creation of a powerful new German state in the heart of the Continent, no larger European-wide conflict occurred. Certainly, the earlier attempts to overthrow the system, whether by Louis XIV, the French Revolutionaries, or Napoleon Bonaparte, had occasioned powerful and generally effective responses by the other major powers.

Three factors prevented these wars from igniting a catastrophic European war that might have resembled the American Civil War. The first and most obvious was the brilliant statesmanship and strategic vision of Otto von Bismarck.[40] But Bismarck alone would have been incapable of achieving his strategic revolution had the Prussians not developed a military

---

[40] Ironically, Bismarck's successors in Germany would largely emphasize the military component in explaining Prussia's success in uniting the Reich rather than Bismarck's understanding of the political and strategic realities. Erich Eyck, *Bismarck and the German Empire* (New York, 1960) remains the classic study on the Iron Chancellor's strategic approach. A.J.P. Taylor's *The Struggle for Mastery in Europe, 1848–1918* (Oxford, 1954) is particularly useful for understanding the larger political and strategic issues of this period.

system more advanced technologically and *professionally* than the European armies they faced.[41] As a result of the military reforms of the 1808–1812 period, the Prussians developed a military culture that allowed their army to adapt to the extraordinarily rapid technological changes occurring.[42]

Admittedly, the generalship of Graf Helmut von Moltke has deservedly received much of the credit for the success of Prussian arms in the 1860s and 1870s. But the general staff system provided the Prussians a major advantage in mobilizing, deploying, and then coordinating the movements of their army. Moreover, one should not discount the incompetence that Prussia's enemies brought to the table, both in the realm of statesmanship and on the field of battle.[43] Thus, it was a unique set of circumstances that allowed Bismarck to set Prussia's opponents up for catastrophic military defeat and then to utilize the results to achieve ends, which were truly revolutionary in strategic terms.

Bismarck's appointment in 1862 as chancellor reflected the breakdown of Prussia's constitutional system. Given his reputation for ferocious partisanship and deep personal hatreds, only a complete political deadlock and the king's desperation served to bring him to power. Bismarck made clear from the first that he had big plans for Prussia. In a speech to the Prussian Chamber's budget committee in September 1862, he announced: "The great questions of [our] time will not be decided through speeches and majority votes – that was the great error of [the revolutions of] 1848 and 1849 – but through blood and iron."[44] Neither the representatives of the Prussian people nor those of the other European powers paid much attention.

To fund the army in the face of the refusal of Prussia's parliamentarians to provide sufficient tax revenue, the chancellor simply collected what the army needed from Prussia's obedient burghers. A war against Denmark over Schleswig–Holstein, with Austria as Prussia's ally, allowed Bismarck to rally patriotic sentiment to the monarchy while the army received its

[41] For the technological choices and advances that the Prussian Army made in mid-century, see Dennis E. Schowalter, *Railroads and Rifles: Soldiers, Technology, and the Unification of Germany* (Hamden, CT, 1975).
[42] For the roots of this development, see Charles Edward White, *The Enlightened Soldier – Scharnhorst and the Militärische Gesellschaft in Berlin, 1801–1805* (New York, 1989).
[43] For the most part, historians have been unwilling to recognize the fact that incompetence dominates the course of human events rather than competence. For a further discussion of this topic, see Williamson Murray, *The Change in the European Balance of Power, 1938–1939, The Path to Ruin* (Princeton, 1984), pp. 358–359.
[44] Otto von Bismarck, *Bismarck: Die gesammelten Werke* (Berlin, 1928), vol. 10, p. 140.

baptism of fire. The small but professional general staff that the reforms of Gerhard von Scharnhorst and others had created in response to the disastrous defeat Prussia had received at French hands in 1806 had not yet achieved a position of dominance within the army. Yet, with trained, professional officers at his disposal, Moltke was able to complete the army's adoption of the needle-gun, the breech-loading rifle, and prepare the army's combat units for deployment by railroad. The results, at least in the Danish War, were spotty, but with an organized, trained general staff, the Prussians were able to do something that no other European army could do at the time: they learned from their combat and logistical experiences in a coherent, effective fashion.

Within two years after the end of the conflict with Denmark, Bismarck had so annoyed the Austrians by Prussia's behavior during their joint occupation of Schleswig–Holstein that war broke out between the two powers.[45] In brilliant fashion the Iron Chancellor either persuaded the other European powers the coming war with Austria was not of their concern, or in the case of the French, that there would be suitable rewards for them down the line. The Austrians declared war. The Prussians then deployed effortlessly and smoothly. Not only did their forces roll up on the frontier of Bohemia and Moravia to launch a major thrust into Austria's Czech provinces, but they had already defeated Austria's two major German allies, Hanover and Saxony, by the time major operations against Austria began.

To make matters worse, the Austrians conducted a lackadaisical campaign, while their commander, General Ludwig Benedek, placed his forces on the far bank of the Elbe River in tactically indefensible positions. The Prussian needle-gun then turned the Austrian Army's hopeless operational position into catastrophe at the Battle of Königgrätz, one more in the long tradition of Austrian defeats. In a single day's hard slogging, Prussian forces turned the Austrian Army into a mass of dead, wounded, and fleeing soldiers, incapable of further resistance.

The road to Vienna lay open, one that Moltke and his generals fully expected to take. To their astonishment – as well as Europe's – Bismarck persuaded the Prussian king to order a halt all along the line. In short order, the chancellor negotiated a peace with the Austrians that cost the latter nothing except the territory of their German allies and a recognition

---

[45] For the course of the war from Austria's perspective, see the outstanding study by Geoffrey Wawro: *The Austro-Prussian War, Austria's War with Prussia and Italy* (Cambridge, 1997).

of Prussia's hegemony over the "Germanies."[46] Moltke and his generals were furious because Bismarck's decisions had robbed them of the glory of occupying Vienna. From an operational perspective, an advance on Vienna would have allowed the Prussian Army to complete the destruction of the Austrian state after the destruction of its army. But Bismarck had good reasons for doing what he did. From his point of view such an action stood the considerable risk of bringing other major powers into the conflict, thus not only prolonging the war but exercising an uncontrollable influence over the settlement. It certainly would have encouraged French intervention in south Germany to support the Bavarians, which would have made the manipulation of the south German states that much more difficult. Thus, the strategic perspective demanded an immediate halt to the war – a halt which left Napoleon III holding a very empty bag.

For the next four years the French caused a series of difficulties, but in fact they had little room for maneuver. The Austrians were undoubtedly unhappy about their defeat and the loss of their centuries-old influence on "the Germanies," but their experiences at the hands of the Prussian Army certainly discouraged ideas of immediate *revanche*. Moreover, Bismarck's lenient treatment made them relatively willing to accept the results, given the alternatives. On the periphery, the Russians remained disinterested in Austria's fate, especially considering Austria's behavior during the Crimean War.[47] Britain also remained disinterested in Prussia's gains, particularly since Bismarck had done nothing to aggrandize Prussia outside of what appeared to be its "own backyard."[48]

Yet, it was soon apparent to Bismarck that the settlement of the Seven Weeks' War was anything but stable. The south German states were now Prussia's "allies," but they remained open to French and Austrian intrigues. Nor was Russia likely in the long run to remain disinterested in Prussian hegemony over "the Germanies." In 1870 Bismarck took the considerable risk of war with France, when Napoleon III was so

---

[46] The Prussians swallowed Hanover entirely and received substantial pieces of Saxony as well. Moreover, they now forced the south German states to join the North German Federation, dominated by Prussia, thus putting the Germanies on the eventual road to unification into a single German state.
[47] Saved from dissolution during the troubles of 1848–1849 by the arrival of a Russian Army to put down the rebellious Hungarians, the Austrians had turned around and proffered the Russians no aid during the Crimean War five years later. The Austrian foreign minister had then made matters worse by egregiously suggesting that the world would be astonished by Austria's ingratitude. It was.
[48] A phrase the British would use in March 1938 to characterize Germany's forcible annexation of Austria.

intemperate as to turn a relatively minor squabble over who was to succeed to the Spanish throne into a major confrontation between France and Prussia. For a time the Prussian king appeared willing to accept an amicable settlement – to Bismarck's considerable horror. But the French ambassador at the instruction of his government carried matters too far in an interview with Wilhelm I.

Bismarck then produced a report on the conversations between his king and the French ambassador at Bad Ems that was so cleverly worded the French believed Wilhelm I had insulted their ambassador, while the Prussians believed the French ambassador had insulted their king. The manner in which the war broke out persuaded the south Germans, not just their rulers, that the French were the aggressors. Moreover, Bismarck delightedly fanned the flames of German nationalism by appealing to memories of the war of liberation of 1813–1814 – an appeal that resonated among many Germans, who still remembered the decade-long occupation by the French during the Napoleonic Wars. On the other side of the Rhine, Napoleon III was equally enthusiastic in appealing to French nationalism and the memories of French victories under his uncle, the great Napoleon. Thus, from the first there was considerable danger that this war was going to turn into a war of the peoples.

Why it did not turn into a protracted struggle along the lines of the American Civil War is a story that would have great influence on the form that the First World War would take. In summer 1870 there was every prospect the war would turn into a protracted struggle, given the nationalist fervor the conflict occasioned on both sides of the Rhine. However, the war began with a series of catastrophic defeats for the French.[49] In effect, those defeats rendered prolonged French resistance impossible in spite of the immense nationalist support for the war throughout France. Ironically, the fact that the Imperial soldiers of France looked much like those of the Grand Army reflected an army firmly anchored in the distant past.

But there was no great Napoleon to lead the French to victory in this war. Instead, a dismal set of generals botched the war from the opening engagements, while, unlike the Prusso–Germans, the French possessed nothing that one could properly term a staff. Thus, the defeats of Sedan

---

[49] The best account of the campaign still remains that of Sir Michael Howard: *The Franco-Prussian War* (London, 1961). Geoffrey Warrow's *The Franco-Prussian War, The German Conquest of France in 1870–1871* (Cambridge, 2003) is also definitely worth consulting.

and Metz that opened up the conflict reflected a general lack of professionalism in the French officer corps as a whole. From the beginning French staff work was abysmal. The mobilization was a shambles. Officers were sent to Algeria to join regiments that had already arrived in France. The army never properly mobilized its reserves. The French secret weapon, the first true machine gun, the *mitrailleuse*, was so secret that virtually none of the army's commanders knew of its existence. Moreover, there was no clear plan for the campaign except to advance into Germany with several army corps with no one in overall command and each corps fighting separately – in sharp contrast to how the great Napoleon had attacked 65 years earlier in his great sweeping movement that had trapped the "unfortunate General Mack" and his entire Austrian army at Ulm.

On the other hand, the Prussian Army had a clear idea of what it wanted to do. Its mobilization went like clockwork, its planning considerably aided by the mobilizations for war in 1864 and 1866. Prussian staff work also got the armies of the south German allies to their destinations on time. So well did mobilization go that the Prusso–German forces were on the French frontier before Napoleon III's armies, despite the greater distance the former had to travel. In this conflict, the Prussians enjoyed less of an advantage in firepower against the French than they had against the Austrians: their needle gun was distinctly inferior to the Chassepot rifles French soldiers carried. However, Prussian artillery, reequipped by Krupp since the Seven Weeks' War, was superior to that possessed by the French. Not surprisingly, poor staff work ensured that the French Army's logistics remained chaotic and badly planned throughout the conflict.

The prime Prussian advantage lay in the superiority of generalship in the conduct of wide-ranging military operations. In a swirling series of contact battles along the Franco–German frontier, the Prussians lost every skirmish. But the French lacked an overall command structure, so that the corps commanders failed to reinforce successful tactical fights, while German commanders marched to the sound of guns. Breaking the French armies apart, Moltke led a great encircling drive that trapped French forces commanded by Marshal Achille Bazaine in Metz. Two ferocious encounter battles occurred at St. Privat and Gravellote, where the French severely damaged the aggressive Prussians and came close to breaking out of the enclosing arms of the encircling Prussian forces. At St. Privat the Prussian Guard Corps attacked across open ground and within 20 minutes French infantry equipped with Chassepots had inflicted 8,000 casualties on the attackers, as heavy a casualty rate as anything that would occur in the First World War. But Bazaine displayed not the slightest grasp of operational leadership, and French forces fell back into the fortified city of Metz. Thus, Moltke had trapped a substantial portion of the Imperial army.

Worse was to come. Napoleon III and Marshal E. P. M. de MacMahon gathered the remainder of the Imperial Army to relieve French forces besieged in Metz. MacMahon and the emperor not only failed to relieve Metz but managed to get themselves and their army trapped in the fateful city of Sedan.[50] There, Prussian artillery battered the French forces into surrendering, as a despondent French emperor confronted Bismarck and the collapse of his empire. As had happened against Austria, the Franco–Prussian War seemed over before it began. But in the case of this war, despite the loss of virtually the entire French Army in the opening moves, the French continued to resist. They proclaimed a republic in Paris and refused all overtures from Bismarck for peace negotiations.

The Prussians now confronted the possibility of a long war. Almost immediately after Moltke's armies had trundled down the dusty roads to Paris, the Iron Chancellor demanded a bombardment of the French capital. Moltke refused because, he claimed, the army was not yet ready. Bismarck, however, was considering the strategic situation. How much longer could he count on Austrian neutrality? Might the Russians also reconsider their position? He was so worried about the possibility of British intervention that he forbade Prussian troops from approaching either the English Channel or the Belgian frontier, thus allowing the French to import arms directly through the Channel ports. But Bismarck understood British sensibilities about the Channel and German operations remained limited to the heart of France.

While the Prussians besieged Paris, their lines of communication and supply were under constant attack from *francs-tireurs* (the French equivalent of Spanish guerrillas), while the French called up new armies, supplied with considerable equipment imported from abroad. These armies launched a series of major offensives throughout winter 1870/1871 in attempts to relieve Paris and batter the Prusso–German armies back. Their efforts failed, and the French suffered heavy casualties. But the new republic displayed the same ability to mobilize the French populace that its predecessor had during the French Revolution.

[50] Sedan would also be fateful for French history with the events that occurred in that frontier city on the 13th and 14th of May 1940, when Heinz Guderian's XIX Panzer Corps broke through French defenses along the Meuse and began the encirclement of Allied armies in the Low Countries that would lead to the collapse of France and the withdrawal of the British Expeditionary force from Dunkirk.

But two factors had changed from eight decades earlier. The gross incompetence of Napoleon III's generals had lost the entire French Army: generals, staff officers, combat officers, and NCOs, lock, stock, and barrel. Thus, the French had few trained cadres on which to rebuild their army. In the 1792–1793 period, while most of the nobility, who provided the army's top leaders, had fled, junior officers, like the great Napoleon, and NCOs had remained to form a solid corps on which to build the revolutionary armies. But now that body of trained leadership was in Prussian prisoner of war camps. Equally important was the fact that the Prussian Army represented "the nation in arms." It was not an army of long-serving professional soldiers. In fact, in the early battles, the Prussian Army was better able to take heavy casualties than Napoleon III's largely professional army. In effect, the defeats at Metz and Sedan, with the wholesale destruction of the French Army and its junior officers and NCOs, ensured that the French could not mold the soldiers mobilized into an effective military instrument for an extended war. Finally, increasing radicalism in Paris pushed the republic's leaders toward peace and confrontation with the radicals in Paris and brought an end to the conflict.

Conclusion: The Results of Bismarck's Wars

The long-term of Bismarck's successes proved disastrous for Germany as well as Europe. At least Disraeli recognized that the unification of Europe had entirely upset the European balance of power. For the short term Bismarck, especially after the war scare of 1875 which had threatened to ally the other European powers at the side of France, placed his skills in ensuring the peace and stability of the new Europe. The consequences of this great Prusso–German victory were enormous, and they bear on any understanding of why World War I would evolve into such a terrible calamity. In the largest sense, it broke the pattern of great European wars that had been occurring approximately every half century, since the War of Spanish Succession in the early eighteenth century. The ingredients certainly were there for another great European war, especially once Bismarck and Napoleon III turned the contest into a war between their peoples. But the peculiarities of that struggle, namely the abysmal performance of French military institutions and the superbly functioning Prussian Army, resulted in an unequal and relatively short contest that prevented the French from drawing on the nation in arms. The relative quickness of the war, as well as Bismarck's enormous strategic and diplomatic skills, prevented the other European powers from intervening.

Had any of these circumstances not happened, a longer and more costly contest would inevitably have occurred. The consequences would have been considerable. On one hand, German generals and statesmen would have had a second great war, interweaving the French and Industrial Revolutions, as a warning (the American Civil war being another). Whether such a lesson would have been sufficient to prevent a great conflict in the twentieth century is open to question. After all, the outbreak of World War II occurred only 25 years after the outbreak of the Great War. Nevertheless, one suspects that European statesmen might have been more careful about unleashing the dogs of war in 1914, had the Franco–Prussian War exploded into a great conflict combining the French Revolution and the Industrial Revolution, as had been the case in the American Civil War. It is unlikely that such a war, even if it had occurred, would have brought the likes of Mussolini, Stalin, and Hitler to power.[51]

The second factor that one needs to consider would have been the fact that no European statesmen would have been under the illusion that war is necessarily short or beneficial to their states. Certainly, Europe's military organizations would have been less willing to believe that decisive battle would bring a future war to a quick end. Admittedly, the prevailing belief among politicians and economists that the modern state could not stand the strain of a long war drove the European general staffs to their belief in the short-war scenario. Thus, anything less than a short war would result in economic and political collapse, followed by revolution. The outbreak of revolution in Tsarist Russia in 1905 as a result of the Russo–Japanese War certainly lent credence to that point of view.

In fact, as we now know, the modern state is capable of extracting extraordinary sacrifices from its citizens, to the point of forcing them "to bear any burden, pay any price." Moreover, modern economies have proven equally resilient in producing vast amounts of ammunition and weapons in support of war. In the end revolution did occur in the three great monarchies of Central and Eastern Europe, but even the ramshackle Austro–Hungarian monarchy was able to survive the pressures of four terrible years of war.

Equally disastrous for Europe was the impact of increasingly rapid technological change in weaponry and ammunition that accompanied the next four decades of peace. Superficially, there were a number of obvious lessons from the colonial wars and the Russo–Japanese conflict that the

---

[51] See particularly Knox, *Common Destiny*, chaps. 2 and 4.

European armies did not ignore.[52] In 1914, they certainly understood the killing power of modern small-arms weapons. But the long period of peace following the Franco–Prussian War added immensely to the tactical and operational problems European armies had to solve, when war broke out in 1914.

In that period, European and American engineers, chemists, scientists, and inventors further developed the machine gun, invented smokeless powder, made the first reciprocating, gasoline-powered engines for locomotion, designed recoil mechanisms that greatly increased the range and accuracy of artillery, invented nitroglycerin and other explosives, constructed the first heavier than air flying machines, designed increasingly sophisticated barbed-wire entanglements, and designed and built gigantic ships which approached 25,000 tons and reached speeds of more than 20 knots. The guns of those great *Dreadnoughts* and battle cruisers could reach more than 20,000 yards. In effect, the Europeans and Americans had invented virtually all the technological pieces of modern war. But no one had the slightest idea of how to put the pieces together. They would learn how to do so during the next four years and in the process invent modern war. But in so doing they would slaughter a whole generation of Europe's youth.

---

[52] For the larger lessons they failed to learn, see Jonathan Bailey's essay on the failure of the Russo–Japanese War to influence the thinking of Europe's armies in the period between 1905 and 1914 in sensible directions in Williamson Murray and Richard Hart Sinnreich, eds., *The Past as Prologue, The Importance of History to the Military Profession* (Cambridge, 2006).

9

The Problem of German Military Effectiveness, 1900–1945

The first half of the twentieth century was the time of the German problem. Emerging from centuries as "the Germanies," Bismarck's Second Reich had by 1900 established itself as the dominant power on the European Continent. Its leaders had every expectation that Germany would become a world power. On the weight of its industrial development, the educational level of its population, its cultural and national discipline, and geographic location, Germany seemed on the verge of emerging as a superpower, overshadowing its European rivals, including Britain, and perhaps even challenging the United States. But this failed to come to pass. In two great world wars, Germany caused its own downfall, and in the resulting disaster drowned itself, its neighbors, and much of the world in a sea of blood.

The nature of that European catastrophe had much to do with Germany's attitude toward its military services, especially the army, the peculiar cultural and intellectual forces that shaped those institutions, and a combination of battlefield brilliance mixed with a myopic strategic vision. That last combination proved deadly, and in both 1914 and 1939 Germany embarked on conflicts that offered only the slightest chance of victory. As early as the failure before Paris in September 1914 and the disaster in front of Moscow in December 1941, Germany reached turning points that made defeat inevitable. Yet, the tactical and operational competence of German military forces ensured that the final defeat in both

---

This work appeared as the opening chapter in a collection of articles published by Nautical and Aviation Press in 1992 that had a small print run. It is reprinted here with the permission of that publishing house. I have added several new footnotes.

world wars would not come for four more years and at a horrendous cost to all involved.

By definition, military institutions in the Western world exist to protect their nations from both internal and external threats. The nature of the birth of Bismarck's Reich, built on the victories over Austria in 1866 and France in 1870, ensured that its military institutions acquired a unique reputation and place in German society: a reputation that was ironic, given that the real reason for success in 1866 and 1870 lay in the masterful strategic and political policies managed by the Iron Chancellor Otto von Bismarck and the appalling incompetence of Prusso–Germany's opponents. In fact, the generals, for all their tactical and operational virtuosity, had again and again attempted to thwart Bismarck's vision in pursuit of ephemeral battlefield success. This had especially been the case after Königgrätz, when the chief of the general staff, Helmut von Moltke, had sought to pursue the beaten Austrians to Vienna – thereby risking bringing the other European powers into the conflict to mitigate the consequences of Prussia's overwhelming victory and endangering the strategic and political possibilities that Bismarck's diplomacy had created.[1]

The economic success of succeeding years helped cover up the serious political and constitutional weaknesses of the Bismarckian Reich – especially after Wilhelm II ascended to the throne. In effect, Bismarck managed to fence the military off from any form of parliamentary control; this was not so serious a matter as long as he and the aged Kaiser were in control. But Wilhelm II possessed neither political nor strategic sense, defects that only magnified a deeply flawed personality, one which gloried in uniforms and military pomp. Without any input, except financial, from the civilian world, German military culture, already distorted by the successes of the wars of unification, moved steadily toward a separation from German and European society at the turn of the century.

Geography and history have also played a crucial role in the approach which German military leaders took in tackling the problems they confronted. The Reich's position at the center of Europe brought the German nation important advantages. Germany was at the crossroads through which not only economic but cultural and intellectual currents flowed across the Continent. But this position at the center also had its disadvantages. While the mountains to the south provided some shielding,

---

[1] For the most recent study of the course of the Seven Weeks' War, see Geoffrey Warrow, *The Austro-Prussian War, Austria's War with Prussia and Italy in 1866* (Cambridge, 1996).

The Problem of German Military Effectiveness, 1900–1945

the Reich's position on the north German plain opened the Reich up to invasion from both east and west. Moreover, historical divisions dating from the Middle Ages made German territory tempting to other powers. By the eighteenth century, armies from virtually all the major European powers – Sweden, France, Britain, Russia, and Austria – found themselves engaged in fighting on German territory. Consequently, due to geographic position alone, the German military always had to think of war at its immediate doorstep. Not surprisingly, the result has been an emphasis on operational and battlefield performance, while their counterparts in Britain and the United States have always had to think in terms of projecting military power.

Finally, history has also exercised considerable influence on the perceptions of the German officer corps. Above all, the catastrophe of Jena-Auerstedt, where in fall 1806 Napoleon's brilliance and the Grand Army's tactical excellence destroyed the Prussian Army and state in one day, reinforced the importance of battlefield performance for the Prussian officer corps.[2] As a result, the Prussians and their successors in the German Army, particularly in the general staff, undertook the study of the military art with a seriousness that did not occur in other armies. Unfortunately for their nation and Europe, that study concentrated on operational and tactical concerns to the exclusion of strategy. Not surprisingly, Napoleon Bonaparte lay at the heart of that study and, like the great master, the German military were soon to confuse battlefield success with strategic wisdom.

Political Effectiveness

Military institutions by nature are highly structured organizations that must often interact with each other in the joint arena and with the political authorities who determine national policy. What is indeed astonishing about the history of the German military in the first half of this century is the relatively poor organization of its external and internal bureaucratic structures. Not only did they work at cross purposes with each other, but its internal structures suggest a surprising unwillingness to think through basic administrative problems. Under the Bismarckian

---

[2] For the clearest description of the Jena-Auerstedt disaster, see David Chandler, *The Campaigns of Napoleon* (New York, 1966). For the recovery of the Prussian Army after that defeat see Peter Paret's two brilliant studies: *Clausewitz and the State* (Oxford, 1976) and *Yorck and the Era of Prussian Reform* (Princeton, NJ, 1966).

Reich, three independent army authorities, the Prussian War Ministry, the military cabinet, and the general staff all reported directly to the emperor.[3] The fact that the general staff did not deem it necessary to inform the war ministry about the scale of its plans for a campaign against France until 1912 suggests how little cooperation occurred among the three.[4] The navy possessed no more coherent organization, while the two services generally failed to coordinate their plans for war. To add to the bureaucratic nightmare before World War I, Wilhelm II gave the right of immediate access to his person to no fewer than 40 generals and eight admirals.

Consequently, there was an almost complete absence of understanding of, or realism about, policy and strategy in the highest levels of the German government as the nation stumbled into war in July 1914. In place of a national strategy, there was a single, completely unrealistic war plan and no mechanisms for the coordination of strategy, military force, and diplomacy. No larger body similar to the Committee of Imperial Defence in Britain existed. As the last prewar chancellor, Theobald von Bethman Hollweg, lamented after the war: "There never took place during my entire period in office a sort of war council at which politics were brought into the military for or against 'consideration.'"[5]

Without a political system capable of making sophisticated strategic judgments, the German Army seized *de facto* control of the war's direction after August 1914. The result was that Germany had no strategy for fighting the war other than fighting the next battle. Moreover, in virtually every case where important decisions had to be made, "military necessity" overruled political and strategic concerns. By the end of the war, even tactics were overruling operational concerns. This only compounded the kinds of mistakes that had dragged the empire into the quagmire in summer 1914; the decision in late 1916 to embark on unrestricted submarine warfare and bring the United States into the war is a case in point.

The Weimar Republic's constitution sought to bring some order to the administrative chaos that had characterized the empire. According

---

[3] Holger Herwig, "The Dynamics of Necessity: German Military Policy during the First World War," in *Military Effectiveness*, vol. 1, *World War I*, ed. by Allan R. Millett and Williamson Murray (London, 1988), p. 81.
[4] Holger Herwig, "Strategic Uncertainties of a Nation State: Prussia–Germany, 1871–1918," in Williamson Murray, MacGregor Knox, and Alvin Bernstein, eds., *The Making of Strategy* (Cambridge, 1994), p. 258. Earlier in his essay, Professor Herwig lays out the extraordinary administrative chaos that marked the German military under Wilhelm II's reign. Ibid., pp. 243–245.
[5] Quoted in Herwig, "The Dynamics of Necessity," p. 79.

to the new order, a defense minister supposedly reported directly to the chancellor. As such, he was responsible for defense matters before the *Reichstag*, with the army and the navy working under his supervision. This system of cabinet responsibility represented a system similar to that used by other European nations. Unfortunately for the republic, the system did not function as designed. The first defense minister, Otto Gessler, deferred to the military on most issues and in effect became its spokesman rather than serving as a directing force. Only during the republic's last years under Wilhelm Groener, one of the few sophisticated general staff officers in the First World War, did a coherent defense policy emerge in accordance with the resources available and Germany's foreign policy.[6] But Groener's short tenure and the troubles plaguing the republic in its last years negated any lasting impression he made on either military strategy or organizational conceptions.

Adolf Hitler's first defense minister (after 1935 renamed the war minister), General Werner von Blomberg, attempted to establish a coherent military structure to support the rapid buildup of Germany's military forces. But Hitler had no intention of allowing such a concentration of power in the hands of one individual – other than, of course, himself – while the three services actively sought to thwart Blomberg's efforts. Moreover, given the war minister's past record and understanding of strategy, one may doubt his chances of successfully bringing strategic coherence to the Third Reich even with Hitler's wholehearted support.[7]

After the Fritsch–Blomberg purge of January 1938 (where Hitler purged both the army's commander-in-chief and the war minister), the Führer assumed the position of war minister himself, created a high command staff (*Oberkommando der Wehrmacht*, *OKW*) with only coordination powers, and drew complete control of the larger strategic and military problems confronting the Third Reich entirely within his purview. Thereafter, Hitler added to the administrative chaos by eventually appointing himself commander-in-chief of the army (December 1941), and even army group commander (September 1942). By 1942, two entirely separate army staffs, the *OKH* (*Oberkommando des Heeres*, the former army high command) for the east and the *OKW* for the Mediterranean and the west ran the ground wars, while the *Luftwaffe* and navy ran their

---

[6] See in particular Wilhelm Deist, *The Wehrmacht and German Rearmament* (London, 1981), chap. 1.
[7] For a discussion of Blomberg's understanding of strategy, see Williamson Murray, "German Net Assessment in the Interwar Period," in Williamson Murray and Allan R. Millett, eds., *Calculations, Net Assessment and the Coming of World War II* (New York, 1992).

own separate wars. Only Hitler possessed a relative understanding of the general situation – exactly the situation he desired.

Many historians have blamed the organizational nightmare on Hitler, and given his inclinations, he certainly deserves a substantial portion of the blame for the administrative chaos. Nevertheless, from the outset of German rearmament, the three services balked at all of Blomberg's attempts to coordinate their activities. On one side, the army, jealous of its traditional role as the Reich's premier service, refused to tolerate interference from the defense ministry (and later from the OKW) in what it regarded as its private preserve, the formulation and conduct of the Reich's ground defense. On the other hand, Hermann Göring's unique position as the number two man in the hierarchy as well as the *Luftwaffe*'s commander in chief ensured that Blomberg exercised little influence over that service. The navy sailed in the lee, shielded by Hitler's ignorance of naval matters. The combination of these factors resulted in the German military being unable to wage war in a unified, joint manner. Each service went its own way, contributing further to the failure to provide sound strategic advice.

In the Anglo–Saxon world a substantial portion of political effectiveness rests on the ability of military organizations to articulate their financial and resource needs. For the most part, the German military lacked such concerns. In fact, through 1911 the Prussian War Ministry waged a successful campaign to limit the army's size despite the threatening international situation. Its stand reflected fears among the aristocrats who controlled it that a larger army would require a larger officer corps, one the size of which would require a greater number of middle-class officers. Such a change they feared would seriously damage the position of the nobility within the Wilhelmine state.[8] Only in 1912 did the general staff and the war ministry reach a satisfactory compromise that provided barely sufficient troops to support the former's plans for a campaign in the west.

Even during the Weimar Republic, a government the German military regarded as hostile to its interests, the problem was not that the state was unwilling to provide the resources that the services needed. Rather, the limitations on military spending reflected the demands of the Treaty of Versailles; indeed, the republic and its ministers generally supported efforts to evade the treaty's restrictive clauses. The extensive financial

---

[8] Gerhard Ritter, *Staatskunst und Kriegshandwerk: Das Problem des 'Militärismus' in Deutschland*, vol. 2 (Munich, 1965), p. 262.

support, all of it secret, that the republic provided the army's clandestine efforts in the Soviet Union is a case in point. With Hitler's coming to power, all previous limitations on spending ceased. The Führer provided the three services (the *Luftwaffe* had now appeared at the table) with blank checks that allowed them to embark on massive programs of rearmament.[9] The wisdom of such a rearmament program with virtually no strategic cooperation among the services and within an economic framework desperately short of raw materials and foreign exchange, however, is open to question.[10]

Germany's military institutions not only confronted few difficulties in acquiring financial resources, they also had access to the manpower and technological resources that modern military institutions require. Particularly in science and technology, the German military had access to some of the world's brightest, best educated minds. However, even with the availability of new technologies, German military institutions often proved slow and cautious in utilizing technological advances to their fullest. In 1910, General Helmuth von Moltke, then chief of the general staff, commented that the possibility of using aircraft to drop bombs was "for the present unimportant."[11] While their conventional munitions and weaponry remained unsurpassed, what was difficult for the Germans to see was the direction toward which technology was driving warfare. In World War I, the Germans responded so late to the use of the tank, first introduced by the British on the Somme in September 1916, that they never managed to produce an effective model. In the next war, only after the Soviet T-34 had appeared on the Eastern Front did the Germans respond with their Tiger and Panther designs; even then, failure to decide on realistic production programs led to innumerable production runs and models.

In many respects German engineering and technological potential far exceeded the capabilities of their opponents.[12] But the failure to establish coherent methods to evaluate technological advances or to set priorities between competing systems often left the German military in the unenviable position of either being equipped with inferior weapons

---

[9] See particularly Deist, *The Wehrmacht and German Rearmament* on this point.
[10] For a more detailed look at the relationship between German rearmament under Hitler and the growing economic crisis in Germany, see Murray, *The Change in the European Balance of Power*, chap. 1.
[11] Herwig, "The Dynamics of Uncertainty," p. 84.
[12] For an excellent discussion of the technological advances involved in German weapons systems development, see Brian Jones, *The Secret War* (London, 1978).

(particularly in the air and sea wars) or failing to utilize available technology to its fullest extent. In the latter case the failure of the Germans to utilize radar in a systemic fashion – as the RAF's Fighter command did during the Battle of Britain – until late 1943 had a significant impact on the *Luftwaffe*'s difficulties with the night bomber offensive. Similarly, Admiral Karl Dönitz and the U-boat high command pursued a tactical rather than a technological approach through May 1943, which had a disastrous impact on the German U-boat campaign, when the Allies were finally able to draw all their technological advances together. To a considerable extent, the problem appears to have been the deep prejudice German officers in all services held toward civilians in general. Thus, they never viewed technologists and scientists as partners instead of subordinates.

Military organizations are also supposed to be servants of the state, at least in the Western world. One of the most disturbing aspects of the German military in the first half of the twentieth century was its penchant for mixing politics with an astonishing naïveté. Before World War I the Prussian officer corps believed that the rising strength of the Social Democrats among the working class threatened their position and that of the monarchy. Kaiser Wilhelm II was given to bloodthirsty pronouncements about settling matters with the left so that blood would run in the streets. A number of senior officers delightedly encouraged the Kaiser's enthusiasms, although he always stopped short of waging war on the working class.[13] Nevertheless, military contempt for even the Bismarckian constitution led to the disastrous affair at Zabern in Alsace Lorraine, where the local military literally took the law into its own hands and created a huge uproar by illegally arresting civilians and flouting the Reich's legal framework.[14]

World War I only served to reinforce the military's contempt for the civilian world. Too many officers believed the nonsense that the home front had not adequately supported the war effort. Almost immediately after the catastrophic collapse of November 1918, the military had propagated the myth that the army had stood unbroken and unbeaten in the field only to be stabbed in the back by Jews and Communists.[15]

---

[13] V.R. Berghan, *Germany and the Approach of War in 1914* (London, 1973), p. 22.
[14] David Schoenbaum, *Zabern, 1913, Consensus Politics in Imperial Germany* (London, 1982).
[15] In terms of the massive effort to create myths surrounding the pernicious activities of the German leadership before and during the First World War, see particularly Holger Herwig, "Clio Deceived, Patriotic Self-Censorship in Germany after the Great War," *International Security*, Fall 1987.

In fact, from the beginning of the war the German military had guided both policy and strategy. By August 1916 General Erich Ludendorff and Field Marshal Paul von Hindenburg had established a virtual dictatorship that excluded civilians and politicians from the Reich's decision-making processes.[16] In the realms of neither strategy nor politics were these two generals competent, but they did provide the German nation with a military ideal that the Kaiser could no longer fulfill. But while Ludendorff's capabilities in dealing with the tactical problems raised by the First World War's battlefield were extraordinary, he was completely incapable of addressing the political and strategic problems raised by the war.[17]

Imperial Germany's collapse in 1918 and the military's reaction to the ensuing political chaos established the most dangerous of postwar political attitudes: a search for a new leader who could replace the Kaiser and provide the bonds of loyalty that the monarchy had failed to maintain during the war. This search would lead many in the officer corps to a wholehearted acceptance of Adolf Hitler's *Führer* state with its *Volksgemeinschaft*. For the time being in the 1920s and early 1930s, the German military had to live in a republic that few of offices respected, much less loved. An uneasy alliance between the Weimar Republic's Social Democrats and the old officer corps enabled the new republic to ward off the danger from the far left, but it also carried the old regime's military over into the new "republican" era. The republic was the loser. Its defenders, now called the *Reichswehr*, carried on most of the traditions and prejudices of the Kaiser's military.

The army's new architect, General Hans von Seeckt, saw to it that the military technicians of the general staff rather than the nobility and the *Frontsoldaten* controlled the new officer corps.[18] That decision ensured the army leadership and culture would be that of the general staff. Not surprisingly, given that institution's emphasis on tactics in the First World War, the Germans were the only European army to study the battlefield of 1918 with great care and thus learn the lessons of combined-arms,

---

[16] For the most thorough critique of the triumph of military influence in Germany during the war, see Gerhard Ritter, *The Sword and the Sceptor*, vol. 3, *The Tragedy of Statesmanship – Bethman Hollweg as War Chancellor (1914–1917)*, and vol. 4, *The Reign of German Militarism and the Disaster of 1918* (Coral Gables, FL, 1972–1973).

[17] For Ludendorff's capabilities in the realm of tactics, see Timothy Lupfer, *The Dynamics of Doctrine: The Changes in German Tactical Doctrine during the First World War* (Leavenworth, KS, 1981).

[18] For Seeckt's role in pushing the army to learn the lessons of the last war, see James Corum, *The Roots of Blitzkrieg, Hans von Seeckt and German Military Reform* (Lawrence, KS, 1994).

decentralized leadership, and exploitation. The military did not, however, provide any analysis of what had gone wrong in the strategic conduct of the war. The result was that a substantial portion of the officer corps not only participated in the propagation of the "stab-in-the-back" myth, but actually came to believe it. It was then an easy step to the belief that the entrance of the United States into the war in 1917 as a result of the navy's unrestricted submarine campaign had not mattered all that much.

Seeckt, thoroughly contemptuous of the republic, responded to Hitler's Munich Beer Hall Putsch by refusing to commit the army to the defense of the republic.[19] As he expressed his attitude to the *Reichswehr*'s senior officers, the army's loyalty must lie with the German state rather than with the republic. After the Third Reich's collapse in 1945, Seeckt's supporters claimed that he had sought to create a military that was above political concerns and that the resulting institution could not deal effectively with Hitler's Third Reich. On the evidence such a judgment is flawed; in fact, Seeckt only attempted to distance the army from the republic. Political involvement, at least in terms of vocal support for a more nationalistic form of government, certainly mirrored his conception about the proper role of the army.

Seeckt would not, however, have approved of the machinations of Kurt von Schleicher, who within the defense ministry played a crucial role in bringing Hitler to power. Schleicher almost singlehandedly forced the resignations of Groener, Chancellor Heinrich Brüning, and Brüning's successor, Franz von Papen. Schleicher eventually manipulated Hindenburg into naming him as the chancellor, but in so doing lost his standing with the president. It is hard to present a more disastrous intervention in politics by the military than Schleicher's.[20]

Ironically, in Hitler, the German military found the leader that they had craved in the First World War – a man who could seemingly unite the German people behind the military and provide the rationale and ideology for German nationalism.[21] The first years of Nazi rule resulted in a honeymoon between the Third Reich and its military institutions. Hitler

[19] There was some justification for Seeckt's reluctance because many of the troops in Bavaria displayed signs of unreliability. For the army and the putsch, see Harold J. Gordon, Jr., *Hitler and the Beer Hall Putsch* (Princeton, 1972).

[20] Peter Hayes, "A Question Mark with Epaulettes? Kurt von Schleicher and Weimar Politics," *Journal of Modern History*, 52, March 1980.

[21] Even some in the eventual military opposition to Hitler, including Klaus von Stauffenberg and Ludwig Beck, were enthusiastic supporters of the Nazis in their first years in power.

provided unlimited funding; and, if he forced the pace of rearmament faster than what seemed prudent to some military leaders, most were delighted to press on with the tasks of the buildup. In the early years the regime took extraordinary diplomatic and strategic risks: withdrawal from the League of Nations in 1933, declaration of rearmament in 1935, and the militarization of the Rhineland in 1936. In each case the failure of the other European powers to respond confirmed Hitler in his strategic assessments and further cemented military support for the regime.

The only significant argument between Hitler and the military came in 1938. In that year, Hitler, taking enormous risks, pushed Germany to the brink of war with Czechoslovakia and the Western Powers.[22] The resulting crisis divided the German military into two camps: the smaller led by the chief of the general staff, Ludwig Beck, the larger consisting of the great majority of the generals and the officer corps. Beck argued that the dangers inherent in Hitler's policy of confrontation over Czechoslovakia represented a strategic and political danger to the nation that the generals must not accept. But most generals believed that the regime should decide the political questions, a surprising change of heart compared to the attitudes of the military in Imperial Germany and during the Weimar Republic. General Erich von Manstein, one of Beck's protégées, wrote his former chief in July urging him not to resign over the Czech crisis, because "Hitler has so far always estimated the political situation correctly."[23] There was also a certain amount of naïveté on the part of the chief of staff. Beck proposed to the generals in mid-July 1938 that they combine with the better, more responsible party leaders to eliminate the SS and the party radicals, restore justice, and re-establish Prussian standards in government, while leaving Hitler as the head of state.[24]

After Hitler's stunning success in destroying the Czech state in September 1938, the military never again confronted Hitler over a strategic issue. Rather, they accepted, sometimes grudgingly, mostly enthusiastically, the Führer's political assumptions. Three years later, Germany's disastrous approach to conquering the Soviet Union resulted to a considerable degree from the generals' ready acceptance of the ideological framework within which Hitler cast *Fall* (Case) Barbarossa (code name

---

[22] For a discussion of the Munich Crisis, see Telford Taylor, *Munich, The Price of Peace* (New York, 1979). For the strategic and military aspects of the crisis, see Murray, *The Change in the European Balance of Power*, chaps. 5, 6, and 7.
[23] Letter from Manstein to Beck, July 1938, Beck Nachlass, Bundesarchiv/Militärarchiv (BA/MA), N 28/3.
[24] BA/MA, N 28/3, Beck Nachlass, "Nachtrag am 19.7.38."

for the invasion of the Soviet Union).[25] The acceptance of Hitler's ideological crusade by the military ensured that the Soviet peoples would almost immediately rally around Stalin's brutal regime and that the German Army would cooperate wholeheartedly with the murderous activities of the *Einsatzgruppen*. In proclamations to their troops, several senior generals made clear what kind of war they were waging – one fully in accordance with their Führer's precepts.[26]

Strategic Effectiveness

According to Clausewitz's much quoted aphorism, "[w]hen whole communities go to war – whole peoples, and especially civilized peoples – the reason always lies in some political situation, and the occasion is always due to some political object.... It is clear that war is not a mere act of policy, but a true political instrument, a continuation of political activity by other means."[27] This was a point of view that senior military leaders in the German military consistently refused to endorse. Thus, they failed to see that effective strategy demands a coherent understanding of the political and economic realities of the external environment that one must weigh in developing an intelligent relationship between political ends and available means. Strategy, at least as the German military defined the concept, almost always reverted to operations. Rather than allowing strategic and political concerns to guide operations, military operations became an end in themselves.

This confusion of strategy with operations helps explain the German military's approach to the First World War as well as its incapacity to address the flawed means-to-ends relationships inherent in Hitler's conduct of the Second World War. The Schlieffen Plan is only one of the more glaring examples of this weakness. Confronted by a complex diplomatic, strategic, and political situation as well as Germany's vulnerabilities on the European Continent with the threat of a two-front war, Schlieffen reduced Germany's options to a simple, massive plan that aimed to knock the French out of the war with a single blow and then solve the Russian

---

[25] In English, see the outstanding article by Jürgen Förster, "Hitler's War Aims against the Soviet Union and German Military Leaders," *Militärhistorik Tidschrift*, 1979; for a more complete discussion, see Horst Boog, et al., *Das Deutsche Reich und der Zweite Weltkrieg*, vol. 4, *Der Angriff auf die Sowjetunion* (Stuttgart, 1983), chaps. 1 and 7.
[26] Ibid., pp. 1052–53.
[27] Clausewitz, *On War*, pp. 86–87.

problem at leisure.[28] Schlieffen saw little need to coordinate his plans with the Foreign Office and had no desire to contemplate the political and strategic consequences of violating Belgian neutrality, to consider the impact of a possible British intervention, or even to inform the Prussian War Ministry, which was responsible for supplying the troops required by his plan. Thus, the general staff reduced the political, diplomatic, strategic, and even logistical problems confronting the Schlieffen to a simple operational formula – one that resulted in a European disaster.[29]

Part of the problem lay in the fact that the German military had by the end of the nineteenth century reached the conclusion that Clausewitz was no longer relevant. As General Leo Geyer von Schweppenburg noted after the Second World War in a letter to the British military pundit, B.H. Liddell Hart, on what passed for education in the general staff before 1914: "You will be horrified to hear that I have never read Clausewitz or Delbrück or Haushofer. The opinion on Clausewitz in our general staff was that of a theoretician to be read by professors."[30] There is no evidence to suggest that the interwar officer corps had any different perceptions or interest in what Clausewitz had to say.[31]

Ludendorff's reply to a question by Crown Prince Rupprecht of Bavaria underlines this confusion of strategy with operations. Rupprecht had asked what the objective of the Michael Offensive of March 1918 might be. Ludendorff replied: "We will punch a hole into [their lines]. For the rest we shall see. We did it this way in Russia."[32] Without a political or strategic vision, the Germans operated in a vacuum, one in which they established military goals with regard only for military criteria, irrespective of strategic or political consequences.

The measure of a military organization's strategic effectiveness lies in its ability to calculate acceptable risks over the long term. Because the

---

[28] For a discussion of the military weaknesses involved in the Schlieffen Plan, see Gerhard Ritter, *The Schlieffen Plan, Critique of a Myth* (New York, 1958).

[29] For the logistical problems confronting the Germans in a campaign in the west, see Martin van Creveld, *Supplying War, Logistics from Wallenstein to Patton* (Cambridge, 1977), chap. 4.

[30] Letter from Leo Geyer von Schweppenburg to B.H. Liddell Hart, King's College Archives, London, 9/24/61, p. 32.

[31] The end of tour report by the future general Albert C. Wedemeyer on his return from a two-year tour in Berlin as a student at the Kriegsakademie makes it clear that German professional military education did not expose its students to Clausewitz. See Albert C. Wedemeyer, "German General Staff School," Report 15,999 dated 17/11/38 from the military attaché Berlin, 1kb, 6/23/39, National Archives.

[32] Quoted in Herwig, "The Dynamics of Necessity," p. 40.

German military so consistently opted for short-term operational gains, the long-term consequences were often catastrophic. The lack of concern before World War I over the possibility Britain might participate in a European War provides an excellent example of the short term over the long term. But the German Navy used equally flawed reasoning in 1916 in attempting to persuade Germany's military leaders to declare unrestricted submarine warfare. In summer 1941 its leaders were urging Hitler to declare war on the United States, so that they could launch their U-boats against America's east coast – a campaign they were largely unprepared to conduct over the long term.[33] As for the economic consequences of such a decision, Germany's naval leaders do not seem to have made any economic analyses at all.

Even more seriously, the Germans tended to evaluate avenues of approach without fully considering whether the benefits of gaining strategic objectives outweighed the costs of failure. The exception was, of course, Beck's arguments against Hitler's inordinately risky policies toward Czechoslovakia in summer 1938. Beck had no doubts that the Czech Republic represented an irritant that Germany needed to be rid of, but the consequences of a 1938 invasion of Czechoslovakia, he argued, would result in Germany once again confronting the rest of Europe. Therefore, Germany should not take the plunge into a war that it could not win in the long run.[34] But few of the others were willing to support the chief of the general staff.

More typical was the approach to the Schlieffen Plan, where the risks and consequences of failure posed concerns only for politicians. Not surprisingly, Hitler mirrored this attitude; as he once argued, it was his business as the nation's leader to calculate the risk, and it was the business of the generals to fight the resulting wars. Consequently, where the military had floundered in the business of making strategy in the First World War due to the abdication of responsibility by the politicians, thus preventing civilian authority from assessing risks, it now turned the assessment of risk over to a political leader whose strategic equation substituted personal will for strategic analysis whenever the means-to-ends equation was out of balance.

---

[33] For the best discussion of German naval attitudes, see Holger Herwig, *The Politics of Frustration, The United States in German Naval Planning, 1889–1941* (Boston, 1976), pp. 225–234.
[34] See "Betrachtungen zur gegenwärtigen mil. politischen Lage," 5.5.38; "Bemerkungen zu den Ausführung des Führers am 28.5.38," 16.7.38; and Vortragsnotiz vom 29.7.38, all in BA/MA N 28/3, Nachlass Beck.

This German approach to war from the bottom up resulted in an inability to connect strategic goals to available forces. Groener conveyed some sense of this assessment in a critique of Reich's strategic conduct of the First World War that he delivered to his officers in early 1919. He suggested that Imperial Germany's defeat had resulted from its attempt to become a world power before it had secured its position in Europe. By attempting both at the same time, Germany had made its defeat inevitable.[35] But Groener's realism, a mark of his tenure as defense minister, did not represent the view of most officers even in the 1920s when the republic possessed minimal military power. More typical was a war game designed by the *Reichswehr* in late 1922 that posited a combined effort with the navy (now reduced to a pre-*Dreadnought* force) to thwart a Franco–Danish invasion of northern Germany. Almost immediately thereafter the French underlined the lack of realism of the game by occupying the Ruhr – an action to which the *Reichswehr* had no reply except to recommend national suicide.[36] And one must not forget the almost universal belief within the officer corps that the army had stood unbeaten and unbroken in the field in fall 1918, only to be stabbed in the back by the Jews and socialists, the so-called *Dolchstoss* legend.[37]

Among other things, strategy demands the consideration of alternatives. If one's assumptions prove faulty, then one must adapt to reality. The leadership of none of the three services displayed such flexibility. The navy proved the most dogged in its refusal to adapt its strategic assumptions to reality. As Holger Herwig has suggested:

> Seapower, in a word, consists of fleet and position: one is useless without the other. Tirpitz either ignored or never grasped Alfred Thayer Mahan's unwritten presupposition that unfettered access to the world's ocean was the cardinal prerequisite for seapower. Given that Britain was Germany's primary potential opponent [especially in view of everything that Tirpitz was attempting to achieve], a brief glance at the map should have confirmed the obvious: the British could bottle up the German fleet, based in either Kiel or Wilhelmshaven, in the North Sea, if they chose to close the Straits of Dover and the waters between Scotland and Norway. Despite this, Tirpitz failed to develop an alternative strategy.[38]

---

[35] Herwig, *The Politics of Frustration*, p. 151.
[36] Michael Geyer, *Aufrüstung oder Sicherheit, Die Reichswehr in der Krise der Machtpolitik, 1924–1936* (Wiesbaden, 1980), p. 80.
[37] There was not a shred of truth in this claim. The army was collapsing as rapidly at the front as it was at home; only logistical difficulties prevented the Allies from flooding into Germany.
[38] Herwig, "The Dynamics of Uncertainty," p. 90.

But Tirpitz's greatest mistake came at the political–strategic level. His "risk theory" rested on three flawed assumptions: first, that in the long run, the British would not match either the manpower or the financial costs of a great naval race; second, that the British would prove incapable of coming to terms with the French and the Russians; and third, that Germany could afford the cost of both Continental defense and a naval buildup. In reality, the British showed their willingness and ability to maintain naval superiority. The *Dreadnought*-class battleships placed the cost of the naval race beyond Imperial Germany's capacity to support. And finally, the ententes with France (1905) and Russia (1907) placed Britain squarely within the great anti-German coalition. Did any of this serve to change Tirpitz's assumptions? Certainly not on the basis of continued German naval policy.[39] Tirpitz's question to the commander of the High Seas Fleet in May 1914 – "what will you do if they don't come out?" – underlines the bankruptcy of the navy's strategic policy through to the outbreak of the world war.[40]

The German Army also proved unwilling to prepare for contingencies or to adapt to strategic realities. In fact, the strategic approach that resulted in the Schlieffen Plan aimed at removing contingencies. In effect, it left only one avenue open to the German military when the crisis broke in summer 1914. Similarly, the army proved incapable of adapting its assumptions to the real conditions of war in its 1941 campaign against the Soviet Union. German planning for Barbarossa rested on several assumptions, few of which, even given the stunning nature of German victories early in the campaign, proved close to the mark. The initial onslaught did not destroy the Red Army in the frontier districts. The Soviets then put far more troops and reserve formations into the field than the Germans expected.[41] Moreover, Stalin's regime, helped by the murderous crusade the Germans waged, weathered the storm created by the invasion. Nevertheless, in spite of the lateness of the season and the serious threat of oncoming winter – the German high command, Field Marshal Walter von Brauchitsch, General Franz Halder, and Field Marshal Fedor von Bock, and their staffs – persisted in a maniacal drive in October and November 1941 to capture Moscow. They refused to address any

---

[39] For the best summary of these issues in English, see Herwig, *'Luxury' Fleet*.
[40] Quoted in Herwig, "The Dynamics of Necessity," p. 91. In other words, what would the Imperial Navy do, if the British mounted a distant rather than a close blockade?
[41] The entry of 11 August in the Halder diary captures this miscalculation most graphically. Franz Halder, *The Halder War Diary, 1939–1942* (Novato, CA, 1988), p. 506.

alternatives, largely due to the pressure of the assumptions they had made at the beginning of the campaign.[42]

The achievement of strategic goals by operational means also demands some connection between logistical capabilities and the industrial support that the national economic structure can support. In terms of war in the industrial age, this may be one of the most important factors in the means–ends equation. Yet, it was here the Germans appear weakest in their approach to war both strategically and operationally. The Schlieffen Plan rested on the logistic assumption that the Belgian railroads would be available. They were not, and the German supply system could not support the drive deep into France – the railheads remained far back in Belgium as German infantry literally staggered up to the Marne.[43]

But it was during the 1941 Russian campaign that German strategic failings had their greatest impact on the strategic outcome. In the planning stages of Barbarossa in fall 1940, a logistical game run by General Friedrich von Paulus, the future commander of the Sixth Army at Stalingrad, made clear that the *Wehrmacht* might run into serious trouble in the depths of the Soviet Union. Logistic calculations indicated that the German supply services would have difficulty provisioning the invading forces much beyond a depth of 500 kilometers east of the frontier – a distance well short of Leningrad, Moscow, and the Donets Basin.[44] But that warning failed to alarm the senior leadership. Even though railroad repair and conversion represented the essential support element in the campaign, those units charged with the task remained at the bottom of the army's priority list in the movement forward into the Soviet Union.[45]

Another significant deficiency in both world wars lay in the military's approach to industrial mobilization. Performance in the First World War was spotty at best. The so-called Hindenburg program that Ludendorff cast in late 1916 was a general economic disaster because it set such unrealistic goals.[46] But the real weaknesses in the military's approach to production and its relation to strategy showed even more clearly in the next war. Admittedly, some senior officers during the interwar period recognized that industrial preparation for a long war would play an

---

[42] In this regard, see particularly Klaus Reinhardt, *Die Wende vor Moskau* (Stuttgart, 1972), pp. 123–171.
[43] Van Creveld, *Supplying War*, pp. 153–157.
[44] Boog, et al., *Das Deutsche Reich und der Zweite Weltkrieg*, vol. 4, p. 117.
[45] Van Creveld, *Supplying War*, pp. 153–157.
[46] See in particular, Gerald Feldman, *Army, Industry, and Labor in Germany* (Princeton, NJ, 1966).

important role in a future conflict. But in the late 1930s the Germans could not prepare the economy for a long war and at the same time meet Hitler's inordinate demands for the immediate buildup of the *Wehrmacht*. Through the French campaign of 1940, economic weaknesses placed severe constraints on what industry could produce for the rapidly expanding *Wehrmacht*.[47] Moreover, there was precious little connection among the Führer's strategy, the *Wehrmacht*'s preparations for war, and the extent of economic preparation and mobilization.[48] German rearmament, massive throughout the late 1930s, caused such severe economic strains that by 1938 it had driven Hitler to embark on an increasingly risky foreign policy.

But the conquest of France in May–June 1940 along with the booty of Scandinavia and the Low Countries put the Third Reich in a more secure economic position. It was in the position to mobilize the whole European Continent. It did not. Instead, while Britain, the Soviet Union, and eventually the United States made desperate efforts to increase production in order to catch up to the Germans, the Germans made no major effort in 1941 to mobilize the resources that had become available to them through their conquests.[49] Admittedly, throughout the war Hitler's unwillingness to pressure the German people for fear of causing a repetition of the 1918 revolution represented a major stumbling block to a fuller mobilization of the Reich's economic resources. But much of Albert Speer's success rested on the fact that the German war economy was able to draw on the resources of the rest of Europe. Had the Germans begun mobilizing Europe's latent economic strengths in the immediate aftermath of the fall of France, they would have been better positioned to fight the terrible battles of 1942 through 1944. However, they did not, and while much of the blame rests on Hitler, the military also failed to think in terms of industrialized war.

The final test of strategic effectiveness involves the capacity of military organizations to work with allies and to utilize allied strengths to the coalition's advantage. Here also, the Germans performed execrably. In the First World War, Germany's chief ally was the Austro–Hungarian Empire. Before the war even started, the Germans had failed to notify their allies about the nature of the Schlieffen Plan. Only upon the outbreak

---

[47] See in particular Murray, *The Change in the European Balance of Power*, chap. 1.
[48] See Williamson Murray, "Force Structure, Blitzkrieg Strategy, and Economic Difficulties: Nazi Grand Strategy in the 1930s," in *German Military Effectiveness* (Baltimore, MD, 1992), chap. 9.
[49] See Williamson Murray, *Luftwaffe* (Baltimore, MD, 1985), pp. 92–104.

of war did the German military attaché in Vienna cable Berlin to suggest that "it is high time that the two general staffs consult now with absolute frankness with respect to mobilization, jump-off time, areas of assembly, and precise troop strength."[50] Things improved little over the course of the war. In 1916 the Austrians weakened their forces on the Russian front to mount an offensive against the Italians. That decision in turn almost resulted in the complete collapse of the Eastern Front when the Russians under General Brusilov attacked the weakened Austrian front lines. To save the situation in the east, the German high command had to shut down the Battle of Verdun.

In World War II the Axis, a supposed alliance among Nazi Germany, Fascist Italy, and Imperial Japan, represented little more than an agreement among thieves whose common interest lay only in their desire to steal what belonged to others. The Axis powers did no common planning before the war and precious little during it. Hitler made his decision to sign the Nazi–Soviet Non-Aggression Pact and to attack Poland without consulting his allies. The Italians fought their own "parallel war" in the Mediterranean until military catastrophes forced them into the embrace of the Germans.[51] Never true allies, the Germans and the Japanese made no coordinated plans, no effort to help each other, and displayed no willingness to work together to affect the course of the war to their mutual benefit. Undoubtedly, geographic distances contributed to the weakness of the bond, but one suspects that the Germans had neither the interest nor the inclination to think in terms of larger alliance issues. Given Nazi attitudes toward other races, this state of affairs is not at all surprising.

Operational and Tactical Effectiveness: The Joint Arena

Moving down a notch from strategy to German battlefield performance in a variety of theaters and conditions, one moves into a different realm of military competence. Despite substantial differences between the services, their strengths and weaknesses remained surprisingly similar. Above all, the Germans displayed a consistent capacity to adapt to the intricate difficulties of modern conflict. Before 1914 their army and navy could not draw on a body of common experience. The operational plans of the First World War revealed little common ground or understanding. The army

---

[50] Herwig, "The Dynamics of Necessity," p. 89.
[51] See MacGregor Knox's excellent study of this relationship in *Mussolini Unleashed, Fascist Italy's Last War* (Cambridge, 1982).

executed the Schlieffen Plan by wheeling inside of Paris, while making no effort to capture the Channel ports. In retrospect, a few cavalry divisions might have brought that crucial area under German control. On the other hand, the navy did not interfere with the transfer of the British Expeditionary Force to the Continent. Those British troops would play a considerable role in arresting the German drive on the Marne in September and in protecting the Channel ports in fall 1914. Four years later when Ludendorff launched his "Michael" offensive on which Germany's bid for world power rested, the navy again did nothing; its battleships remained securely anchored in its North Sea harbors. Consequently, the British found themselves able to rush reinforcements and supplies across the Channel to their hard-pressed forces in northern France.

Much of the failure to cooperate resulted from the lack of a coordinating high command. Moreover, the two services harbored deep suspicions toward each other, the navy even refusing to exchange intelligence data with the army before the outbreak of war.[52] With no tradition of cooperation and with fundamentally different world views, the two services found cooperation almost impossible during World War I. Nevertheless, as Gallipoli underlined, joint matters went no more smoothly on the other side. But in the interwar years, the British, unlike the Germans, created the chiefs of staff system that eventually made effective joint planning possible. As one of the leading officers in the *Oberkommando der Wehrmacht* (*OKW*, armed forces high command) noted after the Second World War: "In fact the advice of the British Chiefs of Staff and the U.S. Joint Chiefs was a deciding factor in Allied strategy. At the comparable level in Germany there was nothing but a disastrous vacuum."[53]

In the Second World War, relations among the army, the navy, and the *Luftwaffe* got progressively worse. Göring lacked any interest in cooperating with the navy to cut Britain's sea lines of communications, nor was the *Luftwaffe*'s general staff any more enthusiastic. Consequently, the air units participating in the maritime campaign represented only a small percentage of the *Luftwaffe*'s overall strength. The navy, for its part, often failed to coordinate air reconnaissance with the disposition of its U-boats. As a result, Dönitz's wolfpacks posed the sole real threat to the Allied sea lines of communication for much of the war.[54]

---

[52] Herwig, "The Dynamics of Necessity," p. 87.
[53] Walter Warlimont, *Inside Hitler's Headquarters* (New York, 1964), p. 54.
[54] British Air Ministry, *The Rise and Fall of the German Air Force, 1933–1945* (New York, 1983), pp. 101–107.

One can only describe the relationship between the army and the navy as tenuous. In early June 1940, even before planning for Operation "Sea Lion" had begun, the navy sent out its last major fleet units, the *Gneisenau* and *Scharnhorst* off Norway's North Cape, not for operational or strategic purposes, but rather, as its war diary makes clear, to influence postwar budget debates.[55] The planning for "Sea Lion" suggests the level of cooperation among the services. The army's high command drew up plans that entirely disregarded the navy's actual strength, with the navy being equally unrealistic in planning to land the army on a minuscule section of Britain's shores.[56] The *Luftwaffe* considered "Sea Lion" irrelevant because it believed its own aerial campaign against the British Isles would win the war against Britain and render a landing unnecessary.[57] As for realism in the *OKW*, General Alfred Jodl, that organization's operations officer, noted in his diary at the end of June that final victory over England was only a question of time.[58] The *OKH* simply regarded the problems involved with "Sea Lion" as no worse than those posed by a "large river crossing."[59]

But the German military could work in the joint environment when operations involved only lower levels of command. "*Weserübung*" (code name for the invasion of Norway and Denmark) represented the best joint performance of German military forces in the war. The *Luftwaffe* dominated the seas around southern Norway, while the navy slipped the army into the major Norwegian ports. While Norwegian defenses blocked naval forces in the Oslo Fiord, *Luftwaffe* paratroopers seized the main airport outside the capital, while transports landed sufficient reinforcements for the invaders to seize Oslo by the early afternoon.[60] Similarly, the seizure of Crete by *Luftwaffe* paratroopers and army mountain troops underlines that at times the German services could skillfully cooperate.

The one area where interservice cooperation reached levels that remained unmatched by Germany's opponents until well into the war was in the development of close air support doctrine by the army

---

[55] Klaus Maier, et al., *Das Deutsche Reich und der Zweite Weltkrieg*, vol. 2, *Die Errichtung der Hegemonie auf dem europäischen Kontinent* (Stuttgart, 1979), pp. 221–224.
[56] For the best description of the German planning for "Sea Lion," see Telford Taylor, *The Breaking Wave* (New York, 1967).
[57] Maier, et al., *Das Deutsche Reich und der Zweite Weltkrieg*, vol. 2, pp. 378–379.
[58] Chef WFA, 30.6.40, "Die Weiterführung des Krieges gegen England," in International Military Tribunal, *Trial of Major War Criminals*, vol. 28, pp. 301–303.
[59] Taylor, *The Breaking Wave*, p. 216.
[60] For the best description of Weserübung in English, see Taylor, *The March of Conquest*.

and the *Luftwaffe*. Unlike most other air forces in the world, the *Luftwaffe* devoted considerable assets to the support of ground forces and to ensuring that those air units received proper training and equipment.[61] But that was a wasting asset as the *Luftwaffe*'s capabilities declined and those of opposing Allied air forces improved.

Operational and Tactical Effectiveness: The Army

At this point, one can best examine the three services' military effectiveness in their separate operational and tactical arenas, starting with the army, given its exalted position within the German military hierarchy. Of all the German military institutions in this period, the army reached the highest levels of battlefield excellence and performance. Yet, it had entered the First World War with serious deficiencies that almost brought defeat to Imperial Germany in the conflict's first two years. In 1914 the general staff exercised sway over only a small portion of the decision-making processes. In particular, it drew up war plans and had some influence over tactical and operational questions. The Prussian War Ministry exercised control over manpower questions as well as budgetary and administrative issues. Significantly, the general staff could not get Lieutenant Colonel Georg Bruchmüller, the great artillery expert who designed a significant proportion of the bombardment plans in the last years of the war, promoted to the rank of permanent colonel over the objections of the war ministry.[62]

The course of the fighting through to 1916 did not suggest any kind of German battlefield superiority. The Schlieffen Plan, whatever its intellectual power, represented a significant departure from the approach that characterized Moltke's efforts in 1866 and 1870. In the latter case, army commanders had possessed great latitude to react to the situation they confronted rather than to follow orders that were no longer relevant. Consequently, Germany reaped the benefits of independent actions taken by commanders on the spot. However, Schlieffen's tightly controlled plan left little room for initiative. In effect, his plan represented an attempt to contradict Moltke's aphorism that "no plan survives contact with the

---

[61] For the development of German close air support capabilities and doctrine, see Williamson Murray, "German Close Air Support," in Benjamin Franklin Cooling, ed., *Close Air Support* (Washington, DC, 1990).

[62] Bradley J. Meyer, "Operational Art and the German Command System in World War I," Ph.D. Dissertation, The Ohio State University, 1988, p. 296.

enemy."[63] To a considerable extent, the defeat on the Marne resulted from the failure of a plan that contradicted operational art and ignored the conditions of ambiguity and uncertainty that characterize war.

The performance of German troops on the tactical level during this early period matched that of their opponents. In the Flanders battles of October 1914, the German high command threw divisions of ill-trained recruits – including university students – who had volunteered on the outbreak of war, against the British and French, an effort that was soon termed "the slaughter of the innocents." It represented as major a tactical disaster for the Germans as that which the French suffered in the opening battles on the frontiers in August 1914 or as the British suffered on the first day of the Somme.[64] By late fall 1916 the Germans confronted a desperate situation on the battlefield. Their attack on Verdun had failed miserably. Moreover, after a disastrous start on the Somme on 1 July 1916, the British Army imposed close to a one-to-one ratio in losses on the German defenders, who continued to pack their frontline trenches with the bulk of their infantry, which exposed them to the devastating effect of British artillery fire.

The Kaiser then brought in Hindenburg and Ludendorff to rectify the situation. On the strategic level, they compounded Germany's problems by agreeing to naval demands for unrestricted submarine warfare – a decision that brought the United States into the war. But for the first time since the conflict had begun, a senior military leader, namely Ludendorff, addressed the considerable tactical problems that the war had raised. First of all, Ludendorff used the general staff system to ensure a reliable flow of information from the battlefield to the German high command. Second, he went out to the Western Front and discovered that conditions there differed substantially from those of the Eastern Front. His memoirs note that, "it was my duty to adapt myself to those conditions."[65] In his fact-finding tour, he demanded that the commanders and staff officers who reported to him speak their minds as to what was really happening and not pass along something "made to order."[66]

---

[63] Robert Debs Heinl, *Dictionary of Military and Naval Quotations* (Annapolis, MD, 1966), p. 239.
[64] For the "Battle of the Frontiers," see Barbara Tuchman, *The Guns of August* (New York, 1962), pp. 163–193. For the first day on the Somme, see Martin Middlebrook, *The First Day on the Somme* (New York, 1972). For the most complete tactical analysis, see Robin Prior and Trevor Wilson, *The Somme* (New Haven, 2005).
[65] Erich Ludendorff, *Ludendorff's Own Story*, vol. 1 (New York, 1919), p. 324.
[66] Ibid., p. 24.

In effect, the Germans invented modern defensive warfare and tactical concepts. They created the concept of the defense in depth aimed at exhausting the enemy's strength at minimum cost to themselves. Successively stronger positions would attrit the attackers, while the bulk of German artillery and infantry strength remained out of range of the enemy's guns. The defense could gauge the location of significant enemy penetrations and then launch counterattacks to seal off any breakthroughs. In 1917, these new defensive tactics, encapsulated in the doctrinal manual "Principles of Command for the Defensive Battle in Position Warfare," allowed the Germans to blunt the Nivelle offensive in the spring, a victory that came close to destroying the French Army. Then, on the basis of lessons learned in these defensive battles with their supporting counterattacks, the Germans developed modern, decentralized, mission-oriented, offensive tactics and operational concepts that allowed them to launch their devastating attacks in spring 1918.

Several factors account for these German successes. The key to modern battlefield performance is decentralized control. Units down to company and platoon level must be able to act on their own. Given the ambiguities of the modern battlefield, higher command levels can at best provide general guidance. They must rely on those at the scene to act in accordance with that guidance. Such an approach depends on a high level of leadership at all levels; it demands that subordinate commanders and their soldiers receive coherent, stringent training; and it demands a coherent doctrine.

Throughout this period the Germans achieved these goals through a variety of means. The general staff system allowed the free flow of information up and down the chain of command. Consequently, the Germans could now adapt more rapidly to changes on the battlefield. The general staff system also allowed a more thorough integration of the combat branches because general staff officers acquired a thorough grounding in, and understanding of, them. Finally, the Germans took their combat doctrine seriously. Once the doctrinal experts in the general staff and at the front had evolved "The Defensive Battle in Position Warfare" in late 1916 and the new offensive doctrine by late 1917, the army established schools throughout the rear areas on the Western Front to ensure that commanders at all levels understood and complied with the new tactical system.[67]

---

[67] This was not the case with the French Army even in the late periods of World War I. By early 1918 Marshal Pétain, commander-in-chief of the French Army, had promulgated

The Problem of German Military Effectiveness, 1900–1945   219

But by the end of 1918, *all* the armies on the Western Front had adapted to the new conditions of offensive and defensive warfare. As the French defense in front of Rheims in July 1918 and the British attacks in the late summer showed, the Allies had learned from the Germans how to utilize defense in depth and employ new offensive tactics. In fact, the British further improved the German system by including tanks in their attacks. However, when the peace came, only the German Army coherently and consistently carried over the lessons of the First World War into the interwar period.[68] By 1930 the French had largely mislearned the lessons of the war by studying only those battles that fit into their paradigm.[69] For their part the British failed to examine the lessons of the war until 1932, far too late to adapt peacetime training to the real world of experience.[70]

The German Army did not make that mistake. Historians often accuse military institutions with the charge that the "Colonel Blimps" study the last war, and that is why they do badly in the next. Nothing could be further from the truth. General Hans von Seeckt, chief of staff in the immediate aftermath of the war, established no fewer than 57 committees to study World War I's lessons.[71] As a result, the Germans prepared for the next war on the basis of a solid understanding of what happened in the last war at the tactical level. By 1923 the Germans had a coherent and intelligent doctrinal manual on the street that incorporated all the major lessons of the last war.

Three senior generals, including Werner von Fritsch, soon to be the army's commander in chief, and Ludwig Beck, soon to be the chief of staff, revised the manual, now called *Truppenführung (Troop Leadership)* in 1934. On the basis of this work, the army prepared for the coming war. Its doctrine, based on a combined-arms approach, emphasized the use of

---

a version of defense in depth as the army's official doctrine. The disastrous pummeling the British took in March and April 1918 should only have served to reinforce the lesson that a defense in depth represented the only way to stop an enemy offensive based on the new German tactics. Nevertheless, General Duchesne, commander of the Sixth Army, entirely disregarded his instructions and ordered his subordinates to pack their infantry in the front lines, where the Germans slaughtered them in the great offensive against the Chemin des Dames. See Barry Pitt, *The Last Act* (New York, 1962), pp. 143–148.

[68] In this regard, see James S. Corum, *The Roots of Blitzkrieg: Hans von Seeckt and German Military Reform* (Lawrence, KS, 1994).

[69] See in particular the outstanding monograph by Robert Doughty, *Seeds of Disaster, The Development of French Army Doctrine, 1919–1939*, (Hamden, CT, 1985).

[70] Michael Howard, *The Continental Commitment* (London, 1972), p. 32. For the best general study of the British Army during the interwar period, see Brian Bond, *British Military Policy between the Two World Wars* (Oxford, 1980).

[71] Corum, *The Roots of Blitzkrieg*, pp. 37–43.

all the combat arms to ensure surprise, exploitation, decentralized planning and execution, and above all, speed. Artillery officers, infantrymen, and support branches could now conceptualize war within a common framework that recognized war as it is:

> Situations in war are of unlimited variety. They change often and suddenly and only rarely are from the first discernable. Incalculable elements are often of great influence. The independent will of the enemy is pitted against ours. Friction and mistakes are everyday occurrences.[72]

By the mid-1930s the Germans could realistically incorporate tanks into a doctrine that emphasized speed, initiative, and decentralized leadership. Thus, the *Wehrmacht* could utilize armor's capabilities to exploit fleeting opportunities on the battlefield. Thus, from the German perspective, there was nothing revolutionary about their employment of panzer units. All the doctrinal pieces were already in place.

What characterized German ground forces in the 1930s was the army leadership's recognition of major flaws and weaknesses within its rapidly expanding organization. From the Anschluss through the French campaign, it never used its operational successes as a standard of measure. No matter how stunning the Polish campaign might have appeared to outsiders, the OKH felt most dissatisfied with the army's performance. In the immediate aftermath of victory over the Polish armed forces, the OKH demanded that army units down to the regimental level render accurate "after action" reports. Within a month the general staff had gathered, digested, and formulated those reports, on which it established a massive program to retrain the entire army.[73] Tireless preparation, lasting from November 1939 through April 1940, turned the German Army into a fearsome instrument of military power that destroyed the Western Front in a matter of days.

Nevertheless, the historian of German military effectiveness would not be accurate in ascribing German battlefield performance in the Second World War exclusively to military factors. In that conflict ideology substantially motivated troop performance, a factor which the army leadership understood even before the war. As early as 1938, the army's commander-in-chief, the future Field Marshal Walther von Brauchitsch, specified that "the officer corps must not allow itself to be surpassed by anyone in the purity and genuineness of its National Socialist

[72] Chef der Heeresleitung, *Truppenführung* (Berlin, 1933), p. 1.
[73] See Williamson Murray, "The German Response to Victory in Poland: A Case Study in Professionalism," *Armed Forces and Society*, Winter 1980/1981.

Weltanschauung."[74] Two years later he wanted "not the slightest doubt about the fact that the training of the soldier is to be a determined and aggressive fighter [can] not be separated from a lively education in the National Socialist sense."[75] The performance of German ground forces on the Eastern Front clearly linked ideological preparation and motivation with combat readiness.[76] Thus, ironically, the very factor that played an important role in the strategic ineffectiveness of the invasion of the Soviet Union, namely Hitler's ideological crusade, also helps to explain why the German soldier fought so well.

The picture outside of battlefield operational tactical effectiveness is not nearly so impressive. Both logistics and intelligence, crucial factors in any modern definition of military effectiveness, revealed enormous weaknesses. In addition to the many crucial logistic mistakes at the strategic level that so bedeviled the German conduct of war, logistical errors and their consequences had an equally serious impact at the operational level. The Schlieffen Plan failed as much for its logistical weaknesses as for any other reasons.[77] The failures in logistical planning and execution had equally serious consequences in the next conflict. Only desperate expedients allowed the Germans to equip the forces for "Barbarossa" up to their basic TO&E (Table of Organization and Equipment) levels. To do this the Germans had to give even the elite panzer and motorized infantry divisions a mixed bag of weapons and support vehicles, many of which had been captured from the British and the French – the rest pulled from Germany's civilian economy. More than half the invading divisions either had shortages of equipment or used equipment captured during the 1940 campaign.[78] French, British, Belgian, and Dutch trucks jostled with Norwegian mountain artillery and Czech tanks to create a logistician's nightmare. Among other bizarre supply estimates, the Germans

---

[74] Quoted in Jürgen Förster, "New Wine in Old Skins? The Wehrmacht and the War of 'Weltanschauung,'" in Wilhelm Deist, ed., *The German Military in the Age of Total War* (Leamington Spa, 1985), p. 305.

[75] Quoted in Jürgen Förster, "The Dynamics of Volksgemeinschaft: The Effectiveness of the German Military Establishment in the Second World War," in Allan R. Millett and Williamson Murray, eds., *Military Effectiveness*, vol. 3, *World War II* (London, 1988), p. 205.

[76] See Omar Bartov, *The Eastern Front, 1941–1945, German Troops and the Barbarization of War* (New York, 1986).

[77] For a particularly good discussion of the operational consequences of the logistical failures in 1914, see van Creveld, *Supplying War*, chap. 4.

[78] See the table, "Die Materiele Ausstattung des deutschen Ostheeres am 22 Juni 1941," in Horst Boog, et al., *Das Deutsche Reich und der Zweite Weltkrieg*, vol. 4, *Der Angriff auf die Sowjetunion* (Stuttgart, 1983), pp. 186–187.

calculated that they would not need more ammunition during their invasion of the Soviet Union than they had used during the French campaign, surely one of the greatest miscalculations in military history.[79]

But of all the logistical miscues of 1941, the advance on Moscow surely represented a mistake with the most disastrous consequences. By late September 1941, the supply system had finally reached the point where the German advance could resume. However, as German logisticians warned, it could only do so by sacrificing the establishment of supply dumps of fuel, ammunition, food, and winter clothing that German troops would require to meet the coming winter. Both the OKH and Army Group Center enthusiastically opted for a resumption of the offensive. Moreover, they do not seem to have consulted Hitler. The defeat in front of Moscow and the terrible trials the army suffered over the winter were the direct results.[80]

The second major area of support where the Germans showed themselves markedly inferior throughout the war lay in intelligence. Like those of the other three services, the army's radio traffic, encoded on Enigma machines, proved vulnerable to British code-breaking efforts at Bletchley Park.[81] In the early part of the war, when the army's communications went largely by land lines, British efforts posed no significant threat. By 1942, however, the results were more damaging. In the North African theater, Ultra, the intelligence gained by the code breaking, played havoc with the movement of supplies from Italy to Libya. Ironically, Ultra decrypts provided the only clear source available to the Western Powers as to what was transpiring on the Eastern Front. By the Normandy invasion, Ultra was providing the Allied high command with intelligence as diverse as the location of the headquarters of Panzer Group West – almost immediately taken out by Allied fighter bombers – and the timing, aim, and direction of the Mortain counterattack in early August.[82]

The most disastrous German intelligence failures came on the Eastern Front. There, at the least from 1942, Soviet *maskirovka* (deception) misled German intelligence about the weight and direction of every single major offensive the Soviets launched through to the end of

---

[79] Van Creveld, *Supplying War*, p. 151.
[80] Reinhardt, *Die Wende vor Moskau*, pp. 123–171.
[81] For the clearest discussion of how and why the German message traffic proved vulnerable, see Gordon Welchman, *The Hut Six Story* (New York, 1982).
[82] The most thorough examination of the direct linkage between Ultra and Allied military operations is Ralph Bennett, *Ultra in the West, The Normandy Campaign 1944–1945* (New York, 1979), pp. 114–116.

the war.[83] For all the vaunted fighting power of German troops on the Eastern Front and the supposed operational performance of senior German military leaders, Soviet deception negated every battlefield advantage the Germans might have enjoyed.

Operational and Tactical Effectiveness: The *Luftwaffe*

Like the army, the *Luftwaffe* enjoyed a high standard of performance on the operational and tactical levels at the outbreak of war in 1939. Of all the air forces in the Second World War, only the *Luftwaffe* possessed a broad-based doctrine that took air power beyond the confines of "strategic" bombing.[84] It was not that the *Luftwaffe* did not take "strategic" bombing seriously. It did. Significantly in the period before the Second World War, only the *Luftwaffe* had prepared seriously to meet the navigational and technological demands for such an air campaign.[85] But the Germans had also learned from their experiences in the Spanish Civil War that hitting targets accurately from the air and the staying power of civilian populations under aerial assault represented difficulties, over which theorists of "strategic" bombing had all too glibly passed. *Luftwaffe* air doctrine recognized the far wider contributions that air power could make to a number of other crucial missions: reconnaissance, interdiction, air superiority, close air support, air defense, and air transport.[86]

In general the *Luftwaffe* prepared itself better than other air forces to contribute to joint operations. Its contribution to the advance and the victories of German ground forces with air superiority, close air support, and interdiction missions was an obvious mark of its effectiveness in early years of the Second World War. Thereafter, it proved a tenacious opponent on the wide frontiers that the *Wehrmacht* defended. And in the

---

[83] For the crucial work that unravels the contribution of Soviet deception to the winning of the Second World War, see David Glantz, *Soviet Military Deception in the Second World War* (London, 1982).

[84] Given the capabilities of air power during the First World War, it is hardly necessary to discuss the German air force as an independent service in that conflict. Nevertheless, it is worth noting that the Germans introduced the concept of "strategic" bombing to the world in 1916.

[85] For a discussion of the Luftwaffe's preparation for "strategic" bombing, see Williamson Murray, *Luftwaffe* (Baltimore, MD, 1985), chap. 1. See also the excellent discussion in Maier, et al., *Das Deutsche Reich und der Zweite Weltkrieg*, vol. 2, pp. 43–49.

[86] I am indebted to Oberst Klaus Maier of the Militärgeschichtliches Forschungsamt for providing me with a copy of the Luftwaffe's basic doctrinal manual: "Die Luftkriegführung (The Conduct of the Air War)," Berlin, 1936.

great air and night battles of 1943 and 1944 against the Anglo–American combined Bomber Offensive, despite being heavily outnumbered, it came close to victory.

Nevertheless, major deficiencies weakened the *Luftwaffe*'s effectiveness throughout the war. At the operational level, the *Luftwaffe*'s high command failed to focus on clearly defined objectives in the Battle of Britain. Consequently, it moved rapidly from one target set to another without achieving any substantive advantages. Its high command remained unrealistically optimistic throughout the war. Admittedly, a substantial part of the problem lay with the *Luftwaffe*'s leader, Hermann Göring, whose general incompetence and slavish devotion to Hitler, not to mention his corruption, led to a series of disastrous decisions.

But while Göring represented much of the problem, others shared in the blame. The young chief of the *Luftwaffe*'s general staff, Colonel General Hans Jeschonneck, fell under Hitler's spell from the beginning. In 1939, when confronted with Hitler's megalomaniacal demand that the *Luftwaffe* expand fivefold – hardly a realistic goal since such a force would have needed 85 percent of the world's supply of aviation gas – Jeschonneck commented to his staff that "in my view it is our duty to support the *Führer* and not work against him."[87] A number of Germany's air commanders also reflected the bizarre assessments of the Reich's political leadership. In early 1943, Johannes Steinhoff reported to Field Marshal Albert Kesselring in Rome before he assumed command of a fighter wing in Tunisia, where the situation was already disastrously deteriorating. He recounted in his memoirs the atmosphere at the field marshal's headquarters in the following terms:

> Never will I forget the Air Fleet situation conference which I was permitted to attend. There was I, a combat officer, witnessing the prognostications and sympathetic portrayal of the future course of the battle of North Africa... Was I allergic to the high command and staff officers? I found their foppish affectation and general superciliousness insufferable. In their presence anyone honored by an interview with the field marshal would be made to feel like a clumsy carthorse;... when it was over we sat down at a large table to an excellent dinner presided over by the field marshal himself. 'As soon as you've familiarized yourself with the theater,' he began, 'it is essential that you convince the people in your group that North Africa must be held – held at all costs. We shall be reinforcing the bridgehead and narrowing the front so that the position can be held without difficulty.'[88]

---

[87] Edward Homze, *Arming the Luftwaffe, The Reich's Air Ministry and the German Aircraft Industry, 1919–1939* (Lincoln, 1976), pp. 223–224.

[88] Johannes Steinhoff, *Messerschmitts over Sicily* (Baltimore, 1987), pp. 59–61.

With such attitudes in his headquarters, it is not surprising that Kesselring would soon be encouraging his aircrew to display Japanese fanaticism in the struggle to defeat Allied superiority in numbers.[89]

Like the army, logistics represented a major weakness in the *Luftwaffe*'s overall effectiveness. At the strategic level its leaders, with the exception of Field Marshal Erhard Milch, dismissed the threat represented by America's productive capabilities. Even as late as March 1942, Jeschonneck was objecting to a Milch proposal that the *Luftwaffe* raise its production of single-engine fighters to 360 per month – a level the British had far exceeded during the Battle of Britain. Jeschonneck commented that he would not know what to do with so many aircraft.[90] By the time the leadership woke to the extent of the Allied air threat, the roof was quite literally collapsing on the Reich.

On the operational and tactical levels, the weaknesses in support areas appear just as glaring. As the leading historian of the *Luftwaffe* suggests, the air force remained so focused on operations that engineering, logistics, and other support areas never received adequate attention.[91] At best the supply system could support a war confined to central and western Europe. Once the war expanded into the depths of the Soviet Union and from the North Cape to North Africa, the *Luftwaffe* found itself in desperate straits. By December 1941 the operational ready rate for bombers had fallen to 32 percent and for fighters to 52 percent.[92] In traveling around the German-occupied air fields in the east, Milch found aircraft needlessly abandoned because of breakdowns in the supply system.[93] While Milch was able to fix a number of problems, the air force's high command continued to take logistics for granted, a fact which had a disastrous impact on its ability to fight a sustained war.

Like the army, the German Air Force shorted its intelligence services in favor of operational and tactical capabilities. The undervaluing of intelligence and the underestimation of enemy capabilities marked *Luftwaffe* operations throughout the war.[94] The basic intelligence study that guided

---

[89] U.S. Army Air Force, *Ultra and the History of the United States Strategic Air Force versus the German Air Force* (Frederick, MD, 1980), p. 13.
[90] David Irving, *The Rise and Fall of the Luftwaffe, The Life of Field Marshal Erhard Milch* (Boston, 1973), p. 148.
[91] Horst Boog, *Die Deutsche Luftwaffenführung, 1933–1945* (Stuttgart, 1982).
[92] Air Historical Branch (Great Britain), "Luftwaffe Strength and Serviceability Tables, August 1938–April 1945," Translation No. VII/107.
[93] Irving, *The Rise and Fall of the Luftwaffe*, p. 134.
[94] Horst Boog, "Higher Command and Leadership in the German Luftwaffe, 1933–1945," in Alfred F. Hurley and Robert C. Ehrhart, eds., *Airpower and Warfare* (Washington, DC, 1979), p. 145.

the *Luftwaffe*'s conduct of the Battle of Britain – produced by its intelligence branch on 16 July 1940 – managed to estimate incorrectly every factor of importance in the coming battle.[95] It estimated Hurricanes and Spitfires as distinctly inferior to Bf-110s, made no mention of Britain's radar defenses, and ended on the optimistic note that "the *Luftwaffe*, unlike the RAF, will be in a position in every respect to achieve a decisive effect this year." Not surprisingly, another estimate calculated it would take the *Luftwaffe* four days to defeat Fighter command in southern England, followed by a four-week period during which its bombers and long-range fighters would mop up the remainder of the RAF and destroy Britain's aircraft industry.[96] The following year, estimates on the Red Air Force and productive capacity of the Soviet aircraft industry immediately before "Barbarossa" were as wildly unrealistic as the army's estimates on the Red Army. Nevertheless, Jeschonneck exclaimed shortly before the invasion began: "At last, a proper war!"[97]

Finally, Ultra's impact on German air operations ultimately spelled disaster for the Germans in a number of areas. A few examples should suffice. It played an important, although not decisive, role in the Battle of Britain by alerting British scientific intelligence to the fact that the Germans possessed blind-bombing technology.[98] Directly, it allowed the Anglo–American air forces to savage the air and sea lines of communications to Tunisia.[99] It also allowed the Allies to wreck the movement forward of the *Luftwaffe*'s fighter squadrons into France at the beginning of the Normandy invasion.[100] In summer and fall 1944 it kept the focus of American strategic bombing on the oil industry and thus cut the *Luftwaffe* off from the fuel it desperately needed not only for air operations but for training replacement pilots to make good the heavy losses it was suffering in combating U.S. long-range fighters.

Operational and Tactical Effectiveness: The *Kriegsmarine*

The navy's effectiveness throughout both world wars remained consistently dismal. While it did considerable damage to enemy shipping,

---

[95] For the study, see Francis K. Mason, *Battle over Britain, A History of German Air Assaults on Great Britain, 1917–1918 and July–December 1940 and the Development of Britain's Air Defenses between the World Wars* (Garden City, NY, 1969), appendix K.
[96] Basil Collier, *The Defence of the United Kingdom* (London, 1957), p. 160.
[97] Irving, *The Rise and Fall of the Luftwaffe*, p. 123.
[98] See R.V. Jones, *The Wizard War* (New York, 1978), pp. 92–105.
[99] Williamson Murray, *Strategy for Defeat, The Luftwaffe, 1933–1945* (Maxwell, AL, 1983), pp. 160–163.
[100] Ibid., pp. 265–266.

particularly with its U-boat force, the damage that it did to Germany's strategic situation was disastrous. One of the greatest historians of the Second World War has in fact gone so far as to claim that Germany would have been better off in that conflict had she never built a single submarine.[101] The conduct of surface operations during the First World War was hardly impressive, since for most of the conflict the High Seas Fleet remained in harbor. The initial contact with the Royal Navy off Heligoland Bight at the beginning of the war was a disgrace. German naval commanders forgot that they needed a high tide to move out into the North Sea, so Beatty and his battle cruisers chewed up the light forces that were out.

Dogger Bank in 1915 only escaped being a catastrophe because of the incompetence of Beatty's subordinates. Nevertheless, the British sank the *Blücher*, while the *Seydlitz* almost blew up. Fortunately for the Germans, swift thinking led to the flooding of her magazines. With the knowledge that only stringent safety measures could prevent a flash fire from running from a burning turret down to the magazines, the Germans were able to prevent a repetition at Jutland. Nevertheless, two German battle cruisers returned to harbor with their decks awash. Whatever tactical advantages the Germans enjoyed at Jutland, the Royal Navy remained in complete control of the exits from the North Sea and thus of the world's oceans.[102] After Jutland the High Seas Fleet remained in harbor for the rest of the war.

The real threat to the Allied strategic position lay in the attack on Britain's commerce by German U-boats. The Germans launched their first attempt at unrestricted warfare in 1915 with completely inadequate means at their disposal – only 28 boats, half of which were ineffective gasoline-powered submarines.[103] They did manage to sink the *Lusitania* after advertising their intentions on the front page of the *New York Times*, an action that almost brought the United States into the war. When the Germans resumed unrestricted submarine warfare in 1917, they still possessed only 100 U-boats, which meant that only 33 could remain on station at any given time – hardly enough to wage an effective campaign. Over the course of the next year, they managed to add nine boats to their fleet – 87 constructed, 78 sunk. Ironically, the naval high command remained hostile to the new force despite its advocacy of unrestricted

---

[101] Gerhard Weinberg in conversation with the author.
[102] For the best treatment of the Battle of Jutland, see Andrew Gordon, *The Rules of the Game, Jutland and British Naval Command* (London, 1996).
[103] Herwig, "The Dynamics of Necessity," p. 99.

submarine warfare. Admiral Eduard von Capelle even suggested that emphasizing U-boat construction would only endanger the capital ship program.[104]

In the interwar period, the German Navy dreamed of recreating the High Seas Fleet and redeeming the shame of the revolution that had broken out on its battle squadrons and the scuttling of the battle fleet at Scapa Flow in 1919. Like the Royal Navy, the Germans spent the interwar period preparing for another Jutland. When Hitler provided large funding increases in 1933, the navy again opted for the big ship, big gun fleet. It showed almost no interest in aircraft carriers, which its leader Admiral Erich Raeder characterized as "only gasoline tankers."[105] As for submarines, the senior leadership believed the obituaries on the weapon that had appeared in British publications. A 1939 study on ship capabilities reported that "the importance of U-boats has considerably declined compared to 1915. One can assume that England has good detection gear which makes torpedo attacks on a secured unit or a convoy impossible."[106] When war came in September 1939, the German surface fleet was still minuscule in size – three pocket battleships and two battle cruisers – and the U-boat fleet numbered only 28 ocean-going submarines.

Condemned to fight on uneven terms, the Germans waged a tenacious struggle that at times appeared to come close to breaking the sea lines of communications between the United Kingdom and the external world. Had the Germans managed to do so, they would have won the war. They failed, however, largely because of the navy's support structure on which a U-boat campaign had to rest. While the navy's signals were more complex than those of the army and the *Luftwaffe*, British code-breakers at Bletchley Park broke into them. In March 1941 the British captured a German weather ship and a U-boat with partial settings for the U-boat Enigma machines for the next several months. In May they captured another weather ship off Iceland with a more complete set of the rotor settings. The British were, thus, able to read the German message traffic to and from the U-boats not only for the next two months, but for the rest of

---

[104] Ibid., p. 99.
[105] Michael Salewski, *Die deutsche Seekriegsleitung*, vol. 1 (Frankfurt am Main, 1970), p. 29.
[106] Bundesarchiv/Militärarchiv, M/31/PG3458, Marine Kriegsakademie, Winterarbeit Kptlt Haack, 1938–1939, "Welche Wege kann die Seestrategie Englands in einem Krieg gegen Deutschland einschlagen und welche strategischen und operativen Möglichkeiten ergeben sich daraus für die deutsche Seekriegsführung?"

the year.[107] British losses of merchant shipping, which had reached well over 300,000 tons per month, dropped off to 100,000 tons per month for the rest of the year. This was the only time during World War II (and perhaps modern military history) where intelligence by itself proved decisive. However, in early 1942, the Germans added an additional rotor to their enigma machines. It took the British code-breakers another year to break back into the U-boat codes. By the end of 1942, the British had then succeeded, and German failures in signals discipline contributed immeasurably to the defeat of the U-boat offensive in the climactic battles in the North Atlantic in winter and spring 1943.[108]

Conclusion

Pictures best capture the strengths and weaknesses of the German military in the first half of the twentieth century. There are innumerable images of long lines of troops captured by the Germans in France and in Russia in 1940 and 1941. But those contrast with the darker images of German cities in 1945: Cologne with its cathedral standing alone in a sea of wreckage, Berlin with its burned-out shells of buildings, or Hamburg looking like the surface of the moon. Despite their defeats the German military performed at extraordinary levels in two world wars. To the bitter end they displayed fighting power and battlefield effectiveness that their opponents found hard to match, even given their enormous superiority in men and material. But down to defeat the Germans went. When it was all over in May 1945, they had come close to bringing the entire edifice of European civilization with them.

It would be unfair to blame the catastrophe entirely on the German military. The political leadership deserves considerable blame for the disasters, as do the German people themselves for providing enthusiastic support for the regimes that dragged the nation over the edge. But the military is accountable for failing to analyze the strategic and operational equations honestly. As an article on military effectiveness has noted:

> [S]trategic wisdom, however deserved, is more important than operational or tactical effectiveness. The best outcome, in which prewar strategic

---

[107] Patrick Beesley, *Very Special Intelligence* (Garden City, NY, 1978).
[108] In 1943 there were other contributing factors to the Allied success beyond code-breaking: the addition of long-range aircraft, more numerous and better trained antisubmarine forces, better tactics, and new technologies, all contributed along with intelligence to winning the Battle of the Atlantic.

analysis helps to make force structures and operational concepts effective in wartime, is as rare in history as wise political leadership. Few 'got it right' in World War I, in uniform or in mufti.... Military success in the earliest stages of modern war does not necessarily testify to strategic judgement. Such an assessment can only be made when the war ends.[109]

When the dust settled in 1918 and 1945, the German military had proven itself inept politically and incompetent strategically. All of their tactical and operational competence could not redress their political and strategic mistakes. In the end those competencies only served to make the consequences more terrible for all concerned.[110]

Additional Readings

A vast number of works and articles have appeared over the past two decades since this piece first appeared in the early 1990s. Among these works, the reader should consult: Gerhard Weinberg, *A World at Arms, A Global History of World War II* (Cambridge, 1994); Isabel V. Hull, *Absolute Destruction: Military Culture and the Practices of War in Imperial Germany* (Ithaca, NY, 2006); the German military history institute's multivolume series: *Das Deutsche Reich und der Zweite Weltkrieg* with a number of volumes translated into English; Holger Herwig, *The First World War: Germany and Austria Hungary, 1914–1918* (London, 2009); Williamson Murray and Allan R. Millett, *A War to Be Won, Fighting the Second World War* (Cambridge, MA, 2000); Williamson Murray, "Net Assessment in Nazi Germany in the 1930s," in Williamson Murray and Allan R. Millett, eds., *Calculations: Net Assessment and the Coming of World War II* (New York, 1994).

---

[109] Allan R. Millett and Williamson Murray, "Lessons of War," *The National Interest*, Winter 1988/1989.
[110] For the extent of the disaster, see particularly Max Hastings, *Armageddon, The Battle for Germany, 1944–1945* (New York, 2004).

10

Reflections on the Combined Bomber Offensive

Of all the major campaigns of World War II, the Combined Bomber Offensive (CBO), the two-pronged attack by the Royal Air Force (RAF) and the U.S. Army Air Forces, still remains the most controversial. On one side there are the arguments typified by the economist and member of the U.S. United States Strategic Bombing Survey (USSBS), John Kenneth Galbraith, who argued that for all the effort and for all its hideous impact on "innocent" civilians, the CBO simply did not achieve anything of commensurate value. According to Galbraith, the CBO was "perhaps the greatest miscalculation of the war":

> German war production had, indeed, expanded under the bombing. The greatly heralded efforts, those on the ball-bearing and aircraft plants for example emerged as costly failures. Other operations, those against oil and the railroads did have military effect. But strategic bombing had not won the war. At most, it had eased somewhat the task of the ground troops who did. The aircraft, manpower, and bombs used in the campaign had cost the American economy far more in output than they had cost Germany.[1]

Galbraith's deprecating comment, that at most the CBO had saved the lives of a few infantrymen, suggests a pervasive view that contrasts such

---

[1] John Kenneth Galbraith, *A Life in Our Times, Memoirs* (Boston, 1981), pp. 206, 226.

This chapter was first published as an article by the Bundeswehr's military history office as "Reflections on the Combined Bomber Offensive," *Militärgeschichtliche Mitteilungen*, 51 (1992), vol. 1. I am indebted to Dr. Colin Grey and the National Institute of Public Policy in Fairfax, Virginia, for sponsoring the original research effort that resulted in this article.

small savings with the wreckage of some of the world's most cultured and beautiful cities.[2]

The purpose of this chapter is to provide the other view – one based on the evidence. In the final analysis, the strategic bombing offensive was essential to Allied victory. To examine why this was so, this chapter will examine the larger questions of how the CBO contributed to the winning of World War II. What exactly was the nature of that contribution both directly and indirectly? What intended as well as unintended consequences did its effort entail? And, finally, what lessons might one draw from the campaign 50 years later?

The Influence of Doctrine

We might best begin with a brief examination of the military doctrines with which airmen embarked on the conflict and how the realities of war led to substantial alterations in the conduct of the campaign. Two substantial theories of air power evolved in the 20 years before World War II. Both had a number of assumptions in common, and those assumptions would play a crucial role in how the air campaigns would begin and almost fail. The theorists of air power in the interwar period argued that the airplane provided a means for nations to escape the terrible killing war in the trenches that had marked the four long years of World War I. By attacking enemy power directly, either in his population or industrial centers, air forces would be able to achieve a quick, easy solution without enormous cost in lives or material. Moreover, these theorists argued that new rules governed the conduct of air war: unlike naval or land war, there was no defense against air attack. The nation that placed its emphasis on bombers could wage a war of annihilation against the enemy. The air forces of the future would not need fighters either to defend their own homeland or to escort the great bomber formations that would attack the enemy directly.[3]

---

[2] In his memoirs Galbraith indicates a contempt for those engaged in the sharp end of fighting the Second World War. On a flight from Europe in summer 1945, "a much decorated sergeant shared a seat with me and asked if I would like to hear of his war adventures. I told him I would not. He made several attempts at conversation which I rejected. Finally he asked me who I thought would win the world series. I asked him what leagues were playing that year." Harvard was indeed a suitable institution in which to keep the great man locked up for most of the next 40 years. Galbraith, *A Life*, p. 225.

[3] Only Billy Mitchell of the early air power theorists saw the need to defeat the enemy's air force before direct attack on the enemy's homeland could begin.

In specifics there were, of course, considerable differences between British and American theories of air power. The British, led by the RAF's first post-war leader, Sir Hugh Trenchard, argued for attacking enemy morale by attacks on cities, particularly working-class districts in urban areas.[4] Trenchard believed that civilian morale was particularly vulnerable, since workers were members of the lower class and *ipso facto* irresponsible, ill-disciplined, and incapable of displaying the stiff upper lip that characterized their betters. Thus, they would not be able to stand up to effects of serious bombing, with the result, he argued, that revolution would break out, and the war would end.

The American version was different; rather than being articulated by one individual, it evolved out of teaching and theoretical work at the Air Corps Tactical School at Maxwell Field, Alabama. There, air theorists argued that industrialized nations contained vulnerable economic sectors on which the economy depended. The destruction of any one of these would cause the economic infrastructure to collapse. In particular, these theorists singled out industrial sectors such as electric power grids, transportation systems, and petroleum production as possibilities where precision bombing attacks would have a synergistic effect. This approach reflected the appeal of technology to Americans; the B-17 and the Norden bomb sight provided further support to those working on U.S. air power employment in the 1930s. Moreover, one also suspects that theorists at the Air Corps Tactical School recognized that targeting enemy populations might destroy the attractiveness of air power to the Congresses of the 1930s, dominated as they were by pacifist sentiments.

There was a general unwillingness on the part of airmen to question or test their hypotheses and assumptions. Crucial to both strategic bombing theories was a set of strategic and operational assumptions. The theories

---

[4] The other prophet of this approach was the Italian Giulio Douhet who argued that Italy must create a strategic bombing capability, if it were really to achieve the status of a great power. During the interwar period, Douhet exercised influence over Italian air policy (distorting it with notions and hopes that Italy had neither the industrial nor the technological capacity to fulfill, but fully in accord with the megalomania of the Fascist regime). It was only in the mid-1940s that he was discovered and resurrected as a prophet of "strategic" air power in the United States. The testimony of RAF leaders is quite specific on this point. "Bomber" Harris, Commander-in-Chief of Bomber Command during the war, stated in an oral interview available at the RAF Staff College, Bracknell, that not only had he never heard of Douhet before the war, but even if he had, he would have paid no attention to his writings because Douhet was an Italian. On the American side, the Italian air attaché provided translations of Douhet's writings to the Air Corps Tactical School in the mid-1920s; there is, however, no evidence that anyone *ever* took these translations out of the library.

implied that modern industrialized societies rested on fragile frameworks which could not sustain punishment. Both theories posited that the enemy could not interpose an effective air defense between the bomber and its target. Consequently, in their view air forces should build as many bombers as possible and as "few fighters [...] as popular opinion [...] will permit."[5] Nor did they perceive any potential difficulty in finding targets at night or in bad weather.

On the macro level, air power theorists assumed that history had little to teach air forces. In other words, technology had made obsolete the lessons of the past. The British air staff made this point explicitly in 1924. It argued that air forces:

> Can either bomb military objectives in populated areas from the beginning of the war, with the objective of obtaining a decision by moral[e] effect which such attacks will produce, and by the serious dislocation of the normal life of the country; or, alternatively, they can be used in the first instance to attack enemy aerodromes with a view to gaining some measure of air superiority and, when this has been gained, can be changed over to the direct attack on the nation. The latter alternative is the method which the lessons of military history seem to recommend, but the air staff are convinced that the former is the correct one.[6]

Such attitudes proved to be misplaced and disastrous in the long run. In fact, the lessons of the air war in the 1914–1918 fighting would prove relevant, if largely ignored by everyone besides the Germans, in the conduct of the air war that began in 1939.[7]

On the tactical level, there were other assumptions on which these theories rested: (1) that the bomber could find its targets easily; (2) that the bomber could drop its weapons with accuracy even in the face of heavy anti-aircraft fire and air opposition; (3) that bombing could do sustained and permanent damage; and (4) that enemy fighter forces could not intercept bombers with any degree of reliability. The problem with these theories was the fact that their advocates failed to see that the relationship between their assumptions rested on probability. The interaction between probability and chance, a dominant factor in war, ensured that

---

[5] Public Record Office (PRO), London AIR 20/40, Air Staff Memorandum No. 11A, March 1924.
[6] Ibid.
[7] Very simply, the main lessons of the aerial combat during the First World War were 1) that air superiority was an absolute necessity for the successful execution of any mission, including strategic bombing; and 2) that finding and then hitting targets accurately was an exceedingly difficult task.

there would be a considerable degradation in the outcome of the theories. Among other factors the airmen should have confronted in peacetime, but did not, were questions such as: What were the difficulties involved in finding enemy targets? What would the impact of weather be? Could an enemy air force mount an effective air defense of its nation? What would be the impact on the morale of the crews of a sustained campaign with heavy losses? Would air forces be able to knock out targets with one attack or would sustained attacks be necessary? Would the enemy be able to disperse his production facilities? There were few clear answers to these kinds of questions in 1939; in fairness to the airmen, only the experience of war could validate or invalidate prewar doctrines.

But in terms of learning from the past, one point does need to be made. Throughout the twentieth century, military organizations have taken preconceived notions of what they believe combat will be like into the next war. Despite the fact that the war they embark on is almost inevitably different from that preconceived picture, they tend to maintain their paradigms and attempt to force reality to conform to their preconceived notions.[8] In both the case of the RAF and the U.S. Army Air Forces (USAAF), most of the leading airmen involved in conducting the CBO allowed their prewar paradigms fundamentally to distort their conduct of operations. They would not, however, pay the price for their unwillingness to adapt to reality. Instead, it would be the young airmen who suffered.

The Campaign

The first lesson that RAF Bomber Command learned on the outbreak of war came in its daylight attack on the German fleet in Heligoland Bight in December 1939. The slaughter of the Wellington bombers by German day fighters was a salutary lesson that the equally costly raid on the M.A.N. works in Augsburg by Lancasters in 1942 confirmed, namely, that daylight bombing, unprotected by fighters, would in most cases result in prohibitive casualties. The British then had to turn to night attacks on Germany with the beginning of active operations on 10 May 1940. For the next ten months, Bomber Command launched its aircraft

---

[8] Two recent books have underlined this phenomenon: see Timothy Travers, *The Killing Ground* (London, 1988), and Andrew Krepinevich, *The Army and Vietnam* (Baltimore, 1988). For a look at a military organization that reacted in a different fashion, see Williamson Murray, "German Response to Victory in Poland: A Case Study in Professionalism," *Armed Forces and Society*, Winter, 1981.

against specific targets in the German petroleum and transportation systems. The hope was that "the accuracy of night bombing [would] differ little from daylight bombing."[9] The Butt report of August 1941 ended such optimism: it underlined that Bomber Command was having difficulty in hitting even cities. The shift to an "area bombing" strategy soon followed; but even then British bombers had difficulty finding targets as large as urban centers.[10]

By winter 1941–1942, Bomber Command's campaign was in serious trouble; it was rescued by Air Marshal Sir Arthur Harris, "Bomber" Harris to his crews and the British population. Harris provided ruthless drive, enthusiasm, and motivational abilities to his task as commander-in-chief of Bomber Command. He was also an intelligent officer who could on occasion show flexibility. Nevertheless, his driving belief was that "area" bombing was the only targeting option open to his command.

In fact, in 1942 he was right – area bombing was the only targeting option open to the British. Harris, moreover, understood that even then area bombing imposed severe limitations on a command still struggling to find cities. Consequently, he selected Rostock, Lübeck, and Cologne more for their ease of location and their vulnerabilities than for their value to the German war effort.[11] By 1943 Bomber Command's capabilities had improved enormously with heavier bombers and increasingly sophisticated technological capabilities. In the spring came the devastation of the Ruhr; in summer Hamburg's catastrophic destruction. German morale bent but did not break. Not only did civilians prove surprisingly resolute, but modern societies, particularly in a totalitarian state, possessed immense capacity to stiffen those who showed weakness.

By now the Americans also had embarked on air operations. Initial attacks on French targets in 1942 had, by 1943, expanded into raids deep onto the Continent against crucial industrial targets, the destruction of which American planners believed would wreck the industrial fabric of the German economy. American attacks singled out ball bearings as

---

[9] Sir Charles Webster and Noble Frankland, *The Strategic Air Offensive Against Germany*, vol. 1, *Preparation* (London, 1961), p. 216.
[10] On 1 October 1941, with Karlsruhe and Stuttgart as targets, British bombers "were reported over Aachen, Eupen, Malmedy, Coblenz, Neuwied, Kreuznach, Frankfurt am Main, Wiesbaden, Limburg, Darmstadt, Mainz, Worms, Trier, Offenburg, Saarfels, Nuremberg, Erlangen, Bamberg, Bayreuth, Coburg, Pegnitz, Aschaffenburg, Schweinfurt, Wurzburg, Regensburg, Welder and Chemnitz." Ibid., p. 185.
[11] Harris accurately described Lubeck as "built more like a firelighter than a human habitation." Ibid., pp. 391–394.

particularly vulnerable. Some senior officers on the British Air Staff urged that Bomber Command follow up American strikes with night attacks on such targets. Harris would have none of it: his force would attack area targets and only area targets. Consequently, on 17 August 1943, after the American daylight raid on Schweinfurt, Bomber Command struck the research installation of Peenemünde at the other end of Germany. The CBO was supposed to be a combined effort of RAF and USAAF strategic bombers against the Third Reich. Harris, however, had no interest in striking "panacea" targets and so refused to help. The Americans, for their part, were no more willing to throw themselves into Harris's night crusade to destroy Berlin over winter 1943–1944. Thus, the CBO remained divided by two very different approaches to attacking the Third Reich. Nevertheless, the pounding by both day and night further stretched the German air defense system.[12]

Beginning in November 1943 Bomber Command went after Berlin.[13] While it did manage to "wreck" much of the Nazi capital, the Third Reich did not collapse. German night fighters, poorly supported by their leadership, nearly broke Harris's force. On the night of 30–31 March 1944, the British lost 108 bombers, a raid symptomatic of the fact that German night defenses were imposing an unsupportable level of attrition on the night bombing offensive.[14] That desperate fact explains why Harris, who had thus far (and would again) resisted every effort to alter Bomber Command's priorities, placed his command at the disposal of the cross-channel invasion in spring 1944 with only mild opposition. He had no other choice, for the continuation of the area bombing campaign would have destroyed his command.[15]

Yet, Harris opposed the bombing of marshalling yards and precision targets in the French transportation system with the argument that Bomber Command's CEP (circular area of probability) was so great that the resulting collateral damage would kill and maim tens of thousands of Frenchmen.[16] He was wrong. By then, Bomber Command had developed

---

[12] For the pressures on the Luftwaffe, see Williamson Murray, *Strategy for Defeat, The Luftwaffe 1933–1945* (Montgomery, AL, 1983), chap. 6.
[13] For the Battle of Berlin, see Martin Middlebrook, *The Berlin Raids, R.A.F. Bomber Command, Winter 1943–1944* (London, 1988).
[14] The most thorough examination of the disastrous raid on Nuremberg is Martin Middlebrook, *The Nuremberg Raid, 30–31 March 1944* (New York, 1974).
[15] Admittedly, a refusal to support Operation Overlord might have been the single issue that would have forced Churchill to replace his obstreperous commander.
[16] For a fascinating discussion of the arguments over the CEP of British raids on French transportation targets, see Solly Zuckerman, *From Apes to Warlords* (London, 1978), pp. 216–258.

blind-bombing capabilities that would enable it to execute its strikes with almost surgical precision. No. 617 Squadron had carried out the famous raid on dams in May 1943, taking out the Mohne dam in the Ruhr Basin and the Eder dam in the Weser Basin with specially developed bombs. Its techniques – low-level marking, pathfinders, among others – gave Bomber Command, within limited range, a better capacity to execute precision raids than Eighth Air Force possessed. The resulting destruction of the French railroad network in spring 1944 and Bomber Command's strikes that helped to isolate the Normandy battlefield during Operation Overlord were among the most important contributions that Bomber Command rendered in World War II.

In September 1944, there were three specific areas on which Allied strategic bombing concentrated: the oil campaign, the transportation plan to shut down the infrastructure of the German economy, and Harris's area bombing effort. The Allied ground drive to the German frontier brought with it two important advantages.

- First, it impaired the German air defense system by destroying the long-range warning network on the Atlantic coast.
- Second, it allowed Bomber Command to move navigational aids forward to the German frontier. It could now bomb accurately deep into Germany with the same accuracy that it had pounded the French railroad network earlier in spring 1944.

Harris, however, largely ignored the changes involved in the improved capabilities and resolutely continued his emphasis on area bombing. Bomber Command contributed only as much to the oil and transportation plans as Harris thought he could get away with. In December 1944 he directly told the chief of air staff that Bomber Command would contribute to the oil plan (a "panacea" target in Harris's definition) only as much as he, Harris, felt he could spare from area bombing.[17] It is, of course, impossible to prove that if Bomber Command had concentrated on oil and transportation, it could have shortened the war. But those two target systems paid enormous dividends in 1944, and Harris's force had the capacity to hit its targets with impressive accuracy.

The American effort evolved over a shorter period and generally displayed more consistency. But there were distinct periods through which American plans evolved in reaction to the realities of the air war. The Americans had a substantial period of peacetime during which they could

[17] Webster and Frankland, *The Strategic Air Offensive Against Germany*, vol. 3, pp. 74–96.

have observed and learned from the combat experience of others. However, there is not much evidence to suggest that this occurred. Rather, their impressions of the Battle of Britain were that the reasons for the defeat of the *Luftwaffe's* bomber formations had been (1) bad formation flying, (2) inadequate defensive armament on German bombers, and (3) inadequate training of aircrew.[18] In no sense did American airmen recognize how dangerous a threat the *Luftwaffe's* fighter force would represent. U.S. employment plans for the European theater, drawn up in August 1941, argued that "by employing large numbers of aircraft with high speed, good defensive power, and high altitude," American bombers could penetrate deep into the heart of Germany in daylight without suffering unbearable losses.[19]

The period of buildup in summer 1942 did not allow sufficiently large forces for deep penetration raids; then, the landings in North Africa siphoned off American bomber strength to the Mediterranean. Thus, it was not until late spring 1943 that the force structure reached a point sufficient in American doctrine to risk deep penetration raids. American airmen embarked on their strategic bombing campaign against Germany with considerable optimism. Lieutenant General Ira Eaker, the first commander of Eighth Air Force, wrote Lieutenant General Carl A. "Tooey" Spaatz in October 1942 that his senior officers were absolutely convinced that 300 bombers [could] attack any target in Germany with less than 4 percent losses.[20]

The initial target sets in 1943 showed the influence of prewar doctrine as well as current realities. The CBO list of targeting priorities was as follows:

1. Intermediate objectives; German fighter strength.
2. Primary objectives: German submarine yards and bases; the remainder of the German aircraft industry; ball bearings; oil (contingent upon attacks against Ploesti [Rumania] (from Mediterranean).
3. Secondary objectives: synthetic rubber and tires; military motor transport vehicles.[21]

---

[18] Williamson Murray, *Luftwaffe* (Baltimore, MD, 1985), p. 60.
[19] Wesley E. Craven and James E. Cate, *The Army Air Forces in World War II*, vol. 1 (Chicago, 1948), p. 149, vol. 2 (Chicago, 1949), vol. 3 (Chicago, 1951).
[20] Bernard M. Boylan, "The Development of the American Long-Range Fighter," University of Missouri Dissertation, 1955, p. 68.
[21] Craven and Cate, *The Army Air Forces in World War II*, vol. 2, p. 367.

The *Luftwaffe*'s position on the list represented a recognition of the enemy fighter threat, while submarines were an immediate and serious danger to the base of air operations. But the emphasis on ball bearings, oil, and synthetic rubber represented a search for the weak link in the Reich's economic system. The August 1943 attack on Schweinfurt represented the culmination of prewar American air power theories. Nevertheless, it also represented the weaknesses of such doctrinal thinking. Half of the raiding force on 17 August struck the Messerschmitt factory at Regensburg; the other half attacked the ball bearing factory at Schweinfurt. The attacks achieved some significant success.[22] American airmen were mostly satisfied with the results; however, heavy losses on the raid (60 bombers) discouraged an immediate re-attack. Not until October did Eighth Air Force's B-17s return. Again, they heavily damaged the target, but German dispersal efforts were well under way; and again the Germans imposed a heavy loss rate on attacking formations (another 60 bombers).

Not until February 1944 did Eighth Air Force strike Schweinfurt again, this time with massive help from Bomber Command. After the war Albert Speer, Hitler's minister for armaments and war production, suggested to Allied interrogators that a concentrated offensive on the ball bearings industry would have resulted in the following effects:

> Armaments production would have been crucially weakened after two months, and after four months would have been brought completely to a standstill. This, to be sure, would have meant:
>
> One: All our ball bearing factories (in Schweinfurt, Steyr, Erkner, Cannstatt, and in France and Italy) had been attacked simultaneously.
>
> Two: These attacks had been repeated three or four times, every two weeks, no matter what the pictures of the target areas showed.
>
> Three: Any attempt at rebuilding these factories had been thwarted by further attacks, spaced at two month intervals.[23]

However, the problem was twofold: Bomber Command refused to cooperate with the Americans, while the punishing losses suffered by Eighth Air Force in the Schweinfurt attack made it impossible to repeat attacks on the target system except after a considerable interval of time. And that interval allowed the Germans to repair the damage and disperse much of the production to other sites.

---

[22] For the most detailed analysis of the Schweinfurt attack, see Friedhelm Gölucke, *Schweinfurt und die strategische Luftkriegführung, 1943* (Paderborn, 1980).

[23] Albert Speer, *Inside the Third Reich* (New York, 1970), p. 285.

Losses inflicted by the *Luftwaffe* on American bombers in fall 1943 forced changes in American air plans. A renewed air offensive deep into Germany began in February 1944. General Henry "Hap" Arnold, commander of USAAF, set the priorities for the coming effort in his Christmas 1943 message: "Destroy the enemy air force wherever you find them, in the air, on the ground, and in the factories."[24] Over a four-month period, USAAF accomplished Arnold's goal. Heavy bombing attacks on production facilities brought German fighters up where American long-range escort fighters could destroy them. Ironically, German fighter production actually increased under the rain of bombs. But historians have largely exaggerated the latter. In fact, over 1944 the weight of German airframe production only increased by slightly more than 20 percent. The reality was that the Germans could only increase fighter production by ceasing production of most other kinds of aircraft.[25] Moreover, much of this production was achieved by double bookkeeping,[26] and what was produced was of generally shoddy workmanship.[27] In the end, it was the attrition of German fighter pilots that eventually broke the back of the day fighter force.[28] The *Luftwaffe* never recovered from the onslaught.

In April 1944 American strategic bombers came under General Dwight Eisenhower's command and saw their priorities shifted to attacks against the French transportation network. However, in May 1944 Spaatz persuaded Eisenhower that Eighth Air Force possessed the excess capacity to take on an additional target set: the German oil industry. On 12 May 1944, 935 B-17s and B-24s attacked synthetic oil plants at Zwickau, Merseburg-Leuna, Brux, Lützkendorf, Bohlen, Zeitz, and Chemnitz.[29] Throughout the remainder of the war, Eighth attacked the synthetic fuel industry on a sustained basis. Crucial to its effort was the fact that Ultra intelligence informed American airmen that these attacks were having a

---

[24] Robert E. Futrell, *Ideas, Concepts, Doctrine. A History of Basic Thinking in the United States Air Force, 1907–1964* (Montgomery, 1971), p. 139.
[25] I am indebted to Dr. Horst Boog of the Militärgeschichtliches Forschungsamt, Freiburg, Federal Republic of Germany, for this point.
[26] The Germans counted the repair of seriously damaged aircraft as new fighter production. In early 1944, this probably totaled as much as 15 percent of production. Moreover, included in German production figures by the U.S. Strategic Bombing Survey were those aircraft produced in Hungary and Rumania.
[27] The Swiss brought a number of Bf 109s in 1942 that they continued flying until the mid-1950s. In 1944 they bought another batch; those, however, were so badly constructed that the Swiss junked them shortly after the end of the war.
[28] See Murray, *Strategy for Defeat*, p. 240.
[29] Craven and Cate, *The Army Air Forces in World War II*, vol. 3, p. 176.

serious impact on German oil production, as well as suggesting the level of success that the Germans were achieving in repair efforts.[30]

One final element in air war planning deserves attention. The success of interdiction attacks on the French transportation network led Eisenhower's chief air expert and deputy, Air Marshal Sir Arthur Tedder, to push for a similar transportation offensive in fall and winter of 1944–1945 to bring the German economy to a halt. Tedder ran into considerable opposition from Harris and Spaatz, the latter now in command of the American strategic bomber force. Nevertheless, he was able to draw some aircraft from Eighth's oil offensive and Bomber Command's area offensive to support his plan, while virtually all the tactical air forces were at his disposal. These attacks on the German transportation system played a crucial role in the sudden collapse of German armed forces on the Western Front in March–April 1945.[31]

This discussion of the evolution of Allied targeting and planning at times reflects the harsh lessons that war and the enemy imposed on Allied air commanders. It is hard, however, to understand the general overconfidence that so many airmen held. Moreover, it is difficult to explain the lack of adaptability, especially when new technology and tactical conceptions provided the air offensive with new avenues. However, the reader must remember that currently we enjoy the benefit of hindsight, while those who conducted the Allied strategic bombing effort operated under the pressure of events, with incomplete and ambiguous information, and against a tenacious and ferocious opponent.

The Failure to Develop Long-Range Fighters

One of the more surprising aspects of the bombing offensive is the fact that equipment availability and increased technological capability exercised relatively little impact on operational choices. As discussed in the previous section, Bomber Command underwent a revolution between 1942 and 1945 in its capacity to hit targets accurately: in 1942 it could barely find

---

[30] The intelligence officer who handled Ultra messages for Eighth Air Force later claimed that intercepts, indicating that fuel shortages were general and not local, convinced, "all concerned that the air offensive had uncovered a weak spot in the German economy and led to exploitation of this weakness to the fullest extent." PRO 31/20/16, "The Handling of Ultra Information at Headquarters Eighth Air Force," Ansel E. M Talbert, Major U.S. Army Air Corps.

[31] See in particular Alfred C. Mierzejewski, *The Collapse of the German War Economy, 1944–1945, Allied Airpower and the German National Railway* (Chapel Hill, 1988).

cities; by 1945 it was able, within certain range limitations, to identify and hit targets with greater accuracy than American daylight bombers. However, as the British official historians admit, Bomber Command failed to use this capability to its fullest extent. Rather, Harris dug in his heels and fought to keep his command's emphasis on area bombing and away from "panacea" targets. The result led to Dresden, while the collapse of the German oil and transportation industries undoubtedly occurred later than might have been the case, had Bomber Command been willing to cooperate in that effort to a greater degree.

On the other hand, the lack of long-range escort fighters came close to shutting down daytime raids at the end of 1943 and nighttime raids in spring 1944. Only the appearance of the P-51 Mustang, largely by fortuitous chance, allowed the resumption of deep penetration raids into Germany in February 1944 and eventually caused the destruction of the *Luftwaffe*.[32] Generally, airmen had refused to believe that technology would allow the creation of a long-range escort fighter. In March 1940, Sir Hugh Dowding, commander-in-chief of Fighter Command, who had a nose for what was technologically possible, pressed the air staff for developmental work on such a fighter. He met the following response from the assistant chief of air staff:

> It must, generally speaking, be regarded as axiomatic that the long-range fighter must be inferior in performance to the short-range fighter [...] The question had been considered many times and the discussion had always tended to go in circles [...] The conclusion had been reached that the escort fighter was really a myth. A fighter performing escort functions would, in reality, have to be a high performance and heavily armed bomber.[33]

In 1941 the chief of air staff, responding to an inquiry from Churchill, told the Prime Minister that long-range escort fighters could never hold their own against short-range fighters. There was, of course, no technological reason for such a view.[34] Churchill's response was that such a view closed "many doors."[35]

---

[32] For the best description of the appearance of the P-51 Mustang and its technological development, see Boylan, "The Development of the American Long-Range Escort Fighter."
[33] PRO AIR 16/1024, Minutes of the 20th Meeting of the Air Fighting Committee, held at Air Ministry, Whitehall, 12.3.40.
[34] In fact, the American and Japanese naval air forces were engaged in a furious race to develop long-range fighters to extend the range of their carrier aircraft at this time.
[35] Webster and Frankland, *The Strange Air Offensive Against Germany*, vol. 1, p. 177.

The Effects

Conventional wisdom suggests that only the oil campaign had a decisive impact on Germany's capacity to wage war. Oil was, indeed, the most vulnerable target; attacks on oil in the last half of 1944 significantly degraded the German ability to wage war. Yet, such arguments simplify a complex problem and beg a number of important issues. Moreover, the fashion in which target subsets were attacked, the persistence with which the CBO followed up attacks, and the understanding as to what was required to damage targets are all issues which need addressing. And one should not ignore the fact that the unintended effects of strategic bombing could be as important as the intended effects.

We might begin with the area bombing offensive – one that conventional wisdom argues did not achieve its aims and may have even increased the German willingness to fight to the bitter end. The actual picture, however, is different, especially if one takes into account the unintended effects that area bombing produced within the German leadership. First of all, evidence suggests a twofold response from the German population. On one hand, the impact of area bombing damaged German morale, particularly in the cities. By 1943 area bombing had caused a dramatic fall in popular morale.[36] Knowledge of the firestorm that swept through Hamburg on 27–28 July 1943 spread throughout Germany. In south Germany, attacks on Nuremberg, Munich, and Augsburg made the population restive, angry, and bitter. How much this translated into direct impact on the war is, of course, another question.

However, another aspect of popular reaction to the bombing is also noteworthy. At the same time that the Germans were gloomy over the bombing, they were extraordinarily angry at their tormentors and demanded retaliation against Britain. Reports by the secret police on the popular mood explain the continued demand of the Nazi leadership for retaliation weapons (V-1s and V-2s), its willingness to throw away the *Luftwaffe's* bomber fleet in winter 1944 in pointless attacks on the British Isles, and its refusal to provide sufficient support to the fighter forces until defeat in the air was a fact. Moreover, distortions in production as a result of V-1 and V-2 programs were enormous. The U.S. Strategic Bombing Survey estimated that in the last year of the war, the

---

[36] This comment is based on a very interesting section of a work on the Hitler myth in Germany, which examines the SD (Sicherheitsdienst, the Security Service in charge of foreign and domestic intelligence and espionage) reports on the morale of the population. See Ian Kershaw, *Volksmeinung und Propaganda im Dritten Reich*, (Stuttgart, 1980), pp. 176–186.

industrial effort expended for these weapons alone equated to production of 24,000 fighter aircraft.[37] The Germans could have found far more productive uses for that effort.

The American Strategic Bombing campaign suggests a number of crucial target systems, some which U.S. bombers attacked, some of which it ignored. Attacks on submarine pens and dockyards were the least effective targets. That fact was understood by airmen at the time; however, the threat posed by German U-boats in the North Atlantic in 1942 and early 1943 was such that political pressures forced Allied airmen to attack those targets regardless of results. There is considerable irony in this fact because at the same time they were wasting sorties in bombing the *Kriegsmarine's* indestructible U-boat pens, they were refusing to provide Allied anti-submarine forces with the long-range bomber aircraft that could have closed the Mid-Atlantic gap and ended the Battle of the Atlantic earlier and at less cost.

The attacks against ball bearing factories in 1943 paid dividends but did not achieve the results hoped. German industry had far greater reserves of bearings than expected. Foreign sources, particularly the Swedes and the Swiss, stepped in and made up some of the losses in production. Finally, the Germans switched to other kinds of bearings, such as roller bearings, where they could. Thus, various expedients allowed the Germans to master temporary difficulties. Eighth Air Force's failure to return to Schweinfurt until October 1943 also helped. Undoubtedly, Bomber Command's intervention in August 1943 might have increased the impact of the initial attack, but Harris was riding high in summer 1943 and was not about to divert his forces to a "panacea" target, whatever the urgings of the air staff.

Attacks on the German fighter industry also began to achieve some success in 1943. But the Germans avoided a complete shutdown of the aircraft industry in early 1944 for a number of reasons.[38] A shift in production from bombers to fighters helped. The creation of a special "Fighter Staff" under the leadership of Field Marshal Erhard Milch and Speer's assistant, Karl-Otto Sauer, extended Speer's reforms to the aircraft industry.[39] And the pressure exerted by combat with American

---

[37] United States Strategic Bombing Survey (USSBS), "V-Weapons (Crossbow) Campaign," Military Analysis Division, Report No. 60 (Washington, DC, January 1947).

[38] For a discussion of the *Luftwaffe* production issues, see Murray, *Luftwaffe*, pp. 238–241.

[39] "...the field marshal's suggestions that Speer's assistant, Karl-Otto-Sauer, head the [fighter] staff, shrewdly insured that fighter production received maximum support from the Armaments Ministry," Williamson Murray, *The Luftwaffe, 1933–1945, Strategy for Defeat* (Washington, DC, Brassey's, 1996), p. 254.

long-range escort fighters placed intolerable pressures on German industry for replacement aircraft. In March 1944, General Adolf Galland, commander-in-chief of fighters, reported that he had only 250 fighters the day before to meet the American onslaught. He pleaded with the fighter staff for "fighters, fighters, nothing but fighters."[40]

Nevertheless, the attack on the aircraft industry was not a particularly profitable line, at least in a direct sense. Such attacks resulted in little collateral impact on the rest of the economy. The aircraft industry was producing an end product; it was probably more profitable to destroy the end product in the air, when one had the opportunity to kill or injure the pilot as well. One factor that worked against the 1944 attacks was the fact that the aircraft industry had been one of the major targets in 1943. Consequently, by 1944 the Germans had undertaken a number of measures, such as the dispersal of facilities, that mitigated the impact of attacks on the Reich's aircraft and engine production.

Coherent attacks on the oil industry did not begin until May 1944. Admittedly, Fifteenth Air Force's B-24s struck Ploesti (Rumania) in summer 1943, but they suffered such catastrophic losses that there were no follow-up raids. Because of excess capacity in the Rumanian refineries, the Germans avoided any serious disruption of the oil supply in 1943. Attacks on the synthetic fuel industry in Germany were another matter; from the first, the Germans understood that destruction of the synthetic petroleum industry might cost them the war. Why it took so long to attack oil facilities is impossible to answer. The most probable explanation lies in mirror imaging. Since the United States did not have serious problems with access to petroleum, American analysts assumed a similar situation existed in the German war economy. Thus, Allied estimates projected far higher reserves of petroleum than was the case. There was also the problem that the oil industry in the Reich consisted of a great number of targets. In 1943 Eighth Air Force did not possess sufficient aircraft for a substantial, coherent campaign against the German oil industry.

From the war's beginning, Germany's petroleum situation had rested on a tenuous basis. Between September 1939 and May 1940, petroleum reserves dropped by nearly 50 percent.[41] Only the conquest of Western Europe and Soviet oil deliveries carried the Germans through the next

---

[40] Bundesarchiv-Militärarchiv, Freiburg, (BA-MA), RL3/1, "Stenogräphische Niederschrift der Besprechungen während des 'Unternehmens Hubertus,'" 11.3.44, p. 21.
[41] Williamson Murray, *The Change in the European Balance of Power, 1938–1939: The Path to Ruin* (Princeton, 1984), pp. 326–330.

year. By 1943 the German production and imports had reached their high point for the war. Over the winter of 1943-44, the Germans were able for the first time in the war to build up a small reserve of aviation gas (119,738 tons). Its existence provided a cushion for meeting the fuel crisis in early summer 1944.[42]

On 12 May 1944, General Spaatz launched Eighth Air Force in its offensive against the synthetic fuel industry. The initial results, while encouraging, were not decisive. The Leuna oil plant at Merseburg, Germany, for example, lost only 18 percent of its preattack capacity. Speer, however, was worried over the implications and warned Hitler: "The enemy has struck us at one of our weakest points. If they persist at it this time, we will soon no longer have any fuel production worth mentioning. Our one hope is that the other side has an air force general staff as scatterbrained as ours!"[43]

Nevertheless, the attention of American air commanders remained firmly on oil, helped because Ultra messages underlined how desperately the Germans were reacting to these strikes. Within days of the May 12th air attacks on Leuna, German flak units were moving throughout the Reich to protect synthetic oil plants.[44] On 21 May, another Ultra decrypt from an unspecified source ordered that "Consumption of mineral oil in every form [...] be substantially reduced [...] In view of effects of Allied action in Rumania [air attacks by Fifteenth Air Force] and on German hydrogention plants; extensive failures in mineral oil production and a considerable reduction in the June allocations of fuel oil, etc., were to be expected."[45] One intelligence officer who handled Ultra at Eighth Air Force later claimed that these intercepts, indicating that petroleum shortages were general and not local, played a crucial role in convincing "all concerned that the air offensive had uncovered a weak spot in the German economy and led to exploitation of this weakness to the fullest extent."[46]

On 28 and 29 May, Eighth Air Force again pounded the synthetic oil factories, while Fifteenth attacked petroleum facilities in Austria. Again the results were apparent through Ultra decrypts:

> Following according to OKL [*Oberkommando der Luftwaffe*, Luftwaffe High Command] on Fifth. As a result of renewed interference with production of aircraft fuel by Allied action, most essential requirements for training

[42] Murray, *Luftwaffe*, p. 257.
[43] Speer, *Inside the Third Reich*, pp. 346-347.
[44] PRO DEFE 3/156, KV 4021, 16.5.44, 05582.
[45] PRO DEFE 3/159, KV 4762, 21.5.44, 20542.
[46] PRO 31/20/26, "The Handling of Ultra Information at Headquarters Eighth Air Force," Ansel E. M. Talbert, Major U.S. Army Air Forces.

TABLE 10.1. *German Fuel Production*

Dates	Percent of Fuel Capacity Produced	Percent of Aviation Fuel Capacity Produced
1944		
August	46	65
September	48	30
October	43	37
November	60	65
December	59	56
1945		
January	51	33
February	40	5

Source: Speer Papers, Vol. 7, Imperial War Museum, FD 2690/45.

and carrying out production plans can scarcely be covered by quantities of aircraft fuel available. Baker four allocation only possible to air officer for bombers, fighters and ground attack [...] No other quota holders can be considered in June. To assume defense of Reich and to prevent gradual collapse of readiness for defense of German Air Force in east, it has been necessary to break into OKW [*Oberkommando der Wehrmacht*] reserves.[47]

May's attacks were a prelude to even more devastating raids in succeeding months. By mid-June, American raids had knocked out 90 percent of aviation fuel production, reducing it to less than 650 tons per day. By mid-July, the Germans had repaired their facilities sufficiently to quadruple production. Alerted by Ultra on repair efforts, more raids, now with Bomber Command support, lowered production to 120 tons per day. By the end of July, Allied air attacks had destroyed 98 percent of the capacity to produce aviation fuel.[48]

While the situation with production of other derivatives was not so desperate, it hardly allowed for optimism. In July, Leuna produced only 70 percent of normal production, while other major centers dropped to between 43 percent and 58 percent of estimated capacity. Continued attacks throughout the summer and fall kept a firm lid on German production (see Table 10.1). These figures underline the enormous impact that the oil campaign had on German fuel production. All the same, we should avoid an overly sanguine belief that this campaign had a decisive

---

[47] PRO DEFE 3/166, KV 6673, 6.6.44, 23562.
[48] Speer, *Inside the Third Reich*, p. 350; and Speer's memorandum to Hitler on the desperate situation, 29.7.44, Imperial War Museum, (IWM), Speer Collection, FD 2690/45 GS, vol. 3.

impact on the course of operations. In the air war, that was probably not the case. By May 1944 the Allies had won general air superiority over Europe, and it is unlikely that continued availability of aviation fuel would have changed that situation, especially given the overwhelming aircraft production advantage enjoyed by the Allies.[49]

Moreover, even in the face of overwhelming air superiority and severe fuel shortages, German ground forces held Anglo–American armies to a virtual stalemate from June 1944 to February 1945 with the exception of August 1944. Consequently, the oil offensive, while contributing considerably to final victory, was not by itself decisive. It impaired but did not prevent the *Wehrmacht* from conducting a sustained and ferocious defense.

The third great impact of the Allied air offensive against the Reich was the effort to destroy the transportation networks of western and central Germany. As articulated by Sir Arthur Tedder, Eisenhower's chief deputy, this plan aimed at two basic effects: first, to limit the logistical support on which the German armies depended; and second, to halt German production by stopping the movement and distribution of goods, raw materials, and fuel within the industrial infrastructure. Generally, such efforts to break the transportation network supporting major military forces have failed. Operation Strangle in the Italian theater in 1944, Operation Strangle against North Korea in 1952, and Rolling Thunder's interdiction efforts to shut down traffic on the Ho Chi Minh trail from 1964 to 1972 – all are notable examples of air power's failure to halt logistical movement. Air operations against the German industrial transportation network, however, suggest that in certain circumstances, this form of targeting represents a profitable avenue of approach.

Tedder was drawn to the transportation plan because of the success of Allied tactical and strategic air forces in France in spring 1944. The result of that effort had seen the virtual cessation of traffic in northern and western France, making German logistical problems in the face of the looming Allied invasion of the Continent immeasurably more difficult.[50] In early June 1944 a *Luftwaffe* intelligence appreciation had suggested:

> In Zone 1 [France and Belgium], the systematic destruction that has been carried out since March of all important junctions of the entire

[49] See Murray, *Luftwaffe*, chap. 7.
[50] PRO AIR 37/12611, Bombing Analysis Unit, 4.11.44, B. A. U. Report No. 8, "Changes in the Volume of the French Traffic, Expressed in Kilometer Tons, as a Result of Air Attacks, January to July 1944."

network – not only of the main lines – has most seriously crippled the whole transportation system (railway installations, including rolling stock)... The rail network is to be completely wrecked. Local and through traffic is to be made impossible, and all efforts to restore the services are to be prevented. The aim has been so successfully achieved – locally at any rate – that the *Reichsbahn* authorities are seriously considering whether it is not useless to attempt further repair work.[51]

On the basis of the experience gained in the spring 1944 campaign, Tedder and his chief scientific adviser, Solly Zuckerman, designed a tactical and strategic rationale and plan to replicate this success. Tedder's close relationship with Eisenhower, along with his astute political sensibilities, allowed him to move transportation up to the number two priority after oil for Allied air attacks.[52]

Beginning in September 1944, the weight of Allied air attacks fell increasingly on the German transportation system because attacks on oil targets could take place only in conditions of good visibility – a condition that was less and less available as winter approached. Air planning divided Germany into nine specific transportation districts, five of which lay to the west of Kassel along the western frontier. In central and eastern Germany, the plan identified transportation districts in Silesia, around Vienna, to the west of Berlin, and in Bavaria.[53] The aim was to break the transportation system among these axes so that raw materials, finished goods, and parts could not move. The hoped for result would be a collapse of the German economy. Crucial to the offensive would be the blockage of not only the *Reichsbahn* (the German railroad system) but also of the canal and waterway systems, on which much of the coal and ore moved.

The Allied transportation offensive had an almost immediate impact on German transport. As the U.S. Strategic Bombing Survey makes clear, loading of railroad cars plummeted from mid-August 1944. For the week ending 19 August 1944, the *Reichsbahn* loaded and dispatched 899,091 cars; by the week of 28 October that figure had fallen to 703,580 cars; and by 23 December the number had fallen to 547,309 despite heavy demands from the Ardennes offensive. By December 1944, marshaling capacity of German rail yards had declined to 40 percent of normal;

---

[51] Air Historical Branch (Great Britain), "Air Attacks Against German Rail Systems During 1944," Luftwaffe Operations Staff/Intelligence, No. 2512/44, "Air Operations Against the German Rail Transport System During March, April and May 1944," 3.6.44.
[52] Mierzejewski, *The Collapse of the German War Economy*, pp. 101–102.
[53] Webster and Frankland, *The Strategic Air Offensive Against Germany*, vol. 3, pp. 245–247 and Map 9.

by February 1945 it had reached 20 percent. The Ardennes offensive indicates that the air offensive against the transportation system was not yet able to prevent the *Wehrmacht* from executing military operations.[54] But its impact was far larger. By early January the attacks "had reduced the available capacity for economic traffic in Germany to a point which it could not hope to sustain, over any period of time, a high level of military production."[55] The loss of transportation gradually strangled the economy by disorganizing the flow of those elements crucial to further production of weapons and ammunition. Under such conditions neither planning nor actual production could take place in an orderly fashion.

The collapse of coal transportation suggests the extent of this situation. In January 1944, the Essen division of the *Reichsbahn* had loaded an average of 21,400 cars daily. By September 1944, that total had dropped to 12,000, of which only 3,000 to 4,000 were long haul. By February 1945, Allied transportation attacks had cut the Ruhr off from the rest of Germany. The *Reichsbahn* often had to confiscate what little coal was loaded just to keep locomotives running. Underlining the impact of transportation attacks was the state of coal production and stocks in the Ruhr between August 1944 and February 1945. Despite the fact that coal production fell drastically from 10,417,000 tons in August to 4,778,000 tons in February, stocks in Ruhr collieries rose from 415,000 tons to 2,217,000 tons; the stocks of coke similarly rose from 630,000 tons to 3,069,0004.[56] The Ruhr was literally swimming in coal it could no longer transport even to the industries in its own region, much less the rest of Germany.

Nevertheless, in retrospect the Allies failed to utilize their full capabilities to shut down German transportation. There were a number of reasons. The commitment by Bomber Harris to area bombing meant that Bomber Command never threw its full weight behind attacking such a "panacea" target system. The Americans were largely committed to the oil plan. Moreover, Ultra information was not properly used to underline the success of transportation attacks. One message in late October 1944 was not passed along until February 1945. It stated: "On October, Reich Minister for Equipment and War Production reported that, on account of destruction of traffic installations and lack of power, from 30 to 50 percent of all works in west Germany were at a standstill."[57]

---

[54] USSBS, "The Effects of Strategic Bombing on German Transportation," Report No. 200, Washington, 20 November 1945, p. 1.
[55] Ibid., p. 3.
[56] Ibid., p. 3.
[57] Mierzejewski, *The Collapse of the German War Economy*, p. 167.

Evidence points to a general collapse of the German war economy beginning in mid-winter 1945. It was not a sudden and cataclysmic collapse; for that reason, it remained difficult to discern even for those who were conducting the campaign.[58] The German Ardennes offensive also misled not only those conducting the campaign but the historians who have subsequently judged the utility of strategic bombing. In July and August 1944, German armies on both the Eastern and Western Fronts had collapsed with losses of massive amounts of equipment. But with German production in summer 1944 remaining largely unimpeded, the *Wehrmacht* was able to reequip those who survived and the new men (mostly boys) culled to fight. There the Germans put up a successful level of resistance and even launched the offensive into the Ardennes in December 1944.

However, that was their last shot. Beginning in January 1945 in the East, followed within a month and a half in the West, German armies collapsed. Neither on the Rhine nor on the Oder were they able to reconstitute for a last stand on the ruins of the Reich. As a result, there was no last, massive *Götterdämmerung*. The cause lay in the fact that the transportation plan had successfully shut down the German war economy by mid-winter 1945, and the *Wehrmacht* simply no longer had the weapons or ammunition to continue the struggle. Even blind fanaticism could not maintain the struggle under such circumstances.

Contributions of the CBO

Virtually nothing happened as prewar airmen thought it would. That statement is not surprising given the fact that neither naval nor land combat has proven easier to predict in pre-war periods.[59] What made the shortfall between expectations and realities so noticeable was the fact that airmen regarded their weapons and their doctrine as a guarantee for victory – one that they could achieve without the terrible attrition that had marked World War I. The greatest surprise of the air war turned out to be the fact that the same conditions and rules that governed air war

---

[58] Part of the problem was the fact that even this late in the war, airmen were still conditioned by prewar air doctrine, which had assumed that the impact of strategic bombing would be quick and decisive.
[59] For the problems predicting naval and land war, and then in adapting preconceived notions to the realities, see Allan R. Millett and Williamson Murray, *Military Effectiveness*, vols. 2 and 3 (London, 1988).

also governed the more traditional forms of combat. As one historian of the CBO has noted:

> Thus we are left with one clear reminder of a painful truth: the laws of war applied as much to the strategic air offensive waged over Europe's skies through five-and-a-half bitter years as they did to the sailors and soldiers on the distant seas or in the mud and sand below. Occasionally, the airman may have felt himself living and fighting in a new dimension, just as the air force commander may have sometimes felt he enjoyed a freedom of maneuver denied to admirals and generals. But the airman died, and the air force commander was defeated and stalemated unless the laws were kept. When they were kept, success came; until they could be kept, hope was kept alive by courage alone.[60]

Enemy air forces could and did interpose themselves between bombers and their targets and inflict an unacceptable level of attrition on attacking forces. U.S. Army Air Force propagandists could claim that once bomber formations were dispatched, they never failed to attack their targets – but such statements missed the larger issue. While Eighth Air Force successfully bombed Schweinfurt in August and October 1943, it was equally clear that its bombers could not return for a substantial period of time because the *Luftwaffe*'s defensive fighters had so successfully devastated attacking formations.

The second major surprise of the air war had to do with the ability of the modern industrial state and its population to absorb huge punishment and still function in an effective fashion. It was not that bombing made workers more efficient, as some superficial critiques of the CBO suggest; rather, modern industrial states, whether totalitarian or democratic, are capable of mobilizing manpower and resources in almost endless quantities. And when popular morale faltered, states possessed the requisite stiffening power to keep things in line. Moreover, excess capacity in industrial infrastructure combined with human ingenuity to adapt and find alternatives to the damage inflicted by strategic bombing attacks.

There were few positive surprises. Perhaps one of some significance was the extraordinary adaptability of technology and the imagination of scientists when applied to the problems that air war posed.[61] But in many cases, especially early in the war, airmen were not receptive to the possibilities that technology and science offered. Nor were they particularly

---
[60] Anthony Verrier, *The Bomber Offensive* (London, 1968), p. 327.
[61] For two outstanding discussions of the contribution that imaginative use of science made to the Allied war effort, see R. V. Jones, *The Wizard War* (New York, 1978); and Zuckerman, *From Apes to Warlords*.

prepared in terms of their educational background to deal with these issues. One of the most important lessons raised by the conduct of the CBO was fundamental to military history: the extraordinary differences between peace (what Carl von Clausewitz termed "war on paper") and the actual conditions of combat. This basic factor makes it difficult for peacetime military organizations to think through the impact of factors such as friction, terror, death, and destruction on the conduct of their operations. Then, when the actual conditions of war turn out to be so new and difficult, the problems of adapting prove almost insurmountable.

In addition to this basic reality, airmen faced a number of other crucial problems. First of all, World War I did not provide much guidance. From our perspective, there was evidence in that conflict of the crucial necessity of gaining air superiority, the difficulties involved in finding and hitting targets accurately, the crucial role of attrition, and a number of other issues. But in fairness, none of these found resolution in World War I. The second great problem that airmen confronted lay in the technological revolution that occurred in aircraft design, capabilities, and performance in the interwar period. Added to that revolution came the development of radar and navigational devices that seemed to expand air power's capabilities geometrically. Consequently, adaptation to change and new capabilities absorbed the energies of air commanders, leaving them little time to think about the impact of those changes in war.

War itself was a harsh teacher. The interrelationship between assumptions proved to be exponential rather than arithmetic. Consequently, the possibilities offered by the applications of air power to attack and destroy discrete target sets as argued by prewar theory, proved considerably less in practice than expected. Compounding the problem was the fact that as with most human institutions, air forces found it difficult to adapt to rapidly changing environments as the air war proceeded. Exacerbating the problem was the fact that each side was adapting technologically, tactically, and operationally to what the other side was doing.

The wisdom in the academic community suggests that the CBO played a relatively unimportant role in winning World War II. This approach argues that the opportunity cost was excessive. The evidence, however, points in a different direction. It suggests that the CBO should rank directly after the Eastern Front in calculations of contributions to Allied victory in World War II. The problem in evaluating the CBO has to do with the excessive claims of airmen and air power theorists in prewar and wartime periods: their claims and expectations were not equaled by reality. While the U.S. Strategic Bombing Survey does not suggest that the bombing offensive was decisive in and of itself, it does provide considerable documentation on the impact that strategic bombing had on the German economy and war production. Moreover, there were a number of unintended effects that the bombing produced.

There is no doubt that area bombing exercised an increasingly severe impact on German morale as the war continued and that it did affect Germany's capacity to produce the elements of military power. In August 1943, Speer warned Hitler that if Bomber Command replicated Hamburg (the devastating raid of the night of 27–28 July) six more times, it would bring "Germany's armaments production to a halt."[62] The problem was that Bomber Command was not capable of replicating its success in succeeding months. It did create another firestorm in its raid on Kassel in October 1943, but by that time, German night fighters were imposing a rising rate of loss, while bad weather made it more difficult to achieve required levels of concentrated bombing.

The contribution of area bombing is equally difficult to measure in a quantitative sense. We can surmise that within areas devastated by Bomber Command, substantial damage was done to German production. How much German production might have increased had the area bombing campaign not occurred is impossible to estimate. What the evidence does suggest is that a German economy, unburdened by such attacks and drawing on the whole of Central and Western Europe, might have accomplished production totals close to those of the Soviet Union. Such success would have had direct and appreciable influence on the fighting, whether on land, sea, or air.

We can, however, estimate Bomber Command's impact more closely in the realm of indirect cause and effect. The British attack on morale led the Nazi government to make two crucial errors in responding to the threat, both of which had important impacts on the course of World War II. On one side, British night raids caused a substantial distortion in the production of artillery and ammunition. The German population drew confidence from the large numbers of anti-aircraft guns blasting away from their cities at the air "pirates" overhead. By summer 1943, no fewer than 89 flak batteries defended Berlin.[63] The overall growth in flak batteries in the anti-aircraft forces was phenomenal in the period from 1940 to 1944. From 791 batteries (88s, 105s, and 128s) in 1940, the number grew to 967 in 1941, 1,148 in 1942, and 2,132 in 1943; such

---

[62] Speer, *Inside the Third Reich*, p. 284.
[63] David Irving, *The Mare's Nest*, (Boston, 1968), p. 109.

forces represented a prodigious investment in resources and manpower.[64] All of these batteries expended ammunition in vast quantities without significant return on investment. The 88 mm flak 36 weapon required an average expenditure of about 16,000 shells to bring down one aircraft flying at high altitude even when bombers were attacking in concentrated streams.[65] The reader hardly needs to be reminded that the presence of approximately 20,000 or more anti-aircraft guns (all highly capable in the anti-tank role) would have had significant impact on ground fighting on the Eastern or Western Fronts in 1944. Moreover, the manning and support of the anti-aircraft air defense force by nearly half-a-million Germans represented an enormous drain on German manpower.

The second impact of area bombing came in the reaction of the Nazi leadership. Ironically, German leaders were the only ones to remain tied to a Douhetan[66] air strategy throughout the war. Their reaction was not to ward off Allied air attacks by defensive measures, or to attack Allied bomber bases. Rather, their reaction was to strike back with terror. Hitler had warned his military aides shortly after the first substantial raid on Hamburg that terror could only be broken with terror. Attacks on German airfields had made no impression on him, he commented, but the smashing of the Reich's cities had been another matter. It was the same thing with the enemy, he added. The German people demanded reprisals.[67] As a result, German production for the first four years of the war up to 1944 had emphasized bomber rather than fighter production.

Hitler's emphasis on retaliation rather than on air superiority resulted in the greatest German production error of World War II. In 1943 both the army and *Luftwaffe* were about to produce retaliation weapons: the army with its V-2, and the *Luftwaffe*, the V-1. The first represents a triumph of German engineering, but it was not a monument to good sense. As a weapon, it demanded extremely complex technology (both in production and combat phases), it was expensive, it used scarce raw materials, and its production overloaded the instrument and electrical components industries.

In summer 1943, German leaders faced the crucial choice of radically restructuring the aircraft industry to ensure day and night fighters at the

---

[64] Gölucke, *Schweinfurt*, p. 157.
[65] Ibid., p. 156.
[66] Refer fn. 3 in this chapter about Giulio Douhet and his influence in the interwar period.
[67] "Hitler zur Frage der Gegenmassnahmen zur Beantwortung der allierten Luftangriffe," 25.7.43, Albert E. Simpson Historical Research Center, (AFSHRC), Maxwell AFB, AL, K 113,312–2, V 3.

expense of bomber production and the development and production of the new V-weapons. The chief of *Luftwaffe* production and logistics, Field Marshal Erhard Milch, had urged Hitler as early as March 1943 to accept a production program of 5,000 fighters per month.[68] But the Nazi leadership, particularly Hitler, was unwilling to meet the strategic bombing threat with a military response. As Göring commented to his staff in October 1943, the German people did not care whether the *Luftwaffe* attacked British airfields. All they had wanted to hear when a hospital or children's home in Germany was destroyed was that the *Luftwaffe* had destroyed the same in England; then they were satisfied.[69] In conversation one month later with Fritz Sauckel, slave labor procurer for the Reich, Göring underlined that the *Luftwaffe* needed bombers as badly as fighters.

> Göring: *Ich kann mich nicht dauernd auf die Verteidigung legen, wir mussen auch zum Angriff kommen. Das ist das Entscheidende.*
>
> Sauckel: *Das einzige Argument, dass auf einen Volksgenossen Eindruck macht, ist das der Vergeltung.*[70]
>
> [Göring: I cannot stand on the defense, we must take the offense. That is the decisive point.
>
> Sauckel: The sole argument that would make an impression on our people is revenge [attacks].]

Hitler himself proclaimed in November 1943 that "our hour of revenge is nigh! [...] Even if for the present we cannot reach America, thank God at least one country is close enough to tackle."[71] Even Speer, normally a shrewd calculator of military and production realities, was an enthusiastic supporter of the V-2 program to pay the British back.

The consequence of this was the emphasis on the V-1 and V-2 weapon programs (the V stands for *Vergeltungswaffen*, retaliation) that distorted air defense programs in the last years of the war. Not only did it prevent development of an effective anti-aircraft rocket, it drained off significant resources from fighter production. The U.S. Strategic Bombing Survey estimated that the German fighter industrial effort and resources

---

[68] David Irving, *The Rise and Fall of the Luftwaffe, The Life of Field Marshal Erhard Milch* (Boston, 1973), p. 202.
[69] "Heimatverteidigungsprogramm 1943, Besprechung beim Reichsmarshcal am 7.10.43, Obersalzberg, Fortsetzung," AFSHRC: K 113.312-2, V 3.
[70] BA-MA, RL 3/61, "Stenographische Niederschrift der Besprechung beim Reichsmarshal am 28.10.43, in Karinhall," p. 88.
[71] Irving, *The Mare's Nest*, pp. 177, 181.

expended for these weapons in the last year and a half of the war equaled the production of 24,000 fighter aircraft.[72] Considering that German aircraft production in 1944 only reached 36,000 aircraft (barely 8,000 more than Japanese production), one can see the impact of revenge weapons on the *Luftwaffe's* air defense capabilities.[73] Here the Nazi regime was reacting to popular pressures and declining morale under the furious impact of area bombing. The regime's resulting decisions responded to political factors rather than to strategic and military realities. Thus, in terms of the V programs alone, area bombing achieved an enormous distortion in the German industrial effort of real consequence to the war's outcome.

The opportunity cost of the American effort is easier to assess because it had specific target sets against which one can measure its success. In 1943 the two crucial target sets were ball bearing and aircraft production facilities. The attacks against the first failed for a number of reasons. Eighth Air Force was never in a position to deliver a sustained and consistent effort against the industry. Consequently, the Germans rebuilt the facilities at Schweinfurt, damaged in the August 1943 attack, dispersed production, and utilized alternatives such as roller bearings. Moreover, German industry itself, facing wartime shortages, possessed a large backlog of ball bearings that helped overcome shortages.

Attacks on German aircraft production in 1943 were more successful. These raids did not defeat the *Luftwaffe*, but they created the preconditions necessary for gaining air superiority in 1944. To begin with, they caused a significant drop off in fighter production in the last half of 1943. Table 10.2 underlines this fact clearly. These American raids on the German aircraft industry, while costly to the attackers, also imposed a high rate of attrition on the defender.[74] But perhaps the most important impact of the American daylight raids on German targets beginning in May 1943 was the fact that by fall of that year they had managed to pull back nearly all the *Luftwaffe*'s daylight fighter force from the theaters of war in order to defend the skies over the Reich. From late summer 1943 German ground forces found themselves with little or no air support, while enemy air forces ruled the skies over their heads.

The American air campaign in 1944 again had specific target sets, the attacks on which again had specific, measurable results. For the first

---

[72] USSBS, "V-Weapon (Crossbow) Campaign," Military Analysis Division, report no. 60, January 1947.
[73] Richard Overy, *The Air War, 1939–1945* (London, 1980), p. 123.
[74] For a more complete discussion of these issues, see Murray, *Luftwaffe*, chaps. 5 and 6.

TABLE 10.2. *Production of New and Reconditioned Fighter Aircraft June–December 1943*

Date	New Bf 109s	New Fw 190s	New and Reconditioned Fighters
June	663	109	1,134
July	704	169	1,263
August	515	159	1,135
September	525	159	1,072
October	556	127	1,181
November	472	114	985
December	350	313	687

Source: USSBS, The Effects of Strategic Bombing on the German War Economy (see fn. 46), Appendix Table 102, p. 277; and "Luftangriffe im Jahre 1943 auf Werke der deutschen Flugzeugindustrie," Albert E. Simpson Historical Research Center, Maxwell AFB, AL: K 113, 312-2, Vol. 3.

five months of 1944, the focus remained on the *Luftwaffe* and its industrial support. Then in May 1944 the focus shifted to attacks on oil, which remained the major target set for American bombers to the end of the war. In both efforts, American attacks achieved the desired effect, although in the first case as much through indirect impact as direct effects. American attacks on German aircraft production achieved notable success, the critics of strategic bombing notwithstanding. As pointed out earlier, increases in German production came at the expense of bomber production. The number of fighters produced in 1944 did increase 55.9 percent from the previous year, but the weight of aircraft produced rose only 23.9 percent, a reflection of the diversion of production from bombers to lighter fighters.[75] The fact that Milch and *Luftwaffe* planners were hoping to produce 80,000 aircraft in 1945 suggests the kind of target that German industry might have reached without the retarding effect of Allied strategic bombings.[76]

The indirect impact of American strategic bombing was no less impressive. The Germans clearly recognized that this offensive aimed to destroy the *Luftwaffe's* capacity to fight. Consequently, *Luftwaffe* fighters had to come up to protect their long-range future, and then American long-range escort fighters were able quite literally to break German air power's

---

[75] USSBS, *The Effects of Strategic Bombing on the German War Economy* (Washington, 1945), Appendix Tables 101 and 102.
[76] Overy, *The Air War, 1939–1945*, p. 123.

back in air battles that lasted from February to May of 1944.[77] That contribution gained the Allies air superiority over the European Continent with two crucial benefits: it allowed daylight bombing of Germany to continue unimpeded for the remainder of the war; and it made possible the Normandy landings with no interference from the *Luftwaffe*.

The oil attacks also had significant direct and indirect effects and placed enormous impediments in the way of German military operations. In the case of the air war, Allied attacks interfered with German air operations; even more importantly, they forced the *Luftwaffe* to reduce the number of flying hours it provided new fighter pilots, making them even less capable of flying and defending themselves in air-to-air combat. The impact on ground operations was also dramatic; without sufficient petroleum, German ground units could not maneuver in the same fashion as in earlier years. For example 1,800 tanks were present to defend Silesia in January 1945, but they were virtually immobilized for lack of fuel. Consequently, they were less able to defend this crucial industrial region than would have been the case the year before.[78]

But whatever impact the oil campaign enjoyed in limiting the maneuverability of the *Wehrmacht*, it did not prevent the Germans from putting up sustained resistance over the war's last years. Both on the Eastern and Western Fronts, over the fall and winter of 1944–1945, the Germans prevented the Allies from achieving their strategic objectives. Moreover, in December 1944 the German army was able to launch a major offensive in the Ardennes that, at least at the time, appeared to have the prospect of achieving significant gains.

Strategic bombing's greatest contribution came in the last months of the war. From 1944 three separate but powerful sledgehammer blows hit the German nation. We have already discussed the oil and area bombing campaigns, but the most crucial effort, in the opinion of this writer, came with Tedder's transportation offensive. That effort could not prevent the Germans from making a last stand on the frontier, one that lasted into the winter of 1944–1945. Nor could it prevent the Germans from assembling their re-equipped forces for the desperate Ardennes offensive in December 1944. But by late fall 1944, it was well on the way to shutting down the German economy. By December 1944, German industry was in a state of collapse with dramatic declines in production in all sectors. And even the weapons and munitions produced were not moving forward in sufficient

---

[77] See Murray, *Luftwaffe*, chaps. 6 and 7.
[78] Webster and Frankland, *The Strategic Air Offensive Against Germany*, vol. 3, p. 239.

numbers to the troops. Movement on the railways and waterways of the Reich ceased, and the armies, starved for munitions and weapons, collapsed. Thus, there was no great *Götterdämmerung* to prolong the war, complete the wreckage of a catastrophic war, and kill millions more. But the contribution of the Allies' transportation plan has largely remained buried in the massive tables and statistics of the Strategic Bombing Survey.

The Opportunity Costs

What then were the opportunity costs of this campaign? As the comments in the previous section suggest, strategic bombing played a crucial role in Nazi Germany's defeat. In fact, victory over Germany is inconceivable without the CBO, just as victory is inconceivable without the victory of Allied navies in the Battle of the Atlantic, or the contribution of the Red Army on the Eastern Front, or the Mediterranean theater and the great invasion of Western Europe in spring 1944. And herein lies much of the problem. By claiming so much for air power before the war (and after the war as well), airmen created false perceptions that documentary and historical evidence simply do not support. The strategic bombing offensives contributed to Allied victory because they supported and were supported by the efforts of Allied ground and naval forces.

Perhaps the best way to address the question of opportunity costs is to ask what alternatives existed to the Anglo–American nations in waging World War II. The answer is virtually nothing. A greater emphasis on ground forces would not have even made an earlier landing on the coast of France possible. And it is difficult to conceive of that landing without either complete air superiority – impossible to achieve without the CBO – or the transportation attacks of April and May 1944 that paralyzed the French transportation network and made the German buildup in Normandy so difficult. Moreover, the lack of strategic bombing against Germany in 1943 would have made much of the German anti-aircraft forces available for deployment on the Eastern Front. Would a quarter of a million men and 5,000 to 7,000 anti-tank guns of heavy caliber have made a significant difference in the great battles of summer 1943 in the east? We cannot say for sure, but the task of the Soviet armies would surely have been more difficult.

The cost of this offensive was high, indeed. Our historical memories are conditioned by the disastrous raids against Schweinfurt (60 B-17s lost on each) and Nuremberg (108 bombers lost). With hindsight we can argue that the CBO was often waged in an unimaginative fashion, that air forces failed to adapt to changing tactical and technological conditions, and that the possible contributions of air power were often minimized rather than maximized. But are those not the conditions under which all wars are fought? Certainly Bomber Command might have increased the effectiveness of the transportation and oil plans from September 1944 to the war's end, if it had abandoned Harris's fixation on area bombing.

What is certain is that the CBO was crucial in causing the final German collapse. An exact measurement is impossible in quantitative terms. We might delineate the issue by recording the response of an expert on Ultra when asked by a German historian as to why, in view of Enigma intelligence, the Allies had not won the war sooner. He replied: "We did!" The same response can be given for the contributions of the strategic bombing campaigns, and that alone justifies the opportunity costs.

Conclusion

A number of key issues are relevant. The first is that many of the assumptions with which prewar airmen entered the war proved wrong. It took an interminable time for air forces and airmen to adapt to the realities they confronted. We should not have the arrogance to believe that our assumptions are any less fallible or that we have thought through our problems in a superior fashion to those who went to war in 1939. In fact, if we are to learn anything useful from the past, we must recognize that our visions of future war may be as flawed.

The second issue is equally applicable. Pre-war theories of air power pictured modern society, either in terms of popular morale and attitudes or in terms of its complex industrial infrastructure, as being fragile and easily disrupted by air attacks. In every respect these theories were wrong. Civilian morale proved an elusive target. The result of being bombed out of one's house or seeing one's relatives or friends killed was, as often as not, anger and a desire to see the war through to the end rather than panic and collapse. Moreover, when morale did show signs of cracking, the modern state, whether democratic or totalitarian, proved capable of providing the necessary stiffening needed to bring things under control. The productive capacity of industry displayed immense flexibility and adaptability in the face of great hardships and difficulties. Not until winter 1944–1945 were Allied air forces in a position to break the industrial and productive links of the German economy, and then only by the most extraordinary effort. Admittedly, the scale of destructive power available to us is exponentially greater.

Another significant lesson has to do with the penchant for airmen to believe that the effective destruction of a target was achieved simply by attacking it. In other words, one application of bombs was sufficient to render a target destroyed. The attacks on Schweinfurt are a case in point. Neither the first nor the second was sufficient to bring production to a halt; after the second, General "Hap" Arnold proclaimed to the American press that "we have got Schweinfurt." Admittedly, the wreckage of 60 B-17s strewn along the entrance and exit routes hardly suggested that Eighth could return to the target, and Arnold may have aimed his remarks as much at reassuring the shattered aircrews as for publicity. But there is a pattern here; all too often the Anglo–American air forces failed to follow up on their attacks. British and American airmen seem to have assumed that one raid was sufficient to cross the target off their list; once crossed off the list one need not return.

This was not the case with the oil or transportation plans from May 1944 to the end of the war. But the focus of American airmen remained fixed on the oil plan by the crucial input of Ultra, input that a) indicated how badly the Germans were being hurt by oil attacks and b) how desperate as well as how successful the Germans were in efforts to repair smashed-up facilities. We need to make an additional point about targeting and the influence that this arcane art exercised on the minds of air commanders in the war. Too often they identified target lists with the actual achievement of strategic purpose.

Harris's November 1943 memorandum to Churchill justifying the coming Battle of Berlin began by listing 19 German cities, including Hamburg, Cologne, Essen, Dortmund, Düsseldorf, Hanover, Mannheim, Rostock, and Kassel, as virtually destroyed; 19 cities as seriously damaged; and a further nine as damaged. "From the above," he concluded, "you will see that the Ruhr is largely 'out' and that much progress has been made towards the elimination of the remaining essentials of German power." Harris's clear intimation was that Berlin was the last remaining target. "We can wreck Berlin from end to end if the USAAF will come in on it. It will cost us between 400–500 aircraft. It will cost Germany the war."[79]

We might end with the observation that of all the vulnerabilities of the German economy that in retrospect appear to have presented the greatest opportunity to the CBO, the electric network and production received virtually no attention (except accidental or collateral damage)

---

[79] PRO PREM 3/14/1, Arthur Harris to Winston Churchill, 3.11.43.

in the course of the last two years.[80] As the Strategic Bombing Survey suggested in August 1945,

> the German electrical utilities system present a target which was unusually vulnerable to strategic bombing attack [...that] vulnerability [...] arises from the lack of any reserve capacity, the relative ease with which electric generating and transmitting equipment can be seriously damaged, the relative difficulty of repairing bomb damage or replacement of destroyed facilities and the construction of electric power production in a relatively small number of plants.[81]

Nevertheless, despite this vulnerability and the consequences of any sustained failure in the German power system for the war economy, Allied air forces never attacked this target system. Given that the Third Reich of 1939 was a relatively open society and that its economic situation was widely known and understood in the West, this failure should suggest to us the magnitude of error that we are capable of making in estimating the vulnerabilities and weaknesses of other economic systems.

Additional Reading

Perhaps the most important book on the Combined Bomber Offensive to appear in recent years does not even have that effort as its main focus. But Adam Tooze's study of the Nazi economy from 1933 through 1945 underlines the crucial importance of strategic bombing, particularly the Battle of the Ruhr to Germany's defeat in World War II: Adam Tooze, *The Wages of Destruction: The Making and Breaking of the German War Economy* (London, 2008). Worthy of examination are also the various volumes and specific chapters dealing with the German response to Allied strategic bombing of the German military history institute's *Das Deutsche Reich und der Zweite Weltkrieg* (many of which have been translated into English). Volume 7 (available in English) is particularly noteworthy. See also Tami Biddle, *Rhetoric and Reality in Air Warfare: The Evolution of British and American Ideas about Strategic Bombing, 1914–1945* (Princeton, 2008).

---

[80] This observation is based on a careful study by the USSBS, "German Electric Utilities Industries Report," Washington, DC, 1945.
[81] Ibid., p. 2.

11

The Air War in the Gulf
The Limits of Air Power

In its immediate aftermath, the Gulf War has received more attention than any other air war, with the exception of World War II.[1] The stunning videos provided by the USAF and the RAF, even while their combat crews were deconstructing Iraq, presented images that remain with us today – bombs disappearing down the air conditioning shaft of Iraqi air force headquarters, bridges collapsing at the first go, hardened aircraft shelters built to withstand the effects of nuclear weapons being smashed, and finally the huddled, helpless equipment of the Iraqi army being blown to smithereens. To many, particularly in the USAF, it appeared that with such capabilities and accuracy, air power had at least come of age, reaching the promises of Douhet, Trenchard, and Mitchell. In the conflict's immediate aftermath, even critics of the USAF exclaimed that Desert Storm "was probably the most frictionless war we have ever fought."[2] In

---

[1] The Gulf War air campaign has not only received the attention of a number of serious monographs and articles, but a major multivolume study by a team of academics selected by the secretary of the air force who provided complete access to USAF documentary sources and allowed editorial freedom in its conclusions. See Eliot Cohen, Director, *The Gulf War Air Power Survey*, eight volumes (Washington, DC, 1993). The author of this piece was the main writer of the "Operations" report, vol. 2. For the most thorough history of the war, see Lieutenant General Bernard E. Trainor and Michael E. Gordon, *General's War: The Inside Story of the Conflict in the Gulf* (New York, 1995).

[2] "Jeffrey Record: Defense Analyst," *Defense News*, March 18, 1991, p. 46.

I delivered this chapter as a lecture during my year as the Centennial Visiting Professor at the London School of Economics in spring 1997. It then appeared two years later in *Strategic Review* (Winter 1998).

fact, it was not. The idea that any human affair – much less war – involving hundreds of thousands of individuals can take place without friction is bizarre. By putting the Gulf War within its operational context, we can access the limitations as well as the actual impact of the air campaign on the course of the war.

Not surprisingly, much, if not all, of the thinking on air power since World War II concentrated on the dark threat raised by nuclear weapons. But the wars waged by air forces since 1945 – and there have been many – all have involved combat in the conventional arena. The result of this dichotomy has been that thinking about air power has confined itself to the theoretical musings of civilian academics about nuclear war, while airmen floundered from one conventional war to the next.

In 1988, a student at the National War College, Colonel John Warden, produced a thesis – later published as a book, *The Air Campaign* – which was to play an important role in the planning and thinking behind the air campaign in the Gulf. Warden has some considerable interest in history. But as with earlier air power theorists, he focused on the influences that air power could bring against the heart of an enemy nation, namely the will of its political leadership. Warden's arguments had two important advantages over most air force "thinking." First, he argued that changes in capabilities provided air forces with advantages in destroying targets that had not been available in earlier periods. Second, Warden recognized that air power represented an operational lever on the enemy's capacity to sustain combat. In making that argument, he was implicitly dissenting with the traditional air force approach of simply racking up targets. Because Warden's thesis represented a serious, if at times flawed, willingness to address the uses of air power in war, *The Air Campaign* received praise as well as derision from senior air force leaders.

The arrival of Lieutenant General Michael Dugan as the chief of plans on the air staff in spring 1988 provided Warden an advocate in the highest places – a position of influence reinforced by Dugan's return from a year in Europe in July 1990 to become the new air force chief of staff. In turn, Warden's position on the air staff as the head of the strategic analysis section placed him in a position to play a major role in developing an air campaign against the Iraqi regime. Those plans and the subsequent ones developed in Riyad, in what became known as the Black Hole, suggest how little the conceptualization of airmen has advanced beyond the thinking of air power theorists of the interwar period. In fact, the course and results of the Gulf War suggest that the natural frictions and difficulties in conducting war, including war in the air, have changed little from the systemic problems confronting commanders and their military forces throughout history.

The Political–Strategic Dimension

The initial efforts to draw up a strategic air plan came as a result of default. Ninth Air Force, based at Shaw Air Force Base, was the air headquarters for any major American deployment to the Middle East. Saddam Hussein's sudden grab of Kuwait resulted in a hurried and massive deployment of U.S. air units to the Middle East. Ninth Air Force not only had more than it could handle in managing such a deployment, but there is little evidence that the command had the capabilities to plan an air campaign beyond racking up targets, starting with the first, and working through to the last. Moreover, for much of August, Ninth's commander, Lieutenant General Chuck Horner, was in command in Saudi Arabia as General Norman Schwarzkopf's deputy, while the latter remained in the United States to make the political and strategic arrangements. Consequently, Horner's concerns remained focused on defending Saudi Arabia, should the Iraqis trump the U.S. move into the Middle East with an all-out attack on the Saudis.

To fill the gap in long-range planning, Schwarzkopf requested air support for an air campaign against Iraq. Warren and his planners on the air staff (most in an organization called "Checkmate") had already began sketching a plan code-named "Instant Thunder." The choice of wording aimed at underlining a major break with how the United States had conducted its air war against North Vietnam. A proposed briefing for President Bush, dated 13 August 1990, argued for a massive first night attack with the explicit aim of decapitating Iraq's political leadership.[3]

Whatever Instant Thunder's weaknesses, other groups within the air force came up with conceptions that displayed no significant advance over Rolling Thunder, the bombing of North Vietnam in the 1965–1968 period. In early August, Tactical Air Command proposed an air campaign against Iraq "with demonstrative attacks against high value targets ... [and then] escalate[ion] as required until all significant targets [were] destroyed." The briefing ended with the bizarre note that such a

[3] "'Instant Thunder,' Proposed Strategic Air Campaign," 13 August 1990, 2300 hrs, Gulf War Air Power Survey Archive, CHP 35-6. While the air staff did not give the briefing to President Bush, it does appear that General Colin Powell, chairman of the joint chiefs of staff, may have used the slides to brief the president on 15 August.

"strategy allows time and opportunity for Hussein to reevaluate his situation and back out while there is something to save."[4] This replay of the past disappeared from the scene almost immediately, but its appearance suggests a general lack of conceptual thinking in Tactical Air Command.

The navy was little more forthcoming than planners in Tactical Air Command in offering innovative possibilities for an air campaign. Some in the naval aviation community suggested a return to the route package formula of the Vietnam War in which the navy and air force received their own individual sections of North Vietnam to execute entirely independent air campaigns. The result had been an air campaign marked with little cooperation and no coherence. Few navy commanders felt comfortable with the concept of a joint forces air component commander (JFACC), particularly since it seemed to give the air force a superior position in the allocation of missions. But as a senior naval officer pointed out after a trip to evaluate the war in February 1991

> several senior officers... were concerned that independent naval operations were threatened by... participation [in the JFACC system] because the carrier's missions were tasked by the JFACC using the... ATO [air tasking order] system. But the navy has no alternative to the ATO system. Without it the campaign would have been planned and directed manually. Sortie rates would have been far lower and strike deconfliction much less certain.[5]

In fact, the navy had a number of other problems that contributed to its lesser role in the Gulf War. First, the geographic circumstances of the theater, which to all intents and purposes was landlocked, forced the navy to use air force tankers to refuel the bulk of its missions. Second, while the Atlantic carriers worked well with the air force – undoubtedly due to their extensive previous experience – the Pacific carriers ran into a number of problems. In fact, their lack of experience in working with the air force almost allowed two Iraqi Mirages to break out into the Gulf and fire their missiles at U.S. ships. When that incident occurred early in the war, the F-14s flying combat air patrol had not received the frequencies on which the Airborne Warning and Control System (AWACS) operated and, consequently, entirely missed desperate attempts by AWACS controllers

---

[4] Interestingly, Tactical Air Command lost the entire briefing before the war was over and then claimed that no such briefing had ever been offered. The slides were found in Checkmate files. Fax from Major General John Griffith TAC/XP to Major General Alexander AF/XOX, 11 August 1990, "CENTCOM Air Campaign Plan," GWAPS Archive CHSH-14.

[5] Letter from Captain Steven U. Ramsdell to Director, Naval Historical Center, Subject: Trip Report, 14 May 1991.

to alert them to the threat posed by the Mirages.[6] Finally, as with much of the air force's fighter bomber fleet, few of the navy aircraft had precision guided munition capabilities, a factor that would limit their effectiveness throughout much of the war.

The planners of Instant Thunder aimed their air campaign to "conduct powerful and focused air attacks on [the enemy's] strategic centers of gravity." The air offense would involve "round-the-clock operations against leadership, strategic air defense," and electrical targets with the aim of achieving "strategic paralysis and air superiority." Besides the command and control centers and other strategic "centers of gravity," Instant Thunder gave heavy attention to the Iraqi electrical system in the belief that its destruction would damage Iraqi morale, as well as affect communications and other systems. While hoping that destruction of the electrical system would have considerable impact on morale, the plan emphasized that under no circumstances was the air campaign to target Iraq's population directly.[7]

Interestingly, Instant Thunder briefings made virtually no reference to the presence of large Iraqi ground forces in Kuwait, poised as they were to launch a major invasion of Saudi Arabia. The planners estimated that with sufficient aircraft and capabilities, Central Command's air forces (CENTAF) could complete the campaign successfully in five or six days.[8] What was not clear was whether the end state of Instant Thunder was to be the removal of Iraqi forces from Kuwait or the destruction of Saddam's regime.

Part of the initial optimism that an air campaign would need only five or six days resulted from U.S. intelligence being able to identify only 84 major targets. The target list in fact eventually expanded to over 300 by the start of Desert Storm, as increasingly sophisticated intelligence became available. But as UN inspections of Iraq revealed after the war, coalition

---

[6] Charles E. Chambers, "Desert Storm Reconstruction Report," vol. III, "Antiair Warfare," Center for Naval Analyses, 1991.
[7] Interview, Colonel John Warden with GWAPS personnel (Williamson Murray, Barry Watts, and Thomas Keaney), 21 February 1992. See also briefing Colonel Warden for General Schwarzkopf, "Iraqi Air Campaign Instant Thunder," 17 August 1990, GWAPS Archive, CHSH 7-11.
[8] The individual who would control much of the planning throughout the conduct of the war, then Brigadier General Buster Glosson, heard the Instant Thunder briefing on 23 August in Riyadh and noted in his diary, "need air campaign for fifteen rounds not three; six days is dumb." Glosson Journal, 23 August 1990; interview Major General Buster Glosson with GWAPS personnel (Williamson Murray, Barry Watts, and Thomas Keaney), 9 April 1992.

intelligence never got a handle on the redundant nuclear facilities the Iraqis had constructed in their cover programs to develop the bomb.[9] The point here, however, has less to do with the lack of accurate target intelligence than with the general underestimation of the political stability of Saddam's regime and the extreme overestimations of the Iraqi military forces on the basis of Iraq's "success" in its lengthy and inconclusive war with Ayatollah Khomeini's Iran.[10] These crucial miscalculations, which ground commanders as well as air commanders held throughout the war, carried with them several dangerous consequences in the planning of the air campaign and might even have skewed the results of the war into a Western political defeat. At a minimum, they explain why the coalition waged such a long air campaign, the length of which carried with it the possibility that Iraq might abandon Kuwait before coalition ground forces revealed Iraq's forces for what they were: a rag-tag military force with little staying power against the training and technical skills of Western armies.

Ironically, Iraq's strengths and weaknesses were the obverse of what U.S. leaders and intelligence expected.[11] Saddam had created a merciless and effective tyranny – one based on a coherent ideology and thoroughly imbued with repressive tools that had made Stalin's regime so effective.[12] This was not a government that could be overthrown by concerns about the destruction of the nation's infrastructure or prospects of defeat. Only a campaign aimed at undermining Saddam's position by the ruthless

---

[9] Among others, see Report, International Atomic Energy Agency, Seventh Inspection in Iraq under UN Security Council Resolution 687, 14 November 1991, GWAPS Archive NA 3.

[10] This overestimation of Iraqi military capabilities caused senior army leaders to miss the significance of the success of the marines and air power in masking the only Iraqi attack of the war, their ill-fated attack on Khafji. The marines after Khafji at least recognized that not only were the Iraqis militarily incompetent, but the air campaign had already wrecked the morale of Iraqi ground units.

[11] The report on effectiveness in the Gulf War Air Power Survey suggests that "few, if any, of the U.S. commanders or planner involved in the conduct of Desert Storm seem to have anticipated that Saddam Hussein's regime might long survive decisive battlefield defeat." Barry D. Watts and Thomas Kearney, *Gulf War Air Power Survey*, vol. 2, Report 2, *Effects and Effectiveness* (Washington DC, 1993), p. 15.

[12] It is worth noting that in summer 1989 a careful, scholarly study of the nature of Iraqi tyranny had appeared in the United States. Its author, writing under the pseudonym of Samir al-Khalil, was thoroughly conversant with the ideological roots of the Ba'athist party in Fascism, communism (of the Stalinist model), and varieties of Arabic nationalism, and the result is a book that lays bare the nature of Iraqi ambitions and the extent of the threat. Samir al-Khalil, *The Republic of Fear, The Politics of Modern Iraq* (Berkeley, CA, 1989).

application of force, including the occupation of much of the country, would have much prospect of overthrowing the tyrant.[13]

On the other hand, the demands of political survival in an Iraq whose history before Saddam had largely been dominated by military coups was such that the regime placed military competence low on its list of priorities for military commanders. Like Stalin between 1937 and 1941, Saddam appointed his generals largely on the basis of political reliability and loyalty. The results in terms of battlefield competence were similar. The inability of American military and political leaders to recognize the real vulnerabilities of Iraq had an important impact on the conduct of the war and might well have led to political disaster.[14]

Warden's conception of a sudden and brief air campaign that would destabilize and perhaps overthrow Saddam's government or at least force the Iraqis to disgorge Kuwait almost immediately ran into two significant criticisms from senior U.S. military leaders. On the one hand, General Colin Powell, chairman of the joint chiefs of staff, recognized that the Iraqi Army represented Iraq's main threat to its neighbors. As early as 11 August he commented to several air force officers: "I won't be happy until I see those tanks destroyed.... The campaign I laid out for the President: sweep the air and leave the tanks to [be] pick[ed] off piece-meal – if we go this far...I want to finish it: destroy Iraq's army on the ground."[15] For Powell, destruction of Iraq's ground forces in Kuwait and southern Iraq became the most important focus of the air campaign and the eventual ground offensive.

But there was a second element in Warden's conception of the importance of Iraqi ground forces in the air campaign – one that would find

---

[13] In fact, my comment here has proven wrong with the availability of Iraqi documents, which indicate that with minimal American help in 1991, the revolt would have overthrown Saddam's Ba'athist regime.

[14] Yet, one should note that the Iraqis made an even greater set of miscalculations about the political will of their opponents as well as the actual balance of forces between Iraq and its potential enemies as the coalition gathered its strength. As one observer has noted, Saddam "remained intractable to the end, being willing to risk war, and believing until relatively late into Operation Desert Storm that Iraq would acquit itself well on the battlefield." Dr. Norman Cigar, "Iraq's Strategic Mindset and the Gulf War: Blueprint for Defeat," *Journal of Strategic Studies*, p. 23.

[15] Memo, Subj: "Instant Thunder," Briefing to Chairman Joint Chiefs of Staff, 11 August 1990, Lieutenant Colonel Ben Harvey, GWAPS Archive, CHSH 14. In a memorandum for the record Harvey put Powell's remarks more pithily: "I don't want them to go home – I want to leave smoking tanks as kilometer posts all of the way to Baghdad." Memo for record, Lieutenant Colonel Ben Harvey, subj: Instant Thunder Briefing to CJCS, 11 August 1990, GWAPS Archive, CHP 7-4.

an echo in the thinking of air planners even late in the air campaign.[16] This was the belief air power by itself could force Saddam to abandon Kuwait without requiring a ground campaign, an idea that was particularly attractive to many who rated the Iraqi Army highly. What such arguments missed was the reason why coalition political leaders were hazarding the dangerous possibilities of war: to remove the military and especially the political threat Iraq posed to its neighbors. Any such political aim necessitated a ground campaign to convince world public opinion – and particularly the Arabs – of the complete defeat of Saddam's army. Without TV pictures showing Iraqis surrendering in droves, Saddam would soon have claimed that his army had remained in the field, bloodied but unbeaten, too formidable for the cowardly Americans to attack. Such propaganda would have played all too well in many parts of the Arab world, in much the same fashion that the *Dolchstoss* legend persuaded the Germans that their army had stood unbroken in November 1918.

Warden's concept of a sudden, quick, and decisive air campaign ran into the solid roadblock of Horner. The latter, as the on-scene commander, confronted the immediate prospect of an Iraqi invasion of Saudi Arabia – not particularly an enticing prospect, given the slow buildup of coalition ground forces: "The idea was that we were to deter an Iraqi invasion of Saudi Arabia, and if an invasion did come, we were prepared to defend.... Those were some of the worst nights of my life, because I had good information as to what the Iraqi threat was, and, quite frankly, we could not have issued speeding tickets to [their] tanks as they would have come rolling down the interstate highway on the east coast."[17]

Horner dismissed Warden's conception as theoretical nonsense. He was particularly furious at what he regarded as Washington's interference in his command responsibilities. But he also felt that the Instant Thunder plan carried unacceptable risks in its strategic, political, and operational assumptions. As he asked Warden at the end of a briefing in Riyadh: Did he [Warden] know when sufficient supplies would exist in theater to support such a campaign? What would happen if the Iraqi regime did not collapse after a five- or six-day campaign, and CENTAF had used up its weapons supplies in theater? And what could CENTAF

---

[16] Interview, Lieutenant Colonel David Deptula with GWAPS personnel (Williamson Murray, Barry Watts, and Thomas Kearney) 20–21 December 1991.
[17] Speech by Lieutenant General Chuck Horner to Business Executive for National Security, 8 May 1991, GWAPS Archives, Horner Files.

do against the Iraqi army with so few ground forces presently in the theater?[18] These questions represented the harsh world of the operational commander bumping up against the theoretical constructs of the air power advocate. The general won because no one in the political world was willing to embark on a course of action that rested on such chancy assumptions.

The Air War against Iraq

The larger question of what exactly the air campaign was supposed to do to the Iraqi regime is, indeed, an interesting one. At the highest level there was considerable ambiguity in the U.S. position on the end state that military operations were supposed to create. At times President Bush enunciated a position that seemed to advocate the overthrow of Saddam, but the framework within which the U.S. military worked remained limited to inflicting a significant defeat on Iraq and liberating Kuwait. As of early August, the aims of the United States and its allies were "1) To effect the immediate, complete and unconditional withdrawal of all Iraqi forces from Kuwait; 2) to restore Kuwait's legitimate government; 3) to protect the lives of American citizens abroad; and 4) to promote the security and stability of the Persian Gulf."[19]

The result was a bifurcated air campaign against the Iraqis: First, a strategic air campaign: 1) to destroy the Iraqi air defense system and air force; 2) cripple the electric systems; 3) ensure the destruction of Iraq's nuclear, chemical, and biological warfare programs; 4) prevent the Iraqis from using their SCUD missiles against Israel, and (very much the last priority); and 5) attack Iraq's political and command and control system. The second was a tactical campaign – almost entirely separate from the first and aimed at wrecking Iraqi forces deployed in the KTO (the Kuwaiti Theater of Operations, roughly Kuwait and the surrounding Iraqi territory to the north and the west).

Let me address the strategic campaign first. The attack on the Iraqi air defense system was a brilliant piece of operational planning that wrecked Iraq's complex air defenses over the course of the opening night, all at the

---

[18] Interview, Major General Larry Henry with GWAPS personnel (Williamson Murray and Barry Watts), August 1992; Lieutenant Colonel Harvey notes, 20 August 1990, both in GWAPS Archives.
[19] "Presidential Address to the Nation Announcing the Deployment of United States Armed Forces to Saudi Arabia," 8 August 1990, in *Public Papers of the President of the United States. George Bush, 1990* (Washington, DC, 1991), p. 1108.

cost of a single coalition aircraft. Stealth, precision weaponry, complex tactics, and the extraordinary capabilities of coalition aircrews destroyed Iraq's capacity to defend itself against an attack in the first hours of war.[20] What made the planning of the first night's attacks particularly devastating was the understanding of the planners that what mattered was not the absolute destruction of targets but sufficient destruction to render them ineffective. Thus, each of the sector air defense centers received only one precision-guided munition rather than the seven required to cause absolute destruction. The assumption was that one hit would prove sufficient to discourage the Iraqis from further use of the facilities. In the case of one center, postwar examination indicated that a near miss had been sufficient to close the center down for the remainder of the war. In turn, deconstruction of Iraqi air defenses allowed the air campaign to continue with minimum loss of aircrews and aircraft.

The attack on Iraq's electrical system proved equally effective but raised interesting questions on both tactical and political levels. The initial raids targeted transformer stations rather than generators; special mission cruise missiles with package of carbon filament wires were able to take down most of the electrical network in the first several days, but the means left no visible signs of damage that intelligence could pick up. As a result, over the course of the campaign a large number of reattacks took place. Despite explicit orders from CENTAF that generator halls were not to be targeted, the attacking aircraft squadrons eventually did so, partially because they had lost track of their instructions in the mass of paperwork occasioned by the war. The attack on Iraqi chemical/nuclear/biological programs underlined the problems of intelligence in an uncertain world. The failure to identify much of the Iraqi program in weapons of mass destruction resulted from the fact that the Iraqis had disguised the extent of their programs before the war, were able to dissemble what they had, and then hid much of their equipment during the period of Desert Shield. The air campaign undoubtedly set the Iraqi program back, but it was not able to destroy the program.

In the end, the pursuit of mobile SCUD launchers was a success story, but one that again suggests the limits of technology. After the war, the Defense Science Board suggested that there was no evidence that air attacks had destroyed any of the SCUD mobile launchers during the war. Thus, the air effort appears at best to have been one that suppressed the

---

[20] For a fuller discussion of these issues, see Williamson Murray, *Air War in the Persian Gulf* (Baltimore, MD, 1995).

Iraqis' ability to launch their grossly inaccurate missiles at Israeli and Saudi cities. But again, we are dealing with indirect effects; whatever the actual impact of the suppression effort, it was the perception that coalition air forces were making a major effort against SCUDs that prevented Israeli air strikes against Iraq, which would have had potentially dangerous political consequences to the coalition's stability.

The Attacks on Iraqi Leadership

The attacks on Saddam's regime and its "popular support" proved far less successful. While the defeat of the Iraqi Army in the war eventually led to rebellions in both northern and southern Iraq, the center held. There are a number of reasons for this. Politically, the ambiguities about U.S. and coalition policy on whether Allied efforts should aim at overthrowing Saddam prevented a clear strategic and operational focus toward that end.[21] While coalition air forces embarked on considerable psychological efforts to undermine the morale of the Iraqi army in the KTO, similar efforts were distinctly missing in the attacks on Iraq. There were plans to drop anti-regime leaflets over downtown Baghdad early in the air campaign; but such plans were cancelled and never resurrected.

Fundamental to all the various ends that the coalition air campaign pursued was an emphasis on reducing "collateral damage incident to military attacks, taking special precautions to minimize civilian causalities."[22] As the report in the *Gulf War Air Power Supply on Effects and Effectiveness* suggests:

> From President George Bush on down, there was widespread agreement from the outset of the planning process that directly attacking the people of Iraq or their food supply was neither compatible with U.S. objectives nor morally acceptable to the American people, whose support was felt, in light of the Vietnam experience, to be essential to the war effort. Thus, the coalition's "targeting" of the will of Iraq's civilian population was limited, for the very best of reasons, to psychological operations and indirect effects stemming from the bombing of other core target categories.[23]

---

[21] The authors of the effectiveness volume in the *Gulf War Air Power Survey* indicate that "while attacking the Iraqi leadership was a military objective of the U.S.... plan, the removal of Saddam Hussein was not stated as a political objective of either the United States or the Coalition." Watts and Keaney, *Effects and Effectiveness*, p. 76.
[22] National Security Directive, 54, 15 January 1991, pp. 2-3, GWAPS Archive, NA 247A.
[23] Watts and Keaney, *Effect and Effectiveness*, pp. 268-269.

There were two exceptions to the coalition's efforts to limit the collateral damage to civilians: the RAF attack on the bridge of Nasiriyah and the F-117 bombing of the Al-Firdos bunker.[24] Both involved considerable, although unintended, civilian casualties and both had a significant impact on the ability of the air campaign to pressure the Iraqis. The result of the Nasiriyah bridge incident was that Colin Powell ordered attacks on bridges in downtown Baghdad to cease. We will turn to the implications of the Al-Firdos in a moment, but the point here is that with the strictures on avoiding civilian casualties, the air campaign had relatively little direct impact on the lives of Iraqis other than putting out the lights.

That fact explains why the regime had little trouble during the war in maintaining its hold over the center. One of the few testaments we have on the war from the point of view of those living in Baghdad comes from the diary of an Iraqi woman, Nuha Al-Radi. Her comments suggest how little the air war impacted the lives of most Iraqis:

> DAY FOUR... Suha is experimenting with a recipe for *basturma*. The meat in our freezers is thawing so it's a good thing the weather is cold. In the evening we cook potatoes in the fireplace... I make a dynamite punch with Aquavit, vodka, and fresh orange juice....
>
> DAY FIVE... Apparently people take off for the countryside with their freezers loaded on their pick-up trucks and barbeque the food as it defrosts. Only Iraqis would escape from a war carrying freezers full of goodies....
>
> DAY SEVEN... The worst has happened: we have to drink warm beer. I cleaned out the freezer and removed a ton of different kinds of bread.... We have to eat everything that will spoil.... I finished Mundher's painting and we had little party to celebrate its unveiling. We opened a bottle of champagne and ate *meloukhia* and a million other things. I wish that our stock of food would finish so that we could eat a little less....
>
> DAY TEN... Everyone talks endlessly about food. While eating lunch the conversation is about what we are having for dinner. We have cooked up all the meat we had....
>
> DAY THIRTEEN... The peasant's life we now lead is very hard, and the work never stops. I get up, come downstairs, collect the firewood,

---

[24] See Williamson Murray, *The Gulf War Air Power Survey*, vol. 2, report 1, *Operations*, (Washington, DC, 1993), pp. 206–208, 221–222.

clean the grate and make up the evening fire. I clean the kitchen and boil water for coffee. Suha and Amal cook the meals. Ma makes the bread and cakes. I do the soup and salads.

DAY TWENTY... It has now been three weeks. Forty-four thousand air raids. I have another leak in the water system.

DAY TWENTY-TWO... There is a sameness about the days now. I saw the Jumhuriya Bridge today; it's incredibly sad to see a bombed bridge – a murderous action, for it destroys a link. The sight affects everyone that sees it; many people cry. Children play in the streets without traffic. The have never had it so good....

DAY THIRTY-FOUR... Tim brought faxes from Sol, Dood, and Charlie, our first contacts with family and friends – a break in our isolation. We had a super barbeque lunch today, a lovely day but quite noisy.[25]

From the earliest days coalition planners as well as senior commanders had recognized the constraints that Western sensibilities had placed on the conduct of an air campaign against Iraq. In fact, CENTAF's chief planner noted in his diary at the end of August that "the American people would never stand for another 'Dresden.'"[26] And, indeed, there is no doubt that any campaign that resulted in heavy civilian casualties would have caused serious political problems not only in the United States but throughout the coalition. But American qualms about casualties, particularly at the higher levels of the Bush administration and in the Pentagon, had a significant impact on the ability of air power to destabilize Saddam Hussein's tyranny. The first three weeks of the air campaign concentrated on destroying the Iraqi air defense system, managing the SCUD menace, attacking the Iraqi air force in its hardened aircraft shelters, and attempting to deconstruct Saddam's nuclear/chemical/biological programs.

But on the night of February 12–13, the planners turned the focus of the air effort against the administrative structure of the Iraqi regime, particularly the secret police apparatus. Over that night, among other targets, F-117s struck the air force headquarters (two hits); the ministry of defense (two hits); the Ba'ath Party headquarters (four hits); the Baghdad directorate of internal security (one hit, one "no guide"); the Baghdad

---

[25] Nuha Al-Radi, "Baghdad Diary," *Granta*, 1992, No. 42, pp. 209–229.
[26] Glosson Journal, 25 August, interview with GWAPS personnel, 9 April 1992 (Williamson Murray, Barry D. Watts, and Thomas A. Keaney).

directorate of military intelligence (two hits); the Iraqi intelligence service headquarters (three hits); and the Baghdad presidential bunker (two hits).[27] This bombing effort represented what was to be the opening of a substantial attempt to target and destroy the mechanisms by which Saddam and the Ba'ath Party controlled the Iraqi people.

Unfortunately, it proved to be the last night of the effort, because two bombs dropped by an F-117 hit the Al-Firdos bunker. Coalition intelligence had identified no fewer than 25 bunkers, including the Al-Firdos site, that the Iraqis had built as redundant, backup capabilities should the main control headquarters of the regime's secret police organizations and military headquarters be destroyed. In early February, intelligence indicated that one of the Iraqi administrative organizations had activated the Al-Firdos bunker and was using it as a major center. Consequently, it found its way onto the target list.

What was not known to intelligence was that the Iraqi political elite was also using the bunker as a shelter. The Ba'athist regime had *not* prepared a vast system of shelters for the population of Baghdad, much less Iraq. Those who were in the Al-Firdos bunker were there because they had political connections. Ironically, they would have been safer had they sheltered in their homes in the civilian districts of Baghdad, which was where Saddam spent much of the war. The ensuing uproar, as CNN carried the recovery of bodies live on worldwide television, was sufficient to terminate efforts to attack Saddam's means of controlling the Iraqi population. And when the Gulf War was over, that administrative structure of redundant and ruthless secret police organizations, along with the remains of the Republican Guard, were sufficient to crush the revolution that broke out among the Kurds and Shi'ites. Saddam's survival, despite his miscalculations and defeat, was partially the result of the inability of the coalition to attack the support structure of the tyranny for fear of civilian casualties that might occur.[28]

There is another irony in the reaction at the highest political levels in the United States to the Al-Firdos bunker incident. Those killed in the bunker were from the families of the Iraqi leadership – those responsible

---

[27] GWAPS Mission Data Base, GWAPS Archive.
[28] When the Clinton administration decided that the Iraqi attempt to blow up former President Bush in Iraq was beyond the bounds of acceptable international behavior, it responded with a night cruise missile attack that at most was going to kill washerwomen and janitors rather than the real authors of the attempted assassination and risk having their bodies – undoubtedly tailored in the best suits from Saville Row tailors – on display on CNN as "innocent civilians."

for the ruthless, cruel imposition of the Ba'ath tyranny on the people of Iraq. Yet, at the same time that the West was reacting so viscerally to the Al-Firdos incident, coalition air forces were into the 26th day of blasting Iraqi forces deployed in the KTO, and they would continue that effort for almost another two weeks. Those Iraqi ground forces were for the most part – with the exception of the Republican Guard – conscripts, drawn from the poorest elements in Iraqi society and the victims rather than the perpetrators of the tyranny. It would be from this group that the revolution in Iraq drew. Yet, there would be little outcry in the First World, much less the Arab world, about what was happening to them and little recognition that by wrecking those Iraqi forces, the coalition was undermining the possibility that a successful revolution might occur.

There is another depressing story of the failure of coalition attacks to undermine the political stability of the Ba'athist regime. In early February, as the planners turned to attacking the political apparatus of the regime, they attempted to place several major symbols of the regime – namely the great monument of arms bearing crossed swords through which so many Iraqi military parades took place, as well as several of the statues of the great man himself – on the target lists. However, the legal "experts" at the Tactical Air Command in the United States raised and sustained the bizarre objection that such sites were "cultural monuments" and therefore by the strictures of international law could not be attacked.[29]

Toward the end of the war, the planners again raised the possibility of attacking such targets. This time army lawyers in the Pentagon objected that such attacks would have no significance, since the war was almost over – an argument that had nothing to do with their area of expertise. Such is the position of lawyers in U.S. society, however, that when they advise against an action, politicians and generals listen, even when their advice has nothing to do with their area of responsibility. On 25 February, after approving such attacks on Saddam's arches and statues, Powell changed his mind and asked Schwarzkopf to hold off.[30] The chance would not come again.[31]

---

[29] For a fuller discussion of these issues, see Murray, *Gulf War Air Power Survey*, vol. 2, report 1, *Operations*, pp. 240–245.
[30] Norman Schwarzkopf with Peter Petre, *It Doesn't Take a Hero* (New York, 1992), pp. 457 and 468.
[31] Even after the war was over, Horner was still under the mistaken impression that attacks on such edifices as Saddam's statues were forbidden by international law. *Air Force Times*, 8 March 1991.

Numbers, Numbers, and the KTO

The conduct of the air war against the Iraqi army in the KTO stands in stark contrast to the efforts to seek an operational handle in the offensive against Iraq proper. This reflected several factors, chief of which was that the air war in the KTO received considerably less attention from the chief planners both in Desert Storm and during the course of the war. There was never any attempt to seek leverage against the Iraqi forces occupying Kuwait and stationed in southern Iraq. Yet, the air war against Kuwait raises a number of interesting issues, including the fascination with numbers as well as the fact that what may be efficient may not be the most effective utilization of air power.

At the beginning, Schwarzkopf set astonishingly high goals for the air effort against Iraqi forces deployed in the KTO; he wanted no less than 50 percent of the deployed Iraqi tanks and artillery destroyed before he would let the ground campaign begin.[32] What is even more surprising is the fact that the air commanders agreed to the target figure without any qualms. This focus on numbers on both the ground and air sides was to begin a furious series of rows that would last up to the beginning of the ground campaign, when the results thereafter finally terminated the quarrels – at least until the postwar budget debates began.

Because the most general aim was only attriting tanks and artillery with a special emphasis on Saddam's Republican Guard, the air planners divided the KTO into a series of kill boxes and then funneled aircraft into each specific box on a set of priorities established in the Black Hole. In the best air force tradition, the effort represented a racking up of targets and then going after them on the basis of numbers of sorties and tonnages of bombs dropped by kill box without a coherent plan to achieve some larger effects.[33]

The initial weeks of the air offensive against Iraqi forces in the KTO were none too successful. Few of the attacking aircraft had the capability to employ precision-guided munitions; and to hold losses down to manageable levels, they were flying their missions above the level of Iraqi flak and hand-held, heat-seeking missiles. The result was that large numbers of bombs were dropped all over the desert but minimal damage was done

---

[32] See HQCENTCOM, *Combined Operations Desert Storm*, 17 January 1991, para. 3.d(3)(c), GWAPS Archive, CHP 18–1.

[33] For a further examination of the issues involved in the campaign against Iraqi ground forces, see Murray, *Operations*, pp. 254–326; and Watts and Keaney, *Effects and Effectiveness*, pp. 159–264.

to the Iraqi ground forces. To add to the difficulties, the B-52s funneled into the attacks on the KTO were using different grid coordinates and consequently the bombing bias was approximately 600 yards short of what they were attacking, a fact that was not discovered until late in the war. This is not to say that these attacks were useless. (We will turn to their psychological impact in a moment.) But even in a physical sense, the attacks inflicted some damage: one B-52 strike hit the Tawakana Division's ammunition supply and the spectacular results suggested to some outside observers of the war that someone had lit off a nuclear weapon in the theater. But the crucial point is that over the course of the first two weeks of the air campaign, there was little evidence of damage to Iraqi equipment deployed in Kuwait.

In early February, that state of affairs changed when Schwarzkopf ordered Horner to deploy his F-111s with their precision-guided munition capabilities against the Iraqi Army. F-111 drivers quickly discovered that their forward-looking infrared receivers could pick up the heat differential between Iraqi equipment and the surrounding desert. They could then use laser-guided 500-pound bombs to strike at the dug-in equipment with considerable effect.[34] Thus began what F-111 aircrews termed the tank "plinking" effort. Schwarzkopf ordered that air force pilots no longer use the term "plinking," but that order only ensured that it gained general currency among the pilots.[35] A steady attrition of Iraqi equipment began, but there also ensued an ongoing and furious debate between the air planners and the ground commanders about exactly how much equipment the air attacks were destroying and whether the air campaign was reaching the agreed-upon levels of equipment destruction. Generally these arguments did not reflect well on either the wisdom or the degree of inter-service cooperation between the participants.

What is in fact important is that these arguments were entirely irrelevant to the matter at hand – destroying the Iraqi ground forces in KTO. What mattered was not what air attacks did to the Iraqi equipment in the theater but what it did to the minds of the Iraqi soldiers who were going to have to use that equipment. Here, evidence indicates that the massive, unceasing air assaults had substantially affected the prisoners captured in the ground forces in the KTO. Ironically, the most inaccurate weapon on the coalition air inventory, the B-52, was the air weapon that

---

[34] TACC, Current Operations, Log 6, February 1991, 0730Z, GWAPS Archive NA 215.
[35] TACC, Current Operations, Log 8, February 1991, GWAPS Archive NA 215.

Iraqi solders cited again and again as the most terrifying of those whose attacks they had to endure.[36]

> The persuasive impression left by the interrogation reports of prisoners who deserted or who were captured was the sense of futility felt by the Iraqis after weeks of extensive bombing. When the bombing started, their ground transportation began to crumble. They ran short of water, food, fuel, and spare parts. Some units had their supply stocks destroyed. Training in the units ceased. Soldiers moved apart from their equipment because they well understood what the targets were. Many captured Iraqis stated they thought the air campaign would last several days to a week at most. When it did not, the sense of futility and inevitability of the outcome became apparent.[37]

In the end, it was the psychological impact of air attacks that mattered. And how could one measure the impact on morale during the course of the campaign? For the most part one could not, although there was considerable evidence in the Khafji attack – mostly ignored by senior army generals – that the Iraqis, at least their front line divisions, were in serious trouble. As in previous wars, it was the imponderables, the unmeasurable that mattered, not the mathematically calculable.

Additional Reading

The Iraqi perspectives project at the Institute for Defense Analyses has published an important work on the 1991 Gulf War from the Iraqi point of view and based on Iraqi documents, including transcripts of a number of Saddam's meetings with his ministers and generals: See Kevin M. Woods, *The Mother of All Battles: Saddam Hussein's Strategic Plan for the Persian Gulf War* (Annapolis, MS, 2008).

---

[36] See among others, Department of the Army, 513th Military Intelligence Brigade, Joint Debriefing Center: The Gulf War: An Iraqi General Officer's Perspective," JDC Report #0052, 11 March 1991.

[37] Watts and Keaney, *Effect and Effectiveness*, chap. 4.

12

Thoughts on British Intelligence in World War II and the Implications for Intelligence in the Twenty-First Century

The Greek Thucydides, the greatest of all historians, suggested in the early passages of his work on the Peloponnesian War that it "will be enough for me, however, if these words of mine are judged useful by those who want to understand clearly the events which happened in the past and which (human nature being what it is) will, at some time or other and in much the same ways, be repeated in the future."[1] The problem with Thucydides' claim is that history rarely suggests exact patterns. At best, it can provide illumination to help in understanding the complex problems that confront today's policy makers and military leaders. The best one can hope for from history is that it will suggest the right questions, or how to think more coherently and intelligently about current problems.

This chapter examines the development of British intelligence over the course of the Second World War for insights into how America's present-day intelligence organizations might consider and address their own problems. Admittedly considerable differences exist between the challenges the British faced and those confronting Americans today. Yet, there are also similarities that may help address the complex and intractable problems of the twenty-first century. At the least, the success of British intelligence in the Second World War would seem to suggest lessons adaptable to today's conditions.

Indeed, the British intelligence effort in the Second World War was among the most massive – especially in terms of percentage increase in manpower and resources – mounted by any major power in history.

---

[1] Thucydides, *History of the Peloponnesian War*, translated by Rex Warner (London, 1954), p. 48.

It was also among the most effective, if not the most effective. Just in terms of signals intelligence against the Germans, the British confronted no less than 30 different variants of the Enigma codes and five other codes produced by a machine the British termed Fish.[2] And every day at 2400 hours, the British had to begin again the business of breaking into those codes.[3] That, of course, represented only the first step, because they then had to separate the significant and important from the chaff the *Wehrmacht*'s transmitting stations spewed out every day.[4] Then, that usable intelligence had to be transmitted as quickly as possible to operational commanders in a useful form.

Even with the advantages that the breaking of the Enigma codes conveyed, the picture of what the Germans were doing more often than not remained opaque and ambiguous.[5] Then, as now, the business of intelligence analysis was similar to the problems historians or lawyers confront, both of whom must take disconnected pieces of evidence and develop patterns that approximate what they believe happened in the past as well as what might happen in the future.[6] Thus, intelligence is more art than science in its attempt to make sense of what is always an incomplete and

---

[2] Sir Harry Hinsley, "The Influence of ULTRA in the Second World War," address to Security Group Seminar, 26 November 1996.

[3] A number of works make clear that *the* essential element in breaking the Enigma codes was the carelessness with which German operators transmitted their messages and the overconfidence with which senior officers *believed* that the Allies would not be able to break German codes on a continuing basis.

[4] The volume of messages the Germans transmitted every day was a major factor that enabled the British to break into the German codes to begin with; without that volume, the British would never have been able to find the cribs necessary to break into the various codes. Many messages were timely and important; others, however, were of little importance, or should never have been transmitted by Enigma. The author of this chapter remembers coming across a message from a German naval trawler off Norway requesting permission to return to Trondheim because one of the sailors on board had a bad case of venereal disease.

[5] The breaking of German codes involved a difficult and massive effort – helped considerably by German arrogance and inexcusable sloppiness. The Enigma encyphering machine that the Germans used should have remained unbroken; the British success in breaking into a number of the codes used by the different services in turn yielded the Ultra intelligence that would affect so much of the conduct of the Second World War. There are a number of first-class works dealing with Enigma and Ultra, some of which we will discuss during the course of this chapter.

[6] The majority of academic historians would disagree with that statement, because most believe that history has little relevance to policy makers. Moreover, many believe that using history in thinking about current problems is somehow a violation of professional ethics. Nevertheless, such a belief was clearly the intention of Thucydides in writing his history of the Peloponnesian War.

ambiguous picture. Much of the British success during the Second World War lay in the art of taking the bits and pieces of successful intercepts and decrypts as well as other intelligence and stitching them together into an understandable picture.[7]

The most important reason for using British intelligence in World War II as a model lies in the level of excellence the British achieved.[8] Over the last half of 1941, British intelligence against Dönitz's U-boat offensive was *by itself* decisive in lowering convoy losses significantly.[9] Rarely, if ever, in military history has intelligence achieved a similar level of success. At the same time German arrogance and carelessness created the conditions that led to the breaking of Enigma and then to the refusal to believe that the British had compromised Enigma – a deduction that should have been obvious, given the extraordinary Allied ability to show up at the right place and right time.[10] What clearly should have been detectable to the Germans was how the Allies acted, and those actions, having proved suspiciously successful over and over, should have raised questions not once or twice, as was the case, but innumerable times.

What then might be the similarities or differences between the challenges of 1939 and those that confront America's intelligence agencies in the global war on terrorism? In September 1939 Britain possessed only the barest infrastructure of intelligence, despite the fact that the British had been in the business in a relatively serious fashion since before the First World War. Therein lay both advantage and disadvantage in comparison with the current situation of the United States. The British had to begin with only a small bureaucratic framework, while U.S. intelligence agencies today possess a vast array of analysts and capabilities. Nevertheless, both the British of 1939 and the Americans of today confronted the need to make major changes in the culture of their intelligence agencies.

---

[7] This would be called in current terminology "all source analysis," and for the most part, the British excelled at putting various sources together to create a coherent picture.
[8] One might, of course, use the model of American intelligence in the Second World War, but then one would have to make constant references to the British system, since the British passed much of their organizational and other skills to their American allies. This was not true in the Pacific where the Americans dominated the gathering and dissemination of intelligence.
[9] This chapter will discuss these successes and suggest why they were important.
[10] Along these lines, it is worth noting that on the Eastern Front, Soviet maskirovka (deception) efforts were so successful that from 1942, German intelligence failed to predict the location of every single major offensive the Soviets launched through the end of the war. For Soviet deception efforts, see particularly David Glantz, *Soviet Military Deception in the Second World War* (London, 1989).

And the Britain of 1939, like the United States at the beginning of the twenty-first century, confronted a war of interminable length in the conflict with the Third Reich, and eventually Italy and Japan.

The sparseness of their prewar intelligence organizations forced the British to raid their universities for the best talent available – a major advantage. Given the threat to Britain's existence, there were few impediments to recruiting the "best and the brightest" – especially in the early years of the war as the nation mobilized. The Second World War was about Britain's very existence, its values, and its way of life.[11] The Nazi enemy had already established a substantial lead both in military and psychological terms.[12] Moreover, the British had focused their intelligence efforts through 1939 on diplomatic and economic aspects of the rise of the Third Reich as opposed to its military buildup and capabilities, although the latter played a role as much for its contribution to British debates over defense budgets as for interest in and understanding of German combat capabilities.[13]

On the other hand, the supporting structure for a massive intelligence effort did not exist. Thus, the British had to create that bureaucratic structure at the same time that they grappled with the strategic and operational problems raised by the catastrophes of the 1939–1941 period. This effort involved changing the existing prewar intelligence culture to make intelligence organizations more responsive to the challenges Britain confronted.[14] One of the more valuable lessons of comparing the two periods lies in the fact that cultural and intellectual understanding was

---

[11] Only Winston Churchill, of all Britain's politicians, recognized that Nazi Germany represented not only a strategic danger to Britain, but a moral danger as well. For most of the 1930s, he was a pariah among British politicians for holding such old-fashioned views. Only after the seizure of the remainder of Czechoslovakia in March 1939 did the British public begin to take him seriously again.

[12] The large number of bizarre stories that accompanied the German invasion of the Low Countries and France in 1940 underline the sinister menace that the Nazis were able to convey to their opponents in the late 1930s and that affected French and British intelligence.

[13] This chapter will focus on this factor in a separate section. What is important here is that Britain's intelligence agencies were forced to make a radical shift in their focus in September 1939, and the weaknesses in intelligence culture had an important impact on British intelligence in the war's early years. In the prewar period even military intelligence focused on supporting aspects of the British diplomatic effort such as the Anglo–German Naval Treaty of 1935.

[14] One might argue that the British confronted an easier problem than that which America's intelligence agencies confront today. They were creating a new culture in intelligence organizations that was expanding exponentially, and thus much of the cultural change occurred not only through the nature of the threat, but due to the newness of most of

as important to successful estimates of German capabilities and potential actions as were the hard decrypts of top secret messages from one *Wehrmacht* headquarters to another. What was important here in the contribution that intelligence made to the war effort – especially in regard to the U-boat war in the North Atlantic – was an increasing understanding of the German military's culture, something British analysts and military leaders could only gain through constant, long-term experience in inferring the mind of the enemy through his moves and action in various battle spaces.

Equally important was the translation of raw data into actionable intelligence – estimates that suggested German intentions. The problem then was to move that intelligence to those who needed it and could act on it. Initially, this involved persuading operators that intelligence really had something to offer. Given German successes in the early months of the war, few of which intelligence predicted, this represented no easy task. In fact, in the first war years some senior officers in the British military may have agreed with Clausewitz's characterization of intelligence: "Many intelligence reports in war are contradictory; even more are false, and most are uncertain.... In short most intelligence is false, and the effect of fear is to multiply lies and inaccuracies."[15] Nevertheless, in a relatively short period of time, British intelligence established a substantial level of trust between itself and the users of its products. It was then able to incorporate American intelligence into overall Allied efforts and to buttress U.S. military operations by passing its products directly to American commanders.

By late 1941, the British had created a highly effective, sophisticated intelligence system, based almost entirely on the careful recruitment of analysts from the civilian world. It was already making major contributions to operations on land, at sea, and in the air. Unfortunately for the Allied cause, it was still not able to make up for the tactical and conceptual failures in British military forces – particularly on the ground – but it had already tilted the playing field substantially against the Germans. Much of that success lay in personnel policies and decisions that British leaders made in the last months of peace and the first months of the war. Again, how the British established a winning team and then kept it working

---

the personnel. The American intelligence agencies, however, confront the problem of imposing a new culture on old and large bureaucratic organizations.

[15] Carl von Clausewitz, *On War*, trans. and ed. by Michael Howard and Peter Paret (Princeton, NJ, 1976), p. 117.

at an effective level has important implications for thinking about intelligence in the twenty-first century.

Nevertheless, despite all its skill and effectiveness, there were still substantial intelligence failures.[16] Those failures are also useful for thinking through the problem of intelligence in an ambiguous and uncertain world. Even with the advantages gained by breaking most of the important German military codes – especially those dealing with the *Luftwaffe* and navy – there were still substantial problems in understanding German intentions. The crucial point here is that intelligence is *always* prone to make mistakes even in the best of circumstances. Consequently, those who use intelligence should not expect too much, nor should intelligence agencies promise too much. In most cases, the best that policy makers and military leaders can expect are reasonable and plausible explanations of what the enemy might do with the understanding that he always has other courses of action open. And the incompleteness of the information available to intelligence analysts makes it inevitable that errors and misunderstandings will occur.[17]

This chapter aims to examine these issues. It begins by examining the heavy demands on British intelligence organizations, confronting in the late 1930s the devastating military capabilities the *Wehrmacht* possessed in the first years of the Second World War.[18] Addressing this threat required drastic changes in culture and personnel policies, which will be a major theme. We will do this by highlighting the careers of several leading British intelligence analysts as well as the general approach the British used in recruiting and using the talent on which they built their

---

[16] In the end what matters in war is the useful but often incomplete intelligence that gets into the hands of military leaders in time to be of use. Three outstanding books that bridge this gap are the memoirs of the British government's scientific adviser, R.V. Jones, *The Wizard War, British Scientific Intelligence, 1939–1945* (New York, 1978); the memoirs of one of the analysts at Bletchley Park, Ralph Bennett, *Ultra in the West, The Normandy Campaign, 1944–1945* (New York, 1980); and the official history of British deception efforts during the Second World War by the great British military historian Sir Michael Howard, *British Intelligence in the Second World War*, vol. 5, *Strategic Deception* (London, 1990).

[17] In this case, one must understand that those who analyze the past will always know what has happened. Thus, they inevitably find it easy to see what was important and what intelligence analysts should have seen but missed. Moreover, such observers, historians, and others possess the advantage of both time to sift the evidence of raw intelligence and the luxury of having none of the pressures under which intelligence analysts and policy makers inevitably work.

[18] For a discussion of those military operations, see particularly Williamson Murray and Allan R. Millett, *A War to Be Won, Fighting the Second World War* (Cambridge, MA, 2000).

intelligence capabilities. Finally, we will discuss the overall implications for thinking about intelligence in the twenty-first century.

My purpose is also to suggest parallels and approaches to intelligence that can inform those who confront the new challenges of the twenty-first century. To paraphrase Clausewitz, history can then form "a guide to anyone who wants to learn about [intelligence]...; it will light his way, ease his progress, train his judgment, and help him avoid pitfalls."[19] It cannot provide answers, but it can suggest the kinds of personnel and cultural questions that policy makers need to consider in addressing the emerging threats to the security of the United States and its allies.

The Problem: British Intelligence before the Second World War

From the vantage point of the twenty-first century, the interwar period between 1919 and 1939 possesses a clarity coherence that was clear to none of those who lived through those tumultuous years. To military planners and intelligence analysts, the interwar period represented a period of constant adjustment to shifting circumstances. Throughout the 1930s British intelligence focused on economic, diplomatic, and ideological issues. Military capabilities and developments remained within the purview of military attachés and the weak intelligence organizations the services maintained. Moreover, as with Britain's military capabilities, its intelligence efforts received minimum funding and attention from political leaders.

Not surprisingly, intelligence analysis was of inferior quality. This was particularly true of scientific intelligence, where the operatives of the Secret Intelligence Service – SIS or M.I.6 – swallowed the most bizarre stories of death rays and other such nonsense, supposedly being developed by the scientists of the Third Reich.[20] The products of British intelligence that are available in the open documentary records in the Public Record Office suggest analytic capabilities far inferior to those possessed by the Joint Planning Staff of the British Chiefs of Staff Sub-Committee.[21] Through

---

[19] Clausewitz, *On War*, p. 141.
[20] Jones, *The Wizard War*, pp. 63–64. As Jones suggests, the average SIS operative "was a scientific analphabet." Ibid., p. 63.
[21] In this regard see the paper prepared by the SIS (Secret Intelligence Service – now known as M.I.6) at the height of the Czech crisis in late September 1938 and compare it to the strategic assessments written for the Chiefs of Staff by the Joint Planning Committee at the same time: PRO FO 371/21659, C 14471/42/18, Secret Intelligence Service, 18.9.38. For the types of analysis that the service planners were capable of producing – in this case contradictory analyses despite the fact they were published one day apart – see PRO CAB 55/13, JP 315, 23.9.38., Joint Planning Committee, "The Czechoslovak Crisis;"

1938, British strategic analysis consistently overestimated German military and economic capabilities, sometimes wildly.[22] In 1939, however, those estimates and assessments suddenly shifted to providing a far more negative view of Germany's strategic situation, one that missed almost entirely the fact that the Third Reich's battlefield capabilities had now reached a tipping point, where the *Wehrmacht* would enjoy a substantial advantage over its opponents. Thus, estimates in 1939 emphasized German economic and military difficulties, which, however, were not sufficient to prevent the Germans from waging devastating operational campaigns.[23]

There was considerable irony in this swing because through fall 1938, German military capabilities were far weaker than British assessment depicted them; but in 1939, they were increasingly superior to British estimates. Why? It appears that the consistent under-funding of Britain's defenses drove British estimates more than a real feel for the German threat. In 1939, two factors interacted to alter the assessments at the time when the *Wehrmacht* was becoming really dangerous: first, in the aftermath of Munich, British intelligence received a considerable number of reports underlining German economic and military weaknesses in September 1938. Second, the radical altering of budget priorities in favor of defense in reaction to the German occupation of Prague in March 1939 seems to have generated a feeling of euphoria within Britain's military and intelligence organizations, despite the fact that the loosening of the budget strings on defense would have no real impact on British capabilities for at least a year, if not longer.

On 3 September 1939 Prime Minister Neville Chamberlain declared war on Germany in response to the Nazi invasion of Poland. Understaffed and underfunded, Britain's intelligence agencies now scrambled to make up for 20 years of neglect.[24] Moreover, the underfunded service

---

and PRO CAB 53/13, JP 317, 24.9.38., Joint Planning Committee, "The Czechoslovak Crisis." These documents underline how complex the business of estimating what an opponent might do as well as what his real military capabilities are, given the incomplete information available. The basic problem was that failures in analysis in the prewar period carried over into the wartime period.

[22] This aspect of British strategic assessment is discussed in Williamson Murray, *The Change in the European Balance of Power, 1938–1939, The Path to Ruin* (Princeton, NJ, 1984).

[23] The swing in British estimates between the 1935–1938 period and 1939 is ably laid out in Wesley Wark, *The Ultimate Enemy, British Intelligence and Nazi Germany, 1938–1939* (Ithaca, NY, 1985).

[24] In the immediate aftermath of the Anschluss – the German occupation of Austria – the British government authorized an increase in the intelligence budget. But six months

intelligence agencies had little understanding of how their opponents would fight beyond what they had observed during the First World War. Army intelligence throughout the Second World War never seems to have grasped the basic principles of German tactical or operational doctrine, in spite of the fact that much of the German approach to war was available in open source literature.[25] The RAF, for that matter, entirely ignored the lessons of what had happened in the air during the Civil War in Spain.

In terms of understanding the importance of intelligence and acting on it, only the Royal Navy was really prepared for the coming war. This was largely due to the fact that the navy's failure to utilize the decrypts produced by Room 40 at the Battle of Jutland in 1916 had cost the Grand Fleet an opportunity to destroy the German High Seas Fleet. A whole generation of British naval officers had relentlessly analyzed Jutland and Jellicoe's failures throughout the interwar period. As a result, senior officers proved more adaptable and willing to incorporate special intelligence directly into the conduct of naval operations. Nevertheless, one should note that the Royal Navy's archivists had destroyed all of the anti-submarine studies of World War I in the 1920s to save space on library shelves. There was a mad scramble to find those studies in 1939 with no success.

The British, whatever their weaknesses, had one enormous piece of luck in the immediate months before the war. In late August 1939 senior officers of the British, French, and Polish intelligence agencies met to discuss common problems in a war against the Third Reich. The Poles, unbidden by anything other than alliance spirit, provided their allies with the details of their work in breaking the German Enigma enciphering

---

after the Anschluss, in the aftermath of the euphoria over the "success" at Munich, the Chamberlain government again cut intelligence funding to previous levels. Not until the German seizure of Prague in March 1939 did significant increases occur in intelligence spending. F.H. Hinsley, *British Intelligence in the Second World War, Its Influence on Strategy and Operations*, vol. 1 (London, 1979), p. 51.

[25] Because the British Army had undertaken a lessons-learned analysis of the First World War too late (in 1932), it possessed no real understanding of the radical change in tactical concepts the Germans brought to their spring offensives in 1918. The Germans encapsulated those lessons in their basic doctrinal manual *Truppenführung (Troop Leadership)* (Berlin, 1933) that remained in force throughout the Second World War. Written by three of the most senior officers in the German Army, it told much about how the Germans were going to fight the coming war, but unfortunately it exercised little influence over the British Army's understanding of their German opponents throughout the Second World War. For a recent translation of the manual, see Bruce Condell and David T. Zabecki, eds., *On the German Art of War, Truppenführung* (Boulder, CO, 2001).

machine over the previous decade and a half. They included in the windfall two working Enigma machines, which arrived in London on 16 August 1939, barely two weeks before the German invasion of Poland.[26] Along with the Enigma copies, the Poles provided their mathematical work and the supporting machines they had designed to help break earlier versions of the Enigma.

During the interwar period, the British concentrated their code-breaking efforts in a single organization, the Government Code and Cypher School (GC and CS), under the Foreign Office. This proved most advantageous when war came because there was one central organization charged with code-breaking. Despite efforts by the services to regain control over code-breaking early in the war, GC and CS never lost control of that effort.[27] On the other hand, in the words of its prewar head, GC and CS became during the period before the war "an adopted child of the Foreign Office with no family rights, and the poor relation of the SIS [Secret Intelligence Service], whose peacetime activities left little cash to spare."[28]

As a result, even by the standards of Britain's overall intelligence effort, GC and CS was underfunded.[29] Ironically, that fact worked to the advantage of the British because even more than other intelligence agencies, GC and CS had to reach out to the civilian world to acquire the talent to break the German ciphers and then to turn raw intelligence into useful products when war came. Thus, in the last months before the outbreak of war, British intelligence was involved in a desperate effort to recruit talent to fill the void of what Churchill aptly termed "the locust years." Moreover, with the outbreak of war, British intelligence also had to address a new context – one vastly more complex and difficult than its efforts aimed at diplomatic and economic intelligence. Britain now confronted a world war against a German nation that had been preparing for war with a

---

[26] David Kahn, *Seizing the Enigma, The Race to Break the German U-Boat Codes, 1939–1943* (New York, 1991), pp. 80–81.

[27] This stands in contrast to what happened in Germany, where there were a number of different code-breaking efforts, which, while achieving some success, in the end led to a dilution of scarce intelligence resources.

[28] Quoted in Hinsley, et al., *British Intelligence in the Second World War*, vol. 1, p. 25.

[29] The problem is, of course, different with the current U.S. intelligence agencies, which are not underfunded, but misfunded. The funding during and after the Cold War has emphasized technology rather than intellectual capital, and thus they have found it difficult to adapt to a different environment. What is similar is that U.S. intelligence, as with the British before the Second World War, must figure out how to acquire substantial new intellectual capital.

ruthless, single mindedness over the previous six-and-a-half years. At the time, no one could predict how long the new war would last.

Expanding Intelligence and Changing Culture

This section examines not only how the British expanded their intelligence organizations, but also the personnel philosophy they adopted to create an extraordinarily responsive and adaptive system of analysis. To do so, we will consider the careers of three of the most important figures who came into the system either shortly before or immediately after the outbreak of war. In the largest sense, British intelligence mounted a massive trolling effort throughout the nation's leading universities and research establishments to recruit outstanding talent. To a considerable extent, this effort relied on old school ties and academic connections to identify the "best and the brightest" and to funnel scientists, mathematicians, and others who senior academics thought might be of use into the intelligence effort.[30] Admittedly, the old boy system would later contribute to the Philby-MacLean-Burgess-Blunt-Cairncross debacle of the early Cold War period that so damaged Western intelligence, but it worked exceptionally well in establishing the intelligence capabilities that contributed so much to the defeat of Nazi Germany.

The official history of British intelligence during the Second World War underlines the impact that this recruiting drive had on the culture and organization of Britain's intelligence agencies:

> [M]any of the new recruits had been drawn from the universities and similar backgrounds. Professors, lecturers and undergraduates, chess masters and experts from the principal museums, barristers and antiquarian booksellers, some of them in uniform and others civilians on the books of the Foreign Office of the Service ministries – such for the most part were the individuals who inaugurated and manned the various cells which had sprung up within or alongside the various sections. They contributed by their variety and individuality to the lack of uniformity.[31]

If that lack of uniformity carried with it the seeds of considerable conflict and disagreement between the new interlopers and careerists in the

---

[30] The extent and success of the trolling effort is suggested by the fact that one of the most successful cryptanalysts recruited to work at Bletchley Park was Mavis Lever, an 18-year-old student of German at London University. Upon arriving at Bletchley she received the greeting: "Hello! We're breaking machines! Have you a pencil? Well, here you are." Kahn, *Seizing the Enigma*, p. 139.

[31] Hinsley, *British Intelligence in the Second World War*, vol. 1, p. 273.

intelligence world – which it did – it also brought crucial advantages. As the official history argues:

> It was difficult for the Service directorates to distinguish between the real and growing need for a stronger higher administration at GC and CS, one that would be more effective in negotiating... about the unavoidable clashes of priority and personality that accompanied GC and CS's increasing importance to the intelligence effort, and, on the other hand, the value of accepting and preserving the conditions of creative anarchy, within and between the sections, that distinguished GC and CS's day-to-day work and brought to the front the best among its unorthodox and 'undisciplined' war-time staff.[32]

Not surprisingly, there was considerable tension between the bureaucratic norms of those still enveloped in peacetime practices and those driven by the needs of the war. The latter won and a number of senior intelligence officials from the prewar period found themselves replaced by those more amenable to the new culture and atmosphere of wartime intelligence – a culture where wartime results counted for more than bureaucratic niceties.[33]

The head of the Royal Navy's Intelligence Division in the immediate prewar period, Commander Alistair Denniston, played a major role in the recruitment effort. He understood that the navy needed exceptionally talented individuals – "astute men," as he noted to his seniors.[34] Beginning in 1938, he raided the leading British universities – particularly Oxford and Cambridge – for talented professors and lecturers in fields ranging from mathematics – of obvious importance to breaking codes – to history and German literature. GC and CS had an obvious need for mathematicians such as Alan Turing and Gordon Welchman in the cryptanalysis business, and their contribution to the breaking of the Enigma is well known in intelligence circles. What is not so well known except by the afficionados of the Enigma story is the crucial role played by the softer academic disciplines in the actual turning of the intercepted message traffic into usable intelligence through an understanding of the Germans and their military system.

One of the interesting aspects of those recruited was how well lawyers and historians performed in the business of intelligence analysis. The

---

[32] Ibid., pp. 273–274.
[33] Churchill himself remarked – after a visit to Bletchley Park – to Sir Stewart Menzies, the head of the SIS: "I know I told you to leave no stone unturned to find the necessary staff, but I didn't mean you to take me so literally!" Kahn, *Seizing the Enigma*, p. 185.
[34] Patrick Beesly, *Very Special Intelligence, The Story of the Admiralty's Operational Intelligence Centre, 1939–1945* (Garden City, NY, 1978), p. 11.

crucial attribute possessed by those who worked in these two fields was the ability to put together coherent explanations on the basis of incomplete information. In the largest sense, first-class historians and lawyers must build their cases in reconstructing the past by getting inside the minds of those whom they study. Denniston returned to Oxford and Cambridge in summer 1939, this time to recruit undergraduates – those whom their professors recommended as having special talents and imagination. Among them was a young Cambridge undergraduate, Harry Hinsley, whose career this chapter will examine later.[35]

But it was not just academics to whom British intelligence reached out during this period. It also recruited from among well-connected lawyers and even a leading editorial writer for the *Times*.[36] Most fit into the expanding intelligence bureaucracy with little or no difficulty; they would make useful contributions to the overall war effort, but remain cogs in the great, vast empire that British intelligence analysis became. However, there were a few individuals of exceptional talent and effectiveness, who, as the war unfolded, proved themselves to have unusual abilities to understand the Germans and how the pieces of intelligence fit together. The system treated them differently. As they emerged as key players, they received positions of major importance, and on their recommendations and interpretations the British and American military would make increasingly momentous decisions.

Because of the Chamberlain government's unwillingness to expend significant resources on national defense, the intelligence agencies identified many of these individuals before September 1939 but could not bring them into government service or even give a clear idea of what their tasks might be. R.V. Jones, a government physicist with a deep interest in national security, was partially responsible for the effort to enlist physicists for future service in the prewar period. In March 1938 he wrote D.R. Pye, Director of Scientific Research at the Air Ministry, that "if war were to break out tomorrow, the scientific directorates of the services would find themselves overwhelmed by volunteers, and much valuable time would be wasted in finding out what posts they are best suited for, and the necessary – and as far as I know unforeseen – expansion would

---

[35] Ibid., p. 72.
[36] The point here is not that they were picked because they were well connected, but rather within the ranks of the British society there existed some areas of meritocracy, the members of which were willing to give honest and ruthless evaluations of individuals. This was particularly true in the British academic world and is still true today, where a letter of recommendation by a British academic actually means something.

have to be effected."[37] Pye, as a good bureaucrat serving in an Air Ministry, which was to display an astonishing disinterest in technological change, expressed little interest in Jones' suggestion.[38] Luckily, Sir Henry Tizard, one of Britain's leading scientists, took up the proposal, and by the time war broke out, Britain's leading physicists had been enlisted in British scientific efforts, including intelligence.

R.V. Jones: The Scientist as Intelligence Analyst

Jones himself had sacrificed a promising academic career to participate in top secret research that supported the creation of the air defense system.[39] Thus, he had a clear idea of how the bureaucracy did or did not work. At the outbreak of the war, he found himself assigned to the Air Ministry's intelligence branch and immediately proposed creation of a section devoted to uncovering what new weapons the Germans were developing, coordinating the intelligence work between the services on scientific matters, and executing deception efforts to mislead the Germans as to what the British were doing. In particular, he suggested that the organization be small and "that quality was much the most important factor."[40] His memorandum received general approval except from the Admiralty, the bureaucrats of which argued that the scientists working on its programs were more than sufficient to keep up with the Germans. As Jones points out in his memoirs:

> The fallacy in the argument was to be shown up by future episodes in the war. Plausible as it seems, the scientific experts in one country are not necessarily as good at assessing evidence as independent intelligence officers. It may happen for some reason that they have not developed a particular weapon either because they have not thought of it or, more likely, they have thought of it but have done some careless work which has led them to the wrong conclusion and have decided that the development is not feasible.[41]

Jones himself ran into such opposition in 1940 – an opposition that came close to costing the British the war. Before the war, the Germans

---

[37] Jones, *The Wizard War*, p. 33.
[38] This is not to suggest that extraordinary scientific work was not being performed in Fighter Command under its inspiring leader Air Marshal Sir Hugh Dowding. But Dowding was the exception among senior RAF officers in his interest in and acceptance of the potential of new technologies throughout the interwar period.
[39] Because he was involved in secret research, he could not publish any of his work in academic journals, and hence had no published research work to qualify him for an academic position in one of Britain's universities.
[40] Jones, *The Wizard War*, p. 74.
[41] Ibid., p. 75.

had managed to develop blind bombing capabilities far in advance of anything possessed by their opponents by using radio beams.[42] Alerted by their analysis of what had happened in both the ground and air war of 1914–1918, the Germans were further warned by their experiences in Spain that bombing accuracy at night or in periods of bad weather was not a matter of hundreds of yards, but tens of miles. In the late 1930s they set out to develop radio beams to intersect over a target as a means of solving the blind bombing problem. They succeeded. In the prewar period, British intelligence picked up none of their work along these lines because none of the British scientists had conceived of such a use of technology – nor was anyone worried in Bomber Command about bombing accuracy.[43]

Nevertheless, early in the war Jones had gotten some hints of *Knickebein*'s existence from shot down German aircraft and prisoner interrogations that the Germans had some kind of blind bombing capability that was carried on certain bomber aircraft in a specialized squadron.[44] These were skimpy leads at best. In mid-June 1940 he received from Bletchley Park one of the early decrypts of the *Luftwaffe*'s signal traffic that simply said: "Cleve Knickebein [crooked leg] is confirmed (or established) at position 53 degrees twenty-four minutes north and one degree west."[45] On the basis of that information and earlier ambiguous evidence, Jones surmised the Germans were preparing to use intersecting radio beams to guide night time bombing attacks on Britain in the near future.

With a few other pieces of evidence gathered in the succeeding week, Jones stood virtually alone against almost the entire scientific and military establishment of Britain. Nevertheless, Churchill's scientific adviser, Lord Cherwill (Professor Frederick Lindemann at the time) provided Jones support and access to the prime minister. But for Churchill's intervention,

---

[42] Jones' account is particularly useful to see how far individuals will go to disprove ideas with which they do not agree. Ibid., chap. 11.

[43] Nor for that matter did any of the senior officers in the RAF believe that bombing accuracy at night or in bad weather was going to be a problem. Not until summer 1941 did Bomber Command discover how inaccurate its bombing efforts against the Germans had been so far in the war. The Butt Report, commissioned by Churchill, examined night-time photos taken by British bombers and discovered that only one in three British bombers were capable of hitting a target with an area of 75 square miles. For the actual Butt Report, see Sir Charles Webster and Noble Frankland, *The Strategic Air Offensive Against Germany*, vol. 4, *Appendices* (London, 1962).

[44] That squadron turned out to be the first pathfinder squadron. The RAF would not create a similar squadron until 1942, and then over the protests of the head of Bomber Command's chief, Air Marshal Arthur Harris – who had also dismissed the possibility that the Germans were using radio-guided bombing devices in June 1940.

[45] Ibid., p. 93.

Jones' surmise would have been dismissed out of hand. The showdown came when Jones, a 28-year-old scientist, briefed RAF leaders, senior governmental scientists, and the prime minister himself. Churchill reports the scene in his memoirs: "When Mr. Jones had finished [his case for the existence of the beams] there was *a general air of incredulity*.... Being master, and not having to argue too much, once I was convinced about this queer and deadly game, I gave all the necessary orders that very day in June for the existence of the beam to be assumed" (my italics).[46]

Churchill somewhat overstates what happened in the meeting because, in fact, he only ordered the RAF to carry out airborne tests to evaluate Jones' analysis. Nevertheless, the prime minister recognized that Britain could not take the chance of simply dismissing the possibility that the Germans possessed blind bombing capabilities, even though that was what most of his senior advisers wished to do. The balance of forces was too tenuous to allow intelligence and technological assumptions to determine the fate of the nation.[47] At least Jones had some evidence to back up his arguments for the existence of the beams.

The ensuing tests in turn proved the existence of the beams, and that knowledge played a critical role in allowing the British to develop counter measures over summer 1940 to blunt the effectiveness of the *Luftwaffe's* blind bombing capabilities.[48] Jones' reputation was so enhanced by his analysis that from that point on he played a major role in Britain's scientific intelligence throughout the remainder of the war. In the end, it was Churchill who had provided the drive that consistently overruled a hidebound bureaucracy with a demand "for action this day."

F.H. Hinsley: The Undergraduate as Key Intelligence Analyst

Despite the fact that he was still an undergraduate at Cambridge when the war broke out, F.H. Hinsley already possessed the highest admiration of his academic supervisors, who recommended him to Denniston in the last month of peace.[49] After the war, he returned to Cambridge where he

---

[46] Winston S. Churchill, *The Second World War*, vol. 2, *Their Finest Hour* (Boston, 1949), p. 386.

[47] Had the British not jammed the blind bombing beams on which the Luftwaffe's bombers depended, the "Blitz" bombing of British industry and cities would have been far more effective.

[48] For the importance of British foreknowledge of the beams during the German night Blitz of the British Isles, see Williamson Murray, *Luftwaffe* (Baltimore, MD, 1985), chap. 2.

[49] In fact, in one of the great ironies of the Second World War, Hinsley was in Germany in the last days of peace working on his German. He only got out in the last moments

would become professor of international history and gain an academic reputation as a major military historian.[50] In between he became one of the key figures in the interpretation and analysis of signals intelligence that supported the Royal Navy. At first, however, as a junior recruit Hinsley was shuffled off to what was regarded as a relatively unimportant job – namely the arcane business of traffic analysis of the German Navy's signal communications. Hinsley threw himself into his work, and by early 1940 he and the others in the naval section had sketched out the framework for the *Kriegsmarine*'s organization, including the call signs of its individual ships.

In early April 1940 Hinsley picked up a major increase in German radio traffic in the Baltic that indicated movements into the Heligoland Bight were afoot, as well as the fact that the Germans had introduced an entirely new Enigma code in the area.[51] While he did not predict the German invasion of Norway and Denmark, he certainly did suggest that something big was in the works. However, the Admiralty's Operational Intelligence Centre (OIC) disregarded his analysis. After all, in their eyes he was still a young Cambridge undergraduate. On 9 April 1940 the German invasion of Denmark and Norway began, and the British were caught entirely flat footed.[52] As a result, the Germans were able to seize Norway's major ports and airfields on the first day and thereby win the campaign.

In early June 1940, Hinsley warned that heavy units of the German fleet were at sea – possibly the *Scharnhorst* and the *Gneisenau* – and that they might take "offensive action."[53] Although Hinsley did not know it, the Royal Navy was at that time engaged in a massive withdrawal from

---

of peace between Britain and the Third Reich on 1 September 1939 two days before Chamberlain's declaration of war. The Germans did nothing to stop a harmless British university student from exiting the Reich – a mistake that would cost them dearly in the coming years. Hugh Sebag-Montefiore, *Enigma, The Battle for the Code* (New York, 2000), p. 47.

[50] He was also to become the head of the effort that produced the official history of British intelligence in the Second World War.

[51] Kahn, *Seizing the Enigma*, p. 121.

[52] Had the Royal Navy been alerted that the Germans were coming out, there is little doubt that the Germans would have lost much of their fleet at the beginning of their attack on Norway and the whole invasion might have failed. The one place where the British reacted quickly was at Narvik, where a small force of British destroyers sank or damaged five German destroyers and their oiler, thus ensuring that the other five could not be refueled and thus could not escape – they were all sunk by the battleship *Warspite* several days later.

[53] Ibid., p. 122.

northern Norway. Again, the OIC ignored his analysis. The result was that German battle cruisers caught the Royal Navy's carrier *Glorious* with inadequate escort and sank both the carrier – with a full squadron of Hurricanes and their pilots on board – as well as its accompanying destroyers.[54]

From this point on, the Admiralty and the OIC paid the closest attention to Hinsley. Hinsley himself, 50 years after the loss of the *Glorious*, admitted that "I was a young civilian who as [the Admiralty] correctly assumed, knew nothing about navies." What still caught his attention in the 1990s was "the alacrity" with which the OIC responded to the loss of the *Glorious*. He was immediately invited to London to see how the OIC and the Admiralty worked. The navy then sent him to Scapa Flow for one of what turned out to be several visits to the Home Fleet, where he had the opportunity to talk extensively not only with the commander-in-chief's staff but also with Admiral Tovey himself. He was even taken to sea on a sortie by the Home Fleet. Finally, the Admiralty ensured that Hinsley would be invited to London on a regular basis to exchange ideas on what the *Kriegsmarine* was up to.[55]

By 1941 Hinsley was a major figure at Bletchley Park. This is not to say that everyone was happy to see such a young "junior" civil servant regarded so highly by senior officers of the Royal Navy. Even in the OIC, where the senior leadership was now eagerly seeking Hinsley's advice, some of the watch keepers at OIC were still attempting to freeze him out. As one of his colleagues noted in October 1941: "That [many middle rank at the OIC] should be jealous of [Hinsley's] success is understandable, and that they should dislike him personally is a small matter, but that they should be obstructive is ruinous."[56] With his background in German fleet dispositions and communications, Hinsley understood what Alan Turing and others involved in the mathematical analysis of Enigma needed to enable them to break into the German U-boat codes. As he suggested in a speech in 1996: "And that is where people like myself who were

---

[54] The captain of the *Glorious* appears to have been the worst kind of senior naval officer, entirely ignorant of carrier capabilities and flying operations and unwilling to take any advice from his subordinates. Thus, he was caught with no sailors on watch for possible enemy units and with not all of the *Glorious'* boilers in operation. The first warning that the British had that German battle cruisers were in the area came when 11' shells began falling among their ships. For a fuller discussion of the incident, see Murray and Millett, *A War to Be Won*, p. 65.

[55] F.H. Hinsley, "BP, Admiralty, and Naval Enigma," in F.H. Hinsley and Alan Stripp, eds., *Code Breakers, The Inside Story of Bletchley Park* (Oxford, 1993), p. 78.

[56] Sebag-Montefiore, *Enigma*, p. 126.

non-mathematical came into the story. It was because I was in close touch with [Alan] Turing, for example, that I was fully aware of what he had to have before the machine [the bombe – the first step on Turing's road to inventing the computer] which he had developed could exercise its powers."[57] In spring 1941 the relationship with his fellow Cambridgite Turing paid large dividends. It led to the most important coup of the Second World War, the one place in the war where Ultra intelligence by itself exercised a decisive impact on the course of events.[58]

In spring 1941 the U-boat offensive was swinging into high gear and the monthly losses of British and Allied merchant vessels in the Atlantic had reached well over 300,000 tons. Meanwhile, Bletchley Park appeared no closer to breaking into the U-boat Enigma traffic. Turing made clear to Hinsley that if the cryptanalysts could acquire the settings for a sustained period of time, they would have a shot at breaking the U-boat traffic over the long haul.[59] One day, Hinsley suddenly had "a passing thought" and remembered that German weather ships off the north coast of Iceland had been transmitting their reports on weather conditions in the same Enigma code as the U-boats were using.[60] And since they were on station for sustained periods of time, he surmised that it was likely that they carried the Enigma settings for the whole period they were at sea.

Because of the strain on the Royal Navy in fighting the Battle of the Atlantic, no one had thus far thought it necessary to take the *Kriegsmarine*'s weather ships out. Now on the recommendation of a 21-year-old Cambridge undergraduate, the Royal Navy executed a major cutting out operation to seize the weather ships. So highly did its leaders think of Hinsley and his advice as to where they could capture the Enigma

---

[57] Hinsley, "The Influence of ULTRA in the Second World War," p. 3.
[58] Not all historians of Ultra agree on this point, but Hinsley makes a compelling argument in favor of Ultra's impact in diverting convoys to avoid U-boat lines and thereby decreasing merchant ship losses by approximately 200,000 tons per month over the next six months. See Hinsley, *British Intelligence in the Second World War*, pp. 168–176.
[59] What such a period would give British cryptanalysts was a sense of the cribs in the German system, which they had not been able to gain thus far in their efforts. It was this developed sense of the weaknesses in the German efforts to protect the Enigma that allowed the British to break into the U-boat message traffic even when they no longer possessed the settings. The addition of a fourth rotor to the Enigma machines on U-boats closed Bletchley Park off from reading the U-boat traffic for most of 1942. Nevertheless, that six-months experience of reading the traffic played a major role in creating the second break into the U-boat traffic – a success that was one of several contributing factors to victory in the Battle of the Atlantic in May 1943 and a period that lasted the remainder of the war.
[60] Kahn, *Seizing the Enigma*, p. 154.

settings that the operation was mounted on short notice and counted three cruisers and four destroyers from the home fleet under a vice admiral.[61] The resulting capture of the weather ship *München* provided the British with significant Enigma materials, including settings for the next two months. That capture was followed almost immediately by the capture of U-110, captained by Julius Lemp, one of the great U-boat aces, with more Enigma material. Neither was sufficient, and the British mounted a further cutting out operation that netted a second weather ship, the *Lauenberg*, in late June. This yielded more cipher material, according to the Admiralty, of "inestimable value."[62]

As a result of these seizures, Bletchley Park was able to break into the U-boat Enigma on a regular basis for the next six months. Armed with key decrypts indicating where Dönitz was positioning his U-boat patrol lines, OIC was able to maneuver Allied convoys around the U-boats into open ocean. British losses of merchant shipping dropped by two-thirds – a dramatic reduction that removed much of the growing tension on Allied shipping. However, in early 1942, the Germans introduced a new rotor into the Enigma machine and another period of terrible trials entered into the Battle of the Atlantic.

Not surprisingly, given his contributions thus far in the war, Hinsley's career at Bletchley Park continued to prosper. Yet, there were times when his reputation was not sufficient to deflect senior leaders from making mistakes that cost sailors their lives. In July 1942 he reported that the *Tirpitz* was not at sea; nevertheless, Admiral Dudley Pound, the First Sea Lord, surmised that the great battleship was out and ordered convoy PQ 17 to scatter – a decision that led to the destruction of virtually the entire convoy. There were, however, relatively few such episodes. When Hinsley spoke, the Admiralty listened – a remarkable achievement for one who had yet to achieve even an undergraduate degree.

---

[61] Ibid., 156.
[62] Beesly, *Very Special Intelligence*, p. 74. Beesly rates the success of these operations in the following terms: "Nor was the German confidence that, once the validity of the current settings had expired our cryptanalysts would be again defeated, justified; we continued to read Hydra, albeit with varying time lags when periodically new settings had to be cracked, throughout the war. The penetration of this cipher, just when our other sources of information were also beginning to produce greatly improved results, at last enabled O.I.C. to function as it had always been hoped that it would. It was equivalent to a major victory in itself, but in addition led [Bletchley Park] on to successes with other ciphers, such as Neptune, the operational cipher for the heavy ships, and Sud and Medusa in the Mediterranean. The intelligence scales, which had hitherto been heavily weighted in favor of the Germans, were beginning to swing to our side." Ibid., pp. 74–75.

Commander Rodger Winn, R.N.V.R.

Apparently, from his earliest days Rodger Winn had dreamed of becoming an officer in the Royal Navy, but a bout of polio in his youth left him with a twisted back and a severe limp. With a career in the military not in the cards, he chose to become a barrister. By the outbreak of the war he had the reputation of possessing one of the sharpest minds in the British legal profession.[63] Despite his considerable infirmities and his age of 37, he was recruited as a civilian to serve in the tracking of German submarines at the war's outset.[64] In that capacity his extraordinary intelligence *and* ability to piece together estimates from scanty evidence (the Enigma codes for the U-boat fleet had yet to be broken) brought him to the attention of senior officers in the OIC. By summer 1940 it was clear to those officers that the current head of the submarine tracking room, despite his accomplishment in organizing and training the effort, was simply not up to wartime demands. They recommended that Winn take over the position. To do so, the Royal Navy had to commission him a commander in the Royal Naval Volunteer Reserves – an extraordinary mark of confidence in a man whose physical disabilities were such that he could not stand for long periods of time.[65]

By late summer 1940 Britain was confronting a growing threat from German U-boats, about which Churchill noted the following in his memoirs: "The only thing that ever really frightened me during the war was the U-boat peril."[66] Intelligence would prove the key to victory or defeat in the navy's ability to address the growing ferocity of German attacks on the convoys. Little over a year after his assignment to naval intelligence and the submarine tracking room, Winn found himself in charge of developing the entire intelligence picture of U-boat operations in the North Atlantic. One of the factors in Winn's assignment to this critical

---

[63] After the war Winn returned to the legal profession, ending his career as a Lord Justice of Appeal, one of the highest positions in the British legal system. Beesly, *Very Special Intelligence*, p. 58. It is worth noting that the buildup of America's intelligence agencies during the war also involved the wholesale incorporation of many of the best legal minds on Wall Street into the higher levels of intelligence work. Alfred McCormack, a major figure in legal circles on Wall Street, received the task of assessing U.S. signals intelligence procedures immediately after Pearl Harbor. Other major legal figures included Telford Taylor, a major prosecutor at the Nuremberg trials, and Lewis Powell, a future justice on the Supreme Court.

[64] Again, the old-boy system seems to have been working.

[65] Beesly, *Very Special Intelligence*, p. 58.

[66] Winston S. Churchill, *The Second World War*, vol. 2, *Their Finest Hour* (Boston, 1949), p. 598.

position was the fact that, even before Bletchley Park broke the U-boat Enigma, his sixth sense, based on traffic analysis, allowed him to assess accurately the potential rerouting of ships to avoid German submarines with much greater success than anyone else.[67] Single-mindedly, he concentrated his mental powers on following and then determining how Dönitz was deploying his U-boats to catch the great convoys of Allied shipping. That focus day-in and day-out provided him with a unique and irreplaceable understanding of how the German U-boat command was operating.

The breaking of the operational Enigma code for U-boats in summer 1941 provided Winn and his subordinates with a vantage point not only to affect the Battle of the North Atlantic directly by maneuvering convoys around the U-boat patrol lines, but an opportunity to get inside the decision-making cycle of the U-boat command itself. Thus, the six months during which the British were reading the U-boat Enigma in 1941 created a deep understanding among Winn and his team of the thinking that lay behind the decision making of the U-boat high command. When the Germans introduced another rotor into the U-boat Enigma machines in early January 1942, they shut Bletchley Park out of decrypting their transmissions for most of 1942. But the insights gained during the first six months of reading the U-boat traffic exercised a continuing, though less successful, impact over the Battle of the Atlantic.

Winn's chief subordinate, Patrick Beesly, has best captured the extent of his boss's contribution to the intelligence war against the U-boats:

> The task of handling Special Intelligence was by no means a simple one, despite impressions to the contrary given in some recent books, but it certainly was not beyond the capabilities of ordinary intelligent individuals. What could not be replaced were Winn's own unique gifts: his ability to read Dönitz's mind, his knack of swiftly sorting the wheat from the chaff, and selecting from a mass of evidence that which was of prime and immediate importance and that which was of real significance: his ability to put forward unpopular or at least inconvenient views and above all his forensic skill in persuading the naval staff to accept and rely on his judgment, and indeed also on the judgment of his subordinates.[68]

Beside his immense contributions to the British side of the U-boat war, Winn would make a significant contribution to the American effort. During the first six months after the United States entered the Second World War, Dönitz concentrated his U-boats off the east coast of North America;

---

[67] Beesly, *Very Special Intelligence*, p. 59.
[68] Ibid., p. 159.

quite simply, the Germans slaughtered American shipping, which the U.S. Navy was unprepared to protect.[69] German submarine skippers characterized Operation "Drumbeat" as "the second happy time."[70] Beside the general unpreparedness of the Americans to protect their shipping from U-boat attack, the U.S. Navy had nothing to equal the Royal Navy's OIC. Thus, it was unable to translate the raw data of intercepts, direction finding, and traffic analysis into intelligence on which its anti-submarine forces could act.

Desperate because of German successes, which were severely threatening the vital sea lines of communication to the United Kingdom, the British sent Winn over to the United States to provide guidance and advice on how the Americans might establish the equivalent to the O.I.C.'s submarine tracking room. He immediately ran into a brick wall. But whatever his disabilities, Winn was a tough and unusually blunt Englishman. When a senior American admiral suggested to Winn "that the Americans wished to learn their own lessons and that they had plenty of ships with which to do so," Winn replied with considerable heat: "The trouble is, Admiral, it's not only your bloody ships you are losing; a lot of them are ours."[71] Within a matter of weeks, Admiral Ernest King had ordered establishment of the equivalent to the Admiralty's OIC to help run the war against the U-boats.

Thinking about the Future: What the Past Suggests

Like Britain in 1940, the United States today confronts a war of indeterminable length against an opponent who is both skilled and tenacious. Clearly, given the nature of that opponent, it appears that intelligence will be one of the critical enablers in the American response.[72] Yet, the nature of the opponent, who appears to be following Mao's strategy by swimming in the sea of the Islamic masses, suggests that the understanding

---

[69] This represented one of the least excusable defeats U.S. forces would suffer during the course of World War II. For a popular account of the U-boat campaign along the east coast of the United States, see Michael Gannon, *Operation Drumbeat, The Dramatic True Story of Germany's First U-Boat Attacks Along the American Coast in World War II* (New York, 1991). See also the excellent chapter in Eliot A. Cohen and John Gooch, *Military Misfortunes, The Anatomy of Failure in War* (New York, 1990).

[70] The first "happy time" had come in summer and fall 1940, when most of the Royal Navy's destroyers were tied up on Channel duty to protect against SEALION.

[71] Beesly, *Very Special Intelligence*, pp. 114–115.

[72] It also appears that victory, at least in conventional military terms, may not be possible. At best, success may simply involve keeping terrorist attacks by Al Qaeda and its like actions down to tolerable levels.

gained through cultural studies, linguistic capabilities, historical analyses, and pattern analyses will be every bit as important as the massive technologies that America's intelligence agencies were able to build up during the decades of watching and analyzing trends in the Soviet Union during the Cold War. Technology will undoubtedly play an important role in the decades long war against terrorism, but it will be only a portion of what will be necessary to hold the enemy at bay.

There are two aspects to this. The British certainly depended for their great success in intelligence over the course of the war on the mathematical and computing skills of those who contributed to the breaking of codes at Bletchley Park as well as to the scientific knowledge of first-rate scientists, such as R.V. Jones and Solly Zuckerman.[73] Yet, they also depended on individuals who possessed a cultural and historical knowledge of their German opponents. Thus, on one hand the British recruited and emphasized intelligence skill sets on the basis of the fact that they were confronting an opponent who was fully their equal – and in some respects their superior – in scientific and technological capabilities.[74] On the other hand, even though the Germans were Britain's neighbor across the North Sea, there still existed enormous cultural and historical differences between the two nations. British intelligence could cross that cultural divide only by bringing to its intelligence efforts a number of individuals whose intellectual skills had nothing to do with science, technology, or mathematics, but rather whose expertise dealt with the language, history, literature, and cultural aspects of the German nation and military.[75] That latter group proved so crucial in turning raw data into intelligence that it could and did tip the playing field against the Germans.

---

[73] This chapter has not examined Zuckerman's contribution and background, but it was every bit as interesting and important as that of R.V. Jones. Like Jones, Zuckerman was a first-class scientist, but a biologist rather than a physicist. He would become the chief scientific adviser to Air Marshal Arthur Tedder, who was the RAF's commanding officer in the Mediterranean and then became Eisenhower's deputy at Supreme Headquarters Allied Expeditionary Forces Europe. As Tedder's adviser, Zuckerman developed the concept of the transportation plan, which crippled Rommel's defense of Normandy and then the transportation plan that brought about the collapse of Nazi Germany's war economy in February 1945. For Zuckerman's career see his autobiography: Solly Zuckerman, *From Apes to Warlords, The Autobiography (1904–1946) of Solly Zuckerman* (London, 1978).

[74] In some respects their superior, which ironically worked to the advantage of the British because the Germans overestimated their own sophistication, while underestimating the British capacity to develop workarounds.

[75] In this respect, a weakness in British intelligence analysis was that no one in the analytic community appears to have really understood the doctrinal framework of decentralized

One should also note that the British were careful in how they chose and then directed their analysts. For the most part, analysts remained in the areas to which they were assigned at the beginning of the war. Even after the combined efforts of the British, Canadian, and American navies mastered the German U-boat menace in the climactic battles of May 1943, Winn remained at his post, running the submarine tracking branch of the OIC. Even in the desperate days of summer and fall 1940, there was no effort to surge analysts from one threat to another. The result was that first-rate analysts like Winn were able to gather a deep understanding of how their opponents were likely to act.

Winn clearly managed to acquire a sixth sense – what the German military refer to as a *Fingerspitzengefühl* – about how Dönitz was maneuvering his patrol lines of U-boats in the North Atlantic. But there were many others, including Jones and Hinsley, who could piece together obscure pieces of information to build a coherent picture of German intentions, precisely because they remained focused on one specific aspect of the intelligence puzzle throughout the entire course of the war.

Equally important to thinking about what the experience of British intelligence during the war suggests is the nature of the personnel policies that drove the British system of recruitment and promotion. We have already quoted Jones's memorandum on the personnel that Britain needed to recruit for analyzing the Third Reich's scientific effort – "quality was much the most important factor."[76] This more than any other single principle drove British recruitment and personnel policies throughout the war in regard to intelligence. There were no short cuts in this regard. Moreover, the British were willing to seek out individuals, such as Winn, whose career field (in Winn's case the law) appeared to have little to do with the business of intelligence. Nor was age necessarily a factor where quality was concerned. Hinsley was barely out of his teenage years, while Winn was approaching middle age.

Nevertheless, no matter how impressive the talent pool that the British recruited might have appeared on the surface, most of those recruited

---

command and control in which the German Army worked. Thus, when the OKH (German Army high command) ordered Rommel in North Africa to undertake certain actions, British analysts assumed that he would obey those orders. In fact, he rarely paid attention to what Berlin ordered him to do. Hence, British intelligence about the intentions of the German high command were correct, but it miscalculated the actions Rommel might take, because no British commander would ever disobey explicit instructions from London.

[76] Jones, *The Wizard War*, p. 74.

were simply going to provide talent at the middle level. Only a few were going to possess the level of "imagination" – to use the *9/11 Report's* emphasis on the key factor in the 2001 failure – that could make a significant contribution to the war against the Germans. In the largest sense, the British problem resembled that of a major league baseball team in terms of its initial draft of high school and college players. Most of those it drafts will prove to be adequate ball players: 250 hitters, good fielders, adequate pitchers. But what really matters is the identification and then the care and feeding of future stars, such as Derek Jeter and Mariano Rivera, both of whom the Yankees drafted in 1994 and who were in the big time within two years, and who within four years were emerging stars. Clearly, the British were able to do this – in spite of the jealousy that occurred among the many left behind, including those who had put long years in the bureaucracy of peacetime intelligence.[77]

What seems of critical importance in meeting the intelligence challenges of the coming decades is the need for greater attention to the recruitment of fewer but more talented individuals.[78] This would partially focus on the recruitment of truly exceptional undergraduate and graduate students straight from the university campuses. But as with Winn, America's intelligence organizations should also think about bringing in exceptional talent at the middle and upper levels. Such individuals would have proven their capabilities in other fields such as business, the law, and academics. And they would be brought in with both financial inducements as well as the inducements of responsibility in charting intelligence for the nation's security.

What does not exist in the peacetime atmosphere in which the federal government's bureaucracy – or the great majority of the nation for that matter – is a career path similar to that which marked Hinsley's rise from a 20-year-old undergraduate to a position as one of two or three key naval

---

[77] This was certainly the case also with the U.S. Army in the Second World War. The army promoted people on the basis of competence regardless of seniority. Moreover, George C. Marshall in 1940 in the midst of starting the massive mobilization of the U.S. Army felt strongly enough about education to assign Colonel W.H. Simpson and Major J. Lawton Collins to serve as instructors at the U.S. Army War College. Four years later Simpson would find himself a three-star general in command of Ninth Army in the European Theater of Operations, while Collins would be one of the most successful corps commanders in the war – one of the few to serve in both the Pacific and in Europe. He would be chief of staff of the army after the war.

[78] There is, of course, a fine line between recruiting what is necessary to keep the bureaucracy functioning in a period of stress and recruiting the best for the long-term struggle. To a great extent, the British did both. One of the major challenges confronting U.S. intelligence is how to do both, given the demand for short-term results.

analysts at Bletchley Park with access to the highest levels of the British government within a year. Nevertheless, America's intelligence agencies need to identify the future stars that it recruits off campuses, and then as the truly exceptional individuals begin to identify themselves, they should be protected from the invidia of those less capable.

In addition, the future Hinsleys should be provided considerable opportunities to further their schooling – to attain PhDs in fields that support their analytic work.[79] If they already possess doctorates, they should be allowed to pursue post-doctoral research and other academic work that will continue their education. Moreover, the personnel systems should provide extensive language training and opportunities for the best analysts to live, where possible, in the nations and areas in which their special interests lie. Some of these opportunities could come from assignments within the government. Others would allow them to work and observe independently in various parts of the world. Assignments to U.S. embassies simply cannot provide the inside knowledge of other cultures and peoples that U.S. intelligence will need in the twenty-first century.

Beyond recruiting of exceptional individuals and personnel policies that contribute to a deepening of their analytic insight and understanding of particular areas of the world, it seems that U.S. intelligence needs to reach out to the exceptionally talented in the world beyond Washington. The British were able to bring exceptional individuals like Jones and Winn directly into the work of intelligence because of the nature of the threat. The current situation now appears quite different. Yet, the understanding that exceptional academics, business leaders, or legal minds possess would be every bit as useful to addressing today's threats as those recruited by the British in the late 1930s. Here, the federal government needs to create the possibility of real exchanges with academic and other worlds that understand the world outside the Beltway, and even more important, outside the United States. This will, of course, bring about considerable resistance from many in the intelligence agencies, not to mention many academic institutions.[80] Yet, given the vast flow of information across the frontiers that at one time sharply delineated nation states, such an ability

---

[79] Here we are not talking about sending hundreds or even tens of analysts off for graduate type work. Five or six per year would be more than sufficient. One might also note that such tours for the exceptional would not only serve to keep them on board, but serve as periods to prevent burnout of the best analysts, while at the same time improving the depth and breadth of their analytic skills.

[80] For many of the same reasons, it is not just left-wing prejudice in academia that would hinder such contacts, but the jealousies of colleagues about those who actually were thought important enough to consult with the government.

to fold external sources into the processes of American intelligence seems absolutely essential.

There are no easy, short-term solutions to the problems and challenges that confront American intelligence in the first decade of the twenty-first century. But it seems that American intelligence needs new cultural emphases. Britain's example in the Second World War suggests some of the paths that might be usefully explored in pushing those changes on bureaucracies that are comfortable and inevitably resistant to change.

13

The Meaning of World War II

One cannot look across the long, seemingly endless rows of crosses and Stars of David that dot the cemeteries at Omaha Beach, St. James, and elsewhere in Europe and the Pacific without a sense of the terrible cost of victory in World War II. The cold stone memorials underscore the ages of those whose lives war cut short at eighteen, twenty, twenty-four, thirty years – men who never again saw their families and homes. And as each year passes, fewer and fewer visitors come to these lonely corners of America.

As the past recedes from memory to words printed on a page, historians will start to depict victory in that terrible conflict in soft, ill-measured words. They will suggest that our efforts were nothing more than the reverse side of a coin – that in fact there was little moral worth to the Allied cause, that for every German or Japanese war crime there were similar American or British crimes (a Hamburg, Berlin, or Dresden), the refusal to bomb the rail lines to Auschwitz, the starvation of German POWs at the war's end, or Hiroshima – undoubtedly this summer we will hear ceaseless comments about dropping the atomic bomb on Japan as a "crime against humanity."

These purveyors of moral equivalence are wrong. It is well that we realize, in considering its human cost, why the war was fought and why there is a moral dimension to the Allied victory. Perhaps nothing delineates the

---

This chapter was originally written for *Joint Forces Quarterly* in 1994 for publication on the 50th anniversary of the end of World War II. Having spent much time walking the long rows of crosses in American cemeteries in Normandy and the Low Countries, I felt particularly honored to be asked to write the this work.

character of World War II better than the ambitions and actions of our opponents. Adolf Hitler aimed, in the words of one historian, at nothing short of a "biological world revolution" – the conquest of Europe and beyond, the enslavement of Slavs, the elimination of all differently abled (to use the modern euphemism for handicapped), the extermination of European and possibly world Jewry, and the creation of a great Aryan empire that would rule from Gibraltar to the Urals and last "a thousand years."[1] Japanese objectives were perhaps less coherent, but propaganda about a "Greater East Asian Co-prosperity Sphere" suggests a dramatic plan to restructure Asia – including the enslavement of much of China, an effort that, if not equal to the viciousness of Hitler's "New Order," certainly resulted in extraordinary crimes against humanity.

Thus, behind the murderous execution of operational campaigns came ideological and racial baggage in both the European and Pacific theaters that made the war phenomenal even in the long, violent history of the human race. German attacks on Warsaw, Rotterdam, London, and Belgrade were out-and-out attempts to intimidate opponents into surrendering through the wholesale murder of civilians by air power; and the *Luftwaffe* was highly successful in that endeavor, killing 17,000 Serbs in a single day.[2] In the late 1930s the Japanese lacked the capabilities for strategic bombing, but the "Rape of Nanking" illustrates Tokyo's contempt for international law and the treatment of civilians at the outset of what eventually turned into its war against every ethnic group in Asia.

Moreover, from the outset German forces displayed a callousness toward both civilians and prisoners of war that represented a sharp break with the practices of World War I. The killing of over a hundred British POWs at Le Paradis in May 1940 was the first in a series of incidents involving the *Waffen SS*.[3] The execution of Canadians by the murderous juvenile delinquents of the 12th SS Panzer Division, *Hitler Jugend*,[4] the

---

[1] See MacGregor Knox, "Conquest, Foreign and Domestic, in Fascist Italy and Nazi Germany" *Journal of Modern History*, vol. 56, no. 1 (March 1984), pp. 1–57.

[2] In the case of Belgrade, Operation Gericht (Punishment) killed some 17,000 Serbs. On German attitudes toward strategic bombing at the beginning of the war, see Williamson Murray, *German Military Effectiveness* (Baltimore, MD, 1992), pp. 39–52.

[3] At Le Paradis, soldiers of the *SS Totenkopf* Division killed no fewer than 110 members of the Royal Norfolk Regiment, but the authorities never investigated the incident. George H. Stein, *The Waffen SS, Hitler's Elite Guard at War* (Ithaca, NY, 1966), pp. 76–78.

[4] Guides to Normandy indicate that 18 Canadian bodies were found at Abbe d'Ardennes, headquarters of the 12th SS Panzer Division outside Caen. A recent visit to the site revealed that 27 bodies now have been discovered, and according to a local construction foreman the number goes up each year.

slaughter of French civilians at Oradour-sur-Glan by troops of the 2nd SS Panzer Division, Das Reich,[5] and the slaying of Americans at Malmedy by Peiper's SS troops in late 1944[6] typified behavior among Hitler's ideological legions in the west. The east was an order of magnitude greater in the level of criminality displayed by German forces. As *Waffen SS* soldiers told their interviewer Max Hastings, Oradour-sur-Glan was small potatoes compared to what had happened in the east.

But the largest military crime – one that makes other incidents pale – was the treatment of Soviet POWs by the *Wehrmacht*, not the SS. By the end of the 1941 campaign, the Germans claimed to have captured over 3.6 million Soviets in the great encirclement battles of Operation Barbarossa.[7] What ensued was a calculated policy of starvation and murder, of which the infamous commissar order represented only the tip of the iceberg.[8] In March 1942 Field Marshal Keitel received a memo indicating that of the approximately 3.6 million POWs captured in operations against the Soviet Union barely a hundred thousand were fit to work. The vast majority had already perished from starvation, exposure, or disease.[9] By 1945 only 100,000 of the Soviets captured in 1941 had survived the maltreatment inflicted on them in work camps. Throughout the war, particularly in the 1941 campaign, the German army was delighted to undertake "special action" (*Sonderbehandlungen*) against East European Jews.[10] Beyond the villainy of the military lay the ferocious crimes of the Nazi regime that resulted in the extermination of 6 million Jews solely

---

[5] See Max Hastings, *Das Reich, The March of the 2nd SS Panzer Division through France* (London, 1993) for a further discussion of the murderous activities of the division as it moved north from Toulouse to Normandy.

[6] Peiper and fellow criminals were condemned to death by an American military court, but the sentence was commuted to life imprisonment through the efforts of Senator Joseph McCarthy, and they were then almost immediately released by the post-war West German government.

[7] The Soviets, not surprisingly, contested that number, but even their figures suggest that millions of their soldiers fell into German hands during the course of the campaign.

[8] For details on the savage treatment of Soviet POWs by the German army during the war, see *Kristian Streit, Keine Kameraden, Die Wehrmacht und die sowjetischen Kriegsgefangenen* (Stuttgart, 1979).

[9] Ibid., p. 9.

[10] On the German army's enthusiastic support for the final solution, see Horst Boog et al., *Das Deutsche Reich und der Zweite Weltkrieg*, vol. 4, *Der Angriff auf die Sowjetunion* (Stuttgart, 1983), pp. 413–51; Jürgen Förster, "Hitler's War Aims Against the Soviet Union and the German Military Leaders," *Militärhistorik Tidshrift* (1979), pp. 83–93; Christian Streit, "The German Army and the Policies of Genocide," in *The Policies of Genocide: Jews and Soviet Prisoners of War in Nazi Germany*, ed. by Gerhard Hirschfeld (London, 1966).

on the basis of their race, the murder of 3 million Poles, and the death of more than 20 million plus Soviet citizens – a record unequaled even by Stalin and Mao.

Japanese crimes in the Pacific never reached the levels of German atrocities, though not for lack of trying. The "Rape of Nanking" set the standard for the Imperial Army's conduct in China. Throughout the war the Japanese carried out extensive experiments in biological warfare, including conducting live vivisections and dropping bubonic agents on Chinese villages.[11] One suspects, given the lack of control that Tokyo exercised, that the military would have unleashed terrible plagues in China if it had developed the capabilities.[12] What Japan did inflict more generally on occupied Korea and China has yet to be fully examined by historians.

Thus, there was a moral as well as strategic dimension to the war that the Allies waged in Europe and Asia. Unfortunately, only Churchill among the leaders of Western democracies had recognized in the 1930s that Nazi Germany represented a strategic as well as moral threat to the survival of democratic values and regimes. But conventional wisdom had considered his views old fashioned and no longer relevant in a world where intelligent people recognized that war was no longer an instrument of statecraft. Even Churchill's stirring words after the ruinous Munich agreement could not shake the government or citizens out of the complacent belief that surrendering Czechoslovakia "had achieved peace in our time." The British continued a policy of appeasement for six months and refused to mobilize for the coming struggle. Because Europe was so far away, American policy makers were even less willing to recognize the threat and support measures needed to prepare the nation.

Fortunately, geography and the enemy's stupidity allowed the Anglo–American powers to escape the full consequences of their folly. When France fell in 1940, Britain's position seemed hopeless. It was not. Churchill galvanized the will of a nation outraged by Nazi aggression.[13]

---

[11] See Peter Williams and David Wallace, *Unit 731: Japan's Secret Biological Warfare in World War II* (New York, 1989).

[12] One of the most disgraceful post-war decisions was not to bring those Japanese involved in bacteriological warfare to trial. Instead, the authorities decided to enlist their help in the American program. This undoubtedly raised the suspicion of the Chinese and explains why they accused the United States of using such weapons during the Korean War.

[13] No one at the time foresaw how extraordinary German actions would be in the war. One historian argues that London could have reached an acceptable accommodation with Berlin in 1940 to save the empire. But Churchill supposedly dragged Britain down a road of slavish surrender to American interests – one that inevitably spelled destruction

Fighter Command, under Air Marshal Sir Hugh Dowding, provided that measure of effectiveness to keep Britain in the war and allow the United States more than a year to repair its considerable military deficiencies.

In 1941 the Germans turned a favorable situation against themselves. First, they launched a great racial crusade against the Soviet Union, one that aimed not only at the extermination of Jews but the enslavement of Slavic peoples on Soviet territory. Ironically, the ferocity and ruthlessness with which the Nazis waged ideological war drove the Soviet peoples to support Stalin's criminal regime, which many of them would have been delighted to overthrow. In the end Barbarossa also foundered on German intelligence misestimates and logistic mistakes that still take one's breath away. An August 1941 quotation from the diary of General Franz Halder, chief of the general staff, suggests the extent of the Nazi intelligence failure:

> The whole situation makes it increasingly plain that we have underestimated the Russian colossus, who consistently prepared for war with that utterly ruthless determination so characteristic of totalitarian states.... At the outset of the war, we reckoned with about 200 enemy divisions. Now we have counted 360. These divisions are not armed and equipped ac-cording to our standards, and their tactical leadership is often poor. But there they are, and if we smash a dozen of them, the Russians simply put up another dozen. The time factor favors them, as they are near their resources, while we are moving farther and farther from ours. And so our troops... are subject to the incessant attacks of the enemy.[14]

The logistic mistakes accumulated from the first step into Russia to wreck what little chance the Germans might have had to overthrow Stalin's regime in 1941. Quite simply, even as winter approached in November 1941, and every step in the advance on Moscow prevented the Germans from building up supply dumps to meet the trials of a Russian winter or even from moving winter clothes to the front, Halder could only idly hope that perhaps it would not snow until January.[15]

The evidence suggests that the Japanese surprise attack on Pearl Harbor, followed shortly by Hitler's declaration of war on the United

---

of the empire. What such an argument misses, of course, is the nature of Hitler's regime and that any accommodation, as Vichy France illustrates, would have led to a surrender of the British soul. For an exposition of this position, which reveals how far historians can be removed from reality, see John Charmley, *Churchill: The End of Glory: A Political Biography* (New York, 1993).

[14] Franz Halder, *The Halder War Diary, 1939–1942*, ed. by Charles Burdick and Hans-Adolf Jacobsen (Novato, CA, 1988), entry for August 11, 1944, p. 506.

[15] Klaus Reinhardt, *Die Wende vor Moskau, Das Scheitern der Strategie Hitlers im Winter 1941/1942* (Stuttgart, 1972), p. 140.

States, sealed the fate of the Axis. Certainly that was how Churchill saw the strategic situation in December 1941 before meeting with Roosevelt in Washington. But whatever economic and military advantages America, Britain, and the Soviet Union had over Germany, Japan, and Italy, victory could only come after great land, sea, and air campaigns with terrible casualties. Given the nature of the opposition, there was no other road.

Moreover, the defeat of the Axis required the use of force in a fashion that more squeamish times – when the fundamental survival of the West was less directly threatened – have found repugnant. The Combined Bomber Offensive against Germany is perhaps the prime example; critics of that great Anglo–American effort have seized on its supposed immorality in killing and maiming hundreds of thousands of "innocent" Germans as well as its supposed lack of effect. In fact, that effort was not pretty; it did lead to the death of civilians. And it did not reach the over-optimistic goals that its advocates had intended.

But the bomber offensive was essential to winning the war in Europe: it broke the back of the *Luftwaffe*, and without that achievement it is doubtful whether Allied forces would have made a lodgement on the French coast in June 1944.[16] It wrecked the French transport system, a key element in the success of the Normandy landings. It diverted more than 20,000 high-velocity anti-aircraft guns and half a million soldiers to the defense of the Reich – assets that would definitely have played a more useful role in the ground battle. It had a direct impact on the morale of German civilians, although how that impact actually translated into an Allied advantage is difficult to calculate. It wrecked the German oil industry and from summer 1944 on had a significant impact on the mobility of German ground forces.[17] Finally, the destruction that it wreaked on the transportation network in fall and winter of 1944 prevented the Nazis from making a last stand among the ruins of the Thousand Year Reich.[18] Consequently, it is clear that the strategic bombing of Germany was as

---

[16] For a detailed exposition of the Combined Bomber Offensive, see Williamson Murray, "Reflections on the Combined Bomber Offensive," *Militärgeschichtliche Mitteilungen*, vol. 51 (1992), Heft 1.

[17] For example, when the Soviets hit Silesia in January 1945 the Germans had 1,800 tanks to defend the province, but no fuel. As a result, most of Silesia fell into Soviet hands in less than a week. Sir Charles Webster and Noble Frankland, *The Strategic Air Offensive Against Germany*, vol. 3 (London, 1962), p. 239.

[18] See in particular Alfred C. Mierzejewski, *The Collapse of the German War Economy, 1944–1945; Allied Air Power and the German National Railway* (Chapel Hill, NC, 1988).

vital to victory as the battles on the Eastern Front, or the struggle to control the sea lanes of the North Atlantic, or Allied ground operations in Western Europe after June 6. There was nothing pretty or redeeming about the effort itself; but there was *no other choice.*

Similarly, when it comes to dropping the atomic bomb on Japan, one must look beyond the horror of that event to examine what other courses of action were available. The argument that the enemy was ready to surrender at that point in the war, to put it bluntly, is virtually unsupported by the evidence except in unrealistic proposals that the Japanese foreign ministry sent to Moscow. It was careful not to inform its military masters about the proposal because of the consequences.

By August 1945 the American military had determined on an invasion of the Home Islands that would begin with Kyushu. The estimates provided by MacArthur's command appear to have been unrealistic in light of Okinawa and Iwo Jima, especially when intelligence already indicated that the Japanese were concentrating most of their forces on Kyushu along southern beaches where landings would occur.[19] But even MacArthur's estimates, however low they appear in retrospect (approximately 40,000 killed and 200,000 total casualties), were equivalent to the casualty level suffered by the U.S. Army from Normandy to the Bulge.[20] As one historian pointed out, any president who allowed U.S. forces to suffer such casualties without first using the atomic bomb would have faced immediate impeachment, given the political realities of 1945.[21]

But the most terrible results of a refusal by America to use the bomb would have impacted the Japanese themselves. Fighting on Kyushu would have visited a terrible fate on that island's peasant population, and not only would the fighting have killed tens of thousands, but starvation in the Home Islands as well as mass suicides aided and abetted by the Japanese military (as happened on Okinawa) would have swollen the number of civilian casualties. Finally, one might also note that prolonged combat on Kyushu would undoubtedly have resulted in Soviet operations against

---

[19] It is more likely that the level of ferocity and losses would have replicated Okinawa. But instead of 200,000 casualties, America would probably have suffered as much as twice that among its ground and naval forces.

[20] Americans in the Pacific had fewer illusions about the level of casualties in an invasion of the Home Islands than MacArthur's staff or historians born years later. See Paul Fussell, "Thank God for the Atomic Bomb: Hiroshima, A Soldier's View," *The New Republic* (August 22–29, 1981), pp. 26–30.

[21] Peter Mazlowski, "Truman, the Bomb, and the Numbers Game," *Military History Quarterly*, vol. 7, no. 3 (Spring 1995), pp. 103–07.

Hokkaido and perhaps the main island itself with a resulting Soviet zone of occupation in the north that would have had a devastating impact on post-war Japan.

The terrible war on which the survival of democracy depended did not halt the endless struggles that Thucydides foretold in *The Peloponnesian War*; but democratic values survived and, under the leadership of the United States, those values were maintained throughout another great contest that lasted almost to the end of this century. But the great victories of 1945 and 1989 were attributable to the will of America to defend its values and traditions with the lives of its young men and women. The long white rows of markers in Arlington and cemeteries across Europe and the Pacific bear mute testimony to that courage and dedication.

Index

Abraham, Plains of, 109, 177
Adolphus, Gustavus, 87–89, 104
air power
  nuclear weapons and, 266
  theories of, 58, 232–235, 252–254, 262, 266
Aix-la-Chapelle, 176
Albania, 124
Alexander the Great, 33
Alma, Battle of, 184
Al-Radi, Nuha, 276–277
Al Qaeda, 17n15, 36
Alsace Lorraine, 202
Angell, Norman, 26
Afghanistan, 7, 13
Airborne Warning and Control System (AWACS), 268
American Civil War
  French Revolution and Industrial Revolution, fusion of, and, 169–170, 182, 193
  planning and, 113–115, 135, 146
  principles of war and, 73–74
American Independence, War of, 110, 134, 177
Amherst, General Jeffrey, 109
Anglo-German Naval Treaty of 1935, 286n13
Annapolis. *See* United States Naval Academy
An Nasariyah, 92n32
Anschluss, 220, 290n24
Archidamnus, King, 8n11, 23, 55

Ardennes Forest, 149, 151, 250–252
Armies, U.S.
  Third Army, 77
Arnold, General Henry, 241, 263
Athens, 24–25, 53–56, 132
Atlantic, Battle of the, 127, 131, 229, 301–302, 304
atomic bomb, 311, 317
Auschwitz, 311
Austerlitz, Battle of, 14n2, 46
Australia, 130
Austrian Empire, 116, 133, 185, 187–188
Austrian Succession, War of, 108, 134, 175
Austro-Hungarian Empire, 183, 193, 212–213
Austro-Prussian War. *See* Seven Weeks' War

Balkans, 20n23
battle space dominance, 4, 30, 68–69
BARBAROSSA, Operation
  Hitler and, 123, 205–206
  logistics and, 150, 221, 315
  Luftwaffe and, 226
  Moscow, advance on, 222, 315
  planning and, 90, 210–211
  red teaming and, 150, 160
  Roosevelt and, 129
  war crimes and, 313, 315
  Wehrmacht and, 150, 160
Bazaine, Marshal Achille, 190–191
Beatty, Vice Admiral David, 227
Beaufre, General André, 162n70

Beck, Ludwig, 122, 156n49, 204n21, 205, 208, 219
Beesly, Patrick, 304
Belgium, 118, 148, 173, 211
Belgrade, 312
Benedek, General Ludwig, 187
Berlin, Battle of, 263
Berlin Wall, 117n48, 170
Beyerchen, Alan, 66
bureaucracies, 34
  conformity of thought and, 36–37
  nature of, 35
  overregulation of, 37
Bismarck, Otto von
  Franco-Prussian War and, 188–189, 191–192
  Seven Weeks' War and, 187–188
  statesmanship of, 10, 182–183, 185, 195–196
  strategic vision of, 10, 115–117, 185–186
Blenheim, Battle of, 106n22, 173
Bletchley Park, 222, 228, 293n30, 300–302, 304. *See also* Ultra intelligence
Blomberg, General Werner von, 199–200
Blount, Major General Buford, 5
Blitzkrieg, 143, 154
Bock, Field Marshal Fedor von, 210
Bolshevik Revolution, 19n19, 170
Bomber Command, 11, 235
  area bombing and, 236, 238, 255
  OVERLORD, Operation, and, 238
  target accuracy and, 242–243, 297
  targeting priorities and, 237, 251
Bonaparte, Napoleon, 73, 75, 110–112, 134, 179
Borodino, Battle of, 14n2, 46, 180
Braddock, General Edward, 108, 176
Bradley, Omar, 13
Brauchitsch, Field Marshal Walter von, 210, 220–221
Britain
  air power and, 233–235. *See also* Royal Air Force
  Air Ministry and, 296
  appeasement policy and, 314
  Austrian Succession, War of, and, 175–176
    strategic bombing and, 11. *See also* Combined Bomber Offensive
  Committee of Imperial Defence and, 125
  Crimean War and, 112–113, 183–184
  expeditionary warfare and, 106, 108
  French Revolutionary and Napoleonic Wars and, 110–112
  Gallipoli Campaign and, 51, 120, 214
  Higher Command and Staff Course and, 145
  intelligence organizations of, 12, 283
    Admiralty Operational Intelligence Centre (OIC) and, 299–300, 302, 305
    analysis of intelligence and, 284, 287, 289–291, 299–301
    bureaucratic framework of, 285–286
    civilian recruitment and, 286–287, 292–296, 298, 303, 306–307
    Cold War and, 293
    culture of, 286(nn13, 14), 293–294
    Enigma machines and, 292, 301–302
    effectiveness of, 284, 285, 287, 306–307
    funding of, 289–292
    Government Code and Cypher School (GC and CS) and, 292, 294
    interwar period and, 289, 292
    Secret Intelligence Service and, 289
    scientific development and, 296–298
    signals intelligence and, 284
    U-boat offensive and, 285, 300–305
  merchant shipping and, 227, 229, 302
  Mesopotamian River Valley rebellion of 1920 and, 5–6
  military institutions of,
    adaptation in war and, 41
    Chiefs of Staff and, 214
    naval power. *See* Royal Navy
    red teaming and, 157–159
  resistance movements and, 127
  Runciman mission and, 27
  Seven Years' War and, 108–110, 175–177
  Spanish Succession, War of, and, 105–107, 172–175
  strategic shifts and, 20–21
  World War I and, 26–27, 119–120, 125, 135
Britain, Battle of, 202, 224–226, 239
British Expeditionary Force, 41, 148, 191n50, 214
Brodie, Bernard, 76

Bruchmüller, Lieutenant Colonel Georg, 216
Brüning, Chancellor Heinrich, 204
Bulge, Battle of the, 93
Burnett-Stuart, General Sir John, 158
Bush, President George H.W., 68, 267

Caesar, Julius, 102
Canada, 109
Capelle, Admiral Eduard von, 228
Caribbean, 173–174, 177
Caucasus, 20n23
Central Command Air Force (CENTAF), 269
Central Intelligence Agency (CIA), 13, 36
Chamberlain, Neville, 13, 41–42, 125, 290
Charles XII of Sweden, 15n5
China
  emerging threats and, 34, 36, 78,
  World War II and, 124, 312, 314
Colonies, British North American, 108–110
Churchill, Winston
  British intelligence and, 286n11, 297–298
  Dardanelles and, 119–120
  Gallipoli Campaign, 51, 120
  leadership of, 126, 166, 314, 316
  Royal Navy and, 93, 119
  World War I and, 17–18, 119–120, 170–171
  World War II and, 126, 151, 243, 263, 292, 297–298, 303, 314
Clausewitz, Carl von
  conduct of war and, 3
  friction and, 29, 50–52, 254
  intelligence and, 287
  policy and, 206
  relevancy of, 31, 59, 66
  revolutionary war and, 168–169, 178–179
  theory of war and, 47–50, 74
  works on, 60, 66
Clinton, Sir Henry, 110
Clive, Robert, 109
Coalition Force Land Component Commander (CFLCC), 5, 76
Cold War, 20, 34, 64, 99, 164
Collins, Major J. Lawton, 308n77
combined arms tactics, 120–121, 154, 203, 219

Combined Bomber Offensive, 11, 224, 316
  area bombing offensive and, 244, 255–256, 258, 262
  attrition of aircraft and pilots and, 253, 258
  blind bombing capabilities and, 238
  divided approaches and, 237, 240
  Eighth U.S. Air Force and, 238–240, 242n30, 258
  industrial dispersion and, 240
  long range fighters and, 243, 246
  oil campaign and, 241–242, 244, 246–249, 259–260, 263
  targeting priorities and, 237, 239, 241, 250–251, 258, 263
  transportation campaign and, 241–242, 249–252, 260–261, 263
  Ultra intelligence and, 242n30, 247–248, 251, 263
Combined Joint Task Force-7, 76
Constantine, Emperor, 86
Corcyra, 54–55, 57
Corps, U.S. Army
  Third Army, 77
  V Corps, 77
Corinth, 54–55
Crimean War, 112–113, 183–184, 188
Cromwell, Oliver, 172
Czechoslovakia, 27, 42, 205, 208, 290, 314

Dardanelles, 119–120
De MacMahon, Marshal E.P.M., 191
Denmark, 186, 215, 299
Denniston, Commander Alistair, 294
DESERT SHIELD, Operation, 274. See Gulf War
DESERT STORM, Operation, 265, 281. See also Gulf War
Dien Bien Phu, 64
Dill, Field Marshal Sir John, 158, 161
Division, U.S. Army
  3rd Infantry Division, 5
Division, U.S. Marines
  1st Marine Division, 5, 130
Dogger Bank, Battle of, 227
Dönitz, Admiral Karl, 123, 202, 214, 302, 304, 307
Douhet, Giulio, 58, 233n4
Dowding, Air Marshal Sir Hugh, 29n55, 243, 296n38, 315
Drumbeat, Operation, 305

Dugan, Lieutenant General Michael, 266
Dunkirk, 191n50
Dutch Republic, 105–107, 172–174

Eaker, Lieutenant General Ira, 239
Edward III of England, 103–104
effects-based operations, 31n64
Einsatzgruppen, 206
Eisenhower, President and General Dwight D., 63–64, 130, 132, 241
Elizabeth I of England, 104n18
Enigma encryption
    code-breaking and, 229, 284–285, 294, 299, 302
    Poland and, 291–292
    U-boats and, 300–304
    weather ships and, 228, 301–302
    Wehrmacht and, 222. See also Ultra intelligence
Enlightenment, 106n22
England, 86, 104, 134n97
Eugene of Savoy, Prince, 106–107, 173
Euripides, 16

Falkenhyn, General Erich von, 33n71, 117n49, 149
Fascism, 15n5, 21
Federal Bureau of Investigation (FBI), 36
Fingerspitzengefühl, 138
First World, 24, 26, 78
Fontenot, Colonel Greg, 80n18
Forrest, Nathan Bedford, 73
Fourth Generation War, 33
France, 104. *See also specific named wars*
    Austrian Succession, War of, and, 175–176
    Combined Bomber Offensive and, 241–242
    Crimean War and, 112–113, 183–184
    interwar period and, 39, 143
    Louis XIV, reign of. See Louis XIV
    military effectiveness and, 111
    nationalism and, 178–179, 185, 189
    professional military education and, 39n92, 40
    red teaming and, 143, 145, 149–151, 161n67, 162–163
    Seven Years' War and, 107–110, 175–177
    Spanish Succession, War of, and, 105–107, 172–174

Vietnam and, 15, 80n19
World War I and, 118, 120, 148, 218n67, 219
World War II and, 143, 220, 226, 249, 261, 316
Franco-Prussian War, 115–117, 145, 169, 182, 185, 188–193
Franks, General Tommy, 77
Frederick the Great, 75, 88, 108, 175–177, 179
French Revolution, 21, 106n22, 168–170, 177–178, 182, 193
French Revolutionary Wars, 110–112, 134
Fritsch, Werner von, 156n49, 219
Fuller, Major General J.F.C., 72–73

Galbraith, John Kenneth, 11, 231–232
Galland, General Adolf, 246
Gallipoli, 51, 120, 214
Gamelin, General Maurice, 149–151, 162n70, 163
Gat, Azar, 75
Gavin, Lieutenant General James, 64
George, Prime Minister David Lloyd, 75
Gericht, operation, 312
Germain, George, Lord, 110, 176n18
German operational and tactical effectiveness
    Army and, 216–223
    combined arms doctrine and, 219–220
    decentralized control and, 218
    defensive warfare and, 218–219
    logistics and, 221–222
    intelligence and, 222–223
    Kriegsmarine and
        Enigma and, 228–229, 301–302
        surface operations and, 227
        U-boats and, 227–229, 285, 300–305
    Luftwaffe and, 223–226
        Battle of Britain and, 224, 226, 239
        blind bombing capabilities and, 226, 297–298
        close air support and, 223
        intelligence and, 225–226
        logistics and, 225
        strategic bombing and, 223, 256
        target objectives and, 224
German strategic effectiveness
    allies and, 212–213
    assumptions and, 209–211

confusion of strategy and operations, and, 206–209, 211
industrial mobilization and, 211–212
logistics and, 211–213
politics and, 208, 230
Germany. *See also* Prussia
aircraft production and, 240–241, 246, 256–259
air defense and, 238, 255–258
air force. *See* Luftwaffe
Army Group Prince Rupprecht and, 149
chemical warfare and, 118n52
close air support doctrine and, 215–216
crimes against humanity and, 311–316
Czechoslovakia and, 42, 205
Dolchstoss legend and, 209, 272
Einsatzgruppen and, 206
Enigma. *See* Enigma
geographic positioning of, 196–197
German approach to war and, 10, 206, 209, 291. *See also* German strategic effectiveness
interwar period and, 58–59, 122, 205, 219, 228
industrial dispersion and, 240, 246, 258
Kaiser Reich and, 183, 195–197, 205, 216
Kriegsakademie and, 40
military institutions of
armored warfare and, 201
bureaucratic structures of, 197–200
civil-military relations and, 202–206
financial resources of, 200–201
joint operations and, 213–216
military culture and, 10, 118, 196
military effectiveness. *See* German strategic effectiveness; German operational and tactical effectiveness
red teaming and, 145n17, 148–151, 154–156, 160–161, 164–165, 209
navy and, 209–210, 214, 228. *See also* Kriegsmarine
nationalism and, 204
oil industry and, 241
retaliation weapons and, 244, 256–258
rearmament and, 122, 126, 156, 200–201, 205, 212
Schutzstaffel (SS) and, 205, 312–313
Soviet Union and, *See* BARBAROSSA, Operation

Spanish Civil War and, 223
strategic bombing of, 126, 135, 238, 244, 251–252, 255–259, 316. *See also* Combined Bomber Offensive
technology and, 80, 201–202
Third Reich and, 122, 136, 199, 204–205
12th SS Panzer Division (*Hitler Jugend*) and, 312
U-boat offensive and
merchant shipping and, 127, 227
strategic bombing and, 245
support structure for, 227–228
tactics and, 202
United States and, 208
unrestricted submarine warfare and, 118, 123, 165, 198, 204, 208, 217, 227
unification of, 10, 116
Wehrmacht. *See* Wehrmacht
world conquest and, 27
World War 1 and
mistakes of, 6
disinformation campaign and, 26n45, 121
strategic planning for, 117–120, 135, 207–213
World War II and, strategic planning and, 122–125, 135
Gessler, Otto, 199
Giap, General Vo Nguyen, 25n40, 80n19
globalization, 26, 34, 44, 78–79
Glorious, HMS, 300
Glosson, Brigadier General Buster, 269n8
Göring, Field Marshal Hermann, 200, 214, 224, 257
grand strategy, 8–9
Grant, General Ulysses S., 74, m113
Gravellote, Battle of, 190
Gray, General Al, 67
Great Depression, 19–20, 34
Great Illusion, The, 26
Greater East Asian Co-Prosperity Sphere, 312
Greece, 53–55, 85, 124
Grey, Sir Edward, 17n14
Groener, General Wilhelm, 121, 199, 204, 209
Guadalcanal, Battle of, 124, 130, 136
Guderian, General Heinz, 149–150, 191n50

Gulf War of 1991, 58, 164
  Al-Firdos bunker and, 278–279
  aftermath of, 4
  Ba'ath Party and, 277–279
  Central Command Air Force (CENTAF) and, 269, 272, 274
  coalition policy and, 275–277
  collateral damage and, 275–278
  friction and, 265–266
  intelligence and, 269–270, 274
  Kuwaiti Theater of Operations (KTO) and, 273, 275, 279–281
  RAF and, 276
  strategic air campaign and, 267, 271–273
    air defense systems and, 273–274, 277
    chemical/nuclear/biological programs and, 273–274, 277
    command and control system and, 273, 275, 277
    SCUD missiles and, 273–275, 277
  tactical air campaign and, 273, 280–281
  ground campaign and, 272–273, 280
Gulf War Air Power Survey, 12, 58, 270n11, 275

Haber, Fritz, 118
Hadrian's Wall, 103
Hague conventions, 118
Haig, Field Marshal Douglas, 41
Haldane, Lieutenant General Aylmer, 5
Halder, General Franz, 160, 210
Halifax, E.F.L. Wood, Lord, 27
Halleck, Major General Henry, 73–74, 114
Hamburg, 255–256, 311
Hankey, Sir Maurice, 125
Hanover, 187, 188n46
Hapsburg Empire, 104–107, 172–174
Hardenberg, Baron von, 179
Harris, Air Marshal Sir Arthur, 236–238, 242–243, 251, 261, 297n44
Heligoland Bight, 227, 235, 299
Henderson, Neville, 27
Henry V, 104n17
Herwig, Holger, 209
Hindenburg, Field Marshal Paul von, 203–204, 217
Hindenburg Plan, 120, 211
Hinsley, F.H., 12, 298–302, 308
Hiroshima, 311
history
  bureaucracies and, 36
  deconstruction of, 25, 94
  discontinuities and, 19–21
  historical knowledge and, 16, 42
  human nature and, 23, 26, 35
  military effectiveness and, 8
  military innovation and, 40
  misuse of, 15n5
  relation to future and, 7, 14–17
  study of, 34, 39, 77–78, 81, 95
  war, nature of, and, 17, 78
  Western civilization and, 20, 84–89
Hitler, Adolf
  ascent of, 19, 27, 122–124, 203–205
  Combined Bomber Offensive and, 247, 255–256
  command structure and, 199–201, 205
  Czechoslovakia and, 205, 208
  Greece and, 124
  ideological crusade and, 206, 221, 312
  leadership of, 200, 203–205
  Luftwaffe and, 224, 257
  Poland and, 213
  rearmament and, 212, 228
  retaliation and, 256–258
  Soviet Union and, 122–123, 205–206, 221–222
  United States and, 123, 150, 208, 315
  war crimes and, 170, 312–313
  war gaming and, 150
Hundred Years' War, 86
Ho Chi Minh, 25n40
Hobbes, Thomas, 23
Hollweg, Theobald von Bethmann, 117n49, 198
Hooker, Major General Joseph, 113
Horner, Lieutenant General Chuck, 267, 272–273
Howard, Sir Michael, 44, 66, 135, 159
Hungary, 241n16
Hussein, Saddam, 267, 270–271

Iceland, 301–302
India, 78, 173–174, 177
Indochina, 64, 137
Industrial College of the Armed Forces, 131
Industrial Revolution
  American Civil War and, 113, 169
  Crimean War and, 112–113, 184
  French Revolution, fusion with, and, 177, 182, 185, 193

human condition and, 23
international relations and, 26
revolutionary wars and, 180–182, 184
war and, 21
information dominance, 30
Instant Thunder, Operation, 267, 269, 272
Iran, 270
Iraq, 5, 275
  air defense system and, 273–274
  air force of, 277
  Al-Firdos bunker and, 278
  Ba'ath Party and, 277–279
  cultural monuments and, 279
  ground forces of, 269–271, 279
  military competence and, 271
  Republican Guard and, 278–280
  revolution and, 278–279
  secret police organizations and, 278. See also specific operation names and Gulf War
Irish Republican Army (IRA), 17n15
Iraqi Freedom, Operation, 4, 80
  Coalition forces and, 80
  507th Maintenance Company and, 93n32
  intelligence and, 5
  planning for, 15n4, 23, 76–77
  post-conflict stage and, 5
Islamic world, 34, 78–79
Italy, 124, 185, 233n4
interwar period
  air power theory and, 232–235, 254, 266
  Germany and, 58, 211, 214, 228
  innovation and, 39–40
  intelligence and, 289, 291–292
  military culture and, 96
  professional military education and, 39, 63
  red teaming and, 143, 157
  U.S. Navy and, 128–129, 151–152
  World War I lessons and, 219

Japan
  interwar period and, 128–129
  war crimes and, 311–312, 314–318
  World War II and, 123–125, 130, 136
James II of England, 134n97
Jena-Auerstädt, Battle of, 133, 143, 179, 197

Jeschonneck, Colonel General Hans, 224–226
Jews, extermination of, 313–314
Johnson, President Lyndon B., 2n, 33n71
Joint Forces Air Component Commander (JFACC), 268
Jomini, Baron de Antoine-Henri, 73–75, 77
Jones, R.V., 295–298
Josephus, Flavius, 85
Jumhuriya Bridge, 277
Jünger, Ernst, 27, 173
Just Cause, Operation, 22
Jutland, Battle of, 120n58, 152, 227, 291

Kassebaum Report, 96
Keitel, Field Marshal Wilhelm, 313
Kennedy, Paul, 20
Kennan, George, 63
Kesselring, Field Marshal Albert, 224
Khafji, Battle of, 270n10, 282
King, Fleet Admiral Ernest, 37n84, 63, 130, 305
Königrätz, Battle of, 116, 147, 187, 196
Korea, 314
Korean War, 249
Kriegsakademie, 40, 143–144
Kriegsmarine, 123, 226, 245, 299–301
  Seekriegsleitung and, 150
Kriegspiel, 144–146, 154
Kurds, 278
Kuwait, 267, 269–270

Lawrence, T.E., 15n4
Lauenberg, weather ship, 302
League of Nations, 205
Lebensraum, 161n65
Lemp, Julius, 302
Lend-Lease, 126
Le Paradis massacre, 312
Liege, 148
Lincoln, President Abraham, 113
Linebacker, Operation, 163
Lindemann, Frederick, 297
Lister, Sarah, 94
Louis Napoleon of France. See Napoleon III of France
Louis XIV of France, 105, 107, 172–173
Louis XV of France, 176
Low Countries, 87, 107, 118, 149, 164, 171

Ludendorff, General Erich, 149, 203, 207, 211, 214, 217
Lutz, Oswald, 158
Luftwaffe, 126, 199-200, 214-215, 257-258
   attrition and, 241, 258
   Battle of Britain and, 126, 239
   close air support and, 215-216
   Combined Bomber Offensive and, 240-241, 243-245, 249, 253, 256-260, 316
   command and cooperation, 199-201, 214-215
   daylight fighter force and, 258-260
   effectiveness of, 223-226, 253
   intelligence and, 288, 297-298
   night bomber offensive and, 202
   retaliation weapons and, 256-257
   Sea Lion, Operation and, 215
   technology and, 202
   war crimes and, 312
Lusitania, 227
Luxembourg, 118

MacArthur, General Douglas, 130, 317
McNamara, Secretary of Defense Robert Strange, 2n, 33n71, 65-66, 69, 91
Machiavelli, 87
Magenta, Battle of, 185
Mahan, Alfred Thayer, 58, 209
Malaya, 126
Malmedy massacre, 313
Malplaquet, Battle of, 173
Malta, 124
Manstein, General Erich von, 205
Marcks, General Erich, 90
Marlborough, Duke of, 105-107, 173-174
Marne, Battle of the, 211, 214, 217
Marshall, General of the Army George C., 23n31, 37(nn84, 86), 63, 130, 308n77
Martinet, General Jean, 88
Marxism, 15n5
Mattis, Major General James, 5
Maurice of Orange, 87-88
McCarthy, Senator Joseph, 313n6
McClellan, General George, 113
McCormack, Alfred, 303n63
Meade, Major General George Gordon, 114

Menzies, Sir Stewart, 294n33
Metternich, Clemens von, 182
Metz, siege of 1870, 190-192
Michael Offensive of March 1918, 207, 214
Middle East, 137
Midway, 130
military affairs, revolution in, 30
military institutions
   adaptation in war, 38, 41, 83, 162, 166
   bureaucracy and, 173
   culture of, 8, 61, 78, 83-85, 89, 146, 166
   conformity of thought and, 40
   discipline and, 87-89, 96
   effectiveness of, 38, 42, 83, 96
   experience, value of, and, 21
   innovation and, 22, 38-40, 70, 83, 166
   law and, 87
   peacetime and, 6
   professional military education and, 22, 39-40, 81, 145
   service cultures and, 83
   study of war and, 6-7, 39-40, 121
   tactics and, 89
   technology and, 29, 89, 91
   war games and, 140. *See also* red teaming
military transformation, 38n89
Millett, Allan R., 32, 98, 137
Milch, Field Marshal Erhard, 225, 245, 257
mirror imaging, 20, 246
modern states, 35, 87-88, 173, 253, 262
Moltke, Field Marshal Helmuth von
   American Civil War and, 169
   Franco-Prussian War and, 116-117, 190-191
   leadership of, 186-187
   red teaming and, 147, 149, 155
   Seven Weeks' War and, 187-188, 196
   strategic planning and, 99, 115
   technology and, 201
Muffling, General Phillip Baron von, 144
München, weather ship, 302
Munich Beer Hall Putsch, 204
Murray, Williamson, 2
Mussolini, Benito, 19n19, 123-124

Napoleonic Wars, 110-112, 169, 177-179, 182

Napoleon III of France, 145, 184–185, 188–192
nationalism, 178–180, 182, 185
Nazism, 21, 170
Nelson, Admiral Horatio, 133
New Guinea, 124, 130
Nimitz, Admiral Chester W., 63, 153–154
9/11 Report, 36, 308
Nine Years' War, 172
nonstate entities, 17
Normandy invasion, 226, 261, 316. See also Overlord, Operation
North America
    Queen Anne's War and, 173–174, 176
    Seven Years' War and, 108–110
North German Federation, 188n46
Norway, 215, 299–300
Nurenberg, 261
Nye, Joseph S., Jr., 69

Oberkommando der Wehrmacht (OKW), 199, 214–215, 248
Oberkommando der Luftwaffe (OKL), 247
Oberkommando des Heeres (OKH), 150, 199, 215, 220, 222
Office of Net Assessment, 67
On War, 31, 168
opposition forces (OPFOR), 162
Oradour-sur-Glane, 313
Ottoman Empire, 51, 135, 172, 183–184
Oudenarde, Battle of, 106n22, 173
Owens, Admiral William, 4, 68–69

Panama, 22
Papen, Franz von, 204
Paret, Peter, 66
Passchendaele, Battle of, 41, 135
Paulus, Field Marshal Friedrich von, 211
pax Romana, 103
Peace of Nicias, 55
Pearl Harbor, 123, 124n74, 130
Peiper, *Standartenführer* Joachim, 313
Peloponnesian War, 23, 53–56, 133
Peloponnesian War, The History of, 52
Pericles, 55, 132
Pétain, Marshal Philippe, 218n67
P-51 Mustang, 243
Phillipines, 79, 80n18, 128
Piedmont. See Sardinia, Kingdom of
Pile, General Frederick Alfred, 157
Pitt, William, the Younger, 21, 108–109

Plan Dog memorandum, 129
Plataea, Battle of, 53
Ploesti, 239, 246
Poland, 220, 292, 314
Pound, Admiral Dudley, 302
Portugal, 134, 180
Powell, General Colin, 267n3, 271, 276, 279
Powell doctrine, 67
Powell, Lewis, 303n63
Prague, 290
Prussia
    Austrian Succession, War of, and, 175
    Danish War and, 186–187
    Franco–Prussian War and, 115–117, 188–192
    military institutions of
        bureaucratic structure of, 197–198
        civil military relations and, 202–203
        Kriegsakademie and, 143–144
        Kriegspiel and, 144–147
        military culture and, 186
        Prussian General Staff and, 112, 115, 143, 179, 186–187, 197
        Prussian War Ministry and, 198, 200, 207, 216
    Napoleonic Wars and, 133
    nationalism and, 179, 182, 189
    Seven Weeks' War and, 115–116, 147, 187–188
    Seven Years' War and, 108–110, 175–177
    Social Democrats and, 202
    Spanish Succession, War of, 173
Pye, D.R., 295

Quebec, 109, 177
Queen Anne's War, 173

Raeder, Admiral Erich, 228
Ramillies, Battle of, 106n22
Rape of Nanking, 312
rapid decisive operations, 4
red teaming
    aircraft development and, 153–154
    armored mechanized warfare and, 156–158
    assumptions and, 141–142, 151, 160–161, 164–167
    British Army doctrine and, 157–159
    bureaucracies and, 140, 166

red teaming (*cont.*)
  culture and, 142, 159, 162, 166–167
  deployment and, 147–148
  enemy, understanding of, and, 159–163
  evaluation of officers and, 143–146
  evaluation of results and, 142
  free play and, 142, 155, 162
  German Army doctrine and, 154–156
  history of, 140–142
  imaginative thinking and, 142
  intelligence and, 159, 162
  Kriegspiel and, 144–146, 154
  levels of war, extension to, and, 142
  logistics and, 154
  military effectiveness and, 140–141
  mirror imaging and, 140
  Prussian Army and, 143–147
  service cultures and, 140
  training and, 162–164, 167
  U.S. Navy doctrine and, 151–154
  war planning and, 146–151
Reeves, Admiral Joseph M., 152
Regensburg, 240
Reichsbahn, 250–251
Reich Minister for Equipment and War Production, 251
Reichstag, 199
Reichswehr, 203–204, 209
Richelieu, Cardinal, 104, 185
Ridgway, General Matthew, 64
Rockwell, Kiffin, 17
Rolling Thunder, Operation, 163, 249, 267
Roman Empire, 28, 85–87, 101–103, 172, 174
Rommel, Field Marshal Irwin, 130, 306(nn73, 75)
Roosevelt, President Franklin Delano, 129–130, 131n92, 136, 316
Rosecrans, Major General William, 113
Rossbach, Battle of, 177
Royal Air Force (RAF), 126, 291
  Britain, Battle of, 126, 226
  British Air Staff and, 23
  Combined Bomber Offensive and, 127, 231, 235, 237. *See also* Combined Bomber Offensive
  Gulf War and, 265, 276
  innovation and, 70, 202
  intelligence and, 298
Royal Navy
  anti-submarine studies and, 291
  Austrian Succession, War of, and, 176
  Gibraltar and, 106
  intelligence and, 294, 294, 299–303, 305
  interwar years and, 228
  Napoleonic Wars and, 112
  Seven Years' War and, 177
  Spanish Succession, War of, and, 107
  World War I and, 119–120, 227–228
  World War II and, 126–127
Rumania, 124, 241n16
Rumsfeld, Secretary of Defense Donald, 4n6
Runciman, Lord Walter, 27
Rupprecht, Crown Prince, 149, 207
Russia, 108, 111–113, 180, 183–184, 188. *See also* Soviet Union
Russian Revolution, 19n19
Russo-Japanese War, 193

Salisbury plains exercises, 157, 158n57
Saratoga, Battle of, 110
Sardinia, Kingdom of, 185
Saudi Arabia, 237, 269, 272
Sauer, Karl-Otto, 245
Saxony, 187, 188n46
Scales, Major General Robert H., 79
Scapa Flow, 228
Schleswig-Holstein, 186
Schleicher, Kurt von, 204
Schlieffen Plan, 148, 164, 206–208, 210–214, 216, 221
School of Advanced Military Studies (SAMS), 68
Scott, General Winfield, 113
Schutzstaffel (SS), 205, 312–313
Schwarzkopf, General Norman, 267, 279–281
Schweinfurt, 240, 245, 253, 261
Schweppenburg, General Leo Geyer von, 207
Sea Lion, Operation, 215
Sedan, Battle of (1870), 189, 191–192
Sedan, Battle of (WWII), 191n50
Seeckt, Hans von, 145, 155, 203, 219
Seekriegsleitung, 150
Seven Weeks' War, 115–116, 145, 187–188
Seven Years' War, 108–110, 134, 146, 175–177
Shaara, Michael, 46

Sherman, General William Tecumseh, 24n34, 114
Shi'ites, 278
Sicily, 127
SIGMA war games, 15, 25n40, 165–166
Silesia, 175
Simpson, Colonel H.W., 308n77
Sims, Admiral William, 152
Solferino, Battle of, 185
Solomon Islands, 124, 130
Somme, Battle of the, 41, 89, 120, 135, 201, 217
Soviet Union
    Cold War and, 20, 34, 37, 45, 56, 306
    maskirovka and, 160, 222, 285n10
    Red Air Force and, 226
    red teaming and, 148, 160–161
    Stalin and, 160
    war crimes and, 201, 205, 313, 315–316
    World War II and, 122–123, 126, 129, 131, 160, 206, 221–222. *See also* Barbarossa, Operation
Spaatz, Lieutenant General Carl A., 239, 241–242
Spain. *See also named wars*
    Low Countries and, 87
    Napoleonic Wars and, 78, 111–112, 134, 180
    wars for empire and, 106–107, 110
Spanish Civil War, 291, 297
Spanish Succession, War of, 105, 172–175
Sparta, 53–55, 132
Speer, Albert, 212, 255
Spruance, Admiral Raymond, 63, 152n33
St. Privat, Battle of, 190
Stalin, Joseph, 122, 160–161, 206, 210, 271, 315
Stark, Admiral Harold, 129
Stauffenberg, Klaus von, 204n21
strategic bombing, 11, 231
    assumptions and, 234–235, 252n58, 254, 262
    campaigns and, 235–236. *See also* Combined Bomber Offensive
    effects of, 244, 248–252, 254–255, 260–261
    fighter protection and, 235, 253, 259
    technology and, 242, 253–254
    theory and, 232–235, 252–254, 262
strategic planning, 8–9, 98
    allies and, 105, 111, 120
    articulation of, 99–100
    assumptions in, 110, 117, 136–137
    Bismarck, Otto von and, 115–117
    economic planning and, 120
    Industrial Revolution and, 112–113
    interwar period and, 121–122, 128
    intuition and, 138
    logistics and, 107
    maritime powers and, 132–134
    means and ends and, 136–137
    mirror imaging and, 20, 246
    mobilization and, 110, 112, 115, 133
    political factors in, 98, 100
    Roman Empire and, 101–103
    wars for empire and, 105–112, 173
    Western way of war and, 101
    World War I and, 117–120
    World War II and
        Allies and, 125–132
        Axis and, 121–125
Strangle, Operation, 249
Sun Tsu, 15, 25
Sweden, 104
Swift, Jonathan, 174–175
Switzerland, 86
synchronization, 31n64

Tannenburg, Battle of, 89
Tawakana Division, 281
Taylor, Telford, 303n63
technology
    adaptation and, 6, 29, 242, 253
    air power and, 234
    battlespace dominance and, 4, 30, 68–69, 91
    Cold War and, 67
    Combined Bomber Offensive and, 233, 243
    Crimean War and, 184
    German military institutions and, 201
    Gulf War and, 274
    information dominance and, 30, 70
    intelligence and, 297
    Prussian wars and, 185
    twenty-first century and, 79–80, 94, 306
    United States military and, 6–7, 29–30, 78, 152
    Vietnam War and, 65–66
    war and, 31–32
    World War I and, 40, 201
    World War II and, 202, 233, 256
    Western armies and, 89

Tedder, Air Marshal Sir Arthur, 242, 249–250, 306n73
Thebes, 53–54
Thirty Years' War, 104
Three Emperors, League of, 182
Thucydides
 friction and, 53
 human nature and, 23, 28, 56, 283
 moral parameters of war and, 54, 56
 power and human affairs and, 54
 relevance of, 52, 59
 works on, 60
Tirpitz, Admiral Alfred von, 209–210
Tizard, Sir Henry, 296
Tolstoy, Leo, 14n2
Tooze, Adam, 11
Top Gun, 163
Tovey, Admiral John, 300
Trafalgar, Battle of, 133, 170
Trenchard, Air Marshal Sir Hugh, 58, 233
Turing, Alan, 294, 300–301
Turner, Admiral Stansfield, 18n17

Ultra intelligence
 code breaking and, 284(nn4–5)
 Combined Bomber Offensive and, 241–242, 247–248, 251, 262–263
 Luftwaffe and, 226
 North Africa and, 222
 U-boat offensive and, 301
 Western Front and, 222
United Nations, 269
United States
 ahistoricism of, 81
 Al Qaeda, threat of, 28n50
 bureaucratic state of, 34–37, 308
 civil-military relations in, 90, 94–95, 129, 136
 Cold War and, 67
 culture of, 78
 drive for power and, 24, 25n38
 Gulf War. See Gulf War
 history, view of, 59
 industrial capacity of, 124, 131
 innovation and, 24n37
 intelligence agencies and, 13, 287, 303n63, 305–306, 308–310
 Iraq War. See Iraqi Freedom, Operation
 liberal education and, 25, 54, 66, 81, 94
 military institutions of
  battlespace dominance and, 91–92
  basic training and, 93
  culture of, 29, 61–66, 68, 78, 90, 92–94
  doctrine and, 67, 151, 233–235
  enemy, understanding of, 80–81, 92, 137
  interwar period and, 63, 128–129, 152
  Joint Chiefs of Staff and, 214
  leadership of, 43, 66, 80–82, 96
  logistical capabilities of, 79, 129
  nation building and stability operations and, 79, 80n18, 81
  personnel system of, 81
  professional military education and, 39, 62–65, 68, 71, 81
  red teaming and, 163–166
  service cultures of, 91–93, 95, 137
  technology and, 6–7, 59, 66, 68–70, 91
  training centers of, 67, 163–164
  Vietnam War, effect on, 65–66, 68, 80
 strategic bombing. See Combined Bomber Offensive
 strategy in twenty-first century and, 28, 36–37, 41–42, 79, 81, 139
 Vietnam War and, 6, 25, 78n15, 163
 World War I and, 26–27, 132n93
 World War II and, 123–126, 128–132, 136–137
United States Air Force (USAF), 163, 265
 Black Hole and, 266, 280
 precision guided munitions and, 280–281
 Tactical Air Command and, 267–268, 279
United States Army Air Forces (USAAF)
 Atlantic, Battle of, and, 245
 ball bearing factories and, 245, 258
 Combined Bomber Offensive and, 235–237, 263
 Eighth Air Force and, 238–240, 242n30, 245, 253, 258
 Fifteenth Air Force and, 246–247
 German aircraft industry and, 245
 Ninth Air Force and, 267
 North Africa, and, 239. See also Combined Bomber Offensive

Index

United States Army Command and General Staff College, 62
Unites States Army Industrial College, 39n93
United States Army Infantry School, 63
United States Army War College, 71, 308n77
United States Air Corps Tactical School, 39n93, 58, 63, 233
United States Air War College, 71
United States Department of Defense, 81
United States Military Academy, 62, 77
United States National War College, 63
United States Navy, 127
   Gulf War and, 268–269
   offensive carrier operations and, 152
   red teaming and, 151–154, 163
United States Naval Academy, 62, 77
United States Naval War College, 18n17, 40, 62, 63, 151–153
United States Marine Corps Schools, 40, 63
United States Strategic Bombing Survey (USSBS), 11, 231, 241n16, 244, 250, 254–255, 264
USS Langley, 152–153

Verdun, Battle of, 149, 217
Versailles, Treaty of, 200
Vichy France, 314n13
Victoria, Queen, of England, 170
Vienna, Congress of, 96, 181
Viet Minh, 15, 17n15
Vietnam War, 2, 65, 137, 249, 267
   French Revolution, influence on, 25n40
   lessons of, 71, 139n1
Volksgemeinschaft, 203
V-1 and V-2 programs, 244, 256–258

war
   adaptation in, 29, 41, 99, 115, 142, 253–254, 262
   aims and means in, 43, 98, 206
   conduct of, 3–4, 31–32, 49
   empire, war for, 105, 173–177
   enemy, understanding of, 25, 31, 40, 42–43, 139, 159–162
   friction and, 4–5, 29–31, 50–52, 254
   global war and, 105, 108
   historical analysis of, 7
   information versus knowledge and, 5, 32, 70
   limited warfare and, 175–176
   literature and, 25, 46–47, 95
   maritime powers and, 133
   mobilization and, 38, 110, 253
   moral parameters of, 53, 56
   nature of, 28, 32–33, 53, 80
   non-linear phenomenon and, 8, 31–32, 50
   operational level of, 33, 131, 146
   patterns of, 172–177
   political framework of, 32–33, 42, 49–50, 70, 100, 206
   politico-strategic error and, 33
   principles of, 8, 72–79, 82
   profession, as a, 3, 13, 83–84, 92
   revolutionary war, framework of, and, 177–181
   strategic level of, 3, 6, 32, 164–166, 229–230. *See also* strategic planning; strategic effectiveness
   tactical level of, 33, 146
   technology and, 31, 80, 184, 193–194, 233. *See also* Industrial Revolution
   theories of, 46–50, 74, 232–235
   uncertainties and, 30, 49
   use of force and, 42
   war games and, 140, 147–148, 152. *See also* red teaming
   Western military institutions and, 84–89, 92, 96, 196
War and Peace, 14n2
Warden, Colonel John, 266, 271–273
Warsaw Pact, 164
Washington, General George, 176
Waterloo, Battle of, 170
Wavell, General Archibald, 75
Wedemeyer, Lieutenant General Albert C., 207n31
Wehrmacht
   close air support doctrine and, 215–216
   Combined Bomber Offensive and, 248–249, 251–252, 260–261
   discipline of, 88, 90
   Enigma and, 284, 287–288, 290
   Barbarossa, Operation, and, 122, 150, 160, 211, 313
   rearmament and, 212
   strategic bombing and, 248–249, 251–252, 260–261

Wehrmacht (cont.)
   technology and, 220
   war crimes and, 313
   war gaming and, 150, 160
Weimar Republic, 198–200, 203, 205
Weinburger doctrine, 6n, 67
Welchman, Gordon, 294
Wellington, Duke of, 112, 134, 180
Weltanschauung, 25, 221
Weserübung, 215. *See also* Sea Lion, Operation
Western Way of War, 85–90, 92, 96
Westmoreland, General William, 64
West Point. *See* United States Military Academy
Wilhelm I, Kaiser, 189
Wilhelm II, Kaiser, 17n14, 196, 202
William III of England, 134n97
Winn, Commander Rodger, 303–305
Wolfe, Major General James P., 58, 109, 177
Wolfowitz, Paul, 4n6
World War I
   adaptation and, 41, 62
   Eastern Front and, 217
   Franco-Prussian War, effect on, 192–193
   French and Industrial Revolutions, fusion of, and, 182
   German military culture and, 118, 216
   impact of, 19n19, 20, 26, 117n48, 170–171
   intelligence and, 285, 291
   lessons of, 219
   Michael Offensive of March 1918, 207, 214
   outbreak of, 17, 169–171
   red teaming and, 148, 164–165
   strategic planning and, 117–120, 206, 213
   surface operations and, 227
   technology and, 29, 89
   Western Front and, 119n56, 217
World War II
   Anglo-American allies and, 127
   Axis powers and, 127, 316
   Combined Bomber Offensive and, 11, 231, 242, 249, 252, 254, 261, 316
   crimes against humanity and, 311–318
   Eastern Front, 201, 221, 222, 254, 261, 285n10, 317
   European theater and, 131–132, 220
   strategic bombing and, 231, 255
   strategic mistakes of, 6, 122, 256–258, 315
   impact of, 20
   Mediterranean theater and, 127, 131
   North Africa and, 127, 130, 222, 224–225
   Pacific theater and, 13, 130–131, 136
   World War I, impact on, 19n19, 117n48, 171

Yamamoto, Admiral Isoroku, 124n74

Zabern Affair, 202
Zuckerman, Solly, 250, 306